PEAK
PERFORMANCE
SUCCESS IN COLLEGE AND BEYOND

THIRD EDITION

Sharon K. Ferrett, Ph.D.
Humboldt State University

 Glencoe
McGraw-Hill

New York, New York   Columbus, Ohio   Woodland Hills, California   Peoria, Illinois

Art Credits: Tom Kennedy/Romark Illustrations
Photo Credits:
Cover Telegraph Colour Library/FPG International;
Front Matter: (xii) Michael Kevin Daly/The Stock Market; (xiii) Kevin Vandivier/Viesti Associates; (xiii) Louis Psihoyos/Matrix; (xiv) Gary Buss/FPG International; (xiv, xv) First Image; (xv) John Henley/The Stock Market; (xvi) José Pelaez/The Stock Market; (xvi) First Image; (xvii) Laura Sifferlin; (xvii) T & D McCarthy/The Stock Market; (xvii) Doug Martin; (xviii) Tom Croke/Liaison Agency; (xviii) First Image; (xix) Ken Cooke/Photo Op; (xix) First Image; (xx) Randy Ury/The Stock Market; (xx) Bob Krist/The Stock Market; (xxi a-b) José Pelaez/The Stock Market; (xxii) Chuck Savage/The Stock Market; (xxii) Don Mason/The Stock Market; **Chapter 1:** (1-1) Michael Kevin Daly/The Stock Market; (1-7) Vill Gallery/Viesti Associates; (1-10a) Kevin Vandivier/Viesti Associates; (1-10b) Gary Buss/FPG International; (1-25a) Louis Psihoyos/Matrix; (1-25b) First Image; (1-27) Laura Sifferlin; (1-28) First Image; **Chapter 2:** (2-1) John Henley/The Stock Market; (2-25) Courtesy Lau Technologies; (2-27) José Pelaez/The Stock Market; (2-28) First Image; **Chapter 3:** (3-1) Photri/The Stock Market; (3-20) Gary Buss/FPG International; (3-22) First Image; (3-23) Karl Gehring/Liaison Agency; (3-25) First Image; (3-26) Doug Martin; **Chapter 4:** (4-1) Michael Kevin Daly/The Stock Market; (4-21 a, b) First Image; (4-23, 4-24) Laura Sifferlin; **Chapter 5:** (5-1)Tom Stewart/The Stock Market; (5-5) First Image; (5-10) Laura Sifferlin; (5-21a) Russ Einhorn/Liaison Agency; (5-21b) Scott McKiernan/Liaison Agency; (5-23) Doug Martin; (5-24) Laura Sifferlin; **Chapter 6:** (6-1) Stan Godlewski/Liaison Agency; (6-21) Courtesy Mrs. Fields, Inc.; (6-24) Laura Sifferlin; (6-25) T & D McCarthy/The Stock Market; **Chapter 7:** (7-1) Scott Cuningham; (7-23) Richard E. Schultz/Matrix; (7-25) José Pelaez/The Stock Market; (7-26) First Image; **Chapter 8:** (8-1) Michael Kevin Daly/The Stock Market; (8-13) Tom Stewart/The Stock Market; (8-16) First Image; (8-22) Tom Croke/Liaison Agency; (8-24) First Image; (8-25) José L. Palaez/The Stock Market; **Chapter 9:** (9-1)Ken Cooke/Photo Op; (9-13) First Image; (9-19) James D. Wilson/ Liaison Agency; (9-21) First Image; (9-23) José L. Palaez/The Stock Market; **Chapter 10:** (10-1) Randy Ury/The Stock Market; (10-7) Ariel Skelley/The Stock Market; (10-8) Bryan Peterson/The Stock Market; (10-9) T & D McCarthy/The Stock Market; (10-10) Blaine Harrington III/The Stock Market; (10-28) file photo; (10-28a-b, 10-30, 10-31) First Image; **Chapter 11:** (11-1) First Image; (11-5a) Andrew Holbrooke/ The Stock Market; (11-5b) Chuck Savage/The Stock Market; (11-5c) Joe Viesti/Viesti Associates; (11-11) José L. Palaez/The Stock Market; (11-19) First Image; (11-25) William Waldron/Liaison Agency; (11-27) Tom Stewart/The Stock Market; (11-28) Ted Horowitz/The Stock Market; **Chapter 12:** (12-1) Bob Krist/The Stock Market; (12-20) Alan Weiner/Liaison Agency; (12-22, 12-23) First Image; **Chapter 13:** (13-1) Chuck Savage/The Stock Market; (13-4) First Image; (13-23) Cynthia Johnson/Liaison Agency; (13-25) Laura Sifferlin; (13-26) Bryan F. Peterson/ The Stock Market; **Chapter 14:** (14-1) Don Mason/The Stock Market; (14-27) Timothy Greenfield-Sanders; (14-29) José Pelaez/The Stock Market; (14-30) José Pelaez/The Stock Market.

Ferrett, Sharon K.
    Peak performance : success in college & beyond / Sharon K. Ferrett. — 3rd ed.
      p.   cm.
    Includes bibliographical references (p.) and index.
    ISBN 0-02-804305-7
    1. Academic achievement. 2. Performance. 3. Career development. 4. Success.   I. Title.
    LB1062.6.F47   2000
    370.15'2—dc21   99-23302
                                                            CIP

Glencoe/McGraw-Hill

A Division of The McGraw·Hill Companies

Peak Performance
Success in College and Beyond, Third Edition
Student Text

Send all inquiries to:
Glencoe/McGraw-Hill
936 Eastwind Drive
Westerville, OH 43081

ISBN 0-02-804305-7

Printed in the United States of America

1 2 3 4 5 6 7 8 9 10   079   07 06 05 04 03 02 01 00 99

PREFACE

FROM THE AUTHOR

Why I Wrote This Book

I have spent over twenty-five years working with students as a college professor, advisor, and dean, and over fifteen years as a management consultant. I began my research into personal productivity and human relations early in my teaching career and began compiling data from years of teaching classes in organizational behavior and giving hundreds of workshops to managers and executives. I have always been interested in transitions, which led me to teaching classes to help students successfully make the transition from high school to college and from college to the world of work.

It is apparent that there is a strong connection between the world of college and the world of work. Yet, college is often viewed as separate and distinct from the real world. This book attempts to present the relationship of college with the larger system of work and life. It focuses on responsibility and the consequences of one's decisions and actions. It goes further and shows how decisions and actions can affect others and the larger world. The theme of this book is that it is in the very nature of people to love learning and to strive for peak performance.

Who Are the Peak Performers?

Peak Performers come from all lifestyles, ages, cultures, and sexes. They can be famous individuals such as business entrepreneur Mo Siegel; writer Gary Soto; actress Oprah Winfrey; or Debbi Fields, founder of Mrs. Fields' Cookies. Peak Performers are those who become masters at creating excellence by focusing on determination. They are not perfect or overnight successes. In fact, compulsively pursuing perfection often makes people afraid of mistakes. Peak Performers learn to face that fear and work through it.

Everyday thousands of Peak Performers quietly overcome incredible odds, climb over huge obstacles, and reach within themselves to find inner strength. People from all lifestyles can become Peak Performers by setting goals and developing appropriate attitudes and behaviors to achieve the results they want. Many are not rich or famous, nor have they reached the top in their careers. They are successful because they know that they possess the personal power to produce results in their lives, overcome setbacks, and find passion in what they contribute to life. They are masters, not victims, of life's situations. They control the quality of their lives. Being a Peak Performer involves risk-taking, creative thinking, sound judgment, effective decision making, supportive relationships, skill, confidence, and the motivation to overcome barriers.

The Benefits of Being a Peak Performer

There are many benefits to learning the strategies presented in this book and to becoming a Peak Performer. Here are a few:

- Understanding the connection between college and job success.
- Achieving better grades.
- Having a successful college experience.
- Feeling a higher satisfaction and greater job success.
- Ability to demonstrate SCANS competencies.
- Organizing a portfolio of skills, competencies, and personal qualities.
- Developing a positive and resourceful state of mind.
- Exhibiting more self-confidence.
- Developing healthy relationships.
- Learning effective decision making and problem solving.
- Using time management skills.
- Developing discipline and self-control.
- Showing improved reading comprehension and, consequently, more enjoyable reading.
- Developing an effective learning style that produces results.
- Learning positive habits and personal qualities.
- Finding a balanced life.
- Understanding the importance of integrity, character, and civility.

New to the Third Edition

The third edition of *Peak Performance Success in College and Beyond* has been thoroughly updated and revised in light of the many helpful comments and suggestions of adopters and reviewers of the previous editions. The goal is to help you become a lifelong learner. To be successful, you must adapt to college and the larger community, but also acquire the necessary skills, habits, motivation, and personal qualities to face the challenges of tomorrow's workplace. To that end, this edition reflects the importance of character, ethics, social responsibility, and critical thinking in a world that is increasingly rich in its demographic and cultural diversity. Diversity sections have been expanded.

New features have also been introduced. They are Technology Focus, Career Focus, and the Career Development Portfolio, which allows you the opportunity to begin this essential element.

The major theme continues to stress that success in college and success at work are related. It urges you to think of nurturing all your talents and skills and enhance them by continually learning to learn and work with others. Positive study habits, learning to relate effectively and learn with other students and professors result in positive work habits and powerful organizational teams. Each chapter presents several features to highlight the connection between the world of school and the world of work.

FEATURES

Learning Objectives

Clear and concise objectives and a brief narrative at the beginning of each chapter aid you in identifying and mastering each chapter's key concepts.

Trailmarker Exercises

In every chapter, Trailmarker exercises demonstrate the themes and concepts of each chapter. Many exercises work well in small groups, thus giving you an opportunity to learn together and build on each other's strengths and diversity. You complete self-assessment skills, practice mind mapping, and set goals. Exercises make the chapter material relevant, personal, and active.

Critical Thinking Logs

Critical Thinking Logs help you read, reflect, and think critically. You are asked to observe, evaluate, and apply chapter concepts to your life.

Career Focus

This feature gives you concrete examples of the relationship between the study skills necessary for college success and the skills you'll need for career success. Work situations that directly call on chapter skills are highlighted so that you can see interrelationships.

Technology Focus

This new feature shows you how school assignments, your personal life, and the work of work connect with technology—the computer and Internet. Web site links are provided.

Peak Performance Profiles

Each chapter presents a noted person in the area of business, education, the arts, or public service. These Peak Performers have overcome obstacles and challenges to become successful. You will see that having a positive attitude and perseverance are important for success.

Case Studies

The case studies are examples of students in college that deal with real-life chapter concepts. This feature stresses that the same issues which you will deal with in college exist everywhere and the same skills and strategies that work can be adapted to your job. There are no secrets to college and job success.

Career Development Portfolio

The Career Development Portfolio is a process that shows the best of your skills, competencies, accomplishments, and work. When completed, the portfolio will contain sections on self-analysis, an inventory of transferable skills, SCANS competencies, goals, educational planning, inventory of interests, documentation, cover letters, résumé, a checklist for interviews, and samples of work. You can use the portfolio to create and update your résumé, to gain college credit for prior learning, to help you prepare for an interview, and for job advancement. Your greatest source of job security is a portfolio of skills and personal qualities. The portfolio will give you the opportunity to assess your strengths, set goals, map out a plan of action, and possess an organized system for copies of degrees, certificates, letters of thanks, samples of awards, commendations, job descriptions, and other important documentation. It will also help you to explore possible majors and careers.

Peak Performance Strategies

Each chapter offers affirmations, visualization methods, and a list that summarizes the chapter's strategies.

Chapter Application Worksheets

Practical worksheets will help you apply what you have learned to other classes and situations. These templates provide hands-on application.

APPLYING SCANS

The Secretary of Labor created the Secretary's Commission of Achieving Necessary Skills, or SCANS, in 1990 to encourage the teaching of skills necessary for job success. The Commission identified a set of skills and competencies needed to succeed. These skills and competencies apply to all kinds of jobs in every occupation and they also apply to success in college. SCANS skills and competencies will be highlighted and addressed in each chapter. Students and workers should know:

SCANS COMPETENCIES

BASIC SKILLS (reading, writing, listening, speaking, math)

THINKING SKILLS (critical thinking, creative problem solving, knowing how to learn, reasoning, mental visualization)

PERSONAL QUALITIES (responsibility, enthusiasm, positive attitude, self-management, self-control, integrity, character, civility, sociability, self-esteem)

INTERPERSONAL SKILLS (teaches others, team member, leadership, works well with diverse groups, serves clients and customers)

INFORMATION (acquires, evaluates, organizes, maintains, and uses computers)

SYSTEMS (understands, monitors, corrects, designs, improves systems)

RESOURCES (allocate time, money, material, people, and space)

TECHNOLOGY (selects, applies, maintains, and troubleshoots)

Peak Performance focuses on SCANS requirements to help you connect learning in college with the competencies that will be necessary to demonstrate throughout your working life. Each chapter provides exercises, strategies, case studies, and guidelines that correlate with several SCANS requirements, and systems thinking, diversity, and critical thinking is woven through all chapters.

SCANS COMPETENCY CHART

Competencies and Foundations	Student Edition Chapters That Address SCANS Competencies
Resources: Identifies, organizes, plans, and allocates resources.	
• Managing time	Chapter 3
• Managing money	Chapter 12
• Managing space	Chapters 3, 13
• Managing people	Chapter 11
• Managing materials	Chapters 3, 4, 5, 8
• Managing facilities	Chapters 4, 8, 10, 12
Information: Acquires and uses information	
• Acquiring information	Chapters 4, 5
• Evaluating information	Chapters 6, 7
• Organizing and maintaining information	Chapters 6, 7, 8, 9
• Using computer to process	Chapter 9
Systems: Understands complex interrelationships	
• Understanding systems	All chapters with a strong emphasis in 10
• Designing systems	Chapters 4, 5
• Monitoring systems	Chapters 3, 4, 5, 10
• Correcting systems	Chapters 3, 4, 5, 10
Interpersonal Skills: Works with others	
• Positive attitudes	Chapter 2
• Self-control	Chapter 2
• Goal-setting	Chapter 2
• Responsibility	Chapters 2, 13
• Teamwork	Chapter 11
• Managing stress	Chapter 10
Technology: Works with a variety of technologies	
• Selecting technology	Chapters 8, 14
• Applying technology	Chapters 8, 14
• Maintaining technology	Chapters 8, 14
• Solving problems	Chapter 9
• Staying current in technology	Chapters 13, 14

A 3-PART FOUNDATION

Competencies and Foundations	Student Edition Chapters That Address SCANS Competencies
Personal Qualities: Responsibility, character, integrity, positive habits, self-management, self-esteem, sociability	Chapters 2, 14
Basic Skills:	
• Reading—locates, understands, and interprets written information in prose and in documents such as manuals, graphs, and schedules.	Chapter 5
• Writing—communicates thoughts, ideas, information, and messages in writing; and creates documents such as letters, directions, manuals, reports, graphs, and flow charts.	Chapter 8
• Arithmetic/Mathematics—performs basic computations and approaches practical problems by choosing appropriately from a variety of mathematical techniques.	Chapter 9
• Listening—receives, attends to, interprets, and responds to verbal messages and other cues.	Chapter 4
Thinking Skills:	
• Creative Thinking—generate new ideas.	Chapter 9, Critical Thinking logs in each chapter
• Decision Making—specifies goals and constraints, generates alternatives, considers risks and evaluates and chooses best alternative.	Chapter 9, Case Studies in each chapter, Critical Thinking Logs in each chapter
• Listening—receives, attends to, interprets, and responds to verbal messages and other cues.	Chapters 4, 11
• Seeing Things in the Mind's Eye—organizes and processes symbols, pictures, graphs, objects, and other information.	All chapters with a strong emphasis in Chapter 2
• Knowing How to Learn—uses efficient learning techniques to acquire and apply new knowledge and skills.	Chapter 1
• Reasoning—discovers a rule or principle underlying the relationship between two or more objects and applies it when solving a problem.	Chapter 9

Dedication

To the memory of my father, Albert Lawrence Ferrett, for setting the highest standards.

To my mother, Velma Mary Hollenbeck Ferrett, for her seamless expression of love.

To my husband, Sam, and my daughters, Jennifer Katherine and Sarah Angela, for making it all worthwhile.

Acknowledgments

Dr. Ferrett, the author of *Peak Performance Success in College and Beyond,* also wishes to gratefully acknowledge the contributions of the Glencoe editorial staff—Susan Cole, Executive Editor; Catherine P. Varca, Senior Developmental Editor; and Sue Diehm, Production Editor—whose considerable efforts, suggestions, ideas, and insights helped to make this text a more valuable and viable tool for student success.

She would also like to thank and acknowledge the following advisors and reviewers whose input was also invaluable in this revision.

Reviewers

Paula Adduci
Moraine Valley Community College
Palos Heights, Illinois

Dr. Teresa W. Aldredge
Cosumnes River College
Sacramento, California

Lois Bernhardt
International Business College
Lubbock, Texas

Charlotte Brinneman
Florence, Kentucky

Georgia H. Davis
Shelby State Community College
Memphis, Tennessee

Dr. Thomas Deschaine
Grand Rapids Community College
Grand Rapids, Michigan

Billy S. Ferrell
Education America
Garland, Texas

Edith R. Frazier
ESS—The College for Business
Dallas, Texas

Keeley J. Gadd
Kentucky College of Business
Richmond, Kentucky

Debbie Gentile
Mississippi Gulf Coast
   Community College
Gulfport, Mississippi

Sue Granger-Dickson
Bakersfield College
Bakersfield, California

Judith H. Hammond
Sanford-Brown College
North Kansas City, Missouri

Dr. Sheryl Hartman
Miami Dade Community College
Miami, Florida

Dorothy W. Herndon
National Business College
Salem, Virginia

Gloria Hines
Valencia Community College
Orlando, Florida

Pat Hunnicutt, Ph.D.
ITT Technical Institute
Little Rock, Arkansas

Brief Table of Contents

EXPANDED Table of Contents

CHAPTER 2 ATTITUDE, MOTIVATION, AND INTEGRITY

CHAPTER 3 MANAGING YOUR TIME

PART TWO: BASIC SKILLS AND STRATEGIES

CHAPTER 6   MEMORY   6-1

CHAPTER 7   TEST TAKING   7-1

CHAPTER 8   EXPRESSING YOURSELF IN WRITING AND SPEECH

PART THREE: APPLICATION

CHAPTER 11   BUILDING DIVERSE AND HEALTHY RELATIONSHIPS   11-1

CHAPTER 12   EXPLORING YOUR COMMUNITY'S RESOURCES   12-1

CHAPTER 13   DEVELOPING GOOD HABITS   13-1

CHAPTER 14   CAREER DEVELOPMENT PORTFOLIO 14-1

PEAK PERFORMANCE
SUCCESS IN COLLEGE AND BEYOND

Third Edition

This book was designed for you. Its purpose is to help you to learn and become successful while in school, at work, and in your personal experiences. *Peak Performance Success in College and Beyond,* third edition, uses the following integrated learning system to help you accomplish this:

1. **Concept Preview**—Each chapter's opener introduces key objectives to be learned.

2. **Concept Development**—Each chapter's text explains the concepts in a structured, visual format.

3. **Concept Reinforcement**—Each chapter's text provides examples, graphics, and special features to enhance and strengthen your learning.

4. **Concept Review and Application**—Each chapter's ending exercises and activities encourage you to apply what you have learned.

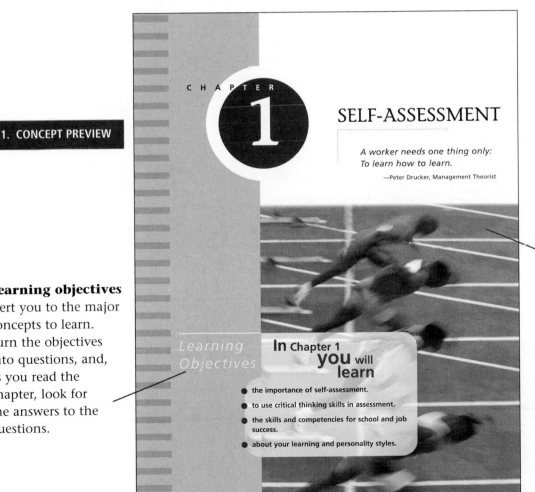

1. CONCEPT PREVIEW

CHAPTER 1

SELF-ASSESSMENT

*A worker needs one thing only:
To learn how to learn.*

—Peter Drucker, Management Theorist

Learning Objectives

In Chapter 1 you will learn

- the importance of self-assessment.
- to use critical thinking skills in assessment.
- the skills and competencies for school and job success.
- about your learning and personality styles.

Learning objectives alert you to the major concepts to learn. Turn the objectives into questions, and, as you read the chapter, look for the answers to the questions.

The **opening photograph** sets the stage for the chapter's content.

2. CONCEPT DEVELOPMENT

The heading structure shows the connection between the topics in a section and organizes the material into easily understandable units of information. To help you understand the structure of the chapter, scan the headings to locate the information that will help you answer the questions you formed from the chapter objectives.

DISCOVERING YOUR LEARNING STYLE

As a lifelong learner, you need to know how to learn. As both a student and an employee, it is important to understand and maximize your learning potential, explore how you learn best, and use this knowledge to your advantage.

Everyone processes information differently. Knowing your preferred learning style can increase your effectiveness in school or at work and enhances your self-esteem. No longer will you ask, *Why am I struggling so hard to learn or to organize information?* Knowing how you learn best can help you to reduce frustration, focus on your strengths, and integrate various styles.

Learning Inventories

Just as there is no "one" or "best" way to learn, there is no "one" instrument, assessment, or inventory that can categorize how you learn best. Any learning style assessment is, at best, a guide.

Two such assessment instruments are

1. The Learning Style Inventory.
2. The Four-Grid Personality and Team Profile.

These instruments have been adapted from various sources and involve twenty-five years of research. They have been given to hundreds of students. They are simple, yet they provide valuable clues and strategies for determining how you learn and process information and relate to others. They will also provide you with possible college majors and careers that fit your personality and style.

The purpose of these inventories is to provide a guide, not to categorize you into a specific box. As you review various assessments, you will begin building a profile of how you process and learn information and relate to other people.

ARE YOU A READER, A LISTENER, OR A DOER?

One way to explore how you learn best is to ask yourself if you are a reader, a listener, or a doer. Do you get more information from *reading and seeing, talking and listening,* or *doing?* Of course, you do all these things, but your learning strength or style may be in one of these areas.

A person who learns better by reading possesses a visual learning style. Someone who learns better by listening is considered an auditory learner, and a kinesthetic learner learns by touch.

Trailmarker 1.1 on page 1–8 has a Learning Style Inventory that will help you discover your learning style.

Visual Learners

Visual learners prefer to see information and read material. They learn more effectively with pictures, graphs, illustrations, diagrams, timelines, photos, pie charts, and visual design. They like to contemplate concepts, reflect, and summarize information in writing. They use arrows, pictures, and bullets to highlight points. Visual learners are often holistic and reflective learners. Visual learners

GETTING ALONG WITH ROOMMATES OR FAMILY

The following suggestions will help you create rapport and improve communication with your roommates or family members:

1. **Clarify expectations.** List the factors that you feel are important for a roommate on the housing application or in an ad. If you don't want a smoker or pets, be honest about it.

2. **Discuss expectations during the first meeting.** Define what neatness means to both of you. Discuss how both of you feel about overnight guests.

3. **Clarify concerns and agree to communicate with each other.** Don't mope or whine about a grievance or leave nasty notes. Communicate honestly and kindly.

4. **Treat your roommate with respect.** Don't give orders or make demands. Communicate openly and calmly. Listen to each other's needs. Treat each other with courtesy and civility. Be especially respectful of your roommate's need to study or sleep. Don't interrupt or make noise.

5. **Don't borrow unless necessary.** A lot of problems result over borrowing money, clothes, jewelry, bikes, cars, and CDs. The best advice is not to borrow. If you do, however, ask permission first and make certain you return the item in good shape or replace it if you lose or damage it. Fill the tank of a borrowed car with gas, for instance. Immediately pay back all money borrowed.

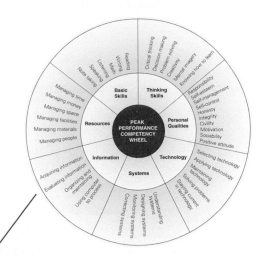

Figure 1-1   The Peak Performance Competency Wheel

Figures help you understand the concepts being presented.

Figure references in the text guide you to illustrations for concept reinforcement.

One of the major reasons people do not succeed in school or in their careers is a lack of willingness to make the necessary effort. If success does not come quickly, they give up and place the blame somewhere else. Some students say that they cannot do mathematics or give speeches. Peak Performers know that learning any new skill requires learning new concepts and basic fundamentals, which means a commitment to time and effort. **Figure 1-2** is the Peak Performance Commitment Pyramid. It will help you assess your willingness to use effort and discipline toward becoming a Peak Performer.

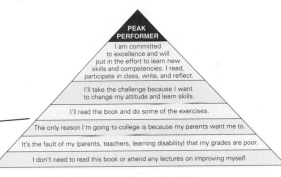

Figure 1-2   Peak Performance Commitment Pyramid

Boxed features highlight important chapter concepts.

Assess Your Skills

Here is a way to assess your skills at various times during your school and work careers. Answer the following questions. Use this list at the end of a term or year or at the beginning of a new job or when considering a job change. Your answers may surprise you. They may remain the same or change dramatically. What is important is that you are assessing, changing, and growing.

- Are you a lifelong learner?

- Are you a creative problem solver?

- Do you know several jobs and have an understanding of many tasks?

- Are you an expert in one area?

- Do you constantly strive to make your job more interesting and improve your productivity?

- Do you add value to the company?

- Do you cooperate and work well with others?

- Do you manage your career professionally?

- Are you efficient, effective, professional, and accurate in your work?

- Are you both people- and task-oriented?

- Are you motivated and a self-starter?

- Do you have excellent communication skills?

- Do you have important personal qualities such as responsibility, character, and integrity?

WORKPLACE TRENDS

Keep a section in the appendix of your Career Development Portfolio for workplace trends that relate directly to your occupation. One of the important trends will be education on the job. Some of this education will be informal and consist of on-the-job-training, acquiring new job skills, learning to complete challenging projects, and shifting your work style so that you can work more effectively with others. Other education will be formal, such as seminars, courses, and workshops designed to improve or add to your job skills. These formal courses may include training in topics such as:

The **Review and Study Notes** summarizes the chapter's major themes. Affirmations, visualization techniques, and peak performance strategies are provided.

Case Studies provide you with student situations and later work experiences that apply the strategies and techniques discussed in the chapter.

CHAPTER

1

Review and Study Notes

Affirmations

* I know how I learn best and I value my strengths.
* I enhance my natural preference by integrating all learning styles.
* Self-assessment helps me to achieve my goals.
* I enjoy using the whole of my intelligence.
* I enjoy keeping an updated portfolio of skills and competencies.
* I am willing to put in the effort to succeed.
* I have what it takes to be a Peak Performer.

Visualization

Find a comfortable and quiet place to which you can retreat undisturbed. Sit upright in a comfortable chair with your feet flat on the floor and your spine straight. Rest your hands, palms up and relaxed, in your lap. Close your eyes and think of your favorite place. Concentrate on this scene as you focus on your breathing. Now see yourself as calm, centered, and committed to excellence in all areas of your life. You know your strengths and are continuously assessing the results you create. See yourself feeling confident and goal-directed and in love with life. See the image of yourself graduating and accomplishing your goals. Feel your sense of purpose and your passion for living. Remind yourself that you can come to this special place within your mind to seek inner strength and peace at any time.

Peak Performance Strategies

1. Self-assessment is essential for success.
2. Connect SCANS competencies to school and job success.
3. Use critical thinking and honesty in self-assessment.
4. Focus on the importance of commitment and effort.
5. Discover your learning and personality styles.
6. Integrate all learning styles.
7. Understand and manage systems and resources.

CASE B   *In the Classroom*

Sonya Green is a freshman at a career school. She talked with an advisor in the career center because she thinks she wants a career in business but isn't certain. She expected to take a vocational test that would match her with a perfect career. Instead, Sonya finds that she is reflecting about her values, beliefs, needs, likes, interests, personal characteristics, and abilities. She is questioning the purpose of all this writing and assessment.

What strategies from this chapter would help Sonya see the value of self-assessment?

_____

_____

_____

In the Workplace

Sonya is now a CPA and has reached a major career crossroads. She has just been offered the position of district manager in a larger branch of a major accounting firm. She is thrilled with the offer. It means a big salary and recognition of all her years of hard work and attending night school while working full-time as a bookkeeper. However, it also means she would have to move away from family and friends, her husband would have to find another job, and her young children would have to adjust to a new school and community. Can she handle the heavy work commitment and still devote the necessary time and energy to her family? In addition, she would be supervising a large staff. She knows she has good management skills, but is she ready to supervise so many people?

1. What strategies from this chapter could help Sonya with all these doubts and questions?

_____

_____

2. How can self-assessment of her values and interests assist her with this major career decision?

_____

_____

Tips and **quotes** appear in the margins to make it easy for you to enhance your understanding.

TIP

Sit in the front, observe, and listen to your instructor. Ask questions, look for patterns, and summarize main points. Continually bring your mind back to the present by pretending that you are in a private conversation with your instructor.

> "Climb the mountains and get their good tidings. Nature's peace will flow into you as sunshine flows into trees. The winds will blow their own freshness into you, and the storms their energy, while cares will drop off like autumn leaves."
>
> —*John Muir*

Career Development Portfolio activities guide you through the important steps of connecting school skills and workplace skills.

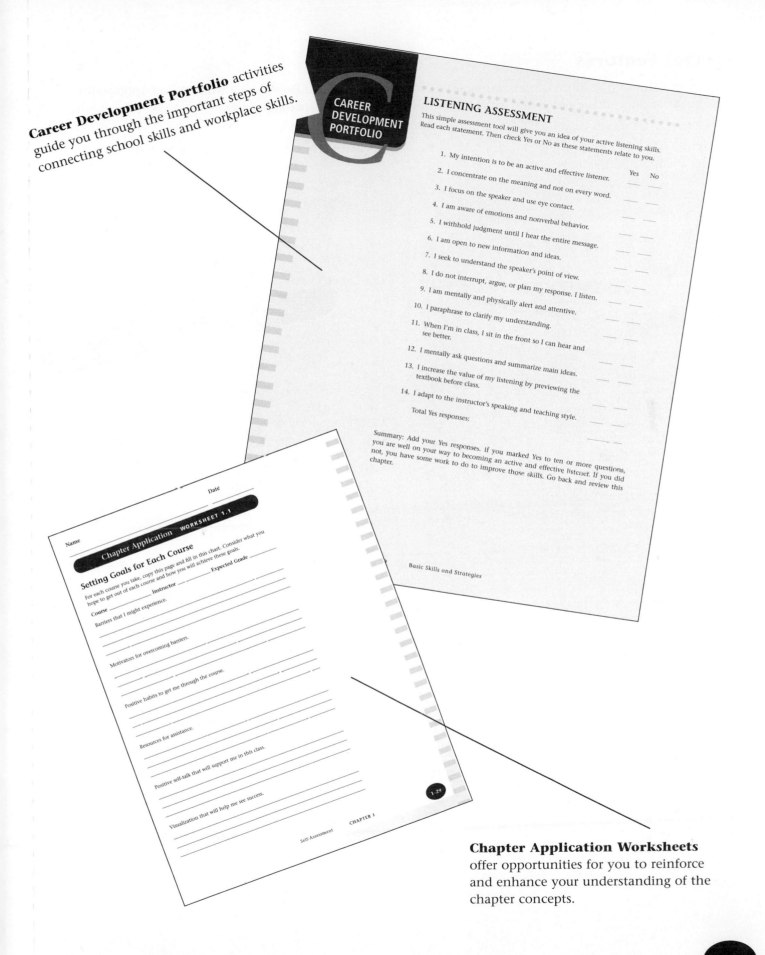

CAREER DEVELOPMENT PORTFOLIO

LISTENING ASSESSMENT

This simple assessment tool will give you an idea of your active listening skills. Read each statement. Then check Yes or No as these statements relate to you.

	Yes	No
1. My intention is to be an active and effective listener.		
2. I concentrate on the meaning and not on every word.		
3. I focus on the speaker and use eye contact.		
4. I am aware of emotions and nonverbal behavior.		
5. I withhold judgment until I hear the entire message.		
6. I am open to new information and ideas.		
7. I seek to understand the speaker's point of view.		
8. I do not interrupt, argue, or plan my response. I listen.		
9. I am mentally and physically alert and attentive.		
10. I paraphrase to clarify my understanding.		
11. When I'm in class, I sit in the front so I can hear and see better.		
12. I mentally ask questions and summarize main ideas.		
13. I increase the value of my listening by previewing the textbook before class.		
14. I adapt to the instructor's speaking and teaching style.		
Total Yes responses:		

Summary: Add your Yes responses. If you marked Yes to ten or more questions, you are well on your way to becoming an active and effective listener. If you did not, you have some work to do to improve those skills. Go back and review this chapter.

Basic Skills and Strategies

Name _____   Date _____

Chapter Application   WORKSHEET 1.1

Setting Goals for Each Course

For each course you take, copy this page and fill in this chart. Consider what you hope to get out of each course and how you will achieve these goals.

Course _____ Instructor _____ Expected Grade _____

Barriers that I might experience.

_____
_____
_____

Motivators for overcoming barriers.

_____
_____

Positive habits to get me through the course.

_____
_____

Resources for assistance.

_____
_____

Positive self-talk that will support me in this class.

_____
_____

Visualization that will help me see success.

_____
_____

Self-Assessment   CHAPTER 1

1-29

Chapter Application Worksheets offer opportunities for you to reinforce and enhance your understanding of the chapter concepts.

Special Features

Throughout the third edition of *Peak Performance Success in College and Beyond,* you will have an opportunity to reinforce the concepts presented in each chapter through a variety of special features.

Critical Thinking Logs allow you to apply chapter theory in individual or small group activities.

Trailmarker exercises provide information about study techniques, preparing for tests, time management, test-taking skills, note taking, or effective speaking skills.

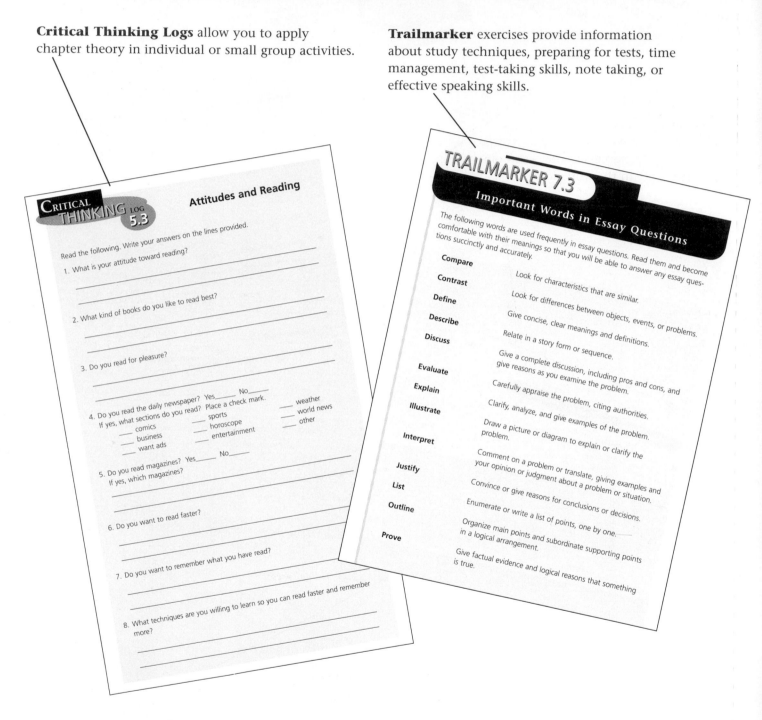

CRITICAL THINKING LOG 5.3

Attitudes and Reading

Read the following. Write your answers on the lines provided.

1. What is your attitude toward reading?

2. What kind of books do you like to read best?

3. Do you read for pleasure?

4. Do you read the daily newspaper? Yes_____ No_____
   If yes, what sections do you read? Place a check mark.
   ____ comics   ____ sports   ____ weather
   ____ business   ____ horoscope   ____ world news
   ____ want ads   ____ entertainment ____ other

5. Do you read magazines? Yes_____ No_____
   If yes, which magazines?

6. Do you want to read faster?

7. Do you want to remember what you have read?

8. What techniques are you willing to learn so you can read faster and remember more?

TRAILMARKER 7.3

Important Words in Essay Questions

The following words are used frequently in essay questions. Read them and become comfortable with their meanings so that you will be able to answer any essay questions succinctly and accurately.

Compare	Look for characteristics that are similar.
Contrast	Look for differences between objects, events, or problems.
Define	Give concise, clear meanings and definitions.
Describe	Relate in a story form or sequence.
Discuss	Give a complete discussion, including pros and cons, and give reasons as you examine the problem.
Evaluate	Carefully appraise the problem, citing authorities.
Explain	Clarify, analyze, and give examples of the problem.
Illustrate	Draw a picture or diagram to explain or clarify the problem.
Interpret	Comment on a problem or translate, giving examples and your opinion or judgment about a problem or situation.
Justify	Convince or give reasons for conclusions or decisions.
List	Enumerate or write a list of points, one by one.
Outline	Organize main points and subordinate supporting points in a logical arrangement.
Prove	Give factual evidence and logical reasons that something is true.

Technology Focus provides you with information linking the computer with school and the workplace.

Technology FOCUS: Computers and Reading Comprehension

Computers can help you with reading comprehension. Use the following techniques when working on a computer.

* After you read a paragraph, section, or chapter, keyboard a brief summary of what you have read on your computer.
* While you read, keyboard computer notes of the important concepts. This will help increase your comprehension and recall.
* Create a computer file which lists questions you think will be on the test and questions to ask your instructor and study team. Bring the list to class or to your study team.
* Explore reading skills on the Internet. Use this book's Web site. http://peak.glencoe.com

Career Focus deals with people in workplace situations and demonstrates how the techniques you are learning for success in the classroom can also apply in the workplace.

CAREER FOCUS: MINDFULNESS AT WORK

Being aware, mindful, alert, and focused in the present are key factors in active listening and are critical for career success. Molly Tyler has just been promoted to conference planner in a large hotel. Her job involves taking accurate notes at meetings and conferences; jotting down directions; and predicting questions, concerns, and potential problems. To be an active listener at work, Molly:

1. Observes verbal and nonverbal messages and clarifies expectations.
2. Is mindful, alert, and aware.
3. Listens actively to main points and seeks to understand.
4. Organizes notes to highlight important information.
5. Reviews details of events and follow-up procedures.

Here's an example of Molly's note taking on the job.

Peak Performers in the Workplace create a positive mind-set for listening by:

1. Suspending judgment about your boss.
2. Adjusting to your boss's style of management.
3. Being prepared for meetings.
4. Developing a partnership with your boss.
5. Listening for understanding.
6. Clarifying instructions.
7. Assessing results.

Initial Meeting for Conference Planning   April 20, 2000
Name of group: National Dental Conference
Dates of Conference: November 28, 29, and 30, 2000

Conference facility needs:
Hotel accommodations
Number of meeting rooms
Hospitality suites
Reception rooms
Size of groups

Equipment needs:
Podium
Head table
Refreshments
Seating
Blackboard
Confirm with master calendar

Follow up with:
Secure budget by _____
Overhead
Audiovisual equipment
Copy machine

Staffing needs:
Secretary
Registration workers
Extra waiters
Dining and reception needs
Coffee and refreshments
Breakfasts, lunches, dinners
Cocktail hour

Profiles of Peak Performers
appear in each chapter and offer
you a story about a public figure
who has succeeded in business,
made a social contribution, or
has overcome the odds.

OPRAH WINFREY

Whether you live in the megalopolis of Chicago, Illinois, or a small town in the middle of Wyoming, you have probably heard of Oprah Winfrey. She is watched by millions of people every afternoon on television, and she has appeared in various television and big-screen movies.

Yet this well-known entertainment personality and executive suffered years of abuse during her childhood and finally ran away when she was a teenager. It was only when she went to live with her father that she finally experienced family structure. Perhaps it was during this supportive time that her love for reading had its beginning. Her father would have her read and do a book report each week. And now many years and many books later, her television viewers listen to her feature a book review during her Book Club segment. This special segment encourages people to read for fun and personal growth.

Oprah truly made an effort to become a Peak Performer. She attended Tennessee State University, where she majored in Speech Communications and Performing Arts. The television persona of today began when she was hired by a radio station in Nashville as a reporter. By 1976, Oprah was a talk show host in Baltimore while continuing to serve as an anchor and news reporter. In January 1984, Oprah landed a talk show host position in Chicago. This show became the *Oprah Winfrey Show* you are familiar with today. By 1985, it became the number 1 talk show and led to Oprah's three daytime Emmy Awards in the categories of Outstanding Host, Outstanding Talk Service Program, and Outstanding Direction. Oprah is not only the youngest person but also the fifth woman to receive the International Radio and Television Society's Broadcaster of the Year Award.

Oprah Winfrey also received praise for her first movie role in *The Color Purple*. She was nominated for the Academy Award and Golden Globe Award for Best Supporting Actress for her performance in this adaptation of Alice Walker's masterpiece.

In spite of a difficult beginning, Oprah has become a true Peak Performer. As the first woman in history to own and produce her own talk show, she also owns a production company called HARPO, which has produced several excellent movies including *The Women of Brewster Place, Kaffir Boy,* and *Beloved.*

Source: See this book's Web site.
http://peak.glencoe.com

BEN COHEN AND JERRY GREENFIELD

What's a Chunky Monkey®? Who's a Cherry Garcia®? If you are an ice cream fan or looked recently in your local grocer's freezer, you know they are popular flavors of Ben & Jerry's Ice Cream. Officially known as Ben & Jerry's, Vermont's Finest Ice Cream and Frozen Yogurt, this corporation was founded by two childhood buddies transplanted from Long Island—Ben Cohen and Jerry Greenfield. From its small beginnings in a renovated gas station, this Vermont-based corporation now distributes its products in all fifty states.

Ben Cohen, who loved ice cream as a kid and liked to experiment by adding cookies and candies to his ice cream concoctions, attended Skidmore College. He studied pottery and jewelry making and taught at a small residential community high school on a working farm. He began experimenting with making ice cream for his students. In the late seventies, he decided to go into an ice cream venture with Jerry Greenfield.

Jerry was a premed major at Oberlin College in Ohio. He worked as an ice cream scooper in the school's cafeteria. After graduation, he applied twice to medical school but was rejected each time. So, he and Ben began researching the ice cream business. They took a correspondence course in ice cream making and finally opened Ben & Jerry's Ice Cream Parlor in Burlington, Vermont, in May 1978 with a $12,000 investment. They soon became well-known for their unusual flavors and socially responsible business practices.

Ben & Jerry's is a company with a strong set of unique values. Its philosophy has been called "caring capitalism." Both Ben and Jerry wanted to be a force for social change and improve the quality of life for their employees. To accomplish this, the Ben & Jerry's Joy Gang was created. It is a group of employees dedicated to bringing more joy into the workplace. Employees plan fun activities that create a strong team spirit and fun work climate.

Ben & Jerry's community spirit is shown by sponsorship for projects that entail creative problem solving and hopefulness. They were recognized with the Corporate Giving Award by the Council on Economic Priorities in 1988, for donating 7.5 percent of their pretax earnings to nonprofit organizations. Their commitment to give back to the community was also recognized by the U.S. Small Business Administration.

Ben continues to be an active founding member of Businesses for Social Responsibility and both he and Jerry speak about these issues publicly.

Ben Cohen and Jerry Greenfield are Peak Performers. They have combined innovation and management skills with compassion, integrity, and character.

Souce: See this book's Web site at http://peak.glencoe.com

Additional Study Resources

Glencoe *Peak Performance Success in College and Beyond*, Third Edition, Web Site

This unique study center contains a wealth of material and multi-reinforcement and assessment tools. Visit it at http://peak.glencoe.com. Here is what you will find:

- A Tip of the Week
- Peak Speak—contains articles for you about student success
- Links to
  — Study and test-taking skills
  — Career development
  — Self-assessment
  — Life skills
  — Other Web links

- Peak Speak—contains articles for you about student success

- Newsletter

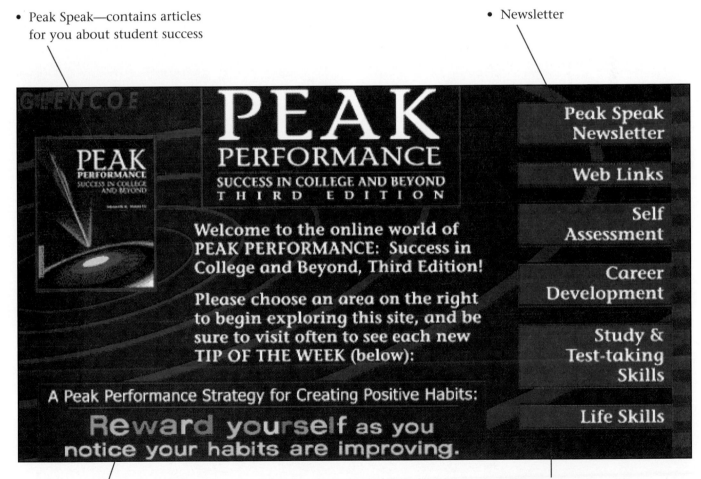

- A Tip of the Week

- Links to
  — Study and test-taking skills
  — Career development
  — Self-assessment
  — Life skills
  — Other Web links

SELF-ASSESSMENT

*A worker needs one thing only:
To learn how to learn.*

—Peter Drucker, Management Theorist

Learning Objectives

In Chapter 1 you will learn

- the importance of self-assessment.

- to use critical thinking skills in assessment.

- the skills and competencies for school and job success.

- about your learning and personality styles.

Learning is a lifelong journey. Successful people or people regarded as Peak Performers are on this journey. They are lifelong learners. It is important for you to think of yourself as a lifelong learner. It is an essential step in your journey toward becoming successful and a Peak Performer.

Today's society is constantly faced with many types of changes—economic, technological, societal, etc. To meet the challenges of these various changes, you will need to learn new skills continually in school, on your job, and throughout your life. You will meet these challenges in your study and learning strategies, in your methods of performing work-related tasks, even in the way you view your personal life and lifestyle.

When thinking about making a change, the first step involved is self-assessment. Self-assessment requires seeing oneself objectively. Although this may sound like a modern concept, it really is not. Centuries ago people asked themselves the universal questions: *Who am I? What shall I do? What shall become of me?* You may have asked yourself these very questions using different words. You may have asked yourself: *What course of study should I take? What kind of job do I want? Where should I go to school? What should I do with my life?*

Throughout this book, as you journey on the road to becoming a Peak Performer, you will discover methods that will help you with the task of self-assessment and change. In this chapter, you start the journey by assessing your learning and personality styles. The chapter's assessment exercises will help you look at your life as a dynamic motion picture rather than as a brief snapshot. These exercises will be the foundation for your Career Development Portfolio. This portfolio will furnish you with a lifelong assessment tool for learning where you are and where you want to go, while documenting the results. Creating this portfolio of skills and competencies will become your guide for remaining marketable and flexible throughout your career.

THE IMPORTANCE AND BENEFITS OF SELF-ASSESSMENT

Self-assessment requires facing the truth and seeing yourself objectively. For example, it is not easy to admit that you procrastinate or lack certain skills. Even when talking about your strengths, you may feel embarrassed. However, honest self-assessment is the foundation for making positive changes in your life. Self-assessment can help you

- understand how you learn best.
- achieve better grades.
- work smarter, not harder.
- work in alignment with your strengths and natural preferences.
- create a positive and motivated state of mind.
- work more effectively with diverse people.
- make sound and creative decisions about school and work.

Success Principle 1:
Focus on **REALITY,**
not *Illusion.*

USE CRITICAL THINKING SKILLS
IN SELF-ASSESSMENT

Self-assessment involves using your critical thinking skills. You may ask yourself: *What exactly is critical thinking?*

Critical thinking is using a logical, rational, and systematic thought process to think through a problem or situation. Since critical thinking determines the quality of the decisions that you make in all areas of your life, it is an important theme throughout this book. To help you fine-tune your critical thinking skills, make a habit of assessing your thinking skills regularly. Also, complete the critical thinking exercises and log entries throughout this book.

As you complete the self-assessment and critical thinking log entries, use the following guidelines in your journey to becoming a critical thinker:

1. Suspend judgment until you have gathered facts and reflected on them.
2. Look for evidence that supports or contradicts your initial assumptions and beliefs.
3. Adjust your opinions as new information and facts are known.
4. Ask questions, look for proof, and examine the problem closely.
5. Reject incorrect or irrelevant information.
6. Consider the source of the information.
7. Remain committed to the truth and not your own beliefs or biases.

SKILLS AND COMPETENCIES FOR SCHOOL
AND JOB SUCCESS

Have you ever asked yourself: *What does it take to be successful on a job?* Many of the skills and competencies that characterize a successful student can also apply to the successful employee. Becoming aware of the connection between school success and job success helps you see how the skills learned in the classroom will eventually apply to the skills needed in the workplace.

Over the years, employers have told educators what skills they want employees to have. In 1990, Elizabeth Dole, who was then the Secretary of Labor, created SCANS (Secretary's Commission on Achieving Necessary Skills). The commission members included business and industry leaders, human resource personnel, and other top advisors in labor and education. The Peak Performance Competency Wheel in Figure 1-1 on page 1-4 illustrates the skills and competencies recommended by SCANS for job success.

The skills and competencies illustrated in the Peak Performance Competency Wheel are necessary not only for job success but also for school success. You can apply and practice them now by completing the Peak Performance Assessment Test that appears on page 1–5. Be honest and use critical thinking skills as you do so.

Notice that Statement 24 on the assessment test deals with commitment and effort. Commitment to your goals, whether they are educational, career-related, or personal, is vital if you are to succeed. Nothing happens without commitment and effort.

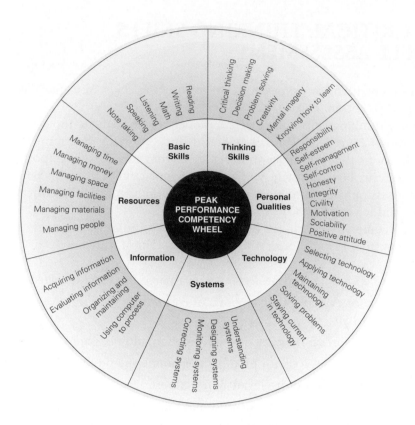

Figure 1-1   The Peak Performance Competency Wheel

One of the major reasons people do not succeed in school or in their careers is a lack of willingness to make the necessary effort. If success does not come quickly, they give up and place the blame somewhere else. Some students say that they cannot do mathematics or give speeches. Peak Performers know that learning any new skill requires learning new concepts and basic fundamentals, which means a commitment to time and effort. Figure 1-2 is the Peak Performance Commitment Pyramid. It will help you assess your willingness to use effort and discipline toward becoming a Peak Performer.

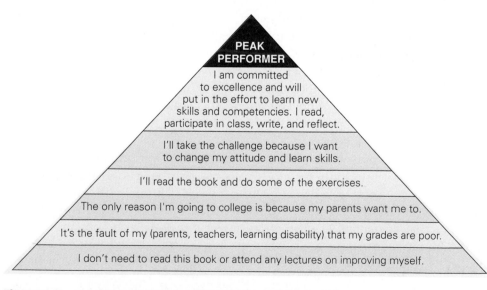

Figure 1-2   Peak Performance Commitment Pyramid

PART ONE   Building Foundation Skills

PEAK performance
ASSESSMENT

Name _____ Date _____

Assess each skill. Rate yourself on a scale of 1 to 5 by placing a checkmark.

	Peak Performance				
Area	**Good** 5	4	**OK** 3	2	**Poor** 1
1. Reading	—	—	—	—	—
2. Writing	—	—	—	—	—
3. Speaking	—	—	—	—	—
4. Mathematics	—	—	—	—	—
5. Listening and note taking	—	—	—	—	—
6. Critical thinking and reasoning	—	—	—	—	—
7. Creative problem solving	—	—	—	—	—
8. Mental visualization	—	—	—	—	—
9. Knowing how you learn	—	—	—	—	—
10. Honesty and integrity	—	—	—	—	—
11. Positive attitude and motivation	—	—	—	—	—
12. Responsibility	—	—	—	—	—
13. Flexibility/ability to adapt to change	—	—	—	—	—
14. Self-management and emotional control	—	—	—	—	—
15. Self-esteem and confidence	—	—	—	—	—
16. Time management	—	—	—	—	—
17. Money management	—	—	—	—	—
18. Management and leadership of people	—	—	—	—	—
19. Interpersonal and communication skills	—	—	—	—	—
20. Ability to work well with culturally diverse group	—	—	—	—	—
21. Organization and evaluation of information	—	—	—	—	—
22. Understanding systems	—	—	—	—	—
23. Understanding technology	—	—	—	—	—
24. Commitment and effort	—	—	—	—	—

DISCOVERING YOUR LEARNING STYLE

TIP There is no *one way* or *best way* to learn.

As a lifelong learner, you need to know how to learn. As both a student and an employee, it is important to understand and maximize your learning potential, explore how you learn best, and use this knowledge to your advantage.

Everyone processes information differently. Knowing your preferred learning style can increase your effectiveness in school or at work and enhances your self-esteem. No longer will you ask, *Why am I struggling so hard to learn or to organize information?* Knowing how you learn best can help you to reduce frustration, focus on your strengths, and integrate various styles.

Learning Inventories

Just as there is no "one" or "best" way to learn, there is no "one" instrument, assessment, or inventory that can categorize how you learn best. Any learning style assessment is, at best, a guide.

Two such assessment instruments are

1. The Learning Style Inventory.
2. The Four-Grid Personality and Team Profile.

These instruments have been adapted from various sources and involve twenty-five years of research. They have been given to hundreds of students. They are simple, yet they provide valuable clues and strategies for determining how you learn and process information and relate to others. They will also provide you with possible college majors and careers that fit your personality and style.

The purpose of these inventories is to provide a guide, not to categorize you into a specific box. As you review various assessments, you will begin building a profile of how you process and learn information and relate to other people.

ARE YOU A READER, A LISTENER, OR A DOER?

One way to explore how you learn best is to ask yourself if you are a reader, a listener, or a doer. Do you get more information from *reading and seeing, talking and listening*, or *doing*? Of course, you do all these things, but your learning strength or style may be in one of these areas.

A person who learns better by reading possesses a visual learning style. Someone who learns better by listening is considered an auditory learner, and a kinesthetic learner learns by touch.

Trailmarker 1.1 on page 1–8 has a Learning Style Inventory that will help you discover your learning style.

Visual Learners

Visual learners prefer to see information and read material. They learn more effectively with pictures, graphs, illustrations, diagrams, timelines, photos, pie charts, and visual design. They like to contemplate concepts, reflect, and summarize information in writing. They use arrows, pictures, and bullets to highlight points. Visual learners are often holistic and reflective learners. Visual learners

- remember what they **see** better than what they hear.
- prefer to have written directions that they can **read.**
- learn better when someone shows them rather than tells them.
- like to read, highlight, and write summaries.
- keep a list of things to do when planning the week.
- tend to be quiet in class and watch facial expressions.
- like to **read** for pleasure and to learn.
- may want to be an interior designer, drafter, proofreader, writer, or artist.

Auditory Learners

Auditory learners rely on their hearing sense. They like tapes, music, and listening to information, such as lectures. They like to work in study teams and enjoy class discussions. They like to talk and recite and summarize information aloud. They like to create rhymes out of words and play music that helps them concentrate. When they take study breaks, they listen to music or chat with a friend. Auditory learners

- remember what they **hear** better than what they see.
- prefer to **listen** to instructions.
- like to listen to music and talk on the telephone.
- plan the week by talking it through with someone.
- use rhyming words to remember.
- learn best when they hear the assignment as well as see it.
- may enjoy being a disc jockey, trial lawyer, counselor, musician.

TRAILMARKER 1.1

Learning Style Inventory

Name _____ Date _____

Determine your learning preference. Complete each sentence by checking *a, b,* or *c*. No completion is correct or better than another.

1. I learn best when I
   a. _____ see information.
   b. _____ hear information.
   c. _____ have hands-on experience.

2. I like
   a. _____ pictures and illustrations.
   b. _____ tapes and listening to stories.
   c. _____ working with people and going on field trips.

3. For pleasure and relaxation, I love to
   a. _____ read.
   b. _____ listen to music and tapes.
   c. _____ garden or play sports.

4. I tend to be
   a. _____ contemplative.
   b. _____ talkative.
   c. _____ a doer.

5. To remember a ZIP Code, I like to
   a. _____ write it down several times.
   b. _____ say it out loud several times.
   c. _____ doodle and draw it on any available paper.

6. In a classroom, I learn best when
   a. _____ I have a good textbook, visual aids, and written information.
   b. _____ the instructor is interesting and clear.
   c. _____ I am involved in doing activities.

7. When I study for a test I
   a. _____ read my notes and write a summary.
   b. _____ review my notes aloud and talk to others.
   c. _____ like to study in a group and use models and charts.

8. I have
   a. ____ a strong fashion sense and pay attention to visual details.
   b. ____ fun telling stories and jokes.
   c. ____ a great time building things and being active.

9. I plan the upcoming week by
   a. ____ making a list and keeping a detailed calendar.
   b. ____ talking it through with someone.
   c. ____ creating a computer calendar or using a project board.

10. When preparing for a math test, I like to
    a. ____ write formulas on note cards or use pictures.
    b. ____ memorize formulas or talk aloud.
    c. ____ use marbles, Legos, or three-dimensional models.

11. I often
    a. ____ remember faces but not names.
    b. ____ remember names but not faces.
    c. ____ remember events but not names or faces.

12. I remember best
    a. ____ when I read instructions and use visual images to remember.
    b. ____ when I listen to instructions and use rhyming words to remember.
    c. ____ with hands-on activities and trial and error.

13. When I give directions, I might say,
    a. ____ "Turn right at the yellow house and left when you see the large oak tree. Do you see what I mean?"
    b. ____ "Turn right, go three blocks, and turn left onto Buttermilk Lane. Okay? Got that? Do you hear what I'm saying?"
    c. ____ "Follow me" after giving directions by using gestures.

14. When driving in a new city, I prefer to
    a. ____ get a map and find my own way.
    b. ____ stop and get directions from someone.
    c. ____ drive around and figure it out by myself.

Scoring: Count the number of check marks for all your choices.

Total *a* choices _____ (Visual Learning Style)
Total *b* choices _____ (Auditory Learning Style)
Total *c* choices _____ (Kinesthetic Learning Style)

The highest total indicates your predominant learning style.

Kinesthetic Learners

Kinesthetic learners are usually well coordinated and like to touch things, and learn best by *doing.* They like to collect samples, write out information, spend time outdoors, and relate to the material that they are learning. They like to connect abstract material to something concrete in nature. When taking study breaks, they go for a walk outdoors. Kinesthetic learners

- create an experience.
- use hands-on activities and computer games.
- build things and put things together.
- use flash cards, models, and **physical activity.**
- draw, doodle, use games and puzzles, and play computer games.
- take field trips and collect samples.
- relate abstract information to something concrete.
- may enjoy being a chef, surgeon, medical technician, nurse, automobile mechanic, electrician, engineer, forest ranger, police officer, or dancer.

Discovering Your Personality and Team Style

The concept of personality and temperaments is not new. Writers and writings that date back for centuries have addressed different temperaments. Hippocrates, the ancient Greek founder of modern medicine, classified people according to personality types. Carl Jung (1875–1961), the psychologist, proposed that people are fundamentally different but also fundamentally alike. He believed that people are made up of two basic types—*extrovert* (energized by people, outgoing, and social) and *introvert* (energized by time alone, prefer world of ideas and thoughts). He also defined two types of perception, or how you gather information: sensing and intuiting. *Sensors* learn best from their senses and like to organize information systematically. *Intuitives* rely on hunches, intuition, and nonverbal perceptions. They dislike routine and structure. Jung defined two ways of relating to the outer world: judging and perceiving. *Judges* prefer orderly, planned, structured learning and working environments. They like control and closure. *Perceivers* prefer flexibility and spontaneity and like to allow life to unfold. Jung also defined two ways of evaluating: thinking and feeling. *Thinkers* depend on rational logic and analysis. They tend to be unemotional and use a systematic evaluation of data and facts for problem solving. *Feelers* are sensitive to the concerns and feelings of others and value harmony. They dislike creating conflict.

These four psychological functions are involved in information gathering and evaluation. Jung suggested that differences and similarities among people could be understood by combining preferences. Although people are not exclusively one way or another, he maintained that they have basic preferences, just as you prefer right-handedness or left-handedness.

Jung's work inspired Katherine Briggs and her daughter Isabel Briggs-Myers to design the Myers-Briggs Type Inventory (MBTI) in 1962. Their work put Jung's theory into practical use. Since then, over 20 million people have completed the MBTI. Later David Keirsy and Marilyn Bates combined the sixteen Myer-Briggs types into four temperaments.

Review Figure 1-3 on page 1-12 to determine the characteristics and likes of **Extroverts, Introverts, Sensors, Intuitives, Thinkers, Feelers, Judges,** and **Perceivers.** It is an adaptation of Keirsy's and Bates's work.

Then complete the Trailmarker 1.2 on page 1-13. This inventory will help you determine your personality style. Find out if you are an **Analyzer, Supporter, Creator,** or **Director.**

Extroverts	Introverts	Sensors	Intuitives
Gregarious	Quiet	Practical	Speculative
Active, talkative	Reflective	Experience	Use hunches
Speak, then think	Think, then speak	See details	See the big picture
Outgoing, social	Fewer, closer friends	Sequential, works steadily	Work in burst of energy
Energized by people	Energized by self	Feet on the ground	Head in the clouds
Like to speak	Like to read	Concrete	Abstract
Like variety and action	Like quiet for concentration	Realistic	See possibilities
Interested in results	Interested in ideas	Sensible and hard working	Imaginative and inspired
Do not mind interruptions	Dislike interruptions	Good at precise work	Dislike precise work

Thinkers	Feelers	Judges	Perceivers
Analytical	Harmonious	Decisive	Tentative
Objective	Subjective	Closure	Open-minded
Impersonal	Personal	Plan ahead	Flexible
Factual	Sympathy	Urgency	Open time frame
Want fairness	Wants recognition	Organized	Spontaneous
Detached	Involved	Deliberate	Go with the flow
Rule	Circumstances	Set goals	Let life unfold
Things, not people	People, not things	Meet deadlines	Procrastinate
Lineal	Whole	Just the facts	Interested and curious

Figure 1-3   Adaptation of Jung's Work

TRAILMARKER 1.2

The Four Grid Personality and Team Profile

The following statements indicate your preference in working with others, in making decisions, and in learning new information. Read each statement with its four possible choices. Rank **4** to the choice **MOST** like you, **3** to the choice **ALMOST** like you, **2** next to the choice **SOMEWHAT** like you, and **1** next to the choice **LEAST** like you.

1. I learn best when I
   a. _____ rely on logical thinking and facts.
   b. _____ am personally involved.
   c. _____ can look for new patterns through trial and error.
   d. _____ use hands-on activities and practical applications.

2. When I'm at my best, I'm described as
   a. _____ dependable, accurate, logical, and objective.
   b. _____ understanding, loyal, cooperative, and harmonious.
   c. _____ imaginative, flexible, open-minded, and creative.
   d. _____ confident, assertive, practical, and results-oriented.

3. I respond best to instructors and bosses who
   a. _____ are factual and to the point.
   b. _____ show appreciation and are friendly.
   c. _____ encourage creativity and flexibility.
   d. _____ expect me to be involved, be active, and get results.

4. When working in a group, I tend to value
   a. _____ objectivity and correctness.
   b. _____ consensus and harmony.
   c. _____ originality and risk taking.
   d. _____ efficiency and results.

5. I am most comfortable with people who are
   a. _____ informed, serious, and accurate.
   b. _____ supportive, appreciative, and friendly.
   c. _____ creative, unique, and idealistic.
   d. _____ productive, realistic, and dependable.

6. Generally, I am
   a. _____ methodical, efficient, trustworthy, and accurate.
   b. _____ cooperative, genuine, gentle, and modest.
   c. _____ high-spirited, spontaneous, easily bored, and dramatic.
   d. _____ straightforward, conservative, responsible, and decisive.

7. When making a decision, I'm generally concerned with
   a. _____ collecting information and facts to determine the right solution.
   b. _____ finding the solution that pleases others and myself.
   c. _____ brainstorming creative solutions that feel right.
   d. _____ quickly choosing the most practical and realistic solution.

8. You could describe me in one word as
   a. ____ analytical.
   b. ____ caring.
   c. ____ innovative.
   d. ____ productive.

9. I excel at
   a. ____ reaching accurate and logical conclusions.
   b. ____ being cooperative and respecting people's feelings.
   c. ____ finding hidden connections and creative outcomes.
   d. ____ making realistic, practical, and timely decisions.

10. When learning at school or on the job, I enjoy
    a. ____ gathering facts, technical information, and being objective.
    b. ____ making personal connections, being supportive, working in groups.
    c. ____ exploring new possibilities, tackling creative tasks, and being flexible.
    d. ____ producing results, solving problems, and making decisions.

Scoring: To determine your style, rank your choices in each column. Then add the column totals. If you have the highest number in the

- choice a column, you are an Analyzer.
- choice b column, you are a Supporter.
- choice c column, you are a Creator.
- choice d column, you are a Director.

	Choice a	Choice b	Choice c	Choice d
1.	_____	_____	_____	_____
2.	_____	_____	_____	_____
3.	_____	_____	_____	_____
4.	_____	_____	_____	_____
5.	_____	_____	_____	_____
6.	_____	_____	_____	_____
7.	_____	_____	_____	_____
8.	_____	_____	_____	_____
9.	_____	_____	_____	_____
10.	_____	_____	_____	_____
Total	_____	_____	_____	_____
	Analyzer	Supporter	Creator	Director

My dominant personality style is _____ (you may be close in two areas). Most people become skilled in one or two areas rather than all four.

CONNECTING LEARNING STYLES AND PERSONALITY STYLES

The following descriptions elaborate on the four personality styles you met in Trailmarker 1.2. You may have discovered that you have a dominant style of personality—Analyzer, Creator, Supporter, or Director.

The next few pages will give you a broader understanding of these personality types. However, remember that inventories only provide clues. People change over time and react differently in different situations.

Analyzer

Analyzers tend to be logical, thoughtful, loyal, exact, dedicated, steady, and organized. They like following direction and work at a steady pace. The key word for Analyzers is **thinking.**

Strengths: Creating concepts and models, and thinking things through.

Goal: Intellectual recognition.

Classroom Style: **Analyzers** relate to instructors who are organized, know their facts, present information logically and precisely. They prefer objective tests rather than essay. They dislike ambiguity of subjects that do not have right or wrong answers. They tend to be left-brained and seem more concerned with facts and abstract ideas and concepts than with people.

Learning Style: **Analyzers** often perceive information abstractly and process it reflectively. They learn best by observing and thinking through ideas. They like models, lectures, textbooks, and working alone. They like to work with things and analyze how things work. They evaluate and come to a precise conclusion.

Effective Traits	Ineffective Traits	Possible Majors	Possible Careers	How to Relate to Analyzers
Objective	Too cautious	Accounting	Computer programmer	Be factual
Logical	Abrupt	Bookkeeping	Accountant	Be logical
Thorough	Unemotional	Mathematics	Bookkeeper	Be formal and thorough
Precise	Aloof	Computer programming	Drafter	Be organized, detached, and calm
Detail-oriented	Indecisive	Drafting	Electrician	Be accurate and use critical thinking
Disciplined	Unimaginative	Electronics	Engineer	State facts briefly and concisely
		Auto mechanics	Auto mechanic	Do not be over friendly
			Technician	
			Librarian	
Bottom Line				
Analyzers want things done right. Their favorite question is "What?"				

Supporters

People who are **Supporters** tend to be cooperative, honest, sensitive, warm, and understanding. They relate well to others. They value harmony and are informal, approachable, and tactful. In business, they place emphasis on people and are concerned with the feelings and values of those around them. The key word for Supporters is **feeling.**

Strengths: Supporters like to clarify values and brainstorm many different ideas.

Goal: to create harmony and cooperation.

Classroom Style: **Supporters** tend to learn best when they like an instructor and feel accepted and respected. They like to integrate course concepts with their own experiences. They relate to instructors who are warm and sociable, tell interesting stories, use visuals, and are approachable. They learn best by observing, listening, and sharing ideas and feelings.

Learning Style: **Supporters** perceive information concretely and process it reflectively. They are intuitive and like to deal with their feelings. They prefer learning information that has personal meaning, and they seek clarity and integrity. They prefer learning in the here and now and like concrete things they can see and touch. They are unhurried and like to listen and observe. They are intuitive and imaginative thinkers and need to be personally involved.

Effective Traits	Ineffective Traits	Possible Majors	Possible Careers	How to Relate to Supporters
Understanding Gentle Loyal Cooperative Sensitive Diplomatic Appreciative	Overly compliant Passive Slow to act Naïve Unprofessional Can be overly sensitive	Counseling or therapy Social work Home economics Nursing Medical assisting Physical therapy Education	Elementary teacher Physical therapist Social worker Therapist Counselor Nurse Medical assistant	Be friendly Be positive Be sincere and build trust Listen actively Focus on people Focus on personal values Create a comfortable, relaxed climate Create an experience they can relate to

Bottom Line
Supporters want things done harmoniously and want to be personally involved. Their favorite question is "Why?"

Creators

Creators are innovative, flexible, spontaneous, creative, and idealistic people. Creators are risk takers and love drama, style, and imaginative design. They like the abstract fresh ideas and are passionate about their work. The key word for Creators is **action.**

Strengths: Creating visions that inspire people.

Goal: Making things happen by turning ideas into action.

Classroom Style: **Creators** learn best in innovative and active classrooms. They relate to instructors who have a passion for their work and are challenging, imaginative, flexible, present interesting ideas, and make the topic exciting.

Learning Style: **Creators** learn by doing and being involved in active experiments. They perceive information concretely and process it actively. They like games, role-playing, stories, plays, illustrations, drawings, music, and visual stimuli. They ask questions and enjoy acting on ideas. They are usually good public speakers. They are future-oriented and good at seeing whole systems.

Effective Traits	Ineffective Traits	Possible Majors	Possible Careers	How to Relate to Creators
Imaginative	Unrealistic	Art	Writer	Be enthusiastic
Creative	Unreliable	English	Politician	Be involved
Visionary	Inconsistent	Music	Travel agent	Be flexible
Idealistic	Hasty	Design	Hotel manager	Be accepting of
Enthusiastic	Impulsive	Hospitality	Cartoonist	change
Innovative	Impatient	Travel	Musician	Focus on
	Fragmented	Theater	Composer	creative ideas
		Communications	Artist	Talk about
			Journalist	dreams and
			Craftsperson	possibilities
			Florist	
			Costume designer	
			Sales	
			Scientist	

Bottom Line

Creators want things done with a sense of drama and style. Their favorite question is "What if?"

Directors

Directors are confident, self-directed, energetic, dynamic, decisive, risk-takers, and results-oriented people. They like to be the leader of groups and respond to ideas of others when they are logical and reasonable. Their strength is in the practical application of ideas. The key word for Directors is **results.**

Strengths: Integrating theory with practice.

Goal: To find practical solutions to problems.

Classroom Style: **Directors** relate to instructors who are organized, clear, to the point, punctual, and results-oriented. They prefer field trips and hands-on activities.

Learning Style: **Directors** learn by hands-on, direct experience. They learn best by practical application. They like classes that are relevant. They work hard to get things done.

Effective Traits	Ineffective Traits	Possible Majors	Possible Careers	How to Relate to Directors
Confident Assertive Active Decisive Forceful Effective leader Results-oriented	Aggressive Pushy Insistent Overpowering Dominating	Business Law enforcement Construction Woodworking Carpentry Business management Wildlife conservationist Forestry	Lawyer Police officer Detective Consultant Banker Park ranger Forest ranger Administrator for outdoor recreation	Set deadlines Be responsibile for your actions Focus on results Focus on achievements Do not try to take control Do not make excuses Have a direction Make known any time or changes in schedule

Bottom Line
Directors want to produce results in a practical manner. Their favorite word is "How?"

INTEGRATE ALL STYLES

The psychologist Henry James believed that people use less than 5 percent of their potential. *Think of what you could accomplish if you could learn to work in alignment with your natural preferences and to integrate different learning styles and techniques.* The Peak Performance Learning Pyramid in Figure 1-4 illustrates how you can maximize your effectiveness by integrating learning styles.

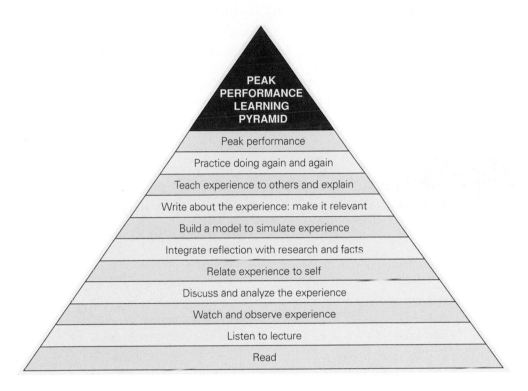

Figure 1-4   The Peak Performance Learning Pyramid

Integrating Both Sides of the Brain

Do you use both sides of your brain? "I use my whole brain!" you might answer. And indeed you do. However, each side, or hemisphere, of the brain specializes in certain functions. Some researchers have suggested that the dominant brain hemisphere may play a significant role in how people learn.

I hear and I forget.
I see and I remember.
I do and I understand.

—*Confucius*

A case study conducted by two researchers from Johns Hopkins discusses the relationship between thought and memory and the brain. This study shows that the brain has two systems by which it classifies information. One is linguistic (left brain), and the other is visual (right brain). People who are left-brain dominant use a logical, rational, and detailed approach, while people who are right-brain dominant use an intuitive, insightful, and holistic approach to solving problems and processing new information. When you integrate both sides of the brain while incorporating all the learning styles, you enhance learning, memory, and recall, and you achieve a synergistic, or whole-brain, effect. Figure 1-5 on page 1-21 integrates the four personality and learning style types and left–right brain dominance.

CRITICAL THINKING LOG 1.1

Reflect on Your Learning Style

Read the following and write your comments on the lines.

1. Describe a time you really enjoyed learning a new skill. You may have been learning how to use a computer, speak a foreign language, or participate in a school or sports event that you really cared about.

_____

_____

2. What helped you to succeed?

_____

_____

3. What was your predominant learning style? Did you listen to directions (auditory), watch others perform the skill or read about it (visual), or practice it yourself (kinesthetic)?

_____

_____

4. Do you practice critical thinking to make effective decisions? Give examples.

_____

_____

PART ONE   Building Foundation Skills

ANALYZER

Logical
Analytical
Literal
Factual
Precise
Accurate
Orderly
Objective
Systematic
Technical
Likes models

Learns by thinking

SUPPORTER

Gentle
Caring
Sensitive
Harmonious
Peacemaker
Emotional
Sociable
Cooperative
Understanding
Adaptable
Seeks meaning

Learns by observing and sharing

Less Assertive

Left-Brain Studying
Neat, organized study area
Daily schedules
Work on one project at a time
Study alone
Study consistently
Plan studying

Right-Brain Studying
Cluttered desk
Flexible study times
Jump from project to project
Study with others
Study in bursts of energy
Cram last minute

Abstract Conceptual

Concrete Experimental

DIRECTOR

Confident
Practical
Realistic
Disciplined
Problem solver
Controlled
Dependable
Results-oriented
Pragmatic
Traditional
Wants results

Learns by practical application

CREATOR

Innovative
Imaginative
Free-spirited
Visionary
Impulsive
Open-minded
Creative
Curious
Energetic
Spontaneous
Wants to create

Learns by trial and error

More Assertive

Figure 1–5

Peak Performance Brain Power

Overcoming the Barriers to Self-Assessment

The biggest barrier to self-assessment is lazy and faulty thinking. A lack of critical thinking keeps you from making a commitment to reality. Look honestly at all areas of your life. You cannot learn positive behaviors and attitudes if you ignore a problem, pretend it isn't serious, hope it will improve magically, or blame it on other people or events. Use critical thinking to assess your performance and creative problem solving for planning innovative ways to overcome discouragement and setbacks. For example, you may have discovered in your assessment exercises that you are often late for class or work. Create ways to help you become punctual. Set your clock ten minutes early and get organized the night before. Establishing positive habits helps you overcome negative behavior. Do not to get discouraged. Acknowledge and work on your shortcomings and focus on your successes.

Technology FOCUS: Computers and Web Practice

Part One

Computers can help you with self-assessment. Keeping a self-assessment journal on your computer allows you to update often. You can identify:

1. Your interests.
2. What is most important for you.
3. Skills.
4. Abilities.
5. Accomplishments.
6. Personal qualities and traits.
7. Strengths and weaknesses.
8. Values and needs.

Part Two

If you have not visited a Web site, pair up with someone in class who can help you. Then show someone else how to do it. Think about what your own Web site would look like. What qualities and skills would you like to highlight?

For more information on sports, travel, and fun ideas, visit this book's Web site at:

http://peak.glencoe.com

Self-Assessment and the Workplace

Self-assessment is important for job success. Peak Performers see self-assessment and feedback as tools for self-discovery and positive change. They keep a portfolio of their successes, awards, letters of appreciation, training programs, and projects that they have completed. They assess their expectations with the results they achieved and set goals for improvement. They keep all their performance evaluations and comments, and a record of informal evaluations. Peak Performers integrate all types of learning styles to enhance their natural learning preference.

For example, they may use tape recorders, flow charts, visual aids, training films, role playing, and small task-force teams to accomplish their work. They may combine planning meetings with retreats or training programs with after-hours bowling teams or receptions.

CAREER FOCUS: BENCHMARK ASSESSMENT

Benchmarking is a management term that describes the process by which a company measures its quality, tasks, and services against the leading competition. You can use benchmarking in your Career Development Portfolio as a guide for establishing performance targets and a plan of action for implementing changes. Benchmarking can help improve study skills in all your classes, your performance in sports, your leadership skills in clubs, and the results you achieve in your job.

Carol Johnson's Benchmark Plan

Meet Carol Johnson. She has just accepted an administrative position for a software company. She wants to overcome shyness and give presentations that are more effective.

To help herself accomplish this, she created a benchmark assessment plan. Carol begins her benchmarking plan by

- gathering information through observation and research about the criteria for excellence in public speaking.
- observing confident people.
- assessing her own skills and attitudes.
- deciding on the skills and attitudes she needs to improve.
- listing the barriers to improvement—fear, resistance, and negative self-talk.
- establishing performance targets.
- recording accurate feedback.
- developing strategies to help her create the results she wants. For example, she videotapes herself and practices confident tone, body stance, and eye contact.
- monitoring results and varying and adjusting strategies.
- establishing measurable performance targets.

Peak Performers in the Workplace Are:

- Ethical and honest.
- Able to perform job skills.
- Able and willing to learn.
- Able to solve problems.
- Able to convey enthusiasm and a positive attitude.
- Flexible and able to adapt to change.
- Able to communicate with diverse people.
- Able to apply high technical expertise.

TRAILMARKER 1.3

Benchmark Plan

Peak Performers regularly analyze and assess their work style, habits, skills, weaknesses, and progress. They know it is important to look at the whole picture, and therefore they include both positive and negative points.

   Now it's your turn to start a benchmark plan. Be honest with yourself and list your strengths and weaknesses. Use Carol's benchmark plan as a guide as you set goals and monitor results.

1. The strengths that work best for me are

_____

_____

_____

_____

2. I am most effective when I

_____

_____

_____

_____

3. I am very good at

_____

_____

_____

_____

4. The skills I would most like to improve are

_____

_____

_____

_____

MORRIS (MO) SIEGEL

Who is Morris (Mo) Siegel? Why is he a Peak Performer?

On a quiet afternoon, you may have tried drinking one of Mo's famous teas. Colorado born and bred, he is the founder and Chairman of the Board for Celestial Seasonings. Headquartered in Boulder, Colorado, this multimillion-dollar company produces a variety of herbal teas that hold a sturdy place in the tea market.

In the sixties, a nineteen-year-old Mo Siegel began his company by picking wild herbs for tea. Joined by his wife and some friends, the tea was packaged and sold in hand-sewn muslin bags to local health food stores. By the early seventies, using his interest in the environment and innate creativity, Mo changed the image of tea drinking. From the beginning, he used environmentally correct teabags packaged without strings and tags.

Applying his creative style of personality to his business, the company prospered, and it was eventually purchased by Kraft. Mo left Celestial Seasonings. However, he continued to stretch his interests in world needs by founding Omega Technologies, Inc., and Earth Wise, Inc. Omega grows algae containing Omega 3, a chemical that helps prevent heart disease, and Earth Wise produces garbage bags from recycled plastic, kitchen cleaner from vegetable oil, and other products.

In the late eighties, management bought Celestial back from Kraft, and Mo returned in 1991. He continues to direct Celestial Seasonings corporate decisions to align with making the world a better place. In addition, the company continues to prosper through his leadership—a man who believes it should be illegal to be boring.

Earlier in this chapter, you read that one of the major reasons people do not succeed in school or in their careers is a lack of willingness to make the necessary effort. Mo Siegel was certainly willing to make the effort. He is a man of vision, ideas, and a great deal of energy. This is why he is a Peak Performer.

Source: http://peak.glencoe.com

Review and Study Notes

Affirmations

- I know how I learn best and I value my strengths.
- I enhance my natural preference by integrating all learning styles.
- Self-assessment helps me to achieve my goals.
- I enjoy using the whole of my intelligence.
- I enjoy keeping an updated portfolio of skills and competencies.
- I am willing to put in the effort to succeed.
- I have what it takes to be a Peak Performer.

Visualization

Find a comfortable and quiet place to which you can retreat undisturbed. Sit upright in a comfortable chair with your feet flat on the floor and your spine straight. Rest your hands, palms up and relaxed, in your lap. Close your eyes and think of your favorite place. Concentrate on this scene as you focus on your breathing. Now see yourself as calm, centered, and committed to excellence in all areas of your life. You know your strengths and are continuously assessing the results you create. See yourself feeling confident and goal-directed and in love with life. See the image of yourself graduating and accomplishing your goals. Feel your sense of purpose and your passion for living. Remind yourself that you can come to this special place within your mind to seek inner strength and peace at any time.

Peak Performance Strategies

1. Self-assessment is essential for success.
2. Connect SCANS competencies to school and job success.
3. Use critical thinking and honesty in self-assessment.
4. Focus on the importance of commitment and effort.
5. Discover your learning and personality styles.
6. Integrate all learning styles.
7. Understand and manage systems and resources.

CASE Studies

CASE A   *In the Classroom*

Peter Davis is a freshman at a community college. He isn't sure if he should be in college. He didn't apply himself in high school and was bored much of the time. He would have liked to travel or work for a while, but his parents really wanted him to go to college. Other students seem to know what they want to be and seem to have better study habits. Peter likes to get involved with projects and has a hands-on approach to learning. He finds it difficult to sit and read or listen to lectures. He likes the outdoors and he is creative. Once he's involved in a project, he is committed.

1. What strategies from this chapter would be most useful to help Peter understand himself better and gain a sense of commitment?

   _____

   _____

2. What would you suggest to Peter to help him find direction and a sense of purpose?

   _____

   _____

In the Workplace

Peter is now a law enforcement officer. He knows that he performs best when he learns by doing. He likes to be active, involved, and physical. He works well on a team. When he is learning a new procedure or writing reports, he bounces ideas off his coworkers. Peter enjoys his job and is amazed at how much learning is involved. He also knows he needs to get more education if he wants to advance but wonders how he'll balance his job, school, and family life. Peter admits that he didn't like his formal education nor did he excel at subjects that were unrelated to law enforcement. He never really learned good study habits and knows that he will have to be committed to going back to school.

What suggestions would you give Peter to help him do better in school and learn faster on the job?

   _____

   _____

CASE B

Sonya Green is a freshman at a career school. She talked with an advisor in the career center because she thinks she wants a career in business but isn't certain. She expected to take a vocational test that would match her with a perfect career. Instead, Sonya finds that she is reflecting about her values, beliefs, needs, likes, interests, personal characteristics, and abilities. She is questioning the purpose of all this writing and assessment.

What strategies from this chapter would help Sonya see the value of self-assessment?

_____

_____

_____

In the Workplace

Sonya is now a CPA and has reached a major career crossroads. She has just been offered the position of district manager in a larger branch of a major accounting firm. She is thrilled with the offer. It means a big salary and recognition of all her years of hard work and attending night school while working full-time as a bookkeeper. However, it also means she would have to move away from family and friends, her husband would have to find another job, and her young children would have to adjust to a new school and community. Can she handle the heavy work commitment and still devote the necessary time and energy to her family? In addition, she would be supervising a large staff. She knows she has good management skills, but is she ready to supervise so many people?

1. What strategies from this chapter could help Sonya with all these doubts and questions?

_____

_____

_____

2. How can self-assessment of her values and interests assist her with this major career decision?

_____

_____

_____

Name

Date

_____   _____

Setting Goals for Each Course

For each course you take, copy this page and fill in this chart. Consider what you hope to get out of each course and how you will achieve these goals.

Course _____ **Instructor** _____ **Expected Grade** _____

Barriers that I might experience.

_____

_____

_____

Motivators for overcoming barriers.

_____

_____

_____

Positive habits to get me through the course.

_____

_____

_____

Resources for assistance.

_____

_____

_____

Positive self-talk that will support me in this class.

_____

_____

_____

Visualization that will help me see success.

_____

_____

_____

Name _____ Date _____

Creating a Semester Calendar

At the start of each semester, take the time to schedule your week.
Planning reduces stress!

Week of:	Sunday	Monday	Tuesday	Wednesday	Thursday	Friday	Saturday

Chapter Application   WORKSHEET 1.3

Self-Assessment Grid

Check the items you assess each month.

	Self-awareness	Motivation	Positive self-talk	Time management skills	Stress management	Listening skills	Note-taking skills	Reading and comprehension	Memory	Learning styles	Writing skills	Research skills	Speaking skills	Creative problem solving	Critical thinking	Decision making	Connecting all your classes	Connecting school with work	Relating to instructor	Positive habits
Term:																				
Month:																				
Week 1:																				
2:																				
3:																				
4:																				
Month:																				
Week 1:																				
2:																				
3:																				
4:																				
Month:																				
Week 1:																				
2:																				
3:																				
4:																				
Overall:																				

AUTOBIOGRAPHY

The purpose of this exercise is to look back and assess how you learned skills and competencies. Write down the turning points, major events, and significant experiences of your life. This autobiography or chronological record will record events that helped you make decisions, set goals, or discover something about yourself. Record both negative and positive experiences and what you learned from them. For example:

1976 Moved to Michigan.   **Learned to make new friends and be flexible.**

1977 First job babysitting.   **Learned responsibility and critical thinking.**

1978 Grandmother   **Helped with care. Learned dependability,**
became ill.   **compassion.**

TIP Soon after you complete a class or leave a job, ask your instructor, advisor, supervisor, or coworker for a letter of recommendation. You can make your request easier by supplying a list of projects, accomplishments, and skills and competencies. Keep these letters in your Career Development Portfolio.

2

ATTITUDE, MOTIVATION, AND INTEGRITY

Nothing great was ever achieved without enthusiasm.

—Ralph Waldo Emerson, American poet, essayist, and philosopher

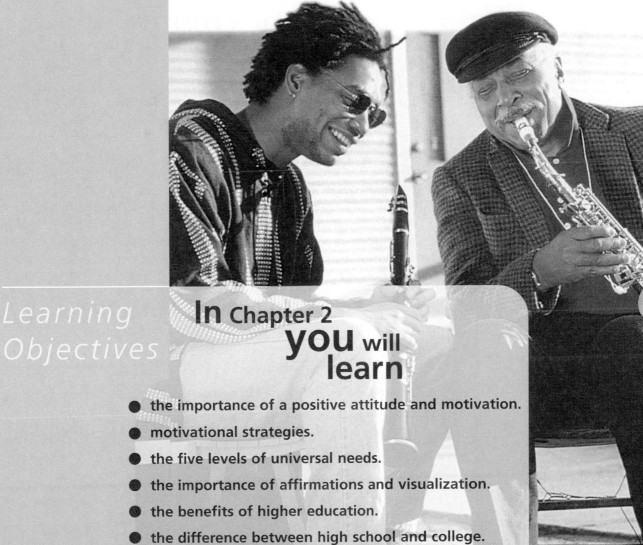

Learning Objectives

In Chapter 2 you will learn

- the importance of a positive attitude and motivation.
- motivational strategies.
- the five levels of universal needs.
- the importance of affirmations and visualization.
- the benefits of higher education.
- the difference between high school and college.
- the importance of synergy.
- to make the connection between school and work.
- the importance of personal qualities.
- to put character first and develop a code of ethics.

The central theme throughout this book is that you can begin to change your thoughts, images, and behaviors to produce the results you want in every aspect of your life. Athletes who make it to the Olympics have the skill, talent, attitude, and motivation to win the gold. Top athletes know that an inner drive is required to be a Peak Performer in any sport and in all areas of life. Why do some people push the limits of their endurance, strive for excellence, and want to test their strength and skill? What do concert pianists, dancers, or gymnasts have that enables them to practice for hours every day, constantly striving to improve and to excel? They have motivation and a positive attitude driven by effort and commitment.

Thus, success in your personal life, school, and career is more dependent on a positive attitude, motivation and effort than on inborn ability or intelligence. To move you toward this concept, you will find motivational strategies in this chapter to help you. You will learn the importance of personal qualities and why character is so important for school and job success. Recognizing the link between school and the world of work is a key motivational strategy.

THE IMPORTANCE OF A POSITIVE AND MOTIVATED ATTITUDE

Nothing is more important for success in school and in your job than a positive attitude. Your attitude influences the outcome of a task more than any other factor.

You also have to be motivated to achieve success in school, in work, and in life. Motivation is the inner drive that moves you to action. Even when you are discouraged or face setbacks, motivation can help you bounce back and keep you on track. You may have skills, experience, intelligence, and talent, but you will accomplish little if you are not motivated to direct your energies toward specific goals.

People with a positive attitude demonstrate enthusiasm, vitality, optimism, and a zest for living. They are more likely to be on time, aware and alert, and able to work well even when they have an unpleasant assignment. There is a strong link between attitude and behavior. You are more likely to change your attitude if you see this connection and recognize the value of a positive attitude. A positive attitude encourages:

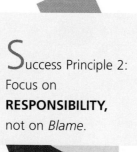

Success Principle 2:
Focus on
RESPONSIBILITY,
not on *Blame*.

* higher productivity.
* an openness to learning at school and on the job.
* school and job satisfaction.
* creativity in solving problems and finding solutions.
* the ability to work with diverse people.
* enthusiasm and a "can do" outlook.
* confidence and higher self-esteem.
* the ability to channel stress and increased energy.
* a sense of purpose and direction.

A negative attitude can drain you of enthusiasm and energy, and it can result in absenteeism, tardiness, and impaired mental and physical health. In addition, people who have a negative attitude tend to

- feel they are victims and helpless to make changes.
- focus on the worst that can happen in a situation.
- blame external circumstances for their attitude.
- focus on the negative in people and situations.
- look at adversity as something that will last forever.
- be angry and blame other people.

HOW NEEDS AND MOTIVES INFLUENCE ATTITUDE AND MOTIVATION

One of the deepest urges in life is to become all that you can be and use all your intelligence and potential. Abraham Maslow, a well-known psychologist, developed the theory of a hierarchy of needs.

According to his theory, there are five levels of universal needs. Figure 2-1 illustrates these levels, moving from the lower-order needs—physiological and safety needs—to the higher-order needs—self-esteem and self-actualization. The lower-level needs must be met first, before considering attaining the higher-order needs. For example, it may be difficult for you to strive for recognition at school or work if you don't have enough money for food and rent.

For some people, the lower-level needs may include a sense of order, power, or independence. The higher levels, which address social and self-esteem factors, may include the need for companionship, respect, and a sense of confidence and belonging.

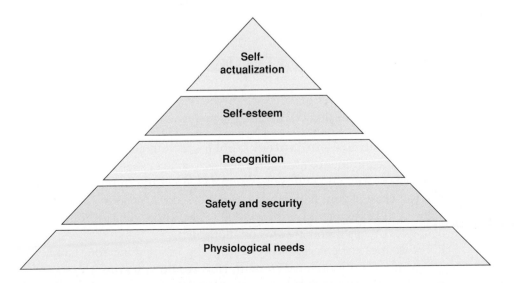

Figure 2–1
Maslow's Hierarchy of Needs

CRITICAL THINKING LOG 2.1

Needs and Motivation

1. What *needs* motivate you at this time?

   _____

   _____

2. What do you think will motivate you in twenty years?

   _____

   _____

3. Complete this sentence in your own words:
   For me to be more motivated, I need

   _____

   _____ .

As your lower needs are satisfied and cease to motivate, you begin to direct your attention to the higher-level needs for motivation. For example, once you feel confident, you will find that you have more energy and focus for defining and pursuing your dreams and goals. You will want to discover and develop your full potential and use the WHOLE of your intelligence. You will not only love learning new ideas, but you will also value emotional maturity, character, and integrity. You will be well on the path to self-actualization.

True happiness comes from possessing the confidence and personal power of knowing who you are and what you want to achieve. You can be a Peak Performer who reaches your full potential and actively achieves the results you want in all areas of your life.

MOTIVATIONAL STRATEGIES

Compare the factors that were involved when you were motivated and the factors you used to get you out of a slump with the following strategies.

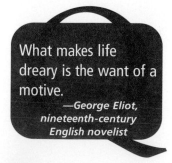

What makes life dreary is the want of a motive.
—*George Eliot, nineteenth-century English novelist*

1. **Act as if you are motivated.** Attitude can influence behavior and behavior can influence attitude. The way you act every day can affect your self-esteem, and your self-esteem can affect the things you do. You can change your behavior anytime. You don't need to wait until your attitude changes or until you FEEL motivated to begin the positive behaviors. *Act* as if you are already motivated.

   For example, pretend you are performing in a movie. Your character is a positive and motivated student. How would you enter the room? Would you be smiling? What would your breathing, posture, and muscle tension be like? What kinds of gestures and facial expressions would you use to create this character? What kind of friends would this person enjoy being with? Try acting out the part when you wake up in the morning and throughout the day. If you develop positive study and work habits and do them consistently, even when you don't FEEL like it, you'll be successful and this will create a positive state of mind. You are what you do consistently. Positive habits create success.

2. **Use affirmations.** Any discussion of motivation must include your self-talk or what you say to yourself throughout the day. Once you start paying attention to your self-talk, you may be amazed at how much of it is negative. Throughout the day, countless thoughts, images, phrases, and self-talk go through your brain almost unnoticed, but they have a tremendous influence on your mood and attitude. Your mind is most receptive just before sleep and when first waking up. The first step, then, is to replace negative self-talk with affirmations. For example, don't say, "I won't waste time today." That just reminds you that you have a habit of wasting time. Instead affirm, "I am setting goals and priorities and achieving the results I want. I have plenty of energy to accomplish all that I choose to do and I feel good when I'm organized and centered."

3. **Use visualization.** Visualization means seeing things in your mind's eye by organizing and processing information through pictures and symbols. When you imagine yourself behaving in certain ways, it becomes real. For example, Calvin Payne knew the power of visualization. He bought his graduation cap and gown and kept them in his room. He visualized himself crossing the stage in his gown to accept his diploma. This visual goal helped him when he suffered setbacks, frustration, and disappointments. He graduated with honors and now uses visualization in his career.

    Most right-brain people are visual and use imagery a great deal. They can see scenes in detail when they read or daydream. In fact, many right-brain people say that their imagery is almost like a movie camera with images of themselves, scenes of how they will react in certain situations, and a replay of what has occurred in the past. These images are rich in detail, expansive, and ongoing. Left-brain people tend to use imagery less, but it is a technique that can be learned and developed. You can learn to be more visual through practice.

    There are affirmations and visualization examples at the end of each chapter, and you may want to combine a morning and evening affirmation with visualization. Visualization will help you to see problems through formulas, read a recipe and see and taste the finished food, read blueprints and visualize the building, and see scenes and characters through narratives. You can also use mental imagery to create a positive, calm, and motivated state of mind.

4. **Use goals as motivational tools.** Just as a climber clearly visualizes the final summit or an athlete visualizes crossing the finish line, you too can visualize your final goal. Peak Performers have written goals. Keep your goals in your wallet and visualize yourself achieving them. Without a specific goal, it is easy to lack the motivation, effort, and focus required to go to classes and complete assignments. Make certain your goals are realistic. Excellence doesn't mean perfection or working compulsively toward impossible or unrealistic goals. If you strive for perfection, you're setting yourself up for frustration, which can lead to decreased motivation, lowered productivity, increased stress, and failure.

5. **Understand expectations.** You will be more motivated to succeed if you understand what is expected of you in college and in each class. Most instructors hand out a syllabus on the first day of class. Review it carefully and keep a copy in your class notebook. Review the syllabus with a study partner and clarify expectations with your instructor. Meet with your academic advisor to review general college and graduation requirements. College is different from high school and the more you understand expectations, the more focused you'll be to reach your goals.

6. **Study in teams.** Success in the business world relies on team skills; and the sharing of skills, knowledge, confidence, and decision-making abilities. Synergy means that the whole is greater than the parts. It means seeing and using the WHOLE system, not just isolated parts. You can increase your school and job success by learning, studying, and working in teams. You can also

   - teach each other material and outline main points.
   - read and edit each other's reports.
   - develop sample quizzes and test each other.
   - learn to get along with and value different people.

7. **Stay physically and mentally healthy.** It is difficult to motivate yourself if you don't feel well physically or emotionally. If you are ill, you miss classes, fall behind in studying, or both. Falling behind can cause you to worry and feel stressed. Talk your problems out, eat well, get plenty of exercise and rest, and create a balance of work and play. Of course, doing these things doesn't make you immune from colds and bouts with the flu, but they will help.

8. **Learn to reframe**. You don't have control over many situations or the actions of others, but you have total control of your responses. Reframing is choosing to see a situation in the best possible light. For example, Joan Bosch works at a fast-food hamburger place. She reframed this experience to focus on essential job skills. She is learning to be positive, dependable, hardworking, service oriented, flexible, and tolerant.

9. **Reward yourself.** The simplest tasks can become discouraging without rewards for making progress and for completion. Set up a system of appropriate rewards and consequences. Decide what your reward will be when you finish a project. For an easier task, the reward might be small, such as a cookie, a hot shower, or a ten-minute phone call to a friend. For a larger project, the reward could be listening to a new CD, going out to dinner, or throwing a small party. Here are some examples of rewards:

Listen to music	Cook your favorite meal	Play sports
Read a novel		Go to a movie
Go to a sporting event	Go to a museum	Visit friends
	Take a walk	Watch television
Take a nap	Work in a garden	Go camping
Take photos		

10. **Make learning relevant.** You will be more motivated if you make the connection between college and the world of work. Make learning relevant.

The Power of Affirmations and Visualization

The motivation cycle in Figure 2-2 illustrates how your self-esteem influences what you say to yourself, which in turn influences your physical reactions—breathing, muscular tension, posture, blushing. These physical reactions influence your behavior—both your verbal and nonverbal responses.

Isn't it amazing how the emotions, body, and mind are linked and interrelated? You cannot change one part without looking at the whole system. Try to remember how important affirmations and visualization are for creating a resourceful state of mind.

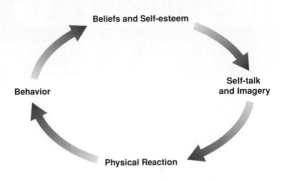

Figure 2–2   The Motivation Cycle

CRITICAL THINKING LOG 2.2   Commitment

1. Describe a time in your life when you were committed to something. You may have been active in sports, a club, a play, a recital, camp, or some other activity from which you really wanted to see results.
   a. What were the factors involved?

   _____

   _____

   b. How did you create this motivated state of mind?

   _____

   _____

2. Review a time in your life when you were depressed and were definitely not performing at your best.
   a. What were the factors involved?

   _____

   _____

   b. What were your feelings?

   _____

   _____

   c. How did you overcome this unmotivated state of mind?

   _____

   _____

TRAILMARKER 2.1

The Differences Between High School and College

In college, you will . . .

- have more responsibilities and must budget your time and money.
- be expected to express your opinions logically, not just give facts.
- be expected to motivate yourself.
- have more freedom and independence.
- have larger classes that meet longer for longer periods but less often.
- be responsible for monitoring your academic progress.
- be responsible for knowing procedures, regulations, and graduation requirements.
- write and read much more than you ever have in your life.
- be required to think critically and logically.
- receive less feedback and be tested less often but more comprehensively.
- have several textbooks and supplemental readings.
- have a greater volume of work and be required to turn in higher quality work.
- take the initiative to make new friends and to resolve conflicts with people.
- be exposed to people of different values, races, cultures, interests, and religions.
- learn to be tolerant and respectful of diversity.
- be exposed to new ideas and critique these ideas in a thoughtful way.
- get involved in the community, campus clubs, volunteer work, and internships related to your major.
- study in teams and work in cooperative learning groups with other students.

The Benefits of Higher Education

You will be more motivated to put in long hours of studying when you feel that the goal is worth it. Higher education is an excellent investment. No one can take your education away from you, and it pays large dividends. College graduates earn an average of well over $700,000 more in a lifetime than do high school graduates. (See Figure 2-3.) Although graduating from college or a career school won't guarantee you a great job, it pays off with more career opportunities, better salaries, more benefits, more job promotions, increased workplace flexibility, better workplace conditions, and greater job satisfaction. Many career centers at colleges make a commitment to help their students find employment.

Besides economic benefits, society and the workplace benefit when people improve their literacy. Various reports from the U.S. Department of Labor indicate that people who attend at least two years of college tend to

- make better decisions.
- be willing to learn new skills.
- have more hobbies and leisure activities.
- have a longer life expectancy.
- be healthier.
- vote more often.
- be more involved in the community.
- have more discipline and perseverance.
- have more self-confidence.
- learn to adapt to change.

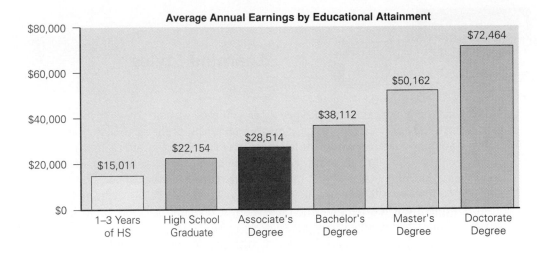

Average Annual Earnings by Educational Attainment

Figure 2–3

Average Annual Earnings by Educational Attainment

Affirmations

Listen to your self-talk for a few days. Jot down the negative thoughts you say to yourself. For example, when you first wake up, do you say, "I can't believe how tired I am" or "I don't want to go to class today"?

Notice how you respond when others greet you and ask how you are. Do you answer, "Terrible, I am so far behind"?

Do your thoughts and self-talk focus on lack of time, money, or problems? Observe when you are positive. How does this change your state of mind and your physical sense of well-being? List examples of your:

Negative Self-Talk	Affirmations
1. _____	1. _____
2. _____	2. _____
3. _____	3. _____
4. _____	4. _____
5. _____	5. _____

Learning Styles

You will feel more motivated and positive when you align your efforts with your learning style. Review your preferences and style and think of the factors that help motivate you. For example, **Auditory learners** may find that they are more motivated when they listen to a tape of their favorite inspirational music and say affirmations. **Visual learners** may find that they are more motivated when they surround themselves with pictures and practice visualizing themselves motivated and positive. **Kinesthetic learners** may be more motivated when they work on activities, dance, hike, jog, and work with others.

List ways you can motivate yourself in sync with your learning, personality, and team styles.

1. _____

2. _____

3. _____

4. _____

5. _____

6. _____

THE CONNECTION BETWEEN SCHOOL AND WORK

The connection between school and job success is a major theme in this book. Focusing on career success is also important for motivation. Successful students are motivated students who know how to connect success in school with success in their careers. They realize that what they learn in school correlates directly with finding, keeping, and succeeding in their chosen career. As you go through school, think about how the skills, personal qualities, and habits you are learning and demonstrating in class are related to job and life success.

As you develop your time and stress management skills, you will see improvements in your behavior in school and on the job. Time management may help you show up for class on time and be prepared every day, thus leading to better grades. Punctuality in school will carry over to punctuality for work. Stress management may help you to get along better with your roommates, instructors, or coworkers. Learning how to succeed in the school or college system will serve as a model for working effectively in organizational systems.

TRAILMARKER 2.2

Skills, School, and Career

Keep the following in mind as you connect school and job success:

Skills	School	Career
Basic skills	Foundation for schoolwork	Foundation for work tasks
Motivation	Motivated to attend classes	Motivated to excel at work
Thinking skills	Solve case studies, equations	Solve work problems
Creativity	Creative experiments	Creative work solutions
Control of time	Homework first	Work priorities in order
Control of money	Personal budget	Departmental budgets
Writing	Writing papers	Writing reports, memos
Speeches	Classroom speeches	Presentations
Test taking	Tests in classes	Performance reviews
Information	Selecting class information	Selecting work information
Learning	Learning for classes	Learning job skills
Systems	Learning college system	Learning organization
Resources	Using college resources	Using work resources
Technology	Using computers for papers	Using computers for work

WHAT KIND OF A STUDENT/WORKER ARE YOU?

A Peak Performer or an *A* student:

1. is alert, actively involved, and eager to learn.
2. consistently does more than is required.
3. consistently shows initiative and enthusiasm.
4. is positive and engaged.
5. can solve problems and make sound decisions.
6. is dependable, prompt, neat, accurate, and thorough.

A good worker or *B* student:

1. frequently does more than is required.
2. is usually attentive, positive, and enthusiastic.
3. completes most work accurately, neatly, and thoroughly.
4. often uses critical thinking to solve problems and make decisions.

An average worker or *C* student:

1. completes tasks that are required.
2. shows a willingness to follow instructions and learn.
3. is generally involved, dependable, enthusiastic, and positive.
4. provides work that is mostly thorough, accurate, and prompt.

A problem worker or *D* student:

1. usually does what is required.
2. has irregular attendance, is often late, or is distracted.
3. lacks a positive attitude or the ability to work well with others.
4. often misunderstands assignments and deadlines.
5. lacks thoroughness.

An unacceptable worker or *F* student:

1. does not do the work that is required.
2. is inattentive, bored, negative, and uninvolved.
3. is undependable and turns in work that is incorrect and incomplete.

The Most Common Reasons Students Fail

Between 30 to 50 percent of freshmen never graduate from their school. Here are the top reasons for failing:

1. Poor study skills and habits.
2. Lack of time management skills.
3. Lack of preparation for the demands and requirements of college.
4. Inability to handle the freedom available at college.
5. Too much partying.
6. Lack of motivation or purpose.
7. Failure to attend class regularly.
8. Failure to ask for help early.
9. Lack of effort and time spent in studying.
10. Failure to take responsibility for education: getting to know instructors, knowing expectations, setting goals, understanding deadlines, making up tests, redoing papers.

THE IMPORTANCE OF PERSONAL QUALITIES

There is a tendency to define intelligence as a score on an IQ test or SAT, or as school grades. Your IQ, however, is only one form of intelligence. School and career success requires more than skills or high IQ. SCANS identifies personal qualities as important competencies for success in the workplace. An awareness of the whole of your intelligence and the ability to demonstrate these competencies to instructors and employers is what defines Peak Performers.

Succeeding in college is not always a matter of ability, but of effort, commitment, motivation, and responsibility. These personal qualities are essential for school and work success.

Complete Critical Thinking Log 2.5. Include in your list personal qualities such as positive attitude, motivation, dependability, and honesty. Personal qualities, especially honesty, become more important when you think of hiring someone to work for a business that you own.

Character First: Integrity and Civility

Employers usually list honesty and character as the top personal qualities they want in employees. Think about Critical Thinking Log 2.5 on owning your own business. Isn't honesty a quality that would be important for you to have in the people who work for you? Did you include it on your list?

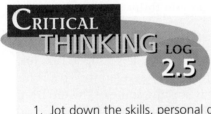

CRITICAL THINKING LOG 2.5
New Skills and Personal Qualities

1. Jot down the skills, personal qualities, and habits you are learning and demonstrating in each of your classes.

Skills	Personal Qualities	Habits
_____	_____	_____
_____	_____	_____
_____	_____	_____
_____	_____	_____

2. Pretend that you own your own business. List the skills and personal qualities you would want in the employees you hire.

Employees' Skills	Employees' Personal Qualities
_____	_____
_____	_____
_____	_____
_____	_____

Let's say that a candidate sends in an outstanding résumé. She has a college degree, experience, and a great personality, and she is positive and motivated, but you find out that she stole from her last employer. No matter how bright or talented someone is, you cannot have a dishonest person working for you.

Character, integrity, civility, and ethics are related. **Character** can be defined as virtuous traits, such as trustworthiness, respect, responsibility, caring, fairness, and citizenship. **Integrity** refers to the tools needed for moral conduct. **Civility** refers to the tools needed for interaction and the sacrifices required for living respectfully with others. **Ethics** deals with more precise and often written standards of conduct and morals in a particular society.

Creating and Following a Code of Ethics

There is no universal code of ethics. However, individuals take actions that are generally viewed as either good and ethical or as wrong and unethical. You will be faced with situations in your personal, school, or business life that will force you to make decisions that will be viewed as either ethical or unethical. Sometimes it is not easy. Everyone is faced at one time or another with situations that demand tough decisions.

Take Peggy Lyons. She has a midterm test to take. This test will determine 50 percent of her final grade. She has been very busy and has not attended class or her study group for the past week. She knows she probably won't do well on this test, but she needs a good grade. She knows the instructor is fair and has been asking if anyone knows where she has been. Someone Peggy met in the cafeteria tells her she can "buy" a copy of the test. She's tempted. What do you think she will do? What would you do?

Meet Rey Armas. Rey goes to the local community college. For the past six months, he has been working part-time in an electronics store. Rey's supervisor, Joe, has worked in the store for ten years. Joe is about fifty and has a family. This is his only means of support. Rey has discovered that Joe is stealing some of the electronics components to sell on the side. Rey likes Joe. What should Rey do? What would you do?

Tora Ueda was walking home from the bus stop one evening. She witnessed a mugging. She knew the mugger and the victim. She was terrified and fled home. When she arrived home, she debated whether to call the police and report the crime. What should she do? What would you do?

Peggy, Rey, and Tora are all faced with tough decisions. Their final decisions will be viewed by others as either ethical or unethical. They will have to call on their own personal code of ethics. When defining their code and their subsequent actions, they may find the following questions helpful. You too may find them helpful when developing a code of ethics.

1. How would I feel about this situation being on the front page of the newspaper?
2. If my mother or child were in this room, would I feel good telling them about this decision or action?
3. Would I feel comfortable telling the truth about this situation?
4. What could be the negative consequences of this decision or action?
5. What could be future repercussions?

6. Is this decision or action illegal or morally wrong?

7. Am I causing unnecessary harm to someone because of this decision?

8. Am I following the Golden Rule of treating others as I would want to be treated?

Character and Ethics

Integrity and honesty are essential qualities. It is important you assess and develop them as you would any skill. Use critical thinking to answer these questions.

1. What is the most difficult ethical dilemma you have faced in your life?

   _____

2. Do you have a code of ethics that helps guide you when making decisions? Explain.

   _____

3. When did you learn about honesty?

   _____

4. Who was your role model?

   _____

5. Do you have a code of ethics at your college? Look it up in your catalog or ask the dean of students for a copy.

   _____

6. Does your company have a code of ethics?

   _____

7. If you were the chief executive officer (CEO) or owner of a small company, what would you want to include in your code of ethics?

   _____

8. How would you make certain that employees understood and honored this code of ethics?

   _____

We know not of the future, and cannot plan for it much. But we can hold our spirits and our bodies so pure and high, we may cherish such thoughts and such ideals, and dream such dreams of lofty purpose, that we can determine and know what manner of men we will be whenever and wherever the hour strikes that calls to noble action . . . . No man becomes suddenly different from his habit and cherished thought.

—Joshua L. Chamberlain, General Commander 20th Maine, Union forces, Battle of Gettysburg

Now let's look at other personal qualities that SCANS and business leaders say are essential for success.

Responsibility

Peak Performers take responsibility for their thoughts, state of mind, and behavior. They don't blame others for their problems, but use their energy to face and solve them. They are persistent and patient. They know they must exert a consistent amount of high effort to achieve their goals. They keep their word and agreements. When they say they are going to do something, they keep their commitment.

People can depend on them. For example, they show up prepared and on time for their study teams; repay student loans; and clean up their messes at home, on campus, and at the workplace. If they make a mistake, they own up to it and do what they can to correct it.

Other personal qualities related to responsibility include displaying a high level of perseverance, punctuality, concentration, attention to details, and follow-through, and setting high standards. What you do or don't do in one area of your

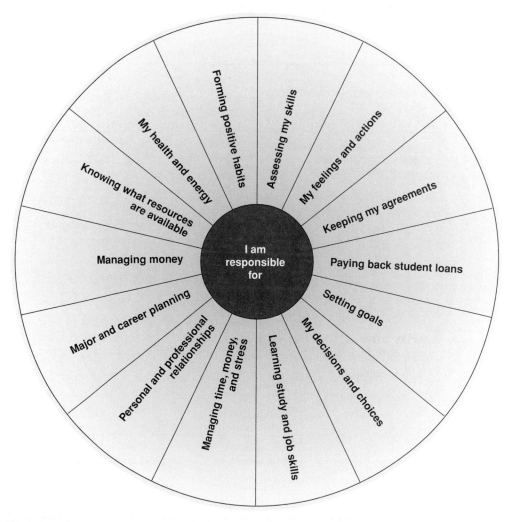

Figure 2–4
Cycle of Responsibility

life affects other areas of your life and other people as well. Peak Performers realize that they are responsible for their attitudes and actions, and they know that they have the power to change them.

A negative attitude is sometimes the result of not coping maturely with change, conflict, and frustration. Emotional, physical, and social changes are part of being an adult. Learning to adjust to frustration and discouragement can take many forms. Some people may withdraw or become critical, shy, sarcastic, or unmotivated and listless. Blame, excuses, justification, and criticism of others are devices for those who refuse to accept responsibility for their behavior and state of mind. Tune in and acknowledge your feelings and attitudes. Decide if they support your goals and, if they do not, take responsibility for choosing a state of mind and actions that support you. Being responsible creates a sense of integrity and a feeling of self–worth. For example, if you owe money to a friend, family member, or bank, take the responsibility to repay the loan. If you have a student loan, repay it on schedule. Not repaying a student loan may keep other deserving students from receiving financial assistance. It can also result in years of guilt and embarrassment for you and debt for the college. It is important to your sense of self-worth to know you are a person who keeps agreements and assumes responsibility. See the model in Figure 2-4. This model is used to remind you that responsibility has a cyclical effect. What you do or don't do in one area of your life affects other areas of your life and other people as well.

Self-Management and Control

If anger were a disease, there would be an epidemic in this country. Road rage, spousal and child abuse, and lack of civility are just a few examples. Emotionally mature people know how to control their thoughts and behaviors and how to resolve conflict. Conflict is an inevitable part of school and work, but it can be resolved in a positive way. Here are a few tips to follow when trying to redirect and transform your anger.

1. **Calm down.** Step back from the situation and take a deep breath. Take the drama out of the situation and observe what is happening, what behavior is triggering angry emotions, and what options you have in responding in appropriate and positive ways. If you lash out without thinking and attack verbally, you may cause serious harm to your relationship. You cannot take back words once they are spoken. Resist the urge to overreact.

2. **Clarify and define.** Determine exactly with whom or what you are angry, and why. What specific behavior in the other person is causing you to feel angry or frustrated? Determine whose problem it is. For example, your instructor may have an annoying tone and style of lecturing. If a behavior annoys only you, perhaps it is your problem.

3. **Listen with empathy and respect.** Understand the other person's point of view. Take the tension out of the conflict by really listening. See if you can restate the other person's position. Listen to yourself as well. Ask yourself how you feel. Are you tired, hot, hungry, frustrated, rushed, or feeling ill? If so, you may not want to deal with your anger until you feel better. Sometimes getting a good night's sleep or having a good meal will put the situation into perspective, and your anger will dissolve.

4. **Use the "I" statement.** Take ownership of your feelings. Using "I" statements—direct messages delivered in a calm tone with supportive body language—can diffuse anger. You are not blaming another person, but expressing how a situation affects you. For example, you can say, "Carlos, when I hear you clicking your pen and tapping it on the desk, I am distracted from studying."

   This is usually accepted better than the statement, "Carlos, you are so rude and inconsiderate. You must know that you are annoying me when you tap your pen."

5. **Focus on one problem.** Don't pounce on every annoying behavior you can think of to dump on the person. Let's continue with the example above. "And in addition to clicking your pen, Carlos, I don't like how you leave your dishes in the sink, drop your towels in the bathroom, and make that annoying little sound when you eat." Take one behavior or conflict and work to resolve it.

6. **Focus on win–win solutions.** How can you both win? Restate the problem and jot down as many different creative solutions as possible that you both can agree upon.

7. **Reward positive behavior.** As you use praise and reinforce positive behaviors, you will find that the person will exert less resistance. You can now be more direct about specific behaviors and ask for a commitment. "Julie, if you could be here right at 8:00, we could get through this study session in two hours. Can we agree on this?" Focus on behavior and not personality or name calling, which just angers you and antagonizes the other person. Don't let anger and conflict create more stress in your life and take a physical and emotional toll. You can learn to step back automatically from explosive situations and control them rather than let your emotions control you.

Self-Esteem and Confidence

Self-esteem is based on how you feel about yourself. Peak Performers have confidence and believe in themselves. They assess themselves honestly and focus on their strengths. They constantly learn new skills and competencies that build their confidence. They accept responsibility for their attitudes and behavior. They know that blame and anger only diminish confidence. They focus their energies on becoming a person of integrity and character.

People with a positive self-esteem have the confidence that allows them to be more open to new experiences and accepting of different people. They tend to be more optimistic. They are more willing to share their feelings and ideas with others and are willing to tolerate differences in others. Because they have a sense of self-worth, they do not find it necessary to put down or discriminate against others.

In contrast, people with low-self esteem tend to mistrust others and reject people who are different. They lack self-confidence and fail to meet their goals. They are often more concerned with their rights than their responsibility to act with respect and integrity.

If you want to change your outer world and experiences, you must begin by looking at your thoughts, feelings, and beliefs about yourself. Assess your self-esteem at the end of the chapter and follow the tips in Trailmarker 2.3.

Peak Performers Who Bounced Back

Thomas Edison was told that he was a slow learner, yet he invented the light bulb.

TRAILMARKER 2.3

Tips to Build Self-Esteem and Confidence

1. Focus on your strengths and positive qualities and find ways to bolster them. Be yourself and don't compare yourself with others.

2. Learn to be resilient and bounce back after disappointments and setbacks. Don't dwell on mistakes or limitations. Accept them, learn from them, and move on with your life.

3. Use affirmations and visualization to replace negative thoughts and images.

4. Take responsibility for your life instead of blaming others. You cannot control other people's behavior, but you have complete control over your own thoughts, emotions, words, and behavior. Value civility and self-control.

5. Learn skills and competencies that give you opportunities and confidence in your abilities. It is not enough to *feel* good about yourself, you must also be able to *do* what is required to demonstrate that you are a competent, honest, and responsible person. The more skills and personal qualities you acquire, the more competent and confident you will feel.

6. Focus on giving, not receiving, and make others feel valued and appreciated. You will increase your self-esteem when you make a contribution.

7. Create a support system by surrounding yourself with confident and kind people who feel good about themselves and who make you feel good about yourself. People who boost your self-esteem generally have high self-esteem themselves.

There is an old story about three men who were working on a project in a large city in France. A curious tourist asked them, "What are you three working on?" The first man said, "I'm hauling rocks." The second man said, "I'm laying a wall." The third man said with pride, "I'm building a cathedral." The third man had a sense of vision of the *whole* system. When college and work seem as tedious as hauling rocks, focus on the big picture. Confidence comes from

- honesty and integrity.
- competence and skills.
- accepting and respecting yourself and your work.
- being responsible for your choices.
- seeing the big picture.
- setting high but attainable goals and expectations.

OVERCOMING THE BARRIERS TO A POSITIVE ATTITUDE AND MOTIVATION

Discouragement is the number 1 barrier to motivation. Even Peak Performers sometimes feel discouraged and need help hiking out of life's valleys. Creating and maintaining a positive state of mind does not happen by reading a book, attending a lecture, or using a few strategies for a day or two. It takes consistent effort. Everyone gets off course now and then, but the key is to regroup at base camp and prepare for the next climb. Realize that setbacks are part of life. Find a formula that works for creating a positive and resourceful mind.

Another barrier to being positive and motivated is the tendency to postpone developing personal qualities. Sometimes students will say, "I'll be more motivated as soon as I graduate or get a real job." Instead try to

- focus on being motivated and positive TODAY.
- focus on your successes and accomplishments.
- surround yourself with positive, supportive, and encouraging friends.
- tell yourself, "This is a setback, not a failure."
- make certain you are physically renewed. Get more rest, extra exercise, and do something every day that you love.
- replace negative and limiting thoughts and self-talk with affirmations and positive visualization.
- collect stories about people who were discouraged, received negative messages, and bounced back.

> The path was worn and slippery. My foot slipped from under me, knocking the other out of the way. But I recovered and said to myself, "It's a slip and not a fall.
>
> —*Abraham Lincoln*

Creating Positive Mind Shifts

Having both a positive attitude and high self-esteem is important, but neither will help you reach your goals if your beliefs or perceptions are wrong. Sometimes a mind shift is necessary to see new possibilities and adjust faulty perceptions. Let's say that you are driving a car to New York. If your map is wrong, positive attitude and self-esteem won't get you to New York. Your beliefs are your mind maps and they influence how you see life. It is important to use critical thinking to assess your beliefs and see if they are accurate and support your goals.

Expectations influence how you see yourself and others. You may let your beliefs, assumptions, or expectations get in the way of seeing a person or situation clearly. Sometimes the closer you are to a situation, the more difficult it is to see it clearly.

Expanding Your Comfort Zone

Your beliefs and expectations about yourself can either limit or expand your success. Other people's expectations of you can make you redefine who you think you are and what you think you are capable of achieving. You may start to believe what you tell yourself or hear from others again and again. Don't allow yourself to become limited in ways of thinking.

For example, Steve Delmay comes from a long line of lumber mill workers. Although they have lived for generations in a college town, his family never had anything to do with the college. Steve was expected to go to work at the mill right

CRITICAL THINKING LOG 2.7

Assess and Reflect

A positive attitude is a habit that requires assessment and consistent practice. It is just as important to assess and develop positive attitudes and personal qualities as it is to learn new skills.

1. Finish this sentence in your own words: "For me to be more motivated, I am waiting for_____.

2. Use critical thinking and creative problem solving to explore and write out possible solutions to these common motivational problems. Add to the list.

   • I've set my goals for the semester and I really want to succeed, but I just lose interest about halfway into the term.

   • I work full-time and also attend school. I just don't have the time to study the way I'd like to, and I always feel behind. There is never enough time to do all that should get done.

   • Is it worth it? I'm busy at school, involved in events, and have a part-time job. My life is full. I just don't know if what I'm working so hard for is really worth it. Will it make a difference?

   • My spouse doesn't support my going to school. I have clear goals, but I worry that they will cost me a close family life. Is this struggle worth it?

   • I am forty pounds overweight, and I really want to slim down. I start a new diet every Monday with great determination, but my willpower sags and I fail to stay on it for even a few days.

   • I've tried time after time to quit smoking, but I feel I have too much happening now, and I'm too nervous and stressed.

   • I get myself psyched up, but I just can't see it through. I feel so weak.

   • I don't know what I want to major in or what career to follow. It's hard for me to see the point of going to college when I lack career direction.

> People are about as happy as they expect to be.
>
> —*Abraham Lincoln*

after high school. He never thought about other options. However, during his senior year in high school, he attended Career Day. He met instructors and students from the local college who were friendly, supportive, and encouraging. His world opened up, and he saw opportunities he had never considered before. Steve experienced a major mind shift. Although he had to overcome a lack of support at home, he is now a successful college student with a bright future.

Creative problem solving can expand your mind and comfort zone and shift your thinking so you can see new possibilities and broader and more exciting horizons. College is an ideal time to develop your natural creativity and explore new ways of thinking. Try these tips:

1. **Create a support system.** Without support and role models, you may question whether you can be successful. First-generation college students, women in technical programs, or men in nursing programs may feel uncomfortable and question whether they belong. Cultural minorities, veterans, or disabled or returning students may feel that they don't belong at certain colleges. Some students were told that they were not college material. You can find encouragement with a support system of positive and

accepting people. Get involved and join a variety of clubs. Make friends with diverse groups of students, instructors, and community leaders.

2. **Reprogram your mind.** Affirmations and visualization can create a self-fulfilling prophecy. If you think of yourself, tell yourself, and see yourself as a success, and are willing to put in the effort, you will be successful. Focus on your successes and accomplishments and overcome limitations. For example, if you need to take a remedial math class, take it and don't label yourself as "dumb" or "math impaired." Labels are self-defeating.

3. **Use critical thinking.** Question limiting labels or beliefs. Where did they come from and are they accurate? Don't be mentally lazy or negative.

4. **Use creative thinking.** Ask yourself, "What if?" Explore creative ways of achieving your goals. Find out how you learn best and adopt positive habits.

5. **Take responsibility.** Don't blame your parents, high school teachers, or counselors for your lack of vision or success. You're an adult now and responsible for your thoughts, beliefs, and actions. You can question, think, and explore. You can achieve almost anything you can dream.

6. **Learn new skills.** Focus on your strengths but be willing to learn new skills and competencies continually. Feeling competent is empowering!

7. **Use the whole of your intelligence.** You are smarter than you think. Use all your experiences and personal qualities to achieve your goals. Develop responsibility, self-control, dependability, sociability, character, manners, and all the qualities necessary for school, job, and life success.

> People who needed a mind shift:
> Everything that can be invented has been invented.
>
> —*Charles H. Duell,*
> *commissioner,*
> *U.S. Office of Patents, 1899*

Technology FOCUS: The Internet

A. Use the Internet to find out what business topics are available on ethics, business etiquette, and codes of ethics. Check out different businesses, the military, government agencies, and colleges to find out if they have a code of ethics. Print some samples and bring them to class. What do they all have in common?

For more information on this topic, visit this book's Web site at:

http://peak.glencoe.com

B. E-mail is an easy way to stay in touch with friends, family, new acquaintances, instructors, your advisor, professional colleagues, and discussion groups. You will feel more motivated when you stay in touch with people and share your joys and concerns. Write at least one letter today.

C. Look up sites that have positive stories and motivational articles. You can begin your search for more information by accessing this book's Web site at:

http://peak.glencoe.com

CAREER FOCUS: POSITIVE ATTITUDES AT WORK

Having a positive attitude is more than just wishful thinking. Your attitude is the single most important factor in job performance and success. A positive attitude can produce success, while a negative attitude often results in failure. Improve your attitude toward your job, your goals, your boss, and your coworkers and you will have taken a major step in improving your working relationships and achieving your goals.

Employees with a positive attitude:

- set high standards of excellence.
- believe in themselves.
- have a sense of enthusiasm.
- see the best in every situation.
- see the best in other people.
- have a healthy self-image.

Employees with a negative attitude:

- do just enough to get by.
- look at the downside of situations.
- see the worst in others.
- have a poor self-image.
- seem indifferent, fearful, and critical.

Motivated, positive people tend to produce outstanding results. Meet Dale Everding. He is a new employee in an automotive company's sales department. He has a list of strategies that he uses every day to get himself into a positive state of mind. Dale spends a few minutes before he gets up in the morning mentally rehearsing his day. He sees himself completing his goals, working well with others, and making sales. He programs his mind with positive self-talk such as, "I am confident and successful. I like to sell quality products."

He pays attention to his appearance and health because he realizes how these factors affect attitude and motivation on the job. In short, Dale knows that he is in charge of his emotions, thoughts, attitude, and behavior. He creates a positive state of mind that produces positive results with this morning routine:

- lay out clothes, briefcase, and snacks the night before.
- wake up early, practice affirmations and visualization.
- exercise, stretch, shower.
- eat a healthy breakfast.
- listen to inspirational tapes on your calm ride to work.

Peak Performance in the Workplace

Attributes of a Positive Manager

- communicates with and motivates others.
- conveys a positive attitude and enthusiasm when working with others.
- accepts people from different cultures.
- adapts cheerfully and skillfully to new situations.
- understands the systems approach to motivation.
- listens and respects others' views and backgrounds.
- increases others' self-esteem.
- bounces back after disappointment and failure.

Your life is not a dress rehearsal.
This life is a test—it is only a test.
If it had been an actual life, you would have received further instructions on where to go and what to do.

Expectations

Complete the following sentences. Write your expectations for being motivated and positive.

1. I intend to _____

_____

_____

_____

_____

_____

_____

_____

_____

_____

_____.

2. I expect the results will be _____

_____

_____

_____

_____

_____

_____

_____

_____

_____

_____

_____.

When you complete this course, return to this log entry. Review any results and behavior changes with the intentions and expectation statements you have written today.

JOANNA LAU

When Joanna Lau immigrated with her parents to the United States from Hong Kong, she was only seventeen. By the time she was thirty, she was already an engineer for General Electric looking for her own manufacturing company to operate.

With this goal in mind, she bought Bowmar ALI Company in the early nineties, a company facing serious losses in the defense industry. Joanna did not let these losses deter her because she saw potential in Bowmar ALI. She saw enough potential to convince twenty employees to buy the company with her, get a bank loan and another $750,000 from a minority-targeted Small Business Administration loan. She remortgaged her house and cashed in her pension. Bowmar ALI became Lau Technologies and Lau became president.

By 1995, Lau Technologies was a very successful company. In those years, revenues grew from $7 million to $49 million. Today, the company continues to grow. Lau's strategy was to focus on quality, customer service, and getting back lost customers. Having many employees as part-owners also helped when commitment and overtime were necessary.

Joanna also set out to define Lau Technologies with a new non-defense line identity. The company branched into new technology. Lau and her team looked at several businesses and decided to make identification cards and drivers' licenses and store the images digitally.

Joanna Lau is one of the most successful Asian-American women in business and has received many awards recognizing her contributions in a male-dominated industry.

At the 1998 commencement at Bentley College in Massachusetts, she received an honory Doctorate of Commercial Science degree. In her commencement address, she told graduates that their education would give them the opportunity to choose what they wanted to do with their lives.

Do you think Joanna Lau's education did this for her?

How did she focus on Win-Win solutions?

Give an example of how she expanded her comfort zone.

Source: http://peak.glencoe.com

2

Review and Study Notes

Affirmations

- I am confident. I like and accept myself.
- I have positive attitudes about school and work.
- I keep my agreements with myself and others.
- I am responsible and have strong personal qualities.
- I have character and integrity and a code of ethics.
- I make friends easily and respect and enjoy diversity.
- I focus on my strengths.
- I have a sense of humor and perspective. I am resilient.
- I am motivated and committed to achieve my full potential.

Visualization

Imagine yourself a confident, motivated, and positive person. You are resourceful, calm, and focused. Your body language is compatible with this enthusiastic state of mind. You walk tall, with shoulders back and head held high, and your eye contact is direct and steady. You know what you want, where you're going, and how to get there. Feel how wonderful it is to be at peace, focused, and motivated. You are happy to be alive and want to reach your full potential. Visualize your goals and see them clearly.

Peak Performance Strategies

1. Focus on the positive.
2. Develop positive personal qualities.
3. Be a person of character and integrity.
4. Use affirmations and visualization.
5. Take responsibility.
6. Be mindful and in the present.
7. Be physically active.
8. Strive for excellence, not perfection.
9. Focus on effort, not ability.
10. Create a balanced life.

CASE Studies

CASE A *In the Classroom*

David Saunders is majoring in forestry. During one of his study groups he made a remark about the men in forestry being real men and that the women studying forestry were real men too. He then passed around suggestive pictures of what he considered to be "real women."

Several members in the study group questioned David's comments and pictures and would not accept the excuse of, "I was only joking." Relationships are now strained in the study group.

1. What suggestions would you have for David to improve his relationship with his group and to relate better to diversity?

_____

2. In the past, women were underrepresented in electronics, engineering, computer, and science classes, but this has changed. Why do you think this has changed?

_____

In the Workplace

David is now a forester in a large company. He really enjoys his work team, and they all have a great rapport. There are only two women on the management team. They are accepted and respected. There is one coworker named Jay, who is always joking. Sometimes, however, his humor crosses the line of good-natured fun. He makes jokes about women and ethnic groups. David decided to have a heart-to-heart talk with Jay and discuss his attitude and behavior. Jay thought he was just having fun and said the women never seemed to mind his jokes. He would never want to make them feel uncomfortable and could now see how his behavior could be misinterpreted.

1. Why do you think David chose to speak with Jay?

_____

2. How do you think Jay will behave now?

_____

3. What have you learned from this chapter that will help you be more respectful of others?

_____

> **Tip From the Classroom:**
> Once I got motivated, I did very well in school. It really came down to setting goals and doing what had to be done every day—no excuses.
> —*First-term student at a business college*

CASE B

Judy Santiago is a drafting major in a career school. She has to work several hours a week and during the summer to pay her expenses. Most people would describe Judy as a motivated person because she goes to every class, is punctual, and works hard at school and in her job. Judy wants to get more out of life and feel as if she is contributing to her community. She likes school, but she doesn't see the connection with real life. As a result, Judy sometimes feels as if she is just marking time and postponing life until graduation.

1. What strategies in this chapter can help Judy find a strong sense of purpose and motivation?

   _____

   _____

   _____

2. What would you recommend to Judy for creating a more resourceful and positive attitude?

   _____

   _____

   _____

In the Workplace

Judy is now a draftsperson for a small industrial equipment company. She has been with the company for ten years and is competent and well liked, and she is a valuable employee. She has a supportive family, is healthy, and travels frequently. Although she likes her job, Judy is becoming bored with the sameness of her work. She wants to become more motivated on the job and also in her personal life.

1. What strategies in this chapter can help Judy become more enthusiastic about work or find new interest in her personal life?

   _____

   _____

   _____

   _____

2. What would you suggest to Judy to get her motivated?

   _____

   _____

   _____

   _____

TIP Many people are good at assessing and continually updating their skills. It is just as important to assess your personal qualities regularly. Set goals and expectations, and adjust them when necessary. Take workshops on motivation and attitude. Document how you demonstrate personal qualities in your Career Development Portfolio. Obtain letters of recommendation from people who can address these qualities.

Chapter Application   WORKSHEET 2.1

Fill in the following contract for one or all the courses you are taking this term. Use this example as a guide.

Reinforcement Contract

Name: Sarah Jones   Date: September 2000
Course: General Accounting

If I: *study for six hours each week in this class and attend all lectures and labs*
Then I will: *reward myself with a long bike ride and a picnic lunch every Saturday.*
I agree to: *learn new skills, choose positive thoughts and attitudes, and try out new behaviors.*
I most want to accomplish: *an A grade in this course so I can qualify for advanced accounting courses.*
The barriers to overcome are: *my poor math skills.*
The resources I can use are: *my study group and the Tutoring Center.*
I will reward myself for meeting my goals by: *going out to dinner with some friends.*
The consequences for not achieving the results I want will be: *to find a new major.*

Reinforcement Contract

Name: _____

Course: _____ Date: _____

If I: _____

Then I will: _____

I agree to: _____

I most want to accomplish: _____

The barriers to overcome are: _____

The resources I can use are: _____

I will reward myself for meeting my goals by: _____

The consequences for not achieving the results I want will be: _____

_____

Chapter Application   WORKSHEET 2.2

Self-Esteem Inventory

Take this simple inventory to find out about your self-esteem. Circle the number that reflects your true feelings.

4 = all the time	2 = some of the time
3 = most of the time	1 = none of the time

1. I like myself and I am a worthwhile person.	4	3	2	1
2. I have many positive qualities.	4	3	2	1
3. Other people generally like me and I have a sense of belonging.	4	3	2	1
4. I feel confident and know I can handle most situations.	4	3	2	1
5. I am competent and good at many things.	4	3	2	1
6. I have emotional control and I am respectful of others.	4	3	2	1
7. I am a person of integrity and character.	4	3	2	1
8. I respect the kind of person I am.	4	3	2	1
9. I am capable and willing to learn new skills.	4	3	2	1
10. Although I want to improve and grow, I am happy with myself.	4	3	2	1
11. I take responsibility for my thoughts, beliefs, and behavior.	4	3	2	1
12. I am empathetic and interested in others and the world around me.	4	3	2	1

Now add up your points. The higher your score, the higher your self-esteem. If you have a high sense of self-esteem, you see yourself in a positive light. The lower your self-esteem, the less confidence you will have to face and solve problems in college or on the job.

Chapter Application   WORSHEET 2.3

Setting Goals for Each Course

For each course you take, copy this chart and fill it in. Consider what you hope to get out of each course and how you will achieve these goals.

Course: _____ **Instructor:** _____ **Expected grade:** _____

Barriers that I might experience:

_____

_____

_____

Motivators to use to overcome barriers:

_____

_____

_____

Positive habits to get me through this course:

_____

_____

_____

Resources that can help:

_____

_____

_____

Positive self-talk that will support me in this class:

_____

_____

_____

Visualization that will help me picture success:

_____

_____

_____

Name _____   Date _____

ASSESSMENT

Assess your attitude in each of the following areas. Remember that your attitude can affect your success. Put a check mark in the **Yes** or **No** column.

Category	Attitude	Yes	No
Assessment	Do I assess myself honestly and positively?		
Test taking	Do I mentally prepare for taking tests?		
Time management	Do I know how to manage my time?		
Note taking	Do I listen and take notes with a positive and open mind?		
Reading	Do I feel confident and positive about my reading?		
Memory	Do I want to improve my memory?		
Responsibility	Do I take responsibility for my attitude?		
Personal qualities	Do I value character and integrity?		
Writing	Do I want to be a good writer?		
Speaking	Do I approach speaking as an important skill to learn?		
Research	Do I approach research with a creative and positive mind?		
Math	Do I approach math with a positive attitude?		
Computers	Do I approach technology with a positive attitude?		
Systems	Do I understand systems and how to work within them?		
Resources	Do I know how to find and use resources?		
Intructors	Do I have a positive and supportive attitude toward my instructors?		
Class	Do I have a positive attitude toward this class?		
Job	Do I have a positive and motivated attitude at work?		

3

MANAGING YOUR TIME

Decide what you want, decide what you are willing to exchange for it, establish your priorities, and go to work.

—H. L. Hunt, financier

Learning Objectives

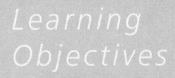

In Chapter 3 **you** will learn

- ● how to create a time-management system.

- ● how to assess your energy level and time wasters.

- ● how to handle interruptions.

- ● how to set goals and priorities.

- ● how to overcome procrastination.

- ● how to work in alignment with your learning style.

This chapter looks at time management with a positive attitude. Instead of controlling, suppressing, or constricting your freedom, time management enables you to achieve the things you really want and frees up time to enjoy life. Peak Performers use a systematic approach that allows them to

- organize projects and achieve results.
- accomplish goals and priorities.
- be effective, not just efficient.
- avoid crises.
- feel calm and productive.
- work smarter, not harder.
- feel a sense of accomplishment.
- have more free time to enjoy life.

Everyone has the same amount of time: twenty-four hours in each day. You can't save or steal time. When it's gone, it's gone. However, you can learn to invest it wisely. This chapter will help you learn how to get control of your life by managing your time wisely and by choosing to spend it on your main goals. It will also help you think about the contributions you want to make during your lifetime and the legacy you want to leave behind after you are gone. You will discover that there is always time to do the things you really want to do. Too many people waste time doing things that can be done in a few moments or doing things that should not be done at all and then ignore their main goals.

As you go through this chapter, think about what you WANT to achieve and how you can use your time skillfully to perform at your peak level. This chapter will help you become effective, not just efficient. Being efficient is about doing things faster. Being effective is about doing the right things in the right way.

As a wise time manager, you can avoid overwhelming feelings of losing control of tasks and falling behind in school, at work, or in your personal life.

ASSESSMENT

Time management is much more than focusing on minutes, hours, and days. Your attitude, energy level, and ability to concentrate have a great impact on the system as well. Try to evaluate clearly situations that may have spun out of control because of your lack of planning or procrastination. Recall how these events affected others. You are part of the whole system. When you are late for class, miss a study-group meeting, or don't do your assigned share of a team project, it affects others.

Let's look at some important questions concerning your present use of time. The answers will help you develop a plan that will fine-tune your organizational and time-management skills—ultimately leading you to become an efficient Peak Performer.

1. Where does your time go? Where are you spending your time and energy?
2. Where should your time go?
3. What strategies can help you?
4. What barriers keep you from being successful?

Success Principle 3:
Focus on **PRIORITIES,**
not *Activities.*

Where Does Your Time Go?

You can divide time into three areas:

Committed Time

This type of time is devoted to school, labs, studying, work, commuting, waiting for the bus, and other activities involving your immediate and long-term goals.

Maintenance Time

This is the time you spend maintaining yourself. Activities such as eating, sleeping, bathing, exercising, or maintaining your home—cooking, cleaning/laundry, shopping, bill paying—use up your maintenance time.

Discretionary Time

The time that is yours to use as you please is discretionary time. Separate your commitments and maintenance from your discretionary time and put all your activities into certain categories. For example, grooming may include showering, styling your hair, cleaning your contact lenses, getting dressed, and so on. Don't spend too much time trying to determine which category an activity fits in. You want to use your discretionary time for the things you value most in life. These important items may include building relationships with family and friends; service to the community; intellectual development; and activities that give you a lot of joy and relaxation and contribute to your physical, mental, and spiritual well-being. These are important goals that tie in with your long-term goals of being healthy, feeling centered and peaceful, and having loving relationships. Make certain your discretionary activities are conscious choices and that you make them top priorities.

Remember this section asked you, Where does your time go? Are you using most of the day for commitments? A good place to determine your answer is with assessment of how your time and energy are spent. Look at Figure 3-1 on page 3-4 and then complete Critical Thinking Log 3.1 on page 3-5. The point of this exercise is to determine the best way to use your time to achieve important goals.

Where Should Your Time Go?

Peak Performers know that the first rule of time management is to set goals to determine what they want to accomplish. Sometimes it's hard to know how to spend time because there are so many things to spend it on. Conflicting demands on your time can be overwhelming and stressful. However, goals help clarify what you want and give you energy, direction, and focus. Goal setting often isn't quick or even easy. You need to take the time to go inward and think about your deepest values and desires.

Complete Critical Thinking Log 3.2 on page 3-6. It will help you create major targets in your life or long-term goals. From these major goals, you can write midterm goals (two to five years), short-term goals (one year), and then immediate goals.

		Activity	Notes	Energy level (high or low)
	6:00 – 7:00	shower, dress	maintenance	low
	7:00 – 8:00	drive kids to school	committed	low
	8:00 – 9:00	make to-do list	committed	high
	9:00 – 10:00	coffee and calls	disc/committed	high
	10:00 – 11:00	write proposal	committed	high
	11:00 – 12:00	meeting	committed	low
	12:00 – 1:00	lunch	maintenance	high
	1:00 – 2:00			
	2:00 – 3:00			
	3:00 – 4:00			
	4:00 – 5:00			
	5:00 – 6:00			
	6:00 – 7:00			
	7:00 – 8:00			
	8:00 – 9:00			
	9:00 – 10:00			
	10:00 – 11:00			

Figure 3–1
Sample Time Log

SET PRIORITIES

There is always time for what is most important. You want to make certain that your days are not just a treadmill of activities, crises, and endless tasks, but that you focus on the important as well as the urgent. Review your goals and jot down your top priorities. If you are in the first month of classes, make certain you are completing items that are top priority.

The First Weeks of College

1. Register and pay fees on time.
2. Buy books and supplies, and obtain an ID card.
3. Make an appointment with your advisor to review requirements.
4. Check deadlines for adding and dropping courses. *Never* just stop going to class.
5. Keep a syllabus in your notebook and review expectations often.

Time Log

	Activity	Notes	Energy level (high or low)
6:00 – 7:00			
7:00 – 8:00			
8:00 – 9:00			
9:00 – 10:00			
10:00 – 11:00			
11:00 – 12:00			
12:00 – 1:00			
1:00 – 2:00			
2:00 – 3:00			
3:00 – 4:00			
4:00 – 5:00			
5:00 – 6:00			
6:00 – 7:00			
7:00 – 8:00			
8:00 – 9:00			
9:00 – 10:00			
10:00 – 11:00			

6. Make a project board with deadlines. Start projects immediately.

7. Keep up with reading and assignments. Preview chapters before class.

8. Make an appointment with each of your instructors.

9. Get help immediately. Don't wait until you're in trouble.

10. Form a study team or get a study partner for *each* class.

11. Go to all your classes on time and sit in the front.

12. Get organized. Keep a file for receipts, grades, and important papers.

13. Keep a daily to-do list.

Chart of Activities

Fill in the following chart to determine how much time you spend on certain activities. Use the information you compiled in Critical Thinking Log 3.1. Typical activities are listed below. You may, of course, change or add activities to the list. Remember, the total number of hours should be twenty-four.

Activity	Time Spent	Activity	Time Spent
Attending class		Eating	
Working		Sleeping	
Commuting		Cooking	
Studying		Shopping	
Attending meetings		Running errands	
Grooming		Socializing	
Exercising		Doing hobbies	
Doing household chores		Talking on the telephone	
Waiting in line		Watching television	
Other		Other	

Time-Management Strategies

1. **Write a daily to-do list.** Use a daily planner to schedule classes, work, priorities, and due dates. Devote a section to your goals and objectives, and devote another section to writing a to-do list. Include shopping, paying bills, making photocopies, cleaning, attending a meeting, seeing an instructor, returning books to the library, and so on. Put number 1 next to the item with the highest priority. Assign numbers to the rest of the items, with the highest number going to the least important item.

   Some people like to write a to-do list for the next day, taking some time at the end of a day to review briefly what they want to focus on for the next day. Others like to write their list in the morning at breakfast or when they first get to school or work.

   Once you have written your list, get going! Begin your day with the first item on your list. Don't do the least important items until the most important ones are done. Check off each item as you complete it. When you see all the items checked off, you'll be inspired. It's okay if you don't get to everything on your list. If there are tasks left over, add them to your next to-do list. The important thing is to work on your top-priority items first and to make this a daily habit. Do first things first! Ask yourself, "What is the best use of my time right now?" You may find the to-do list (Chapter Application Worksheet 3.1) at the end of this chapter to be helpful.

CRITICAL THINKING LOG 3.3

Looking Ahead

Complete this activity and save it in your Career Development Portfolio. Use additional paper if necessary or save it on the computer.

A. Mission Statement

1. Think of what you value most in life, then list those things below.

   _____

2. What is your life's purpose?

   _____

3. What legacy do you want to leave?

   _____

B. Long-Term Goals

Brainstorm all the goals that you want to accomplish during your lifetime. You should include goals for all areas of your life, such as education, career, travel, financial security, relationships, spiritual, community, and personal growth. This list will be long and you will want to add to it and revise it every year. Here are a few incomplete statements that might help you as you brainstorm:

1. My dreams include _____.
2. I most want to accomplish _____.
3. The places I most want to visit are _____.
4. One thing I've always wanted to do is _____.

C. Midterm Goals

Brainstorm the goals you want to accomplish in the next five years. Here are some examples:

1. I will complete my degree.
2. I will graduate with honors.
3. I will buy a new sports car.
4. I will take a trip to Europe.

D. Short-Term Goals

List goals that you want to accomplish in the next year. Consider your answers to these questions:

1. What is the major goal for which I am striving this year?
2. How does this goal relate to my life's mission or purpose?
3. Is this goal in conflict with any other goal?
4. What hurdles must I overcome to reach my goal?
5. What resources, help, and support will I need to overcome these hurdles?
6. What specific actions are necessary to complete my goal?
7. What will be my reward for achieving this goal?

E. Semester Goals

List goals you want to accomplish this semester, for example:

1. I will preview chapters for ten minutes before each lecture.
2. I will go to all of my classes on time.
3. I will jog for thirty minutes each day.

2. **Make a project board.** Refer to Figure 3-2. During the first week of class, mark down deadlines for each assignment, paper, project, and test you must complete for that semester. Set daily and weekly goals for meeting these deadlines. Put your class schedule in your planner and make a copy for your study space. Include your classes, labs, work hours, and sports or club commitments. Once you have recorded your committed time, add in study time and other daily activities such as exercising and commuting. Make certain you build in time for family. If you have children, plan special events that you can all look forward to. Bear in mind that the schedule should be flexible; you will want to allow for free time and unexpected events. Follow this schedule for two weeks and see how accurate it is. For each major project, use a project board. Working your way backward from the due date will indicate the daily and weekly goals necessary for completing the project. Make certain you allow extra time for proofreading and possible computer problems.

Project: Term Paper for Business Class 110

Today's Date: January 23, 2001   Due Date: April 23, 2001

Key Activities	**Date Completed**
Paper finished and turned in.	April 23
Type final draft and proof.	April 15
Proof second draft; revise.	April 10
Additional research, spell-check.	April 5
First draft.	March 27
Detailed outline.	March 15
Detailed library research.	March 10
Library research.	March 5
General outline.	February 22
Initial library research.	February 8
Mind map outline.	February 4
Finalize topic.	January 28
Explore topics.	January 23

Figure 3–2
Sample Project Board

3. **Do the tough tasks first.** Your energy level will be high and you will feel a sense of accomplishment as you tackle your tough tasks first. Start out with your most difficult subjects, while you're fresh and alert. For instance, if you are avoiding your statistics homework because it is difficult, get up early and do it before your classes begin. Start projects when they're assigned. Work first and then play. Using a weekly activity schedule might prove helpful.

4. **Break projects down into smaller tasks.** Begin by seeing the whole project or each chapter as part of a larger system. Then break it into manageable chunks. You may get discouraged if you face a large task, whether it's writing a major term paper or reading several chapters. Getting started is half the battle. Spend just fifteen minutes before you go to bed outlining your chapter for the next day or mind mapping the main ideas for your term paper. If your paper is due on a certain date, plan all the steps necessary prior to that date. Write a summary after each section and at the end of each chapter. You will find inspiration in completing smaller tasks and you will feel more in control.

5. **Consolidate similar tasks.** If you group similar tasks, you can maximize your efforts. For example, if you need to make several calls, make them all at a specific time and reduce interruptions. Set aside a block of time to shop, pay bills, go to the post office, and run errands. Write a list of questions for your advisor, instructor, or study team. Make certain you know expectations so you don't have to repeat tasks. Save your energy and utilize your resources by planning and combining similar activities, such as taking a walk with a friend, thus combining exercise with socializing.

6. **Study at your high-energy time.** Know your body rhythms and study your hardest subjects during your peak energy times. Review the time log to determine the time of day when you have the most energy. See Critical Thinking Log 3.4 on page 3-10. Guard against interruptions and don't do mindless tasks or socialize during your peak energy periods. For example, if your peak time is in the morning, don't waste time by answering mail, socializing, cleaning, checking out books at the library, or doing other routine work. Use your high-energy time to do serious studying and work that requires thinking, writing, and completing projects. Use your low-energy time to do mindless physical work, chores, or easy reading or previewing chapters. If possible, schedule your classes for high-energy times.

7. **Study everywhere and anywhere.** Of course, it is important to have a regular study space, but be prepared to study everywhere and anywhere. Carry note cards with you to review formulas, dates, definitions, facts, and important data. Bring class notes or a book with you and study while waiting. Be prepared for the idle time that is part of every day. Review during the five or ten minutes of waiting between classes, for the bus, in line at the grocery store, or for appointments. Tape important material and lectures and play these tapes while commuting, exercising, dressing, walking, or waiting for class to begin. Avoid crowded times in the library and computer labs. Don't shop on Saturdays or do laundry on weekends unless you have to. Even if you plan well, you will occasionally get stuck in lines but you can make the most of this time.

8. **Study in short segments throughout the day.** Studying in short segments is much more effective than studying in marathon sessions. Your brain is much more receptive to recall when you review at various times in short sessions.

9. **Get organized.** Manage your time by consistently creating good habits. Lay out your clothes and pack your lunch the night before, put your keys on the same hook, put your backpack by the back door, put your mail and assignments in the same space, and keep records of bills, grades,

Daily Energy Levels

Take a more detailed look at your daily energy levels so you can become more aware of your pattern. Keep track of them every day for a week or more.

Energy Level	7:00 A.M.	Noon	10:00 P.M.
100 percent			
80 percent			
50 percent			
25 percent			

1. What tasks do you want to focus on during your high-energy time?

   _____

2. What can you do to increase your energy at your low-energy times?

   _____

> Nothing is so fatiguing as the eternal hanging of an uncompleted task.
>
> —*William James*

etc., in your file. Think of the time that you waste looking for items. Getting organized saves time and reduces stress.

10. **Be flexible, patient, and persistent.** Don't try to make too many changes at once and don't get discouraged if a strategy doesn't work for you. You are striving for excellence, not perfection. Change certain aspects until a strategy fits your style. Be flexible. If it works, do it. If not, try something new. Just make sure you've given yourself at least thirty days to develop new habits. It often feels strange and uncomfortable to do any new task or vary your schedule of daily events. For example, you might discover that you have a habit of getting a donut and coffee every morning and spending an hour or so socializing before your morning classes. Change this habit by doing it only once a week.

Time-Management And Learning Style

Many time-management strategies are designed for people with left-brain dominance. Left-brain people tend to be convergent thinkers because they are good at looking at several unrelated items and bringing order to them. Right-brain people are usually divergent thinkers because they branch out from one idea to many. They are good at brainstorming because one idea leads to another. They are great at focusing on the whole picture. But they can learn to break the global view of the whole project into steps. Break each of these steps into activities. Schedule and organize activities around the big goal. It is very important for right-brain people to focus their efforts on one or two top-priority items instead of being scattered and distracted by busywork. Imagine putting on blinders as you focus on one particular step until it is completed.

A creative way to plan and put your vision into action is to use a mind map and integrate learning styles. Use visual cues and Post-it® notes. When you think of an activity that will help you meet your goal, write it down. Visualize yourself completing the project. Use auditory cues by dictating ideas and planning your project on tape. Talk about the great feeling you will have when you complete this project. Make your project physical by adapting a hands-on approach and working with others to complete your project. Ask yourself, "Is there a way to simplify this task?" Planning is important, even if you are a creative person.

THE MANAGEMENT PROCESS

The management process is a key business concept. Well-run organizations use the management process to ensure efficiency. Every effective manager uses planning, organizing, staffing, delegating, directing and motivating, and evaluating to meet the organization's goals. You can apply the same principles to your education and your job.

Planning

Specify your goals and visualize the results you want to achieve. Break these large goals into semester goals and weekly and daily priorities. Keep these posted by your study area. Detail the steps you need to take to meet your goals. Be prepared for frustrating barriers and setbacks and deal with them calmly. Planning involves knowing how the system works and finding the resources and information that you need. For example, attending college includes seeing your advisor, attending orientation, registering, waiting in lines to pay fees, finding classrooms and parking spaces, getting a library card, obtaining an ID, and so on. This is part of the process. Don't be tempted to take shortcuts or let the little irritations discourage or distract you from your goals.

TIP Planning is powerful.

Organizing

Organize your office, study area, and activities to achieve your goals. Post charts of major projects, due dates, and class schedules. A project board is very important for keeping you on track. Use a detailed calendar and create action steps for your goals. Don't forget to follow through on details.

Staffing

Use the resources available to help you succeed. Your study team members, coworkers, advisors, instructors, and tutors are part of your success team. Know how to reach at least two students in each of your classes. You can take notes for each other in an emergency, share information, ask questions, and study together. Your instructors are key staff in your school career. If you have a choice, pick the best instructors and build supportive relationships with them. Know their names and expectations, take an active part in class discussions, and get to know them as people. Become familiar with support services for students.

Delegating

Every executive knows the importance of delegating tasks to subordinates and coworkers. You can also learn to delegate by assigning certain housekeeping tasks to roommates or family members, and by dividing the workload equally for your study team. If you have children, make certain everyone does his or her share. Delegate whatever you can and build independence, skills, and competencies in others.

Directing and Motivating

Use positive reinforcement to motivate yourself. Keep a list of all the ways you can reward yourself. Take frequent short breaks for walks or exercise. Keep a list of your goals on your desk. Reward yourself and others. Treat yourself to a night out once a week for pizza and a movie. When you are with family or friends, enjoy them totally. Reward yourself after each project and study task. For example, take a few minutes to enjoy time with your children, spouse, or a friend after you complete a study goal.

Evaluating

Monitor your attitude, behavior, expectations, and the results you are creating. Detach yourself and, in a nonjudgmental way, measure your results. Be honest and don't allow excuses or blame to distract you from finding solutions to achieve the results you want. Use creative thinking to overcome barriers.

MANAGE COLLEGE AND YOUR CAREER LIKE A PRO

The same qualities that get you hired and promoted can also help you in school. Your instructor will be just as impressed as your boss with good communication skills, thorough preparation, good manners, and adherence to commitments. Approach your education as if it were a major career move because it is! Try the following strategies to plan your education like a professional.

1. **Plan your course of study.** First, sit down with the school catalog and scan it to review majors, fields of study, resources available, and school requirements. After you have done some planning on your own and made a tentative schedule, make an appointment to talk with your advisor, dean, or department head. Make certain that you have taken the necessary requirements, such as math and English placement tests, and the background courses for certain classes.

2. **Research the best instructors in the subject.** By talking with several students who have had the course, other instructors, and your advisor and staff, you'll get a good idea of who the best instructors are.

3. **Register on time.** You will have a much better chance of getting the classes you need if you register on time.

4. **Be persistent.** If a class you want is closed, go to the first class meeting. Students often drop out and space becomes available. Some instructors will let students in if they show they are committed and interested.

5. **Go to summer school.** You may want to attend summer school for difficult courses or popular courses that are usually full, or getting a few units out of the way so you can get through the program sooner or take a lighter load during the year.

6. **Audit classes.** If a course is difficult, consider auditing it. You can gain a good background and become familiar with the tests, assignments, and requirements. Then you will have a much better chance of getting a good grade when you take it for credit.

7. **Get organized.** Planning your education requires time and organization. Keep an academic file for planning each term. Keep a record of tests, reports, projects, grades, transcripts, and so on. If you need to negotiate a grade, you will have the background information. Invest in big-business tools such as a computer. Videotape your speeches; use a calendar, note cards, and an erasable pen; and market yourself as you would in your career. Write out your short- and long-term goals. Set daily priorities. Plan your work, and work your plan!

8. **Evaluate your performance regularly.** Just as career professionals monitor their performance, you too can welcome feedback from tests and papers to gauge how you are doing in school. You don't need to wait for formal evaluations. See your instructor throughout the term and ask for feedback, suggestions, and ideas for improvement.

ASSESS AND REFLECT

A purpose and clearly defined goals give wings to your dreams. Assess often. Your awareness of where your time goes becomes a continual habit of assessment, planning, and choosing tasks in the order of their importance, and this leads to success. Ask yourself, Do I have a sense of purpose and direction? Are my goals clearly defined? Are any in conflict with each other? Are they flexible enough to be modified and changed as needed? Do I forget to write priorities and phone numbers in my planner? Do I daydream too much and have a problem with concentrating?

OVERCOMING PROCRASTINATION

TIP Get started.

A barrier to time management is procrastination. Some people prefer to do the things they like to do rather than doing what should be done. To avoid procrastination, try these techniques.

1. **Set daily priorities.** Begin by becoming clear on your goals and the results you want to achieve.

2. **Break the project into small tasks.** A large project can seem overwhelming. Do something each day that brings you closer to your goal.

3. **Assess the payoffs for procrastination.** Do you feel important when you are late for class, meetings, or work? Do you get sympathy when you tell friends that you are overloaded? Do you feel as if people won't ask again if you don't say yes to requests? Do you add drama to your life when you are rushed? Complete Critical Thinking Log 3.5 on page 3-14.

4. **Attitude is everything!** When you are positive and focused, you can accomplish a lot in a short time. Negative emotions are time wasters. Anger, jealousy, worry, and resentment can eat up hours of time and sap your energy. Instead, resolve to have a positive attitude.

5. **Work during your high-energy time.** Do what is important first and while you are at your peak energy.

CONTROLLING INTERRUPTIONS

The second biggest barrier to time management is interruption. Interruptions steal your time. They cause you to stop and start projects, and they disrupt your thought pattern, divert your attention, and make it difficult to build momentum again. To avoid wasting time, take control! Don't let endless activities, the telephone, and other people control you. Set every day priorities that will help you meet your goals and reduce interruptions. You may find that you spend a lot of time on the phone. Use the phone for convenience, to save time, or as a reward for accomplishing a task, but don't allow it to become an interruption. For instance, if your friend calls, set a timer for ten minutes or postpone the call until later in the day, after you have previewed your Business 101 chapter or outlined your speech. Set the answering machine if you are studying, or tell the caller that you will call back in an hour. When you return a call, chat for five or ten minutes instead of forty-five minutes. Combine socializing with exercising or eating lunch or dinner. If you don't want to miss a favorite program, turn the set off right after that show. The essence of time management is taking charge of your life and not allowing interruptions to control you. The first step in managing interruptions and time wasters is to identify them.

CRITICAL THINKING LOG 3.5

Delay or Procrastination

Use critical thinking to answer the following questions.

1. What are you doing that doesn't have to be done or could be delayed?

2. What are you doing that could be done by someone else?

3. How can you get control of your time and life?

4. What are you doing during your peak productivity time?

TRAILMARKER 3.1

Investing Your Time in High-Priority Items: The 80/20 Rule

You may be spending 80 percent of your time on activities that produce only 20 percent real benefit to your goals. According to the 80/20 rule of time management, people tend to spend 80 percent of their time on activities that produce only 20 percent of the results that they want. Taking a look at your time wasters may reveal that you are spending too much time on low-priority activities and shortchanging your top priorities. Wasting time on low-priority and unimportant activities is unproductive and a major reason for not accomplishing major tasks. Another way to look at it:

1. 80 per cent of your time is spent on 20 percent of your activities.
2. 80 percent of the clothes you wear come from 20 percent of your favorite wardrobe.
3. 80 percent of the interruptions come from 20 percent of the people.
4. 80 percent of the profits come from 20 percent of the sales.
5. 80 percent of your phone calls come from 20 percent of the people you know.
6. 20 percent more effort can result in an 80 percent better paper/speech, etc.

Sometimes, to increase results by 20 percent, you must exert 80 percent more activity. Other times, increasing your effort by just 20 percent results in a dramatic 80 percent improvement. For instance, you may spend just 20 percent more effort polishing a speech and it resulted in an 80 percent improvement. Can you think of other examples?

TIP Invest your time on items that produce the results you want.

Strategies for Controlling Interruptions

Peak Performers know how to live and work with other people and manage interruptions. Try these tips to help you reduce interruptions.

1. **Create an organized place to study.** A supportive and organized study space can help you reduce interruptions and keep you focused. Have all your study tools—a dictionary, pencils, pens, books, papers, files, notes, calendar, semester schedule, and study team and instructor names and phone numbers—in one place so you won't waste time looking for the items you need. Keep only one project on your desk at one time and file everything else away or put it on a shelf. You can increase your learning by studying in the same space and by conditioning your brain for serious studying and attention. If you have children, include a study area for them close to yours where they can work quietly with puzzles, crayons, or paint. This will allow study time together and create a lifelong study pattern for them.

Interruptions

A. List all the interruptions you experience and their origin. Try to keep a log of interruptions for a few days. Be aware of internally caused interruptions such as procrastination, daydreaming, worry, negative thoughts, anger, and lack of concentration.

Interruptions	Frequency	Possible Solutions
Visitors		
Friends		
Family		
Telephone		
Daydreaming		
Lack of purpose		
Other		

B. Make a list of your most common time wasters. Some common time wasters are:

- socializing
- doing what you like to do first
- watching television
- procrastination
- not setting goals and priorities
- not keeping a calendar
- not writing down deadlines

- losing things and not organizing
- failure to plan
- negative attitude
- complaining and whining
- being overly involved with other people's problems

My common time wasters are:

_____

_____

_____

_____

_____

_____

_____

_____

2. **Create a good time to study.** You will find that when you are focused, you can study anywhere, any time. However, to increase your effectiveness, do your serious studying when your energy level is at its peak. Guard against interruptions and use this time for serious studying.

3. **Create quiet time.** Discuss study needs and expectations with your roommates or family and ask for an agreement. You might establish certain study hours or agree on a signal to let each other know when you need quiet time, such as closing your door or hanging a quiet sign. Make certain that you balance study time with breaks to eat and socialize with your roommates or family.

4. **Study in the library.** If it is difficult to study at home or in the dorm, study in a library. Many students go to the library for quiet time. Once you enter, your brain can turn to a serious study mode. Sitting in a quiet place and facing the wall can reduce interruptions and distractions. You will find that you can accomplish far more in less time, and then you can enjoy your friends and family.

5. **Do first things first.** You will feel more in control if you have a list of priorities that you work through every day. Having a clear purpose of what you want and need to do makes it easier to say no to distractions. Make certain that these important goals include your health. Taking time to exercise, eat right, and relax will not only save time, but will help increase your energy and focus.

6. **Just say no!** Tell your roommate or family when you have an important test or project due. If someone wants to talk or socialize when you need to study, say no. Set aside time each day to spend with your family or roommates, such as dinner, a walk, or a movie. They will understand your priorities when you include them in your plans.

   The key is balance and communication. The next section discusses a few more tips on how to juggle family, school, and job.

JUGGLING FAMILY, SCHOOL, AND JOB

Anyone who lives with children knows how much time and energy they require. Having a family involves endless physical demands that include cleaning, cooking, chauffeuring to activities, helping with homework, and nonstop picking up. Children get sick, need attention, and just want you there sometimes for them. Focus on the big picture as you look at ways to juggle your many roles.

1. **Be flexible.** There are only certain kinds of studying that you can realistically expect to do around children and other kinds of studying that are hopeless to even attempt. If you expect to be interrupted a lot, use this to your advantage. Carry flash cards to use as you cook dinner or while supervising children's homework or playtime. Quiz yourself, preview chapters, skim summaries, review definitions, do a set number of problems, brainstorm ideas for a paper, outline a speech, review equations, match plant specimens, sketch a drawing, explain a chapter out loud. Save the work that requires concentration for time alone.

2. **Communicate expectations.** Children as young as three and four years old can understand that you need quiet time. Make certain that they have lots of quiet activities to keep them busy when you are working. Small children can color, play with clay, or do puzzles when you are working on other projects. After quiet time, you can take a walk, read, or cook dinner together. Clear communication and expectations can save you time at home, school, and work.

3. **Increase your energy.** Find ways to revitalize yourself. Put time into keeping yourself healthy. Exercise, dance, get enough sleep and rest, and eat healthy foods.

4. **Find good day care.** This is essential for school and job success. Line up at least two backup sources of day care. Explore public and private day-care centers, preschools, family day-care homes, parent cooperatives, babysitting pools, other family members, and nannies. Explore renting a room in the basement or attic of your house to a child-care provider. Part of the rent can be paid with child care and light house cleaning. Trade off times with other parents.

5. **Create positive time.** Don't buy your children toys to replace spending time with them. They don't need expensive toys or elaborate outings. You can enjoy each other as you study, garden, shop, do household chores, eat, take walks, read, play games, or watch a favorite television show. The activity is secondary to your uninterrupted presence. Spend time at bedtime sharing your day, talking about dreams, reading a story, and expressing your love and appreciation to them. Make this a positive time and avoid quarrels or harsh words. They will remember and cherish this warm and special time forever. So will you.

6. **Model successful behavior.** Returning to school is an act that sends an important message. You are saying that learning, growth, and being able to juggle family, a job, and school is possible, worthwhile, and rewarding. It is important for children to see their parents setting personal and professional goals while knowing that the family is the center of their lives. You are providing a model by demonstrating the importance of education, setting goals and achieving them, and creating balance.

7. **Delegate and develop.** Clarify expectations with your children so that everyone contributes to the family. Even young children can learn to be team members and important contributors to making the family unit work. Preschool children can help put away toys, fold napkins, set the table, and feel part of the team. Preteens can be responsible for a simple meal one night a week and doing their own laundry. When your children go to college, they will know how to cook, clean, do laundry, get up on time in the morning, and take responsibility for their lives. An important goal of being a good parent is to raise independent, capable, competent, and responsible adults.

8. **Create a support system.** A support system is essential for survival. Check out resources on campus through the reentry center. Set up study teams for all your classes. Make friends with other people who have children.

9. **Get organized.** The night before, take showers; lay out clothes; pack lunches; organize homework in backpacks; and check for keys, books, signed notes, and supplies.

10. **Balance your life.** Make certain that you take time each day to do at least one thing that you like to do. Take time to relax, exercise, meditate, walk, and read for pleasure. Remind yourself that you are blessed with a full and rewarding life.

The Returning Student

The college classroom and workplace are changing. According to the National Center for Education Statistics (August 1997) more than 40 percent of college students are over twenty-four years old. Reentry students are the fastest growing group of college students. Since many reentry students have families and jobs, child care, flexible schedules, relevant classes, and financial aid are all important issues. Many colleges allow people over sixty to take courses for a nominal fee. Older students bring a wealth of experience, practical application, and different viewpoints to the classroom.

The early baby boomers are now past fifty and this large group is changing the nature of the workplace. Many adults change jobs, careers, or start working after raising a family, or do volunteer work. Older adults also bring a wealth of experience and a different perspective to the workplace. Many of these older workers are returning to school, especially to learn computer skills.

Here are a few tips for reentry students. Think how these tips can be applied to the workplace.

1. Observe, read, and notice procedures, deadlines, resources, and policies. Read the catalog and schedule of classes.

2. Explore campus resources. Go to the reentry center, utilize tutoring services, check out campus care, and explore the career center.

3. Explore community and family resources. Create a support system of people who can help. Have backup child care and transportation.

4. Develop an organized record-keeping system. Keep all your grades, transcripts, major contracts, etc., in one place.

5. Join study groups. (This really works!) You will be more effective when you learn to use the talents and skills of others.

6. Integrate *all* learning styles: create experiences, write, reflect, observe, listen, read, summarize, teach, demonstrate, and do.

7. Find a mentor. Build relationships with your advisors, instructors, bosses, and coworkers.

TIP Computers can also waste time if you're not focused and disciplined. You can spend hours surfing the Internet and playing video games. Make certain you have a specific goal to complete when you use the computer.

echnology
FOCUS:
Computer Efficiency

A. Computers can help you save time and be more effective. Use the computer to

1. Keep a daily calendar, a to-do list, and a list of your goals. There are lots of computer application programs that can help you get organized. These include day organizers and class organizers.

2. Write papers and reports. You will save time by brainstorming, writing your first draft, and cutting, pasting, and revising on the computer.

3. Create visual aide for speeches.

4. E-mail friends and family.

5. Do accounting and math problems and use spreadsheets.

B. Use this book's Web site to find more time-management tips:

http://peak.glencoe.com

Balancing Your Life

Take time to reflect on all areas of your life and the time you are presently investing in them. Decide if you are investing too much or too little time in each area. Also, look at the roles you play in each area of your life. In the family area, you may play the role of wife, mother, daughter, husband, father, son, uncle, etc. In the work area you may be a manager, a part-time worker, or an assistant.

Accompanying each role in your life are certain goals. Some goals demand greater time than others. It is okay to make a trade-off for a specific goal, but realize that you may neglect a vital area of your life. For instance, you may have a big term paper due, so you trade off a family outing to accomplish this goal.

Meet Julia Salay. Her health-related goal is to feel more energetic and thus reduce her stress. She plans to exercise twenty minutes each day and eat healthier foods. She also wants to spend quality time with her family. She decides to walk each day with her family so they can talk, spend time together, and be healthier.

Life Area Goals

Several life areas are listed on the chart below. Write one goal you have for each major area. Explain how you can commit a certain amount of time to meeting that goal and still maintain overall balance.

Life Areas	Goals
1. Career (job, earning a living)	_____
2. Educational	_____
3. Spiritual (your inner being, peace of mind)	_____
4. Relationships (your family, friends, associates)	_____
5. Health (weight, exercise, food, stress, personal care)	_____
6. Recreation (hobbies, sports, interests)	_____
7. Financial	_____
8. Home	_____
9. Community involvement and service	_____
10. Personal growth and renewal	_____
11. Other	_____
	_____

CAREER FOCUS: FOCUS ON TASKS, NOT TIME

Developing a reputation as a doer can greatly enhance your career. Successful professionals know it is important to plan, set goals, prioritize their tasks, and achieve results. Therefore, they set realistic and worthwhile goals. Career professionals are more concerned with achieving results than with frantic activity. Successful employees have learned not to procrastinate. They use their natural style and energy to achieve their goals in a flexible way.

Meet Robert Straine. He is a real estate associate. He is primarily a visual learner who uses slides, charts, and overhead transparencies to organize information and set goals. He likes to work with people and uses small teams to accomplish his goals. He tends to be creative, so he plans his day to tap his most creative periods. Robert works when his energy is high, which is often late mornings and evenings. He takes frequent breaks to discuss his projects with coworkers, visit new developments, and read reports of new market trends. Robert knows that paying attention to his commitments and interests outside work helps him create a balanced life and enables him to set realistic goals in all aspects of his life.

BEN NIGHTHORSE CAMPBELL

Ben Nighthorse Campbell is the senator from Iganacio, Colorado. A powerful Native-American leader, he was born in California and did not learn about his heritage until his early youth. Although he quit high school, he earned his GED while serving in the Air Force in the early fifties.

Ben realized that education was the key to success and earned a BS from San Jose State University in California. He also attended Meji University in Tokyo, Japan, as a special research student.

An interest in judo led to becoming the youngest person in the United States to hold the fourth degree black belt. Ben was also a member of the U.S. Olympic judo team in 1964. He later shared his time, talent, and knowledge of this sport with children by establishing one of the first successful judo clubs for children.

A multitalented individual, Ben became a jewelry designer and has won more than 200 first-place and best-of-show awards. He also worked as a rancher who raised, trained, and showed horses.

In 1982, Ben Nighthorse Campbell was elected to the Colorado state legislature and served on numerous committees. He was voted by his colleagues as one of the ten best legislators in the Denver Post News Center survey of 1984 and presented the outstanding legislator award from the Colorado Bankers Association. He was inducted into the Council of 44 Chiefs, Northern Cheyenne Indian Tribe.

On November 3, 1992, Ben Nighthorse Campbell was elected to the U.S. Senate. The only Native-American member in Congress, he has become the spokesperson for all Native Americans. He organizes his time in order to be an active member of a variety of committees and subcommittees. These committees are the Committee on Appropriations, Committee on Energy and Natural Resources, Committee on Veteran's Affairs; Indian Affairs; Agriculture, Nutrition, and Forestry. He also serves as chairperson of the subcommittee on Parks, Historic Preservation, and Recreation.

Throughout his tenure as a senator, he has introduced a variety of bills that have improved training, strengthened housing laws, established historical sites, and helped community development.

Ben Nighthorse Campbell is a Peak Performer who is a major voice in Washington. How do you think he sets his priorities and organizes his tasks?

Source: http://peak.glencoe.com

3

Review and Study Notes

Affirmations

- I have goals and priorities that give me direction and focus.
- I enjoy planning and concentrating on the task at hand.
- I am calm and centered, and I know I have time to do what is important.
- I take time to energize and renew myself.
- I focus on being effective.

Visualization

Envision yourself going through the day effortlessly. You are calm and energetic, and you complete each task. You have control of your time and your life. You have a clear vision of your goals and priorities. You work steadily and consistently until tasks are finished. Visualize your feelings of accomplishment and completion. Imagine yourself in charge of your time and your life.

Peak Performance Strategies

1. Take time to set goals and priorities.
2. Study at your high-energy time and in an organized space.
3. Study everywhere and anywhere.
4. Break projects into smaller tasks.
5. Consolidate similar tasks.
6. Make a schedule.
7. Say no to interruptions.
8. Get organized.
9. Be flexible.

CASE Studies

CASE A — *In the Classroom*

Christina Sato is a returning part-time student. Besides school, she works full-time and has a family. Her husband is verbally supportive of her goal to become a court reporter, but he does little to help her with the children or housework. Their children are twelve and fourteen and have depended on Christina to help them with their homework, drive them to their activities, clean their rooms, and even bake homemade cookies.

Christina prides herself on being a good housekeeper and loves being a mother and a wife. Now that she is in school, however, she has trouble keeping up with classes, homework, job responsibilities, and housework—let alone finding time for herself. Christina has dropped her early morning exercise routine, is getting less sleep, and is feeling exhausted and resentful.

1. What can Christina do to get more control over her life?

   _____

2. What strategies in the chapter would be most helpful to Christina?

   _____

In the Workplace

Christina is now a court reporter. She has always had a busy schedule, but she expected to have more free time after she graduated. Instead, she is just as busy as ever. Her children are active in school, and she feels it is important to be involved in their activities and schoolwork. Christina is also a member of two community organizations, volunteers at the local hospital, and is active in her church. Lately, she has found herself late for meetings and rushing through her day. Because she knows her health is important, Christina resumed her regular exercise program. Since graduation, she has had difficulty finding time for herself.

1. What strategies can help Christina gain control over her time and her life?

   _____

2. What areas of her life does she need to prioritize?

   _____

CASE B

Andy Diehm and Joe Smythe have been friends since high school. They are now roommates in college. They get along well together but have very different personalities and energy levels.

Andy is a morning person. He is up by 7:00 A.M., takes 8:00 A.M. classes, and sometimes gets up even earlier to study or run. He studies during the day and has completed most of his studies by early evening. He uses his evening hours for projects, research at the library, and chores. He goes to bed by 10:00 or 11:00 P.M.

Joe is a night owl. He studies until midnight or later. He has a hard time dragging himself out of bed in the morning and doesn't take a class before 10:00 A.M. Joe has also gotten hooked on the Internet. Some evenings he will surf it for hours.

By recognizing and respecting their differences, Andy and Joe have a system that works for them. Andy is quiet in the morning so Joe can sleep. He doesn't pressure him to get up. Joe is quiet in the evening and doesn't pressure Andy to stay up and talk or go to parties. They both accomplish their goals by supporting their natural learning styles.

1. Do you think Joe has a problem with the time he spends on the Internet?

2. What suggestions do you have to help Joe with his Internet distraction?

In the Workplace

Andy Diehm is now a department head of technology for a plumbing supply company. His life is busier than ever. He attends several meetings a day, writes reports, does presentations, and troubleshoots company problems.
He doesn't know how to deal with the constant flow of interruptions. He often feels behind, frustrated, and rushed. He has three children, and his wife also works full-time. He spends much of his free time attending parent-teacher conferences and athletic games and taking care of sick children. In addition, he is active in his local Rotary Club, and he feels that it is important to contribute to his community and to network with other professionals in the business world. With work, family, and community demands, Andy has little free time. He recently took a computer software class to add to his effectiveness at work, but now he spends hours surfing the Internet.

1. What strategies would you recommend to Andy to gain control of his life and his time?

2. What would you suggest to help him control interruptions?

Chapter Application   WORKSHEET 3.1

To-Do List

Urgent	Priorities	To See or Call

Continuing Attention	Awaiting Developments		
	What	Who	When

Chapter Application   WORKSHEET 3.2

Time Management

Complete the following statements with a Yes or No response.   Yes   No

1. I do the easiest and most enjoyable task first.   ___ ___

2. I do my top-priority task at the time of day when my
   energy is the highest and I know I will perform best.   ___ ___

3. I use my time wisely by doing high-return activities—
   previewing chapters, proofreading papers.   ___ ___

4. Even though I find interruptions distracting,
   I put up with them.   ___ ___

5. I save trivial and mindless tasks for the time of day
   when my energy is low.   ___ ___

6. I don't worry too much about making lists. I don't like
   planning and prefer to be spontaneous and respond as
   events occur.   ___ ___

7. My work space is organized and I have only one project
   on my desk at a time.   ___ ___

8. I set goals and review them each semester and each year.   ___ ___

9. My work space is open and I like to have people wander
   in and out.   ___ ___

10. My study team socializes first and then we work.   ___ ___

11. I have a lot of wasted waiting time, but you can't
    study in small blocks of time.   ___ ___

12. I block out a certain amount of time each week
    for my top-priority and hardest classes.   ___ ___

Scoring

1. Add the number of Yes responses to questions 2, 3, 5, 7, 8, 12.   _____

2. Add the number of No responses to questions 1, 4, 6, 9, 10, 11.   _____

3. Add the two scores together.   _____

The higher the score, the more likely you are to be organized.

Chapter Application   WORKSHEET 3.3

Time Wasters

Getting control of your time and life involves identifying time wasters and determining your peak energy level. It also involves identifying goals, setting priorities, and creating an action plan. Determining what task should be done first and overcoming procrastination are major factors in creating success. All these steps and issues involve critical thinking skills. Use critical thinking to complete the following questions.

1. What are the major activities and tasks that take much of your time?

   _____

2. What activities cause you to waste time?

   _____

3. What activities can you eliminate or reduce?

   _____

4. When is your high-energy time?

   _____

5. When do you study?

   _____

6. Look at your committed time. Does this block of time reflect your values and goals?

   _____

7. How can you increase your discretionary time?

   _____

8. Do you complete top-priority tasks first?

   _____

Chapter Application   WORKSHEET 3.3 (CONTINUED)

9. Look at the common reasons and excuses that some students use for not being organized and focused. Add to this list and use creative problem solving to list strategies for overcoming these barriers.

Reasons	**Strategies**
I ran out of time.	
I overslept.	
I'm easily distracted.	
People interrupt me.	
Instructors put too much pressure on me.	
I feel overwhelmed and panic at deadlines.	
I forgot about an assignment.	
Other	

Name _____   Date _____

Daily Energy Levels

Take a detailed look at your daily energy levels so you can become aware of your pattern. Keep track for a week or more. What tasks do you want to focus on during your high-energy time? Write these tasks on the chart.

Energy Level	7:00 A.M.	Noon	10:00 P.M.
100 percent			
80 percent			
50 percent			
25 percent			

DEMONSTRATING YOUR TIME-MANAGEMENT SKILLS

List all the factors involved in time management. Indicate how you would demonstrate them to employers.

Areas	Demonstration
Dependability	*Haven't missed a day of work in my job*
Reliability	
Effectiveness	
Efficiency	
Responsibility	
Positive attitude	
Persistence	
Ability to plan and set goals and priorities	
Visionary	
Ability to follow through	
High energy	
Ability to handle stress	
Ability to focus	
Respect for others' time	
Ability to overcome procrastination	
Reputation as a doer and self-starter	

TIP Know the expectations and requirements of every class. Keep your syllabus, handouts, instructor's name, his or her office number and hours, sample tests, notes, due dates of projects, tests, project board, and study team's phone numbers in a binder for each class.

ACTIVE LISTENING AND NOTE TAKING

I only wish I could find an institute that teaches people how to listen. After all, a good manager needs to listen as much as he needs to talk . . . . real communication goes in both directions.

—Lee Iacocca, former chairperson of Chrysler Corporation

Learning Objectives

In **Chapter 4** **you** will **learn**

- active listening strategies.
- how to take notes in alignment with your learning style.
- the different note-taking systems.
- effective note-taking strategies.

A ttending lectures or meetings, listening, taking notes, and gathering information are such a daily part of school and work that few people give much thought to the process of selecting, organizing, and recording information. Active listening and note taking are not just tools for school. They are essential job skills. Throughout your career, you will be processing and recording information. The volume of new information is exploding in this computer age, and the career professional who can listen, organize, and summarize information will be sought after. This chapter addresses the fine points of active listening and note taking.

NOTE TAKING

Note taking is an individualized process comprised of a series of complex activities. It is not a passive act of simply writing down words. It is a way to order and arrange thoughts and material to help you remember information. Effective note-taking strategies include highlighting main ideas, organizing key points, comparing and contrasting relationships, and looking for patterns. You will accomplish this by observing, listening, reviewing, organizing, and recording. No two people take notes in the same way because each person's beliefs about the subject and instructor, his or her biases and assumptions, mental state of mind, and listening skills are all factors that affect the others and the individual's note-taking process.

LISTENING TO THE MESSAGE

Before you can be an effective note taker, you must become an effective listener. Most people think of themselves as good listeners. However, listening should not be confused with hearing. Unless you have a medical problem, you can hear the message, but you may not be listening to the intended meaning. Active listening is a decision to be fully attentive and to understand the intent of the speaker. It is a consuming activity that requires physical and mental attention, energy, concentration, and discipline. Not only is listening fundamental to taking good classroom notes, it is directly related to how well you do in college and in your career. As a student, you will be expected to actively listen to other student presentations, small group and class discussions. Active listening is also important for job success. Career professionals attend meetings, follow directions, work with customers, take notes from professional journals and lectures, and give and receive feedback. You can apply the same listening strategies for building effective relationships at school, at work, and in life.

Success Principle 4:
Focus on **INTENTION,**
not your own
Message.

Active Listening Strategies

1. **Desire to listen.** The first place to start is with your intention. You must want to be a better listener and realize that listening is an active rather than a passive process. Is your intention to learn and understand the other person? Or is your intention to prove how smart you are and how wrong the other person is? The best listening strategies in the world won't help if you are unwilling to listen.

2. **Be open and willing to learn.** Be aware of the resistance you have to learning new information. Many students resist change, new ideas, or different beliefs. This resistance gets in the way of actively listening and learning. Be open to different points of view, different styles of lecturing, and learning new ideas. Students sometimes have problems listening to lectures because they have already made up their minds, or they want to prove the instructor wrong and mentally challenge everything that is said. It is easy to misinterpret the meaning of a message if you are defensive, judgmental, bored, or emotionally upset.

3. **Postpone judgment.** Don't judge your instructor or his or her message based on clothes, reputation, voice, or teaching style. Go to class with an open and curious mind and focus on the message, course content, and your performance.

4. **Be mindful.** Being mentally and physically alert is vital for active listening. It's true that everyone's mind wanders during a long lecture, but being mentally preoccupied is a major barrier to effective listening. It's up to you to focus your attention, concentrate on the subject, and bring your mind back to the present. Make a determined effort to stay focused and in the present.

5. **Use empathy and respect.** Focus on understanding the message and viewpoint of the speaker. Look for common views and ways that you are alike rather than different. Listen with empathy, respect, and the intention to understand.

6. **Observe.** A large part of listening and note taking is observing. Observe your instructor and watch for obvious verbal and nonverbal clues about what information is important. If your instructor uses repetition, becomes more animated, or writes information on the board, it is probably important. Overhead transparencies or handouts may also include important diagrams, lists, drawings, facts, or definitions. Watch for examples and connect similar ideas. Observe words and phrases that signal important information or transition, such as "One important factor is . . . ." Review the list of signal words and phrases that appears in Figure 4-1 on pages 4-4 and 4-5.

7. **Predict and ask questions.** Keep yourself alert by predicting and asking yourself questions. Is this story supporting the main topic? What are the main points? How does this example clarify the readings? What test questions could be asked about these main points? Pretend that you are in a private conversation and ask your instructor to elaborate, give examples, or explain certain points. Make certain that you are not taking up too much time in the class daydreaming and that you have previewed the chapter and done your homework.

To Show Addition or Another Fact

again	in addition
also	in fact
and	last
and then	likewise
another	moreover
besides	next
but also	nor
equally important	plus the fact that
finally	second
first	then too
further	third
	too

To Show Contrast or Change an Idea

although	in contrast
anyhow	nevertheless
anyway	notwithstanding
at the same time	on the contrary
but	on the other hand
despite this	
even though	otherwise
for all that	still
however	yet
in any event	

To Show Summary

as has been noted	in essence
as I have said	in other words
finally	in short
in brief	in summary
in closing	on the whole
in conclusion	to conclude
	to sum up

To Show Amount

few	over
greater	several
less than	smaller
many	some
more than	under
most	

To Show Comparison

in like manner	likewise
in the same way	similarly

To Show Purpose

all things considered	to this end
	with this in mind
for this purpose	with this object

Figure 4-1
Signal Words and Phrases

To Show Place

above	here
across	nearby
adjacent to	on the opposite
below	side
beneath	opposite to
beside	over
between	there
beyond	under
farther	

To Show Time

after a few days	immediately
afterward	in the meantime
at last	later
at length	not long after
before	soon
between	then
finally	while

To Show a Specific Case

a few of these	let us consider
are	the case of
especially	the following
for example	you can see
for instance	this in
in particular	

To Show Result

accordingly	so
as a result	then
because	therefore
consequently	thereupon
for this reason	thus
hence	

To Strengthen a Point

basically	undeniably
essentially	without a doubt
indeed	without any
truly	question

Figure 4-1 (continued)
Signal Words and Phrases

8. **Look as if you are listening.** Active listening requires high energy. Sit up, keep your spine straight, and uncross your legs and you will have more energy. Look like you are alert and receptive. Maintain eye contact and lean slightly forward. Don't look at your watch, read the newspaper, lean back and cross your arms, or look bored. Respond with nods, smiles, and open facial expressions. Participate in discussions or when asked questions.

9. **Reduce distractions.** Don't sit next to friends or someone who likes to talk or is distracting. Sit near the front. Bring a sweater if it is cold in the classroom or sit by an open window if it is warm. Carry a bottle of water with you to sip when your energy starts to lag.

10. **Be quiet.** The fundamental rule of listening is to be quiet while the speaker is talking. Don't interrupt or talk to classmates. As a listener, your role is to understand and comprehend. As a speaker, your role is to make the message clear and comprehensible. Don't confuse the two roles. When you are listening, really listen until the speaker is finished.

CRITICAL THINKING LOG 4.1

Active Listening

Use critical thinking to answer the following questions.

1. Do you come to class prepared and with a positive and receptive state of mind? Write down one tip that you would be willing to try to improve your listening.

_____

2. Jot down the name of a person whom you consider to be a good listener.

_____

Think about your feelings toward this person. It is usually difficult not to like someone whom you consider to be a good listener. Active listening shows respect and caring and is one of the best gifts one person can give to another.

3. Write a list of daily situations where active listening is required. Some situations could include talking to your child about his or her day at school, listening to your spouse's or roommate's views on politics, or meeting with a community group to plan a fundraising event. What listening strategies would increase your attention and responsiveness in the situations you've listed?

_____

_____

RECORDING THE MESSAGE

Now that you are prepared and have sharpened your listening and observation skills, let's look at the structure and format of your notes. To help you organize and record information, you will want to use a system that enhances your learning and personality style.

There are several note-taking systems that will help you organize information while you listen and read. Find one that supports your learning and personality style. For example, if you are primarily an auditory learner, listen attentively and consider taping certain lectures (make certain you ask the instructor before you tape). Recite your book notes into a tape recorder and play it back several times. If you are an Analytical type, you may be more comfortable with a lineal and sequential or formal method of note taking.

If you are primarily a visual learner, supplement your lecture notes with drawings, illustrations, and pictures and take special note of material on the blackboard, overhead transparencies, and handouts. Read your notes right after class to reinforce your learning and compare your notes to material in the textbook.

If you are a Creative type, you can look for information that is different and doesn't match. You may like using a creative outline or mind map because they present the big picture visually and allow a creative flair. If you are Supportive, you can process information that is personally relevant and connect similar patterns. You may want to use the Cornell or T note-taking system, where you can jot stories in the margin or create a mind map to connect ideas and patterns.

If you are a Kinesthetic learner, you may also have a Director style personality and like active learning. You can make learning more physical by writing and rephrasing material; working with your study team or study partner; collecting examples, stories, and diagrams; using note cards; and standing to take notes from your textbook. You may find the template system to be practical for use in many classes, or you may want to use a combination of systems that produces the results you want. Here are a few common outline systems.

Formal Outline

A formal outline shows headings, main points, and supporting examples and requires consistency. For example, if you have an A.1, you should have a B.1. Likewise, if you have an A.2, you should have a B.2. Left-brain people like neat, orderly notes and are often comfortable with a sequential format. See Figure 4-2 on page 4-8 for a sample formal outline.

> **TIP** Note taking is really sorting out and organizing information while you listen and read.

Topic: Note taking

Jana Rosa
April 9, 2000

Effective strategies for taking notes

    A. The traditional outline for note taking

        1. Advantages

            a. Occupies your attention totally

            b. Organizes ideas as well as records them

        2. Disadvantages

            a. Too structured for right-brain person

            b. Time consuming

    B. The mapping system for note taking

        1. Advantages

            a. Presents a creative and visual model

            b. You can start anywhere on the page

        2. Disadvantages

            a. Too busy for a left-brain person

            b. Too unorganized for a left-brain person

Figure 4-2
Sample Formal Outline

Creative Outline

If you are a right-brain person, you may feel more comfortable with a creative outline. You can simply divide the paper and use the left side for key words, illustrations, questions, graphs, definition, stories, dates, or formulas. Use the right side to list topics. See Figure 4-3 for an example of a creative outline.

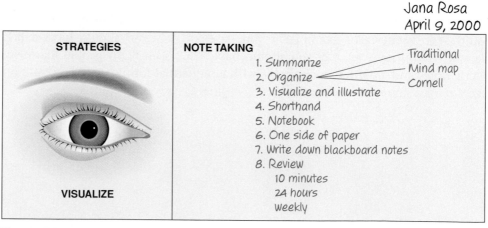

Figure 4-3
Sample Creative Outline

Mind Map

You can also use the creative outline style that is often called mind mapping. See the sample mind map in Figure 4-4. A mind map is a visual and holistic form of note taking. The advantage is that you can see connections and the BIG PICTURE. You can also see connections to the main idea. Mapping starts from the main idea placed in the center of a page and branches out with subtopics through associations and patterns. If you are a right-brain person, you may find that mapping helps you increase your comprehension, creativity, and recall. You can draw a map for each chapter and put them on your bulletin board, or you may want to use a combination of maps and traditional outlines.

A left-brain student may have trouble mapping because the outline is not sequential, it is difficult to follow the instructor's train of thought, there is little space for corrections or additions, and the notes must be shortened to key words and only one page. An option for a left-brain student is to use a map to illustrate the whole chapter but also to use the traditional outline for daily notes.

Jana Rosa
April 9, 2000

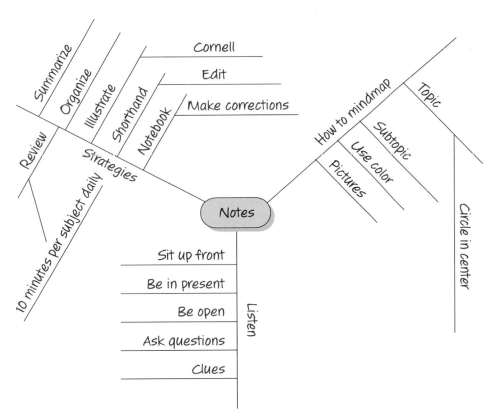

Figure 4-4
Mind Map

Mind Map Template

In certain classes, you will study several different topics that have the same patterns. For example, you may study different cultures, and the categories or patterns are the same for each culture. You can adapt the template in Figure 4-5 to many subjects.

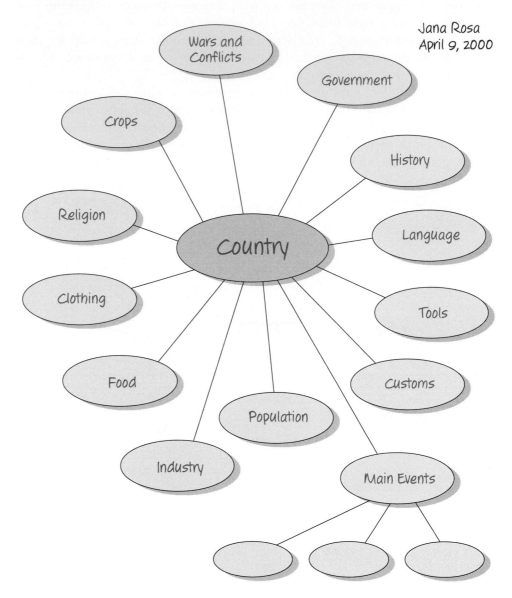

Figure 4-5
Mind Map Template

PART TWO   Basic Skills and Strategies

CRITICAL
THINKING LOG
4.2

Mind Map

Make a mind map of a chapter from your textbook in the space below. Compare it to the mind maps drawn by members of your study group. Use the sample in Figure 4-5 as a guide.

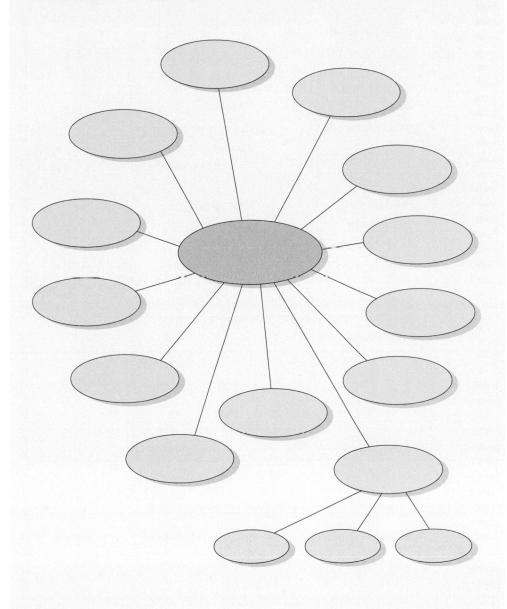

Cornell Method

The Cornell or T note-taking system has been used for more than forty-five years and is effective in integrating text and lecture notes. See Figure 4-6 for an example of the Cornell method of note taking.

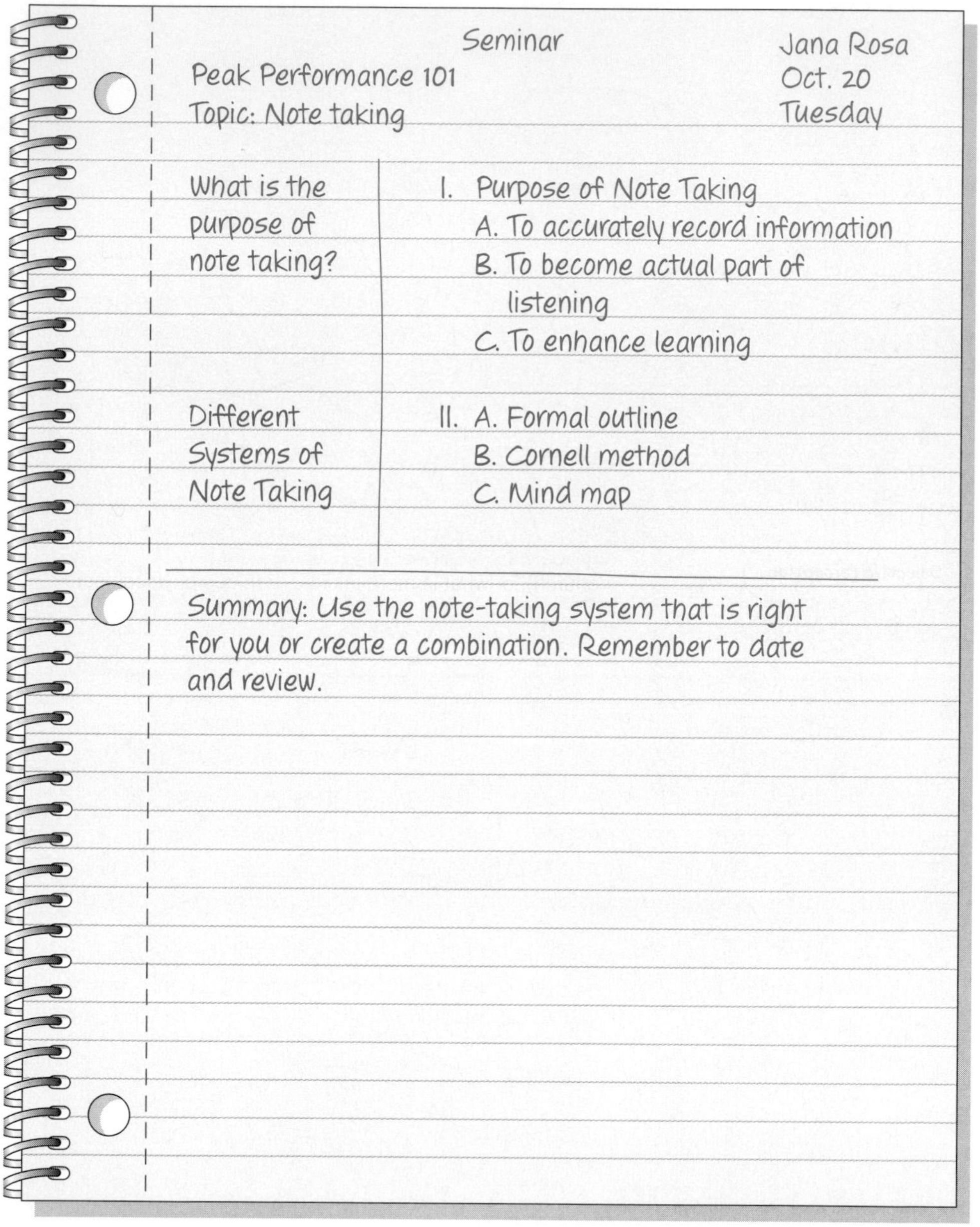

	Seminar	Jana Rosa
	Peak Performance 101	Oct. 20
	Topic: Note taking	Tuesday

What is the purpose of note taking?	I. Purpose of Note Taking
	  A. To accurately record information
	  B. To become actual part of listening
	  C. To enhance learning

Different Systems of Note Taking	II. A. Formal outline
	  B. Cornell method
	  C. Mind map

Summary: Use the note-taking system that is right for you or create a combination. Remember to date and review.

Figure 4-6
Cornell Method

Combination Note-Taking System

The following figure shows the combination note-taking system.

Jana Rosa
April 9, 2000

What is

I. Selective Perception
  A. External
    1. Larger, brighter
    2. Different
    3. Repetitive
    4. Contrast
  B. Internal
    1. Needs
      a. Hunger
      b. Fatigue
    2. Motives
      a. Entertain

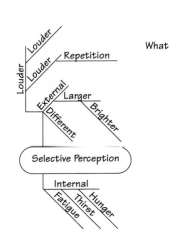

What

Eat here   **Example:**

  1. Needs
  2. Motives   **What**

Summary:

Selective Perception?

Selective perception is the process by which certain events, objects, or information is selected for our attention. Because of selection, we do not process the information required to make decisions or initiate behavior. Perception is selective. We all have the ability to tune out certain stimuli and focus on others or to shift our attention at will. We tend to hear and see what meets our needs, interests, and motivation. We fill in what is missing. We choose what we want to perceive and organize information into meaningful pictures. We block out some information and add to others. What are the factors that cause us to focus on and select certain events and ignore others? These factors tend to fall into two categories: external and internal.

    A.   **B.**

External Factors?

External factors refer to certain events around us that determine whether we notice something or not.
  Many factors affect which objects will receive our attention and focus. Stimuli that activate our senses are noticed more (larger, brighter, louder). Anything that is different and out of the ordinary, colorful, unfamiliar, or that contrasts a background receives more attention. We notice what is different and incongruent (wearing shorts in church), or what is more intense. Besides physical factors, we also notice objects that are in motion or messages that are repetitive. The more information presented (the frequency), the greater the chances that the information will be selected.
  Marketing experts study these external factors and use them in advertisements. If a message is loud or bright it increases the chances that it will be selected. We even use external factors in our daily life. John is a public relations executive and wants to stand out and be noticed in a large company. He wears expensive suits and unusual, interesting ties. Even his office is decorated in a unique, colorful, yet professional style.

Internal Factors?

There are several internal factors that affect perception. Motivation: What we focus on is affected by our current motives or needs. If you've ever attended a meeting close to lunch time you may find yourself concentrating on the aroma of the coffee or the smells coming from a nearby restaurant. You tend to respond to stimuli that relate to your immediate needs (hunger, fatigue). If you are driving down the highway and see a host of signs and billboards, you will notice the ones that are directed to your current motivational state, such as those for food, lodging, or entertainment. Related to your motivational state is your attitude.

Selective perception is the process by which information is selected for our attention. Both external and internal factors affect perception. External factors include stimuli that is larger, brighter, louder, unusual, unfamiliar, colorful, or intense. Internal factors include our motives and needs, such as hunger, fatigue, anger, or our attitude.

Figure 4-7
Combination Note-Taking System

NOTE-TAKING STRATEGIES

The following strategies will help you make the most of whatever note-taking system you use.

1. **Be prepared.** Can you imagine going to an important class without doing your homework; being unprepared to participate; or lacking pen, paper, and necessary material? Preview or skim the textbook chapters for main ideas, general theme, and key concepts. Previewing is a simple strategy that enhances your note taking and learning. In a sense, you are priming your brain to process information efficiently and effectively. You will also want to review previous notes and connect what you have learned to new ideas. Use index cards to jot down key words, formulas, definitions, and important information.

2. **Go to every class.** The most obvious and important part of being prepared is to *attend all your classes*. You cannot take effective notes if you are not there. Having someone else take notes for you is not the same as being in class. Make a commitment that you will go to every class unless you are seriously ill. If you have a cold, stay away from others and cover your mouth. Check bus schedules in case your car breaks down. Have several backup plans if you have children. Don't schedule other appointments when you have classes. In other words, be prepared and make a commitment to treat your education as a top priority.

3. **Be on time.** Walking in late for class indicates an attitude that class is not important and disrupts the instructor and other students. Set your watch five minutes early and arrive early enough to preview your notes and get settled. Punctuality also helps you prepare emotionally and mentally.

4. **Sit up front.** You will be more physically alert and you will see and hear better if you sit in the front of the class. You are also more likely to ask questions and engage the instructor in eye contact when you sit in front. You will be less likely to talk with other students, pass notes, doodle, finish your homework, or daydream when you sit in front.

5. **Use all your senses.** Many people view note taking not only as a passive activity but also an auditory activity. Actually, you will find note taking more effective if you integrate learning styles and use all your senses.

   If you are primarily an auditory listener, listen attentively and capitalize on this style of processing information. You might want to tape lectures. Explain your notes to your study group so you can hear the material again.

   If you are primarily a visual learner, develop mental pictures and your right-brain creativity. Draw and illustrate concepts. Practice visualizing images while the speaker is talking and form mental pictures of the topic. Visualize the whole of the subject and associate the image with key words. Use colored pencils, cartoons, and any illustrations that add humor and make the material come alive. Supplement your lecture notes with drawings, illustrations, and pictures, and take special note of material on the blackboard, overhead transparencies, and handouts. Use visualization to form pictures in your mind about the lecture topics.

> Eighty-five percent of success in life is just showing up.
> —*Woody Allen*

Make note taking more kinesthetic by writing and rephrasing material, drawing diagrams, discussing your notes with your study team, outlining your notes on the board, and standing when you take notes from your textbook. Draw models and charts, and collect samples and write descriptive notes. Take notes on field trips.

Use left-brain organizational skills. Use large, bold headlines for the main ideas, large print for key words, important points, facts, places, and other supporting data. Write your name, topic, and date on each sheet of paper. You may want to purchase a binder for each class to organize notes, syllabi, handouts, tests, and summaries.

6. **Make note taking active and physical.** For your mind to be alert, your body also has to be alert. Physical activity gets your blood flowing throughout your body, including your brain, which is why physical activity enhances academic performance for all learning styles. Observe your body, how you hold your pen, and how your back feels against the chair. Slouching produces fatigue and signals the brain that this activity is not important. Sit straight. When you are at home taking notes and you feel your energy dip, take a walk, stretch, do deep knee bends or head rolls, or jog in place for a few minutes. Exercise also helps relax the body, focuses the mind, and reduces stress.

7. **Link information.** Connect ideas and link similar information. Look for patterns and for information that is different. Compare and contrast; find similarities and differences. Develop associations between what you are hearing for the first time and what you already know. When you link new knowledge to what you already know, you create lasting impressions. Ask yourself how this information relates to other classes or to your job.

8. **Use creative shorthand and focus on key words.** A common mistake students make is attempting to write down everything the instructor says. Notes are like blueprints because they represent a larger subject and highlight main details. The essential element in taking effective notes is to jot down only main points and key words. Let's suppose that you are learning about groups and group dynamics. Your instructor may declare, "The essential ingredient for groupthink to occur is strong group cohesiveness." *Group cohesiveness* is a key phrase that will link to the concept of groupthink. Ask yourself, How does all this new information relate to what I already know? In the above example of groupthink, you might list fraternities/sororities, political groups, sporting teams, and clubs as having strong group cohesiveness.

Focus on key words that link concepts, associate words, and emphasize main ideas. Illustrations, filler statements, stories, introductions, and transitions are important for depth, interest, and understanding, but you don't have to write down every word. Devise your own system for note taking that include abbreviations and symbols. See Figure 4-8 on page 4-16 for examples.

Symbol	Meaning	Abbreviation	Meaning
>	greater than; increase	i.e.	that is
<	less than; decrease	etc.	and so forth
?	question	lb.	pound
w/	with	assoc.	association
w/o	without	info	information
V OR *	important ideas	ex.	example
+	positive		
-	negative		
×	times		
~	lost		
ρ	leads to (motivation ρ success)		
^	bridge of concepts		
#	number		

Figure 4-8
Sample Note-Taking Symbols and Abbreviations

9. **Leave space for revisions and additions.** Leave wide margins and plenty of space to make corrections, add notes, clarify, and summarize. Don't crowd your words or the notes will be difficult to understand. Keep all handouts you receive in class. Use a question mark if you do not understand something so you can ask about it later.

ASSESS AND REVIEW

1. **Summarize in your own words.** When you finish taking text and lecture notes, summarize in your own words. You might want to write summaries on index cards, then check to see what you left out and what you can add. This will also highlight questions you may want to ask. Summarizing can be done quickly and can cover only main concepts. This one small action will greatly increase your comprehension and learning. It is even more effective when you read your summary out loud to others. Teaching is the best way to learn.

2. **Edit and revise your notes.** Set aside a few minutes as soon as possible after the lecture to edit, revise, fill in, or copy your notes. Ask yourself what questions might be on a test. Underline what the instructor has indicated is important. Fill in blanks with new material. Clean up, expand, and rewrite sections that are messy or incomplete. If you are unclear on a point, leave a space and put a question mark in the margin. You can ask for verification from other students in class or in your study group, or you can ask your instructor during office hours or before or after class.

3. **Review your notes.** Even if you have only ten minutes, review your notes for the main ideas and write down any questions you have. Experts say that, unless students review soon after the lecture, much of the new information will be lost within the first half-hour after the class. Research indicates that your memory is at its most receptive within twenty-four hours after hearing new information. You might try going to your next class early and spending five minutes reviewing your class notes from the previous class. Or you can review while the instructor passes out handouts, adjusts the overhead projector, sets up the projector, or organizes. Reviewing right before you go to sleep is also a great strategy to help you remember. Your mind is receptive to new information at that time. Reviewing increases your memory and helps you perform better on exams.

4. **Monitor and evaluate.** Periodically assess your note-taking system. Try different systems and strategies until you find one that works best. Feedback from study group members, your instructor, and tests will help you assess how well your system is working.

CRITICAL THINKING LOG 4.3   Note-Taking Strategies

List the different note-taking strategies and styles of your study group members. Discuss the merits and shortcomings of each. With the group members, brainstorm the best strategies and come up with several styles that work.

_____

_____

_____

_____

_____

_____

_____

_____

_____

_____

_____

_____

TRAILMARKER 4.1

Overcoming Barriers to Effective Note Taking

The first step in overcoming the barriers to effective note taking is to recognize its importance. Some students view note taking as a passive academic skill that they will never use once they graduate from college. As a result, their notes are often disorganized, incomplete, illegible, and of little help in preparing for tests. Effective note taking changes the information that you hear into information that is distinctly yours. You have discarded the unessential, highlighted the essential, and organized information to give it meaning and focus. This process is an important job skill. Follow the simple steps below until discipline and focus become a habit.

- **Observe** your intention and willingness to listen and learn. Observe what is on the board, in handouts, and in overhead transparencies. Sit in the front to avoid distractions and to help you focus and observe.
- **Listen** for understanding and for main points and key words.
- **Organize** the important information. Choose a system that helps you organize and record main points and key words.
- **Record** the date and topic and leave room in the margins for revising.
- **Review** and revise your notes as soon as possible. Review notes with your study team so you can fill in information that you missed and summarize main points.

Technology FOCUS:

Computers and Note Taking

Computers can help you take better notes. Organizing material is essential for recall. Computer programs are available to help you:

- Outline ideas and information in both traditional and mind-mapping outlines.
- Copy your notes and arrange them in an organized outline. After each lecture, you can adjust, reorganize, add, change, and elaborate. You can also incorporate your reading notes. Print out a copy and take it to the next lecture so that you are building on good notes in each lecture. As you type your notes, leave room for questions that you think might be on the test or questions to ask your instructor or study group.
- Explore note-taking skills on the Internet.

Use this book's Web site to find more information about note-taking and study skills.

http://peak.glencoe.com

Reflection

Use critical thinking to answer the following. Write your answers on the lines provided.

1. Do you preview chapters, take textbook notes, and write summaries?

_____

_____

_____

_____

2. Are you prepared mentally to listen and learn?

_____

_____

_____

_____

3. Can you see the whole picture from your notes and gain a general understanding of the material? Explain how.

_____

_____

_____

_____

4. Describe how you can make your least interesting class more interesting and productive.

_____

_____

_____

_____

5. Give some examples of how being an active note-taker can create a positive learning experience.

_____

_____

_____

_____

MINDFULNESS AT WORK

Being aware, mindful, alert, and focused in the present are key factors in active listening and are critical for career success. Molly Tyler has just been promoted to conference planner in a large hotel. Her job involves taking accurate notes at meetings and conferences; jotting down directions; and predicting questions, concerns, and potential problems. To be an active listener at work, Molly:

1. Observes verbal and nonverbal messages and clarifies expectations.
2. Is mindful, alert, and aware.
3. Listens actively to main points and seeks to understand.
4. Organizes notes to highlight important information.
5. Reviews details of events and follow-up procedures.

Here's an example of Molly's note taking on the job.

Initial Meeting for Conference Planning   April 20, 2000
Name of group: National Dental Conference
Dates of Conference: November 28, 29, and 30, 2000

Conference facility needs:
Hotel accommodations
Number of meeting rooms
Hospitality suites
Reception rooms
Size of groups

Equipment needs:
Podium
Head table
Refreshments
Seating
Blackboard
Confirm with master calendar

Follow up with:
Secure budget by _____
Overhead
Audiovisual equipment
Copy machine

Staffing needs:
Secretary
Registration workers
Extra waiters
Dining and reception needs
Coffee and refreshments
Breakfasts, lunches, dinners
Cocktail hour

Peak Performers in the Workplace create a positive mind-set for listening by:

1. Suspending judgment about your boss.
2. Adjusting to your boss's style of management.
3. Being prepared for meetings.
4. Developing a partnership with your boss.
5. Listening for understanding.
6. Clarifying instructions.
7. Assessing results.

MARY KATHLYN WAGNER

Mary Kathlyn Wagner, known by millions today as Mary Kay, did not have an easy childhood. Her father developed tuberculosis when she was seven, and her mother had to go to work early in the morning and did not return home until late at night.

Mary Kay took over running the house—washing dishes, cooking meals, and cleaning—while attending second grade. She would call her mother often to ask questions. Her mother always praised her and ended many conversations with the encouraging words, "You can do it!" These words were to fill her young life with hope and courage and later provide the confidence she would need to start her own business.

Years later, after marriage, children, and a divorce, she became a salesperson for Stanley Home Products. This gave her excellent training in marketing, sales, products, and all aspects of running a business. Even then, her employer saw a special spark and encouraged her to start her own business.

With borrowed money, courage, and amazing determination, she bought a formula for a beauty product and opened a small shop. Beauty by Mary Kay was launched. Mary Kay's philosophy has always been to provide training, skills, and confidence to empower women.

Today, Mary Kay, Inc., is housed in a twenty-story glass tower in Dallas. The international headquarters oversee a multimillion-dollar company. Mary Kay is a Peak Performer. She had the confidence and determination to overcome barriers and become a success. What can *you* learn from Mary Kay?

Source: http://peak.glencoe.com

4

Review and Study Notes

Affirmations

- I enjoy listening to all kinds of lectures and discovering the main ideas.
- I like taking organized notes and making them creative.
- I am alert and aware, and I listen actively during lectures.
- I enjoy digging out key facts when I take textbook notes.

Visualization

Visualize yourself in class, prepared and ready to take notes. Imagine yourself as aware, alert, and actively listening to the lecture. You have previewed the chapter, so you can listen with ease and connect key concepts to what you already know.

Peak Performance Strategies for Active Listening

1. Observe and clarify intentions.
2. Be willing and open to learn.
3. Postpone judgment.
4. Be alert and in the present.
5. Observe patterns and clues.
6. Predict and ask questions.
7. Listen; don't talk.

Peak Performance Strategies for Active Note Taking

1. Make note taking physical.
2. Go to every class and be on time.
3. Sit in the front.
4. Be prepared.
5. Preview the textbook.
6. Write summaries.
7. Organize notes according to your learning style preference.
8. Create an organized system.
9. Visualize and illustrate.
10. Use creative shorthand.
11. Write down all material from the board.
12. Leave space for questions and revisions.
13. Summarize in your own words.
14. Edit notes.
15. Review your notes.
16. Monitor and evaluate.

CASE Studies

CASE A — In the Classroom

Joe Cole hates his personal finance class and thinks his instructor is boring. Class meets at 9:00 A.M. and Joe misses a lot of classes because he's a night owl. When he does go, he is usually late and sits in the back row so he can nap or catch up on his accounting. He never asks questions, volunteers for class exercises, or gets involved in class discussion. Joe is confident that he can cram for the exams. Besides, he plans to be an accountant, not a financial manager. He already knows how to balance his checkbook and do a budget. He can learn everything he needs from the textbook, so he feels like it's no big deal if he misses a few classes.

1. What would you suggest to help Joe change his behavior and attitude?

   _____

2. What strategies in this chapter would help him most?

   _____

3. What is one habit that Joe can adapt to make a real difference?

   _____

In the Workplace

Joe is an accountant with a large firm. He was recently promoted to a supervisor position. He has learned to manage his time, puts a lot of effort into his job, and gets along well with others. Joe has to attend several meetings, which requires him to listen actively and take accurate notes. It is becoming difficult for him to stay awake and alert during long meetings, and Joe often has trouble relating the main content of the meetings to his staff.

1. What would you suggest to help Joe listen more effectively and take better notes?

   _____

2. What strategies in this chapter do you think would help Joe most?

   _____

   _____

CASE B
In the Classroom

Lindsay Monroe is a fashion design student and works part-time in a retail clothing store. She has two roommates, who are also students. Lindsay is an extremely social person. She loves to talk, tells interesting stories, and always tells great jokes. She is the life of the party! Unfortunately, Lindsay isn't a very good listener. In class she is too busy chatting with the person next to her to hear the correct assignments. She always starts off as a popular study team member, but it soon becomes clear that her assignments are always late and incorrect. Her roommates have finally leveled with her. Tension has built up among the roommates because they feel that Lindsay isn't pulling her weight on household chores. One major bone of contention is Lindsay's difficulty in taking accurate phone messages. She never seems to get the information down correctly.

1. What strategies in this chapter can help Lindsay be a more effective listener?

   _____

2. What would you suggest she do to improve her relationships with others and help her become better at taking down information?

   _____

   _____

TIP Sit in the front, observe, and listen to your instructor. Ask questions, look for patterns, and summarize main points. Continually bring your mind back to the present by pretending that you are in a private conversation with your instructor.

In the Workplace

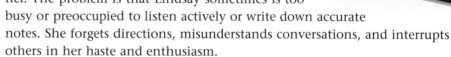

Lindsay is now a fashion designer in a large department store. She loves working with people. She is a talented, responsible employee when she is actively aware and tuned in to others. People respond to her favorably and enjoy being around her. The problem is that Lindsay sometimes is too busy or preoccupied to listen actively or write down accurate notes. She forgets directions, misunderstands conversations, and interrupts others in her haste and enthusiasm.

1. What would you suggest to help Lindsay become a better listener?

   _____

   _____

2. What strategies in this chapter would help her become more aware, more sensitive to others, and able to record information more effectively?

   _____

   _____

Name _____   Date _____

Mind Map for Sorting Information

Use the example below as a guide for developing a mind map of key points from one of your class lectures. Write the topic on the rule and draw lines from it. Write the key points on those lines.

Lecture _____   **Class** _____

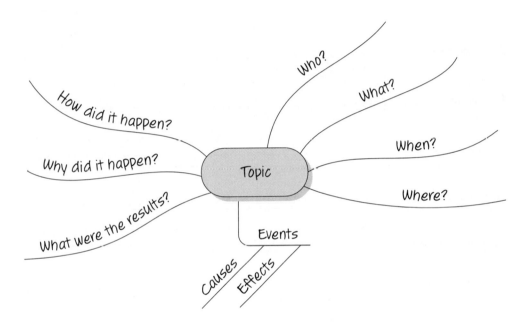

TOPIC
_____

Chapter Application   WORKSHEET 4.2

Taking Notes

Use this guide to focus on creating an outline of the important ideas presented in a class lecture.

Class _____   **Instructor** _____   **Date** _____

Lecture topic: _____

Chapters covered: _____

Main ideas: _____

Supporting ideas: _____

Examples: _____

Vocabulary terms: _____

Key words: _____

Important concepts and theories: _____

Applications: _____

How this information is similar to known information: _____

How this information is different: _____

Overall theme: _____

Summary of lecture: _____

_____

Chapter Application   WORKSHEET 4.3

Note-Taking Checklist

	Observe				Organize				Link				Review			
Prepare Listen Outline Summarize	Maintain a positive attitude.	Be alert and attentive.	Integrate learning styles.	Focus on main points and key words.	Outline material.	Illustrate.	Separate essential from nonessential.	Categorize and compare.	Link familiar with new.	Link similarities and differences.	Link key words and points.	Link questions and summary.	Review information.	Edit and modify.	Summarize.	Recall and evaluate.
Course 1																
Course 2																
Course 3																
Course 4																
Course 5																
Course 6																

Chapter Application   WORKSHEET 4.4

Note Taking in the Work Environment

Indicate how you will demonstrate listening and note-taking skills for future employers.

1. Active listening

   _____

2. Acquiring information

   _____

3. Organizing information

   _____

4. Willingness to learn

   _____

5. Showing interest

   _____

6. Staying alert and in the present

   _____

7. Organized system of note taking

   _____

8. Taking notes at meetings

   _____

9. Attending meetings prepared

   _____

10. Using computer to process information

    _____

11. Other

    _____

Chapter Application WORKSHEET 4.5

Your Legacy

It may help you plan your life today by imagining yourself growing older. Think about the personal qualities, character traits, friends, type of family, goals, and values that may be most important to you in later years. The kind of person you hope to be at eighty-five or ninety years old will not just happen unless you really think about the future. By doing so, you will begin to define more clearly the values and goals you have today. It can also help you determine your current priorities and make decisions that will have an impact on your future.

Think about the legacy you want to leave behind. What do you want to be remembered for? What characteristics and qualities do you want your children and grandchildren to remember about you? Reflect upon them and jot them down. Then try to imagine yourself at eighty or ninety years of age. With this future image of yourself in mind, write your legacy below. Try to include what you think will be most important to you when you are eighty-six years old. Consider values, interests, attitude, abilities, accomplishments, and talents.

_____

_____

_____

_____

_____

_____

_____

_____

_____

_____

_____

_____

_____

_____

_____

_____

_____

Chapter Application WORKSHEET 4.6

Ongoing Assessment and Action Plan

One of the most important skills is to learn what you are good at doing. Focus on your strengths and remove barriers that limit you. An easy way to do this is to keep an ongoing assessment and action plan. Jot down your key activities, tasks, skills, and decisions and what you expect to happen. Review your action plan at the end of the semester and compare expectations with results. Continue this practice in your career. You will soon learn what you do effectively. You will also see patterns of choices and thus identify barriers and limitations. This information will help you improve.

Key Activity	Expectation	Results	Correction
Presentation in class	Earn an A grade	Earned a B grade	Must overcome my nervousness Will join the Toastmasters' Practice

Chapter Application   WORKSHEET 4.7

Good Listening Habits

A. Can you identify good listening habits in a social, small group, or conference setting? Read the following situations. Write Yes or No to identify the listening habits being used.

1. Jake keeps his eyes as much as possible on each person in his study group as he or she speaks. Is Jake practicing good listening habits? _____

2. Kara does not like the way her math instructor dresses, so she never listens very carefully to the lectures. Is Kara practicing good listening habits? _____

3. Donald knows his lab partner, Joe, is shy. He avoids eye contact with Joe whenever Joe speaks. Is this a good listening habit? _____

4. Lucy always tries to decide in advance whether it is worthwhile to listen to the speaker. Is she practicing good listening habits? _____

5. Keisha's boss called her department into a meeting concerning work hours. She paid attention to both his words and his nonverbal cues—gestures, posture, and facial expression. Did she practice good listening habits? _____

B. What would you do in the following situations? Check Yes or No.

	Yes	No
1. I continue to listen even if a great deal of effort is needed to understand what the speaker is saying.	____	____
2. I wait until the speaker has finished before asking for an explanation about an important concept I did not fully understand.	____	____
3. I try to identify the major points of a class lecture and decide if each point has been supported.	____	____
4. I try not to do another activity—like watching television—while trying to listen to what someone is saying.	____	____
5. I try to prepare my response while the speaker is still speaking.	____	____

LISTENING ASSESSMENT

This simple assessment tool will give you an idea of your active listening skills. Read each statement. Then check Yes or No as these statements relate to you.

	Yes	No
1. My intention is to be an active and effective listener.	___	___
2. I concentrate on the meaning and not on every word.	___	___
3. I focus on the speaker and use eye contact.	___	___
4. I am aware of emotions and nonverbal behavior.	___	___
5. I withhold judgment until I hear the entire message.	___	___
6. I am open to new information and ideas.	___	___
7. I seek to understand the speaker's point of view.	___	___
8. I do not interrupt, argue, or plan my response. I listen.	___	___
9. I am mentally and physically alert and attentive.	___	___
10. I paraphrase to clarify my understanding.	___	___
11. When I'm in class, I sit in the front so I can hear and see better.	___	___
12. I mentally ask questions and summarize main ideas.	___	___
13. I increase the value of my listening by previewing the textbook before class.	___	___
14. I adapt to the instructor's speaking and teaching style.	___	___
Total Yes responses:	___	

Summary: Add your Yes responses. If you marked Yes to ten or more questions, you are well on your way to becoming an active and effective listener. If you did not, you have some work to do to improve those skills. Go back and review this chapter.

5 ACTIVE READING

To read a writer is for me not merely to get an idea of what he says, but to go off with him, and travel in his company.

—Andrew Gide, author

Learning Objectives

In Chapter 5 you will learn

- how to define your reading purpose.
- the five-part reading system.
- active reading strategies.
- reading in alignment with your learning style.
- how to build a better vocabulary.
- special strategies for managing language courses.

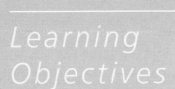

et's approach reading as a climber approaches a towering mountain. In fact, some students have expressed dismay at the mountain of reading that they have to complete each week.

Experienced climbers are alert and aware of the terrain and weather. They are certain of their purpose, goals, and objectives; inspired by the challenge; and confident of their skills. They communicate, in a sense, with the mountain, getting to know the various ridges and feeling the mountain's unique energy and rhythm. They know the importance of concentration and mindfulness. They maintain a relaxed, calm, and centered focus but never allow themselves to get too comfortable or inattentive to even minute details.

This same sense of adventure and purpose, concentration, and attentiveness is necessary if you are going to make reading more enjoyable and increase your comprehension. The amount of reading required in school is enormous and demanding, and it is easy to get discouraged and put off reading until it piles up. In this chapter you will learn to create a reading system that helps you keep up with your reading assignments and increase your comprehension.

THE IMPORTANCE OF ACTIVE READING

When you were a child at home, you may have been told, "This is quiet time, go read a book," or "Curl up with a book and just relax." In school, your instructor may have said, "Read Chapters 1 through 5 for tomorrow's test," or "You didn't do well on the test because you didn't read the directions carefully." On the job, someone may have said to you, "I need your reactions to this report. Have it ready to discuss by this afternoon."

Whether you are reading material for enjoyment, for a test, or for a research project on the job, to be an effective reader you must become actively involved with what you are reading. Previewing, taking notes, outlining main points, digging out ideas, jotting down key words, finding definitions, asking and answering questions, underlining important points, looking for patterns and themes, summarizing in your own words, and reviewing for recall can all greatly improve your comprehension. This is active reading because you, the reader, are purposeful, attentive, and physical.

Many factors affect your reading comprehension. Your skill level, vocabulary, ability to concentrate, the type of distractions, and your state of mind all affect your comprehension and ability to recall what you read. Over the years, you may have developed a reading system that works best for you. One such system is known as the **5-Part Reading System** (Figure 5-1). This system and others will be discussed in this chapter.

THE FIVE-PART READING SYSTEM

1. **Prepare.** Try to prepare yourself mentally for reading by creating a positive and interested attitude. Focus your attention on what you are about to read. Clarify your purpose and how you will use the information you gain from your reading. Think about what you already know about the subject before you begin reading. Prepare yourself physically by being rested and reading during high-energy times. Eliminate distractions by choosing a study area that encourages concentration.

Success Principle 5:
Focus on the **PRESENT,** not the *Past.*

2. **Preview.** A quick survey of the chapter you are about to read will give you a general overview. Pay attention to the title, introduction, chapter objectives, main ideas, connections between concepts, terms, and formulas. This information will set the stage for your reading. Look at the visuals, any illustrations, and key and boldface words. These elements will help clarify the main ideas of the subject. By gaining a general understanding of the assignment, you will be better prepared to read the material actively and to understand the classroom lecture.

3. **Predict questions.** Next, change every section heading into a question. For example, if the section heading is "The Sensory Organs," ask yourself the question, "What are the sensory organs?" As you read, predict test questions and search for answers. Ask yourself Who? What? Where? When? Why? and How? The more questions you ask, the better prepared you will be to find answers and the more prepared you will be for test questions.

4. **Pick out key words.** Outline, underline, and highlight key words, main ideas, definitions, facts, and important concepts. Look for main concepts, supporting points, and answers to the questions you have raised. Develop an outline using either a traditional or a mind map to help you organize the information.

5. **Paraphrase.** Paraphrase, summarize, and review. Write a short summary and then recite it aloud. Practice reciting this summary right after class and again within twenty-four hours of previewing the chapter. Review your summary several times until you understand the material and can explain it to someone else. To integrate learning styles and help you remember main points at the end of each major section, recite aloud and in your own words. During your study team meetings, take turns reviewing and listening to one another's summaries. Carry your note cards with you so you can review questions, answers, and summaries often.

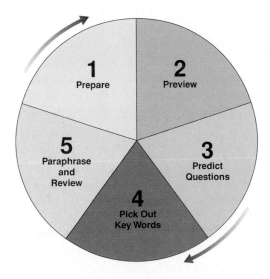

Figure 5-1
The 5-Part Reading System

THE SQ3R READING SYSTEM

The method of reading called SQ3R has helped many students improve their reading comprehension since it was first developed by Professor Francis Robinson in 1941. It suggests that the reader

- **survey** the material before reading it. Quickly peruse the contents, scan the main heads, look at illustrations and captions, and become familiar with the special features in each chapter.
- find the main points and **ask questions.**
- **read** the material.
- **recite** the main ideas and key points in his or her own words.
- **review** the material carefully.

PREPARATION FOR READING

Before you begin a reading assignment, prepare yourself mentally through affirmations. Avoid telling yourself that the book is too hard or too boring. Instead, try saying to yourself, "This book looks interesting," or "The information in this book will be helpful."

If you approach reading with a lack of interest or importance, you will read only what is required. Your ability to retain will be influenced negatively. Retention is the process by which you store information. If you think something is important, you will retain it. *Remember:* Critical reading requires skill accompanied with a positive attitude.

Being in the present means being mindful and keenly aware. Whether you are playing a sport, performing a dance, giving a speech, acting in a play, talking with a friend, or focusing on a difficult book, being in the present is the key to concentration. Keep your reading goals in mind and concentrate on understanding main points. If your mind does wander, take a quick break, drink a glass of water, or stretch. Become aware of your posture, your thoughts, and your surroundings, and then gently bring your thoughts back to the task at hand. Do this consistently.

Since active reading requires energy and alertness, it is important to get enough sleep. Read when you are most rested and alert. Prepare yourself physically by sitting up in your chair, keeping your spine straight, and taking deep breaths frequently. Read at your study area, which by now should be organized and supplied with the necessary study material. Your brain will begin to associate this spot with being alert and producing results. Reading in bed puts most people to sleep.

Determine whether you are reading for pleasure, previewing information, enhancing classroom lectures, background information, understanding ideas, finding facts, memorizing formulas and data, research questions, or analyzing and comprehending a difficult or complex subject. In this way, you clarify your purpose for reading. Determine what you want to get from an assignment, plan the amount of material you intend to read, and set a goal for the time it will take. Ask yourself, "Why am I reading this?" You will be more motivated when there is a set goal and time for completion.

Previewing is a major step in making the most of your reading. Just as an athlete warms up before a jog, previewing warms up your brain for incoming information. Therefore, the goal in previewing is to read quickly for overall understanding of main concepts and ideas. You want to get the big picture and not memorize facts or details. Identify the main idea of each section to get a feel for the chapter. Look at how it is organized; its level of difficulty; and the illustrations, diagrams, pictures, summaries, and graphs. Look for familiar concepts and connections.

READING STRATEGIES

To improve your reading, here are some active reading strategies you may wish to use as you read:

1. **Outline main points.** Organizing information in an outline creates order and understanding. Use a traditional outline or mind map to outline main points quickly. The purpose of a brief outline is to add meaning and structure to material, and to simplify and organize complex information. In addition, the physical process of writing and organizing material creates a foundation that is most useful in committing it to memory. Use section titles and paragraph headlines to provide a guide. Identify main ideas in each paragraph.

2. **Predict questions.** Dig out key points and questions. Jot down questions as you read either in the margin or in your reading notes. Asking questions gets you interested and involved, keeps you focused, organizes information, and helps you prepare for tests. As you preview the chapter, make questions out of chapter headings, sections, titles, and definitions. If there are sample questions at the end of the chapter, review them and tie them in with your other questions. Ask yourself, "What are some possible test questions?" List them on note cards and review them as you walk to classes or while eating or waiting in lines. Exchange questions with your study team or partner.

3. **Read actively.** Stay focused and alert by reading quickly and making it an active experience. Reading phrases instead of individual words and concentrating on main points will help keep you focused. Read difficult material aloud or stand and read. Pretend you are explaining concepts to others or giving a lecture on the chapter. Several readings at different paces may be required to comprehend it. Pay close attention to headings, main topics, key ideas, first and last sentences in paragraphs, summaries, and questions.

4. **Take frequent breaks.** Try to schedule a short stretching break about every forty minutes. A person's brain retains information best in short study segments. Don't struggle with unclear material now. Go back to the difficult areas later when you are refreshed and when the creative process is not blocked.

5. **Make connections.** Try to link new information with what you already know. Ask yourself the questions below. They may help you make associations and jog your memory.

   - What conclusions can you make as you survey the material?
   - How can you apply this new material to other material, concepts, and examples?
   - What information does and doesn't match?
   - What are examples and what are nonexamples?
   - What has been your past experience with reading similar subjects or with reading in general?
   - What do you know about the topic that may influence how you approach the reading?

6. **Talk with the author.** Pretend you are talking with the author and jot down points with which you agree or disagree. When your brain has been exposed to a subject before, it is far more receptive to taking in more information. So jot down in the margins everything you can think of that you already know about this topic, even if it is just a word or an image.

7. **Read in alignment with your learning style.** For example, if you are a visual learner, you can draw pictures, charts, and diagrams, and highlight illustrations as you read. Develop mental pictures in your head. If you are primarily an auditory learner, read out loud or into a tape recorder and then listen to tapes. If you are a kinesthetic learner, collect samples and recite and summarize your material with your study team. Integrate different learning styles. Write your vocabulary, formulas, and key words on note cards. Visualize key words and main ideas, and read them to yourself. Read while standing up.

8. **Identify key words.** Focus on your purpose of finding key words and main ideas. Write in the margins, draw illustrations, underline, sketch, take notes on cards, and become actively involved. Underline or highlight important material. Almost all students use highlighters to emphasize main points and mark sections that are important to review later. Use a graphic device such as wavy lines (~ ~) to indicate difficult material that needs to be reviewed later. Don't underline until you have previewed information. Underline just the key points and words, and think about the ideas expressed. Highlighting is not a substitute for learning. Use a colored highlighter for marking only important material and when you underline, recite out loud.

   Refer to Trailmarker 5.1 on page 5-9 for sample symbols you might find helpful.

SQ3R System

Recall the SQ3R reading system discussed in this chapter. Look at the table below for a quick review. Then do the activity that follows.

LETTER	MEANING	READING ACTIVITY
S	Survey	Survey the assigned reading material. Pay attention to the title, boldface terms, the introduction, and summary.
Q	Question	Find the major heads. Try to make questions out of these heads.
3 R	(1) Read	Read the material section by section or part by part.
	(2) Recite	After reading a section or part, try to briefly summarize aloud what you have read. Make sure your summary answers the question you formed for the section's or part's head.
	(3) Review	After reading the entire assigned reading material, review your question heads. Make sure you can recall your original question and your answers. If you cannot, then go back and reread that section or part.

A. Use the SQ3R system for the following reading selection, then complete the questions that follow.

JOB SEARCHING

Point of Departure

Before you begin to look for a job, it is important to decide what it is you want to do, what you like to do, and what skills and abilities you have to offer.

Self-knowledge is understanding your skills, strengths, capabilities, feelings, character, and motivations. It means you have done some serious **reflection** about what is important to you and what values you want to live your life by. It is very hard to make career decision unless your really know yourself.

Know Yourself

The more you know about yourself, your skills, values, attitudes, and the type of work you like best, the easier it will be to **market your skills.** Your entire job search will be faster and smoother if you

- identify your most marketable skills.
- assess your strengths.
- review your interests.
- identify creative ways you solve problems.

B. **S** - **S**urvey

   1. What is the title of the selection?

    _____

   2. What is the reading selection about?

    _____

    _____

   3. What are the major topics?

    _____

    _____

   4. List the boldface terms.

    _____

C. **Q** - **Q**uestion

   1. Write a question for the first heading.

    _____

    _____

   2. Write a question for the second heading.

    _____

    _____

D. **R** - **R**ead

Read the selection section by section.

R - **R**ecite

Briefly summarize to yourself what you read. Then, share your summary with a study team member.

R - **R**eview

   1. Can you recall the questions you had for each head?

    Yes ___ No ___

   2. Can you answer those questions?

    Yes ___ No ___

Write your answers for each section head question on the lines provided.

   1. Heading 1

    _____

    _____

   2. Heading 2

    _____

    _____

Symbols

Set up a chart of the notations you plan to use in each of your courses this term. A sample chart is provided below. Be methodical about using the symbols by adapt them to your needs.

You may need to use different symbols in each course, although some can be shared.

Symbol	Exploration
>	greater than
<	less than
Q	question
w/	with
w/o	without
V or *	important ideas
+	positive
–	negative
×	times
.-	lost
→	leads to (motivation → success)

Symbols	Math	English	Basic Finance
	= equals	→ leads to	$ American dollars

REVIEW AND REFLECT

1. **Summarize in writing.** After you finish reading, close your book. Write down everything you can recall about the chapter and the main topics. In just four or five minutes, brainstorm main ideas and key points and summarize the material in your own words. Writing is an active process that increases comprehension and recall. Write quickly and test yourself by asking questions like these:

   - What is the major theme?
   - What are the main points?
   - What are the connections to other concepts?
   - What can I summarize in one paragraph?

2. **Recite aloud.** Summarizing aloud can increase learning. Read aloud when you are previewing main points and outlining important material, and when you want to memorize it. Practice giving summaries in front of a mirror. Some students use an empty classroom and pretend they are lecturing. Summarize or explain the material to a study partner. Recite the main ideas to your study team. You can take turns summarizing, and the benefits are enormous. Not only are you reciting the material in your own words, but you are hearing other viewpoints.

3. **Review.** You have previewed your material for an overall view, summarized main concepts, and recited aloud. Now it is important to review for understanding of main ideas and to commit the information to long-term memory. You can increase your comprehension by reviewing the material within twenty-four hours of your first reading session. You may want to review your outline, note cards, key words, and main points. Review headings, main topics, key ideas, first and last sentences in paragraphs, and summaries. Carry your note cards with you and review when you have a few minutes before class or while you wait in lines. Reviewing often and in short sessions kicks the material into long-term memory. Your note cards are the most effective tool for reviewing information.

4. **Review often.** Review weekly and conduct a thorough review a week or so before a test. Keep a list of questions to ask your instructor and a list of possible test questions. Review right before you go to bed when your mind is relaxed and is more receptive to information. As you review, use all your senses. Visualize what something looks like. Look at graphs, charts, and pictures and actively use your imagination. Hear yourself repeat words. Ask for explanations. Read and summarize difficult material out loud. Draw illustrations. Imagine what something feels like or what it smells like.

BARRIERS TO EFFECTIVE READING

The greatest barrier to effective reading is attitude. Many people are not willing to invest the time in becoming a better reader. If the material is difficult or boring or requires concentration, they may not continue reading or complete the reading assignment. Many students were raised in the era of videos and computer games. There is so much action and instant entertainment available that it is easy to watch a movie or television program or listen to the news instead of reading a newspaper or newsmagazine. Reading takes time, effort, concentration, and practice. Some students and career professionals say that they have too much required reading and have little time for pleasure reading. However, it is important to read for pleasure, even if you have only a few minutes a day. Carry a book with you. Keep one in the car and another by your bed. The more you read, the more your reading skills will increase. As you become a better reader, you will find you enjoy reading more and more. You will also find that, as your attitude improves, so will your ability and your vocabulary.

Critical Reading

A. Becoming a critical reader will help you generate meaning and will result in greater understanding. Use critical thinking to draw on knowledge of vocabulary and previous readings. Critical reading will also help you to organize the text, decide what information is important, and take notes on the reading to assist you in recall. Use critical thinking to answer the following questions:

- Do you use headings, subheadings, summaries, and questions to create order and organization?
- Do you recognize key vocabulary and definitions?
- Do you analyze reading goals and use different reading strategies for different reading tasks?
- Do you preview chapters?
- Do you look for connections?
- Do you evaluate the attitude you bring to reading?

B. Below is a list of the common reasons (barriers to reading) that some students use for not reading effectively. Read this list. Then add to it. Use creative problem solving to list strategies for overcoming these barriers.

Reasons for Not Reading	Strategies for Overcoming Reading Barriers
1. My textbooks are boring.	1. _____ _____
2. I can't concentrate.	2. _____ _____
3. I'm easily distracted.	3. _____ _____
4. I fall asleep when I read.	4. _____ _____
5. I never study the right material.	5. _____ _____
6. There is too much information, and I don't know what is important.	6. _____ _____
7. I read for hours, but I don't understand what I have read.	7. _____ _____
8. I don't like to read.	8. _____ _____

TRAILMARKER 5.2

Look It Up! Using the Dictionary

A dictionary can help you spell, find the meaning of, and pronounce a word. Here is a quick guide for using the dictionary.

Guide word: Boldface word at the top of the page indicates the first and last entry on the page.

Main entry: This is the word you want to look up.

Syllabication: Shows the method of forming or dividing a word into syllables.

Pronunciations: Key at the bottom of right-hand page shows pronunciation.

Capital letters: The dictionary will indicate if a word should be capitalized.

Parts of speech: The dictionary uses nine abbreviations for the parts of speech:

n.—noun	**adv.**—adverb
v.t.—transitive verb	**v.i.**—intransitive verb
adj.—adjective	**conj.**—conjunction
pron.—pronoun	**prep.**—preposition
interj.—interjection	

Etymology: This is the origin of the word, which is especially helpful if the word has a Latin or Greek root from which many other words are derived. Knowing the word's history can help you remember the word or look for similar words.

Restrictive labels: There are three types of labels that are used most often in a dictionary. *Subject labels* tell you that a word has a special meaning when used in certain fields (*mus.* for music, *med.* for medicine, etc.). *Usage labels* indicate how a word is used (*slang, dial.* for dialect, etc.). *Geographic labels* tell you the region of the country where the word is used most often.

SPECIAL STRATEGIES FOR MANAGING LANGUAGE COURSES

Building vocabulary is also important if you are taking English as a second language course or learning a foreign language. Here are a few special reading and study tips for students who are studying language.

1. **Practice exercises.** As with math and science, practice exercises are critical in learning another language.

2. **Keep up with your reading.** You must build on previous lessons and skills. Therefore, it is important to keep up your readings, preview chapters so you have a basic understanding of any new words, and then complete your practice sessions several times.

Homographs: The dictionary will indicate when a single spelling of a word has different meanings.

Variants: These are multiple correct spellings of a single word (*ax* or *axe*).

Illustrations: These are drawings or pictures used to help illustrate a word.

Definition: Most dictionaries list the definitions, or meanings, chronologically (the oldest meaning first).

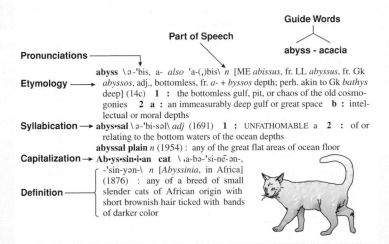

Use this book's Web site to find online dictionaries and reference sources.

http://peak.glencoe.com

3. **Carry note cards with you.** Drill yourself on parts of speech and verb conjugation through all the tenses and practice vocabulary building.

4. **Recite out loud.** Recite new words to yourself out loud. This is especially important in a language course. Tape yourself and play it back.

5. **Form study teams.** Meet with a study team and speak only the language you are studying. Recite out loud to each other, explain verb conjugation, and use words in different contexts. Recitation is an excellent strategy when studying languages.

6. **Listen to tapes.** Play practice tapes while commuting, jogging, exercising, before going to sleep, and so on.

7. **Visualize.** During an exam, visualize yourself listening to a tape, seeing the diagrams you have drawn, and hearing yourself reciting the material.

8. **Model and tutor.** Invite to your study team or out for coffee a student whose primary language is the one you are studying. Speak only his or her native language. Offer to teach the person your language in exchange for private tutoring. You can meet foreign students in classes where English as a second language is taught, usually in local schools and communities.

9. **Focus on key words.** Study words, meanings, tenses, and pronunciation. Keep these drilling exercises on note cards.

10. **Have fun.** Do research on the country of the language you're studying. Make the language come alive for you. Invite your study group over for an authentic meal, complete with music and costumes. Invite foreign students and your instructor.

Technology FOCUS: Computers and Reading Comprehension

Computers can help you with reading comprehension. Use the following techniques when working on a computer.

- After you read a paragraph, section, or chapter, keyboard a brief summary of what you have read on your computer.

- While you read, keyboard computer notes of the important concepts. This will help increase your comprehension and recall.

- Create a computer file which lists questions you think will be on the test and questions to ask your instructor and study team. Bring the list to class or to your study team.

- Explore reading skills on the Internet. Use this book's Web site.

  http://peak.glencoe.com

Attitudes and Reading

Read the following. Write your answers on the lines provided.

1. What is your attitude toward reading?

   _____

   _____

2. What kind of books do you like to read best?

   _____

   _____

3. Do you read for pleasure?

   _____

   _____

4. Do you read the daily newspaper? Yes_____ No_____
   If yes, what sections do you read? Place a check mark.

____ comics	____ sports	____ weather
____ business	____ horoscope	____ world news
____ want ads	____ entertainment	____ other

5. Do you read magazines? Yes_____ No_____
   If yes, which magazines?

   _____

   _____

6. Do you want to read faster?

   _____

   _____

7. Do you want to remember what you have read?

   _____

   _____

8. What techniques are you willing to learn so you can read faster and remember more?

   _____

   _____

VOCABULARY BUILDING

You will need a fundamental vocabulary to master any subject. Developing a good vocabulary is important for reading comprehension and success in college. To succeed in a career, you must know and understand the meaning of words that you encounter in conversations, reports, meetings, and professional reading. People often judge the intelligence of another person by the ability to communicate through words. Words are the tools of thinking and communicating. Try the following methods for building your vocabulary.

- **Realize the power and value of words.** An effective speaker who has a command of language can influence others.

- **Observe your words and habits.** You may be unaware that you fill your conversations with profanity and annoying phrases such as *you know, okay,* and *yeah.*

- **Be creative and articulate.** Use precise, interesting, and expressive words.

- **Develop an interest in words.** Attitude is the key to learning new words.

- **Associate with articulate people.** Surround yourself with people who have effective and extensive vocabularies.

- **Be aware and alert.** Listen for new words. Observe how they are used and how often you hear them and see them in print.

- **Look up words you don't know.** Keep a dictionary and a thesaurus at your desk.

- **Study the word.** How can you use it in conversation?

- **Write new words.** List new words in your journal or write them on note cards.

- **Practice mentally.** Say new words again and again in your mind as you read and think of appropriate settings where you could use the words.

- **Practice in conversation.** Use new words until you are comfortable.

- **Read.** The best way to improve your vocabulary is to read more.

- **Review great speeches.** Look at how Abraham Lincoln, Benjamin Franklin, Winston Churchill, and Thomas Jefferson chose precise words. Read letters written during the Revolutionary and Civil Wars. You may find that the common person at that time was more articulate and expressive than many educated people today.

- **Invest in a vocabulary book.**

- **Look for context clues.** Try to figure out a word by the context in which it is used.

- **Learn common word parts.** Knowing root words, prefixes, and suffixes makes it easier to understand the meaning of many new words. Also learn to recognize syllables. When you divide words into syllables, you learn them faster, and doing so helps with pronunciation, spelling, and memory recall.

Root	Meaning	Example
auto	self	autograph, autobiography
sub	under	submarine, submerge
circum	around	circumference, circumspect
manu	hand	manuscript, manual, manufacture

 **INCREASE YOUR COMPREHENSION**

Increasing your reading comprehension is an essential job skill. The amount of your on-the-job reading increases throughout your career. Besides a mountain of memos, professional journals, letters, forms, manuals, annual reports, legal documents, government requirements, and codes, you will be reading community items, newspapers, and magazines. The employee who reads quickly, has the ability to concentrate, and comprehends accurately has an advantage over an employee who dislikes reading or has difficulty concentrating or comprehending.

Meet Mark Layos. He is a paralegal in a large law firm. To practice active reading on the job, he routinely scans the contents to get the big picture and determine how much time to devote to an article, law brief, specific case, or book. He uses fast reading, previewing, reading summaries, and asking questions as techniques to improve his reading comprehension. He reads hundreds of memos each week and has developed the ability to quickly dig out essential information, deadlines, main points, and action items.

Read the following memo and highlight important information using the active reading techniques in this chapter.

MEMORANDUM

```
November 6, 2000
To:       Faculty, School of Business Administration

From:     Roberta J. Gonzales
          Chair, School of Business Administration


Subject:  Promotional material for community colleges

Our enrollments in Acct. 210 are down substantially. Investigation by
Bob Iato indicates that our number of incoming students selecting
business as an area of study has also declined over the past few years.
This is consistent with the national trend.

In an effort to increase our enrollment, Jack Lawrence and I are
preparing a letter with other material to send to the department chairs
at the community colleges. I am including this material with this memo
and ask that you review it and get back to me as soon as possible with
any suggestions.

Thanks!
```

TECHNICAL READING

Some of the subjects you are taking now or will take as your course of study advances will involve very specific and technical information. Science, math, computer, accounting, and courses involving statistics tend to present their data in specialized formats. You may find yourself interpreting graphs, charts, diagrams, or tables. You may be reading technical material such as the directions for a chemistry experiment, a flowchart for a computer program, the steps for administering medication, or the statistical analysis of a financial statement.

Such material can be complicated and difficult. This is why many readers—and student readers in particular—tend to skip over it or become discouraged. However, there are some reading strategies you can implement when you encounter technical material in your studies or on the job. Use the following list to help you.

1. **Do not** skip over any graphics.

2. Read
   - the graphic title.
   - any accompanying captions.
   - any column titles.
   - any labels or symbols and their interpretations.
   - any data (percentages, totals, figures, etc.).

3. Identify the type of graphic you are looking at. Are you looking at a table, chart, or graph?

4. Decide the purpose of the graphic. Is it demonstrating to the reader likenesses or differences; increases or decreases; comparisons or changes, etc?

5. See a connection or relationship between the topic of the graphic and the chapter or section topic.

6. Explain in your own words the information depicted on the graphic.

7. Finally, using the graphic share your interpretation of it with your study group members. Did they feel your interpretation was clear and *on target?*

TIP Graphics can enhance and help explain the written material that appears in the text.

READING FORMS

Whether you are entering school, applying for a job, needing service at a hospital, or requesting a bank loan, you probably had to fill out some type of form. Although forms differ in many ways, there are many requested elements of information that appear on all forms. You can expect to provide your name, address, social security number, and phone numbers.

Reading the form carefully and accurately can save time and prevent complications. For example:

- Most forms ask for your name. This would not normally be a problem. However, the small printed directions may ask you to print your name in black or blue ink, but you, instead, use a pencil and write your name in cursive handwriting.

- Or, a job application asks that you answer all questions in your own hand writing, but you type out the application.

In both cases, the forms would most likely be returned to you because you didn't read the directions carefully. In the situation with the job application, there may have been a cut-off date for applying, and you missed it because your application was returned.

Some of this carelessness in reading forms can be avoided by using the following reading tips:

1. Scan the entire form before you begin to fill it out.

2. If you are unsure of any questions and what information is actually needed, ask or call the appropriate office or person for clarification.

3. When filling out the form, read the SMALL print directions carefully. Often these directions appear in parentheses below a fill-in blank.

4. Fill in all questions that pertain to you. Pay attention when you read the directions that tell you what sections of the form or application you should fill out and what sections are to be completed by someone else.

5. Make sure you write clearly—particularly your numbers.

6. When reporting somewhere to fill out forms, bring with you any pertinent information that may be needed. Call ahead and ask what you are expected to have with you; for example, social security card, proof of citizenship, dates of employment or schooling, names, addresses, and phone numbers of references, former employees, or teachers.

7. Reread your responses before submitting your form or application.

TIP Bring with you a blue or black pen and a Number 2 pencil when you have forms to fill out.

Filling Out Forms

Here are some data requests that you may encounter on forms. Read the directions carefully and then fill in the blanks.

1. Name _____
   (USE A PENCIL)   (LAST)   (FIRST)   (MI)

2. Address _____
   (USE A BLACK PEN)   (STREET#) (STREET NAME)   (CITY)   (ZIP CODE)

3. Date _____ / _____ / _____
   (USE A RED PEN) (MO)   (YR)   (DAY)

4. Are you a citizen of the United States? (Check) Yes___ No___
   If no, what country?_____

5. Age (Please X one)
   18-25____   26-35____   36-45____
   46-55____   over 55____

6. Why do you want to attend this school? (Answer in your own handwriting.)

   _____

   _____

   _____

   _____

   _____

   _____

   _____

   _____

   _____

   _____

OPRAH WINFREY

Whether you live in the megalopolis of Chicago, Illinois, or a small town in the middle of Wyoming, you have probably heard of Oprah Winfrey. She is watched by millions of people every afternoon on television, and she has appeared in various television and big-screen movies.

Yet this well-known entertainment personality and executive suffered years of abuse during her childhood and finally ran away when she was a teenager. It was only when she went to live with her father that she finally experienced family structure. Perhaps it was during this supportive time that her love for reading had its beginning. Her father would have her read and do a book report each week. And now many years and many books later, her television viewers listen to her feature a book review during her Book Club segment. This special segment encourages people to read for fun and personal growth.

Oprah truly made an effort to become a Peak Performer. She attended Tennessee State University, where she majored in Speech Communications and Performing Arts. The television persona of today began when she was hired by a radio station in Nashville as a reporter. By 1976, Oprah was a talk show host in Baltimore while continuing to serve as an anchor and news reporter. In January 1984, Oprah landed a talk show host position in Chicago. This show became the *Oprah Winfrey Show* you are familiar with today. By 1985, it became the number 1 talk show and led to Oprah's three daytime Emmy Awards in the categories of Outstanding Host, Outstanding Talk Service Program, and Outstanding Direction. Oprah is not only the youngest person but also the fifth woman to receive the International Radio and Television Society's Broadcaster of the Year Award.

Oprah Winfrey also received praise for her first movie role in *The Color Purple*. She was nominated for the Academy Award and Golden Globe Award for Best Supporting Actress for her performance in this adaptation of Alice Walker's masterpiece.

In spite of a difficult beginning, Oprah has become a true Peak Performer. As the first woman in history to own and produce her own talk show, she also owns a production company called HARPO, which has produced several excellent movies including *The Women of Brewster Place, Kaffir Boy,* and *Beloved.*

Source: See this book's Web site.
http://peak.glencoe.com

CHAPTER 5

Review and Study Notes

Affirmations

- I love to read for pleasure and to learn information.
- I am an active reader. I predict, skim, dig out questions, and easily understand the material I read.
- I have confidence in my ability to read and comprehend difficult material.
- It is fun to predict questions and summarize material.

Visualization

Visualize a vivid picture of yourself reading quickly, comprehending what you are reading, and recalling information effortlessly. Imagine yourself thinking, "I enjoy reading. It is easy for me. I will retain this information." See yourself as an explorer digging out information; building on facts, ideas, and concepts; and developing the skill to retain and recall. Feel the confidence and joy you get from the ability to concentrate, comprehend, and recall information from your books.

Peak Performance Strategies for Reading

1. Prepare mentally.
2. Prepare physically.
3. Clarify purpose.
4. Preview.
5. Outline main points.
6. Predict questions.
7. Read actively.
8. Pick out key words.
9. Summarize.
10. Review.
11. Review often.

CASE Studies

CASE A

Kent Smith has problems keeping up with his reading. He is overwhelmed by the amount of reading and the difficulty of his textbooks. He has never been much of a reader and prefers television instead. He reads in bed or in a comfortable chair but often falls asleep. He knows this is not the best way to study, but it has become a cozy habit. Several times he has noticed that after reading for an hour or so, he can recall almost nothing. This has caused him frustration, self-doubt about his ability to succeed in college, and anger at himself for not being able to concentrate.

1. What can you suggest to Kent that would help him improve his reading skills?

   _____

2. What strategies in this chapter would be most helpful?

   _____

3. Suggest one or two habits you think would help him most.

   _____

In the Workplace

Kent is now a stockbroker. He never thought that he would work in this business, but a part-time summer job led him to the finance world and he really likes the challenge. He is surprised, however, at the vast amount of reading involved in his job: reports, letters, magazines, and articles. He also reads several books on money management each month. He is also involved in several community organizations that require a great deal of reading.

What strategies in this chapter would help Kent become a better reader?

_____

_____

_____

_____

_____

_____

_____

TIP From the Classroom

I was totally unprepared for the mountain of reading in my first semester of college. I felt I was always behind. Learning to dig out important facts and ideas helped my comprehension and helped me read faster.
— Junior at University of Michigan

CASE B

Sabrina Toshio is majoring in library services. She has always enjoyed reading books, newspapers, and weekly magazines. Sabrina has difficulty completing her required reading for class. She is a fast reader but has never learned to read textbooks actively and critically. Instead, she treats all books the same and becomes bored or frustrated with textbooks. Sabrina reads the material quickly and feels that she has a fairly good grasp of the material. However, she doesn't do well on tests. She knows she is a good reader and is resentful of friends or instructors who offer advice.

1. What suggestions could you offer that would help Sabrina pick out important information and data?

   _____

   _____

2. What strategies in this chapter can help her read actively and remember the material she has read?

   _____

   _____

> **TIP** From the Workplace
>
> To succeed in business, you have to keep up with journals and professional readings, in addition to memos, reports, surveys, and a stack of daily mail. I had to learn to be a critical and fast reader.
>
> —Recruitment director at a college

In the Workplace

Sabrina is now a library technician who has recently been promoted to supervisor. Because of budget concerns, Sabrina continues to perform many of her old duties as well as a heavy administrative load, and she is amazed at the amount of reading that is required in her new job. In addition to memos, reports, and letters, she is on the editorial board for her professional organization and also likes to review new books that the library has ordered. She feels overwhelmed.

1. What suggestions could you offer Sabrina that would help her skim the pile of daily reading and pick out important information?

   _____

   _____

2. What strategies from this chapter would help her become a more effective reader?

   _____

   _____

Chapter Application   WORKSHEET 5.1

Different Types of Reading

Find a sample of each of the following types of reading:

1. newspaper
2. chapter from a textbook
3. instructions for an appliance, insurance policy, or rental contract

Read each sample. Then describe in your own words how the reading process differs among the three.

The reading process differs _____

_____

_____

_____

_____

_____

_____

_____

_____

Does knowing your purpose for reading affect how you read? Explain below.

_____

_____

_____

_____

_____

_____

_____

_____

Chapter Application   WORKSHEET 5.2

Summarize and Teach

A. Read the section that follows on predicting questions. Underline, write in the margins, and write a one- or two-sentence summary. Compare your work with the work below and with a study partner. There are many ways to highlight, so don't be concerned if yours is different. This will give you ideas on creative note taking.

Predicting Questions

Dig out key points and questions. Jot down questions either in the margin or in your reading notes as you read. Asking questions gets you interested and involved, keeps you focused, organizes information, and helps you prepare for tests. As you preview the chapter, make questions out of chapter headings, sections, titles, and definitions. If there are sample questions at the end of the chapter, review them and tie them in with your own questions. What are possible test questions? List them on note cards and review them. Exchange questions with your study team or partner.

Summary: _____

_____

_____

_____

_____

_____

_____

_____

_____

B. Work with another student-partner in one of your classes. Read a chapter and write a summary. Compare your work with your study partner. Now summarize and teach the main concepts to your partner. Each of you can clarify and ask questions.

Chapter Application   WORKSHEET 5.3

Creating a Reading Outline

Outlining what you read can be a helpful study technique. Develop the habit of outlining. Use the format below as a guide. Eventually you may develop your own format. Outline pages 5-2 through 5-5 of Chapter 5 on the lines below.

Course: _____   **Chapter:** _____   **Date:** _____

I. _____

   A. _____

      1. _____

      2. _____

      3. _____

      4. _____

   B. _____

      1. _____

      2. _____

      3. _____

      4. _____

II. _____

   A. _____

      1. _____

      2. _____

      3. _____

      4. _____

   B. _____

      1. _____

      2. _____

3. _____

4. _____

C. _____

    1. _____

    2. _____

    3. _____

    4. _____

III. _____

  A. _____

    1. _____

    2. _____

    3. _____

    4. _____

  B. _____

    1. _____

    2. _____

    3. _____

    4. _____

IV. _____

  A. _____

    1. _____

    2. _____

    3. _____

    4. _____

  B. _____

    1. _____

    2. _____

    3. _____

    4. _____

PART TWO   Basic Skills and Strategies

Chapter Application   WORKSHEET 5.4

Analyzing Textbook Chapters

As you start to read the next chapter in this book, fill in this page to prepare for reading. Phrase each heading as a question. You may need to add additional headings.

Course: _____   **Textbook:** _____

Chapter: _____

Heading 1: _____

Question: _____

Heading 2: _____

Question: _____

Heading 3: _____

Question: _____

Heading 4: _____

Question: _____

Summary of Section: _____

_____

_____

_____

_____

Summary of Chapter: _____

_____

_____

_____

_____

Chapter Application   WORKSHEET 5.5

Reading Matrix

Use this matrix for the textbook assigned in each of your classes. As you read an assignment, place a check mark in each box when you complete each part of the reading system.

The 5-Part Reading System	Prepare				Preview				Predict Questions				Pick Out Key Words				Paraphrase			
	Create a positive attitude.	Create an interested attitude.	Clarify your purpose.	Prepare yourself physically.	Preview contents.	Preview titles and chapter headings.	Preview for overall understanding.	Preview summary.	Predict topics.	Predict questions.	Predict answers.	Ask Who? What? Where? When? Why? How?	Pick out key words.	Pick out main ideas.	Underline important points.	Develop an outline.	Paraphrase.	Recite out loud.	Write a summary.	Review several times.
Class																				
Class																				
Class																				
Class																				

DEMONSTRATING COMPETENCIES

Looking back: Review your worksheets from other chapters to find activities from which you learned to read and concentrate.

Taking stock: What are your strengths in reading and what do you want to improve?

Looking forward: Indicate how you would demonstrate reading and comprehension skills to an employer.

Documentation: Include documentation of your reading skills.

Inventory: List the books you've read recently and include any classics you have read.

Fill in the chart below. Explain how you demonstrate these competencies.

Competencies	Demonstration
Active reading	_____
Critical reading	_____
Willingness to learn new words	_____
Improving technical vocabulary	_____
Articulation	_____
Expressiveness	_____
Ability to use dictionary	_____
Positive attitude toward reading	_____
Technical reading	_____
Reading forms	_____

TIP Preview before a lecture, summarize after the lecture, explain it to your study partner. If you really want to learn something, teach it to someone else.

MEMORY

*Remember people and learn
their names.*

—Yuki Togo, former president,
Toyota Motor Sales

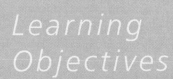

Learning Objectives

In Chapter 6 you will learn

- how to prepare yourself mentally and physically for remembering.

- how to use your senses and learning styles to enhance memory.

- memory strategies.

- how to use mnemonic devices.

- how to recall names.

You may have heard someone say, "I just don't have a good memory." Do you have a good memory? Do you think some people are born with better memories than others are? You will discover in this chapter that memory is a process. As a complex process, memory is not an isolated activity that takes place in one part of the brain; rather it involves many factors that you can control. How well you remember depends on factors such as your attitude, interest, intent, awareness, mental alertness, observation skills, senses, distractions, memory devices, and willingness to practice.

Most people with good memories say that the skill is mastered by learning the strategies for storing and recalling information. This chapter will summarize and highlight specific strategies that help you remember information.

THE MEMORY PROCESS

The memory process involves five main steps:

1. **Intention**—you are interested and willing to learn.
2. **Observation**—you are alert to the information and attentive.
3. **Organization**—you make sense of the information.
4. **Retention**—you record and store the information in the brain.
5. **Recall**—you actually remember the information.

PREPARATION

1. **Intend to remember.** The first step in using memory effectively is to prepare yourself mentally. As with learning any skill, your intention, attitude, and motivation are fundamental to success. Have you ever said, "I wish I could remember names," "I'm just not good at remembering facts for tests," or "I can't remember formulas for math"?

   If you make excuses or program your mind with negative self-talk, your mind refuses to learn new information. If you think a subject is boring or unimportant, you will have difficulty remembering it. Too often students study just enough to get by on a quiz and forget the information immediately thereafter. It is much better to learn a subject so that it becomes interesting and part of your long-term memory. Uncover the facts, interesting points, related material, details, and fascinating aspects of the subject. Ask your instructor for interesting stories to enhance a point. Read a novel on the subject or look for another textbook at the library that explains the subject from a different view. Take full responsibility for your attitude and intention. Realize that you are in control of your memory. Develop an interest in whatever you are studying or in any task or project with which you are working. Make a conscious, active decision to remember and state your intention with affirmations. Use phrases such as

Success Principle 6: Focus on the **WHOLENESS,** not *Fragmented parts*.

- Remembering is easy for me.
- I like to remember people's names.
- Remembering is essential for job success.
- I have developed strategies that help me remember.

2. **Be observant and alert.** Observe and be attentive to details. How many times have you physically been in one place but mentally and emotionally you were thousands of miles away? Mindfulness means being totally in the moment and becoming part of the process around you. Learning occurs when your mind is relaxed, focused, receptive, and alert. Relax, close your eyes, breathe deeply, create a quiet atmosphere, and let your mind flow. Become absorbed in the process and subject. Focus your attention by concentrating on one thing at a time.

3. **Prepare yourself physically.** People often think of learning as a passive activity that happens quietly in the brain. Physical activity increases academic performance by getting the blood flowing and activating the senses. Your mental and physical states are interrelated. Trying to memorize information when you are tired is a waste of time. Get enough rest so that you are alert. Study when you are alert and can concentrate. Sit up straight, take frequent breaks, and exercise every day to build energy and stamina. Practice reciting information while doing physical activity such as showering, walking, or jogging.

4. **Reduce information overload and avoid distractions.** Reduce mental distractions by eliminating unnecessary information. You don't have to memorize certain types of information such as deadlines, telephone messages, and assignment due dates. You just have to know where to find this information. Write deadlines and important information in your organizer or student planner or on a calendar. Write messages in a phone log and not on slips of paper that can get lost. You can refer to any of this written information again if you need it.

   Avoid becoming someone else's memory support. If someone asks you to call him or her with the notes from class, ask the person to call you instead. If a study team member asks you to remind him or her about a study meeting, suggest using the student planner to record important dates. You have enough to remember without taking responsibility for someone else's memory. If something is bothering you, write it down and tell yourself that as soon as your study time is over, you will address it.

   Distractions can keep you from paying attention and, consequently, from remembering what you're trying to learn. One way to avoid distractions is to study in a place designed for serious intent and where you will not be distracted. Libraries and designated study rooms are good places to use for quiet study.

MEMORY STRATEGIES

1. **Use all your senses.** Memory is sensory, so using all your senses (sight, hearing, touch, smell, and taste) will give your brain a better chance of retaining information. Assume that you are taking a medical terminology or vocabulary-building course. You may want to look at pictures and visualize in your mind images with the new terms or words. Actively listen in class, tape all lectures, and play them back later. Recite definitions and information aloud. Rewrite key words and definitions on note cards. Draw pictures and illustrations of these words whenever possible. Use the computer to write definitions or descriptions. Discuss the new terms with your study team. Try to use the new words in your own conversations. Listen for the new words and notice when and how others use them in conversation. Keep a log of new words, definitions, and uses of the word.

2. **Make learning visual.** Consider three students who are preparing for a test in a computer class. The first student is primarily a visual learner and may feel most comfortable reading the manual, reading her textbook, and reviewing her notes. Visual learners recall information best when they see it. They like watching a video and looking at illustrations and pictures.

3. **Make learning auditory.** The second student in the computer class is an auditory learner. He remembers best when he hears instructions and responds more to spoken words. Auditory learners need to hear the message by listening to tapes and CDs, and talking aloud when they study.

4. **Make learning physical.** The third student likes hands-on experience. He writes out commands and directions and gets actively involved. Whether you like to learn by reading or listening, you will retain information better if you use all your senses and make learning physical. Read aloud, read while standing, jot down notes, lecture in front of the classroom to yourself or your study team, go on field trips, draw diagrams and models, and join a study group.

5. **Write information down.** Writing is physical and enhances learning. When you write information down, you are reinforcing learning by using your eyes, hand, fingers, and arm. Writing uses different parts of the brain than does speaking or listening.

   - writing down a telephone number helps you remember it.
   - taking notes in class prompts you to be logical and concise and fills in memory gaps.
   - underlining important information and then copying it onto note cards reinforces information.
   - writing a summary after reading a chapter will also reinforce information.
   - summarizing in your own words helps to transfer information to long-term memory.

6. **Study in short sessions.** The brain retains information better in short study sessions. After about an hour, the brain needs a break to process information effectively. Break large goals into specific objectives and study in short sessions. For example, preview a chapter in your marketing textbook for twenty minutes and mind-map the chapter on sales for twenty minutes. Then take a ten-minute break. Tips for this type of studying include:

   - taking regular scheduled breaks.
   - yourself with a small treat.
   - returning to complete your goal.

   Even when you are working on something complex, like completing a term paper or a major project, you are more effective when you take frequent breaks.

7. **Integrate your left brain and your right brain.** Think of both sides of your brain as members of a team that can cooperate, appreciate, and support each other. By using both sides of your brain, you can enhance your memory. For example, you may have a term paper assignment that constitutes 50 percent of your final grade. You want to turn in a well-researched, accurately written, neatly typed paper. The left side of your brain insists that it be error-free. Your preferred style of learning leans toward the right side, so your reaction to this assignment is frustration, fear, and resistance. Using the word processor can support both sides of the brain. You satisfy the structured side that wants a flawless paper while allowing your creative side to correct mistakes easily by using the spell check.

8. **Organize information.** Organization brings material together and makes sense out of it. Nothing is harder to remember than isolated or unconnected facts, dates, or theories. Use whatever form of outline that works for you, but make certain that information is in sections and units and that you can demonstrate the interconnections and relations between separate units. You cannot retain or recall information unless you understand it. Understanding means that you see connections and relationships in the information you are studying.

- Use index cards for recording information you want to memorize.
- Organize the cards according to category, color, size, order, weight, and other areas.
- Map each chapter.

In your own words, write brief summaries and indicate the main points of each chapter on the backs of note cards. Carry these cards with you and review them during waiting time, before going to sleep at night, or any time you have a few minutes to spare.

9. **Go from the general to the specific.** Many people learn best by looking at the big picture and then learning the details. Try to outline from the general (main topic) to the specific (subtopics). Previewing a chapter gives you an overview and makes the topic more meaningful. Your brain is more receptive to specific details when it has a general idea of the main topic.

10. **Associate and connect.** By associating and linking new material with old material, you make it meaningful. Suppose you are learning about the explorer Christopher Columbus's three ships. Think of three friends whose names start with the same first letter as the ships' names: Pinta, Santa Maria, and Nina (e.g., Paul, Sandy, and Nancy). Associate these names with the three ships and you should be able to recall the ships' names.

11. **Recite.** When you say information aloud, you use your throat, voice, and lips and you hear yourself recite. You may find this recitation technique helpful when you are dealing with difficult reading materials. Reading aloud and hearing the material will reinforce it for you. Reciting may be helpful when preparing to give a speech. Try to practice in the actual place where you will be speaking. Visualize the audience, practice demonstrating your visual aids, write on the board, use gestures and pauses, and listen to how you sound as you practice. Tape your speech and play it back. You can also present your speech to your study team and ask for feedback.

12. **Use mnemonic devices.** Mnemonic devices are memory tricks that help you remember information. However, there are problems with memory tricks. It can take time to develop a memory trick and it can be hard to remember the trick if you make it too complicated. Further, memory tricks don't help in understanding the information or develop skills in critical thinking. They are best used for sheer rote memorization.

- *Use rhythm and rhymes.* In elementary school, you might have learned the rhyme, *In 1492 Columbus sailed the ocean blue.* It helped you to remember the date of Columbus's voyage. Rhythms can also be helpful. Many people have learned to spell the word *Mississippi* by accenting all the *i*'s and making the word rhythmic.

- *Acronyms.* Acronyms are words formed from the first letters of a series of other words, such as *homes* for the Great Lakes (Huron, Ontario, Michigan, Erie, and Superior) and EPCOT (Experimental Prototype Community of Tomorrow).

- *Grouping.* Grouping long lists of information or numbers can break up the task and make it easier for you. Most people can remember up to seven numbers in a row, which is why phone numbers are that long.

- *Association.* If your ATM identification number is 9072, you might remember it by creating associations with dates. Maybe 1990 is the year that you graduated from high school, and 1972 was the year you were born.

- *The method-of-place technique.* As far back as 500 B.C., the Greeks were using a method of imagery called loci—the method-of-place technique. This method is still effective today because it uses imagery and association to aid memory. Memorize a setting in detail and then place the item or information that you want to remember at certain places on your memory map. Some people like to use a familiar street, their home, or their car as a map on which to place their information. The concept is the same. You memorize certain places on your street, in your home, or on your car. You memorize a specific order or path in which you visit each place. Once you have this map memorized, you can position various items to remember at different points.

Being Observant

How observant are you? Try the following experiments to determine if you are really observing the world around you.

Experiment 1
- Look around the room.
- Then, close your eyes.
- Mentally picture what is in the room.
- Open your eyes.

a. Did you remember everything?   Yes ___   No ___

b. If no, what didn't you remember?

_____

_____

_____

Experiment 2
- Look at a painting, photo, or poster for one minute.
- Without looking back, write down the details you remember.
- Then, compare your list of details with the painting, photo, or poster.

a. What details did you remember? Colors? Faces? Clothing?

_____

_____

_____

b. What details didn't you remember?

_____

_____

_____

c. Did you remember the obvious things or did you remember subtle details?

_____

_____

_____

d. Why do you think this happened?

_____

_____

_____

REVIEW AND REFLECT

The sooner and the more often you review information, the easier it is to recall. Ideally, your first review should be within the first hour after hearing a lecture or reading an assignment. Carry note cards with you and review again during that first day. Studies show that within forty-eight hours, you forget eighty-five percent of what you learned. If you review right after you hear it and again within twenty-four hours, however, your recall soars to ninety percent. Discuss, write, summarize, and recite in your own words what you have just read or heard.

Practice information that you want to remember. For example, when you first start driver training, you learn the various steps involved in driving. At first, they may seem overwhelming. You may have to stop and think through each step. After you have driven a car for a while, however, you don't even think about all the steps required to start it and back out of the driveway. You check your mirror automatically before changing lanes and driving safely has become a habit. The information is in long-term memory. The more often you use information, the easier it is to recall. You could not become a good musician without hours of practice. Sports, public speaking, flying an airplane, and learning to drive all require skills that need to be repeated and practiced many times.

Observe when you remember and what strategies or techniques work for you. Acknowledge and reward yourself. Use positive affirmations. Tell yourself that you will remember. Observe ways that you recall information. If you are stuck and can't remember something, tell yourself before you go to sleep that you will remember it in the morning. You might also try brainstorming when you draw a blank or misplace something. Think of similar ideas or retrace your steps. Support your memory by creating rituals. Put your keys in the same spot each night, write information down. In other words, get organized and feel in control.

TIP Most instructors suggest that you devote at least two hours for studying outside of class for each hour you spend in class. Some classes require even more effort. Reviewing often, summarizing, and reciting aloud are the best tips for increasing your memory.

TRAILMARKER 6.1

Mindfulness

Set a timer or clock to go off every half-hour as you are studying or working on a project. Observe and notice the colors, shapes, sizes, sights, smells, and textures of objects around you. Notice if your mind wanders. If so, gently bring it back to the topic at hand. Determine as you do this exercise, if it is easier to keep your mind on the topic.

TRAILMARKER 6.2

Memory Map—A Walk Down Memory Lane

Let's think of your memory map as a beautiful garden and apply the method-of-place technique. This garden is rich in detail and full of lovely flowers representing thoughts, images, and ideas. You always enter the garden through a beautiful white garden gate. But you are not just standing at the white garden gate looking; you are actively involved, attentive to all the details, and in control of your memory. You can see each distinct point in the garden: the garden gate, the birdbath, the gazebo, the fountain, a garden bench, and a flower bed. The key is to set the items clearly in your memory and visualize them. Draw a picture of your garden in detail in the space provided.

Using your drawing of the garden, let's say that you want to memorize four stories that emphasize four key points for a speech you are giving in your Speech 100 class.

The first story in your speech is about a monk, so you draw a monk and place him at the garden gate. You want to tell a joke about a robin, so you place the robin in the birdbath. Your third point involves people of a bygone era, and you have chosen a Victorian woman as the image to represent this key point, so you place her in the gazebo. Your fourth point involves the younger generation, so you choose a little girl and place her playing in the fountain. The essential steps to the method-of-place technique follow:

- Imagine your beautiful memory garden. You know this illustration so well that you can visualize it.
- Imagine each distinctive detail of the location: the white garden gate, birdbath, gazebo, fountain, flower bed, and the flowers arranged by colors.
- Create a vivid image for each item you want to remember and place it at a specific location.
- Associate each of the images representing the items with points in the garden and see the images at each location.
- As you mentally stroll down the garden lane, you create pictures in your mind of each of your items through association.

If you have additional points you want to remember, place one at the garden bench and one at the flower bed. If you have more than six items to remember, you can illustrate a rainbow over your flower bed. Flowers in the various colors of the rainbow can represent each item you wish to remember. It is easier to remember information that is grouped together and associated by categories. The colorful flowers in the flower bed can be arranged according to the colors of the rainbow: red, orange, yellow, green, blue, indigo, and violet.

Be creative and flexible with the method-of-place technique. If a garden doesn't work for you, use a car, a bike, or your home and apply the same concept. Start with the bell on your bike, go to the handlebars, and so on. Just make certain that your illustration is clear and you always start in the same place. Draw it in detail and color it.

Use a Checklist in Your Memory Garden

A checklist is an effective technique to remember items. It provides a way of reviewing and checking off each item you want to remember. You can combine it with the method-of-place technique. For example:

Memory Checklist
1. Garden gate   Monk
2. Birdbath   Bird
3. Gazebo   Victorian woman
4. Fountain   Little girl
5. Garden bench
6. Flower bed

Check off each memory point and the item that you want to remember. By using imagery, association, color, and repetition, you become part of the learning process and take control of your memory.

Go to page 6-20 to see a drawn interpretation of a memory garden.

Learning names is really important in my job. I invested time in getting to know people and developing relationships, and being attentive to detail.

—Sales representative for an ice-cream distributor

CRITICAL THINKING LOG 6.2

Memory Assessment

A. Sometimes your perceptions differ from reality, particularly when you are assessing your skills and personal qualities. Assess your memory and your intention. Then check Yes or No as it pertains to you.

1. Do you remember names? ___ Yes ___ No
2. Do you remember important information for tests? ___ Yes ___ No
3. Did you use your senses more as a child? ___ Yes ___ No

B. Read each statement that follows and write your comments on the lines provided.

1. Write a few lines about your earliest memory.

_____

_____

_____

_____

_____

2. Does it help your memory to look at family photos or hear about your childhood?

_____

_____

_____

_____

_____

3. What smells do you remember most from home?

_____

_____

_____

_____

_____

OVERCOMING BARRIERS TO MEMORY

The number 1 barrier to memory is mental laziness. People often say, "If only I could remember names" or "I wish I had a better memory." Avoid using words such as *try, wish,* or *hope.* You can overcome the barrier of mental laziness by creating a positive attitude, intending to remember, using all your senses, and using memory techniques.

Practice becoming more observant and aware. For example, let's say that you want to learn the students' names in all your classes. Look at each student as the instructor takes roll, copy down each name, and say each name mentally as you look around the classroom. As you go about your day, practice becoming aware of your surroundings, people, and new information.

To make sure your memory skills stay sharp, review and assess your answers to these questions periodically. Can you answer yes to them?

1. Do I want to remember?

2. Do I have a positive attitude about the information?

3. Have I created interest?

4. Have I eliminated distractions?

5. Have I organized and grouped material?

6. Have I reviewed the information often?

7. Have I reviewed right after the lecture?

8. Have I reviewed class notes within twenty-four hours?

9. Have I set up weekly reviews?

10. Have I used repetition?

11. Have I summarized material in my own words?

12. Have I summarized material aloud to my study group?

13. Have I compared, contrasted, and associated new material with what I know?

14. Have I used memory techniques to help associate key words?

It takes effort to learn and remember.

Organization

A mind map will help organize information to be memorized. Use the map figure that follows as a guide and create a mind map of this chapter.

- Take a blank sheet of paper (any size, a note card will do).
- Write the main topic in the middle and draw a circle or a box around it.
- Surround the main topic with subtopics.
- Draw lines from the subtopics to the main topic.
- Under the subtopics, jot down supporting points, ideas, and illustrations.
- Be creative.
- Use different color ink and write main topics in block letters.
- Draw pictures for supporting points.

The point is to draw a diagram that will organize all the information about a particular topic in one place. The mapping style of outlining organizes in a visual and creative form. Not only will the map organize the information, but the physical act of writing will also help you commit the material to memory.

Create your mind map below:

Mind Map

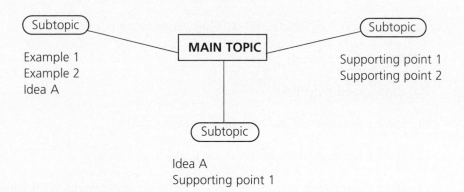

TRAILMARKER 6.3

Remembering Names

Here is a technique that may help you to remember someone's name.

1. Imagine the name. See the name clearly in your mind: Tom Plum.

2. Be observant.

3. Use exaggeration. Caricaturing the features is a fun and effective way to remember names. Single out and amplify one outstanding feature. For example, if Tom has red hair, exaggerate it to bright red and see the hair much fuller and longer than it is.

4. Visualize the red hair and the name *Tom.* See this vision clearly.

5. Repeat Tom's name to yourself several times as you are talking to him.

6. Recite Tom's name aloud during your conversation. Introduce Tom to others.

7. Use association. Associate the name with something you know ("Tom is the name of my cat") or make up a story using the person's name.

8. As soon as you can, jot down the name. Use a key word, or write or draw a description.

9. Use rhyming to help you recall: "Tom Plum is not glum, nor is he dumb."

10. Use your preferred learning style. It may help if you see the name (visual), hear it pronounced (auditory), or practice saying it and writing it several times and connecting the name with something familiar (kinesthetic).

11. Ask people their names. Do this if you forget or say your name first. "Hi, I'm Sam and I met you last week." If they don't offer their name, ask.

12. Relax. Being nervous can make you forget. For example, suppose you are with a good friend and you meet Tom. You may be so anxious to make a good impression that Tom's name is lost for a moment. Learn to relax by being totally in the moment instead of worrying about forgetting, how you look, what others may think, or being nervous.

Imagery and Association

Use critical thinking to answer the following questions. Be prepared to discuss your answers in your study teams.

1. How can you use imagery and association to help you remember something you forget often, such as your keys? Try your techniques for a few days and record the results.

_____

_____

_____

_____

_____

_____

_____

_____

_____

_____

2. Look at the following list of the common reasons and excuses some students use for not remembering. Add to this list and use creative problem solving to list strategies for overcoming these barriers.

Reasons for Not Remembering	Strategies to Overcome Barriers to Memory
1. I don't have a good memory.	_____
2. I can't concentrate and I am easily distracted.	_____
3. This class or book is boring.	_____
4. I never study the right material.	_____
5. _____	
6. _____	
7. _____	
8. _____	

Technology
FOCUS:
Computers and **Y**our **M**emory **S**kills

Use the computer to

- organize lecture and reading notes to help you recall information.
- help you to stay alert while you are studying because it's an active process.
- link ideas and connect known information with new information. Programs are available to help you increase your memory through association games, outlines, visual representations, and mind maps.
- explore memory skills on the Internet. Try this book's Web site:

http://peak.glencoe.com

Left/Right Brain Affirmations

Try integrating these affirmations into your daily life.

1. I choose to finish this project and then I will socialize.

2. I use memory techniques to help me study and recall information.

3. I look forward to completing my projects and taking short breaks.

4. It's fun to hike while I review a few key memory note cards.

5. I look forward to accomplishing my goals in study teams.

Learning Styles and Memory

Read the following and write your comments on the lines provided.

1. How can you use your preferred learning style to enhance your memory?

_____

_____

_____

_____

_____

_____

_____

_____

_____

_____

_____

2. What can you do to integrate both sides of the brain and to use all your senses to help yourself recall information?

_____

_____

_____

_____

_____

_____

_____

_____

_____

_____

_____

CAREER FOCUS: INTEGRATE LEARNING STYLES

The career professional who can learn and recall new information and remember names is in demand. Employees are often called on to learn new information, continue their education, and upgrade their skills.

Meet Kesia Downing. She is a sales assistant for a large software company. She has found that increasing her ability to remember and understanding how she learns best have helped her succeed in her job. Because she is primarily a kinesthetic and visual learner, she uses a hands-on approach to learning about the products she sells. Kesia routinely tries out various computer products and uses many visual aids when demonstrating a new product. She uses memory tips such as visualizing a person's name, repeating the name mentally, or imagining a character to help her remember the names of her clients and customers. As she writes down the names of new contacts and colleagues whom she meets at professional organizations, Kesia is developing good rapport and business relationships. To remember products and specific points when giving presentations, Kesia uses the memory garden technique (discussed in this chapter) and note cards. She is

- observing details and paying attention to main ideas and essential points.
- identifying how the material is organized.
- physically writing these main points on a note card.
- summarizing the information in her own words.
- reciting aloud and reinforcing the auditory learning style.
- connecting and linking material.

Figure 6-1
Memory Garden

DEBBI FIELDS

At twenty, Debbi Fields had just finished a two-year program in English at Foothill, a small community college. With no background in business or money to begin a new company, she set out to open a cookie shop. She loved to bake and had a plan. So with a plate of her cookies and her plan, she went from bank to bank for financing. When she found someone who would back her, she opened her first cookie store, Mrs. Fields Chocolate Chippery.

At the end of her first business day, she had sold only $75 worth of cookies, sales that were the result of giving free cookie samples to people in the streets. Debbi, however, was not ready to give up. Her free cookie samples saved not only the first day of business but became a strategic marketing plan—a plan which ultimately led to Mrs. Fields Cookies, Inc.

Debbi has been acclaimed as an international business phenomenon. And although she has enjoyed success, she has also had setbacks. For example, too many stores were opened too close to already existing locations, so she had to close ninety-seven stores and begin retrenchment. Debbi had been involved in the day-to-day operations of every store, but she knew that she had to remove herself from the details to see the big picture.

One of the marks of a Peak Performer is to learn from setbacks and mistakes. Debbi did that. She used her setbacks as opportunities. She continued to believe in herself and her product. She focused on quality and customer service. She expanded her product line to include gourmet coffee, bagels, biscotti, muffins, sandwiches, and soups. She placed her stores in airports, highway plazas, and college campuses. By being dedicated and continuing to try, Debbi eventually expanded her business to over 600 stores in more than seven countries.

Debbi Fields is a hard-working, creative Peak Performer. What can you learn from her?

Source: See this book's Web site: http://peak.glencoe.com

6

Review and Study Notes

Affirmations

- I remember easily.

- I enjoy remembering facts.

- I make the effort to remember formulas and equations.

- It's fun to read information and recall it easily.

- I never forget anything.

- I work at remembering people's names.

- I relax and allow my natural memory ability to work.

- My memory gets better every day.

- I can see myself successfully remembering whatever I want to.

- I am fully aware of my environment.

- I am attentive to the people around me.

- I am involved in the present.

Visualization

Visualize information and knowledge within you. See yourself recalling this information easily. Imagine yourself calm and relaxed during tests and exams and using your natural memory to remember information. Imagine the confidence and the sense of accomplishment that you feel as you effortlessly retrieve facts, dates, key words, and information. See yourself remembering names, appointments, and dates. It is easy for you to remember, and it gives you a sense of joy and accomplishment.

Peak Performance Memory Strategies

1. Intend to remember.

2. Be observant and alert.

3. Prepare myself mentally and physically.

4. Use all my senses and both sides of the brain.

5. Make learning visual, auditory, and physical.

6. Write down information.

7. Study in short sessions.

8. Organize information.

9. Go from general to specific.

10. Associate and connect.

11. Recite.

12. Use repetition.

13. Summarize in my own words.

14. Compare, contrast, and associate new material and old material.

15. Teach the information to someone else.

16. Review often.

17. Practice.

18. Reward myself.

CASE Studies

CASE A   *In the Classroom*

Trina Wilson is fun, bright, and popular, but she has
a reputation for being forgetful. She forgets appointments, projects, and due dates. She is continually losing her keys and important papers. She is often late and forgets
meetings and even social events. She continually tells herself, "I'm just not good at
remembering names" and "I really am going to try harder to get more organized and
remember my commitments." She blames her poor memory for doing poorly on
tests and wishes that people would just understand that she's doing the best she can.
She insists that she's tried but just can't change.

1. What would you suggest to help Trina improve her memory skills?

    _____

    _____

2. What strategies in this chapter would be most helpful?

    _____

    _____

It takes effort to learn
and remember.

In the Workplace

Trina is now in hotel management. She loves the excitement, the diversity of the
people she meets, and the daily challenges. She has recently been assigned to plan
and coordinate special events, which include catering, parties, meetings, and social
affairs. This new job requires remembering many names, dates, and endless details.

1. What strategies in this chapter would be most helpful for Trina?

    _____

    _____

2. Design a program for her that would increase her memory skills.

    _____

    _____

CASE B

Miguel Farias is majoring in marketing and sales at a business college. He has always been outgoing; he works well with people and does well on team projects, presentations, and essay tests. He has trouble, however, remembering data, formulas, and specific information. Miguel recently took a self-awareness workshop and discovered that he is a visual learner.

1. How can this knowledge about his learning style help Miguel remember dates and class information?

_____

_____

2. What other strategies from this chapter can help Miguel increase his memory skills?

_____

_____

_____

the Workplace

Miguel is now a sales representative at a medical laboratories company. Every day he meets new clients, deals with numerous customers, works with administrators and staff at the main and branch offices, and meets with other sales representatives at medical supply outlets. He is also active in his professional organization and in the community. It is critical for Miguel to remember the names of clients and the people with whom he works. In addition to remembering his standard equipment and supply inventory, he must also remember new products. Memory is important to Miguel's ability to do his job well.

1. What would you suggest to help him keep track of his products?

_____

_____

2. What strategies in this chapter would help Miguel become better at remembering names?

_____

_____

_____

Chapter Application   WORKSHEET 6.1

Connecting Learning Style With Memory

For each course you are taking, consider your best learning style. Write the name of the course in the Course column. Then put a check mark in the column of the learning style that best accommodates the course.

Course	Visual	Auditory	Kinesthetic

Chapter Application   WORKSHEET 6.2

Memory

A. Quickly read these lists once. Read one word at a time and in order.

1	2
the	Disney World
work	light
of	time
and	and
to	of
the	house
and	the
of	packages
light	good
of	praise
career	and
the	coffee
chair	the
and	of

B. Write as many words from the lists as you can remember on the lines that follow.
   Then check your list against the lists in Part A.

_____   _____

_____   _____

_____   _____

_____   _____

_____   _____

_____   _____

_____   _____

_____   _____

_____   _____

_____   _____

_____   _____

WORKSHEET 6.2 (CONTINUED)

1. How many words did you remember from the beginning of the list?

   _____

   _____

2. How many words did you remember from the middle of the list?

   _____

   _____

3. How many words did you remember from the end of the list?

   _____

   _____

4. Did you remember the term *Disney World?*   Yes _____   No _____

   _____

   _____

Most people who complete this exercise remember the first few words, the last few words, the unusual term *Disney World,* and the words that were listed more than once (*of, the,* and *and*). Did you find this to be true about yourself? Yes _____ No _____

C. Remembering Names

   1. Do you have problems remembering names? Yes _____ No _____

   2. What do you think you are still resisting?

      _____

      _____

   3. What are the benefits of remembering names now and in a career?

      _____

      _____

D. What memory techniques will you commit to learning and using?

   _____

   _____

   _____

Chapter Application   WORKSHEET 6.3

To-Do List

Urgent	Priorities	To See or Call

Continuing Attention

Awaiting Developments

What	Who	When

Name _____   Date _____

Chapter Application   WORKSHEET 6.4

Memory Systems

Use this grid when preparing for a test. Place a check mark next to each task as it is finished.

	Observe				Organize				Associate				Summarize			
	Pay attention to details.	Listen and observe.	Avoid distractions.	Stay alert.	Organize with an outline.	Use index cards.	Organize whole to part.	Organize part to whole.	Associate, compare, and contrast.	Link information.	Connect material.	Use imagery.	Summarize.	Recite out loud.	Use repetition.	Review.
Test 1																
Test 2																
Test 3																
Test 4																
Test 5																
Test 6																
Test 7																
Test 8																

APPLYING MEMORY SKILLS

Looking Back

Review an autobiography you may have written for this course or another. Look for ways that you learned memory.

Taking Stock

What are your memory strengths and what do you want to improve?

Looking Forward

How would you demonstrate memory skills for employers?

Documentation

Include examples such as poems you have memorized, Bible verses, techniques for remembering names, etc.

Assessment and Demonstration

Assess your memory skills. Review your life to discover how you learned these various skills. How would you use memory skills at work? Indicate how you would demonstrate these competencies to an employer.

Critical thinking skills for memory include

- preparing yourself mentally and physically.
- creating a willingness to remember.
- determining what information is important and organizing it.
- linking new material with known information (creating associations).
- integrating various learning styles.
- asking questions.
- reviewing and practicing.
- evaluating your progress.

TEST TAKING

The Universe is a grand book which cannot be read until one first learns to comprehend the language and become familiar with the characters in which it is composed. It is written in the language of mathematics.

—Galileo

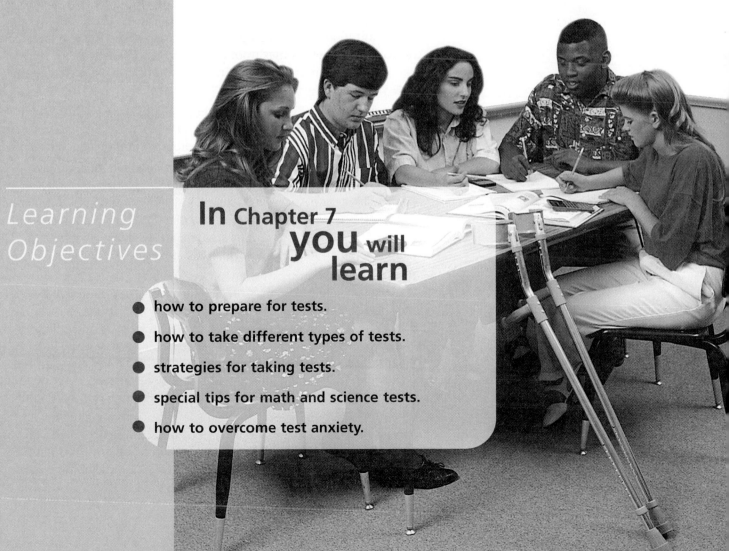

Learning Objectives

In Chapter 7 **you** will **learn**

- how to prepare for tests.
- how to take different types of tests.
- strategies for taking tests.
- special tips for math and science tests.
- how to overcome test anxiety.

All successful athletes and performers know how important it is to monitor and measure their techniques and vary their training programs to improve results. Taking tests is part of school, performance reviews are part of a job, and tryouts and performing are part of the life of an athlete, dancer, actor, or public speaker. In fact, there are few jobs in life that don't require you to assess skills, attitude, and behavior. The goal of this chapter is to explore specific test-taking strategies.

PREPARING FOR THE TEST

1. **Prepare early.** The best way to do well on tests is to begin by preparing on the first day of class. Prepare by attending all classes, arriving on time, and staying until the end of class. Set up a review schedule on the first day. Observe your instructors during class to see what they consider important and what points and key words are stressed. As you listen to lectures or read your textbook, ask yourself what questions could be on the examination.

2. **Know expectations.** The first day of class is important because most instructors outline the course and clarify the syllabus and expectations concerning grading, test dates, and the types of tests. During class or office hours, ask your instructors about test formats. Ask for sample questions, a study guide, or additional material that may be helpful for studying. You are in a partnership with your instructors, and it is important in any relationship to understand expectations. A large part of fear and anxiety comes from the unknown. The more you know about what is expected concerning evaluations and exams, the more at ease you will be.

3. **Keep up.** Manage your time and keep up with daily reading, homework, and assignments. Consolidate your class notes with your reading notes. Avoid waiting until the night before an exam to prepare for it.

4. **Ask questions.** Ask questions in class. As you read, take notes and review chapter material. Chapter summaries, key concepts, reviews, and end-of-chapter questions and exercises all provide examples of possible test questions. Save all quizzes, course materials, exercise sheets, and lab work. Ask if old tests or sample tests are available at the library. This will give you an idea of the format and possible questions.

5. **Review early.** Start the review process by previewing chapters before classes. Take a few minutes to review your class notes immediately after class. When information is fresh, you can fill in missing pieces, make connections, and raise questions to ask later. Set up a schedule so that you have time to review daily notes from all your classes each day. Review time can be short; five or ten minutes for every class is often sufficient. Daily review should also include scanning reading notes and items that need memorization. This kind of review should continue until the final exam.

6. **Review weekly.** Spend about an hour or so for each subject to investigate and review not only the week's assignments, but what has been included thus far in the course. These review sessions should include

Success Principle 7:
Focus on **STRENGTHS,**
not *Weaknesses*.

class notes, reading notes, chapter questions, note cards, mind maps, flash cards, a checklist of items to study, and summaries written in your own words. One of the best ways to test yourself is to close your book after reading and write a summary; then go back and fill in missing material. Make a mind map of the revised summary.

7. **Final review.** A week or so before a test, commit yourself to a major review. This review should include class and book notes, note cards, and summaries. You can practice test questions, compare concepts, integrate major points, and review and recite with your study team. Long-term memory depends on organizing the information. Fragmented information is difficult to remember or recall. Understanding the main ideas and connecting and relating information transfers the material into long-term memory.

8. **Rehearse.** One of the best tips for doing well on tests is to pretest yourself by predicting questions and making up and taking sample tests.

9. **Summarize.** Pretend the instructor said that you could bring one note card to the test. Choose the most important concepts, formulas, key words, and points and condense them onto one note card. This exercise really highlights important material. You will do better on a test even if you cannot use the note card during the test.

10. **Use your study team.** You may be tempted to skip studying one night, but you can avoid temptation if you know other people are waiting for you and depending on your contribution. Have each member of the study team provide five to ten questions. Share these questions and discuss possible answers. Word the questions in different formats—multiple-choice, true/false, matching, and essay. Then simulate the test-taking experience by taking, giving, and correcting timed sample tests.

TEST-TAKING STRATEGIES

1. **Arrive early.** You don't want to be frantic and late before a test. Arrive a few minutes early, practice deep breathing and affirmations, and visualize yourself relaxed and completing the test successfully. While waiting for other students to arrive, the instructor will sometimes answer questions or explain material to those students who are in class ahead of schedule. Use anxiety-reducing strategies to stay focused and positive. Look over your note cards calmly, but don't get into negative conversations. They will make you feel anxious if someone mentions the length of time they have studied.

2. **Organize yourself.** Write words, facts, formulas, dates, principles, or statistics in pencil on the back of your paper or in the margins as soon as you get the test. If you wait until you are reading each question, you may forget important material while under pressure.

3. **Read and listen to all instructions.** Scan the entire test briefly. Preview the questions to see which you can answer quickly and which

will take more time. Some questions may help you answer others. Dates, key words, or related facts may stimulate your memory for another question.

4. **Pace yourself.** Keep moving through the test according to your plan. Make your time count. Look at points for each question and determine the importance that should be given to each section. For example, you will want to spend more time on an essay worth twenty-five points than on a multiple choice worth five. Don't panic if you don't know an answer right away. Leave it and answer all the questions you do know. Build on success and don't block your thinking. Rephrase questions that you find difficult. It may help you if you change the wording of a sentence. Use memory strategies if you are blocked: draw a picture or a diagram, use a different equation, or make a mind map and write the topic and subtopics. Use association to remember items that are related.

5. **Review.** Once you have finished, reread the test and check for careless mistakes or spelling errors. Stay the entire time, answer extra-credit questions, and fill in details, if time permits.

AFTER THE TEST

1. **Reward yourself.** Reward yourself with a treat such as a hot bath, a walk, an evening with friends, or a special dinner. Always reward yourself with a good night's sleep.

2. **Analyze and assess.** When you receive the graded test, analyze and assess it. Be a detached, curious, receptive observer and view the results as feedback. Feedback is critical for improvement. Ask yourself the following questions:

- Did I prepare enough?
- What should I have studied more?
- Did I anticipate the style, format, and questions?
- What didn't I expect?
- What did I do right?
- How was my recall?
- Did I test myself with the right questions?
- Did I handle test anxiety well?
- Would it have helped if I had studied with others?

If you honestly don't know why you received the grade you did, see the instructor. Approach the meeting with a positive attitude, not a defensive one. Remember, a test is information and feedback on how you are doing, not an evaluation of yourself as a person. You cannot change unless you know what you are doing. Learn from your mistakes and move forward. Assess what you did wrong and what you will do right the next time.

TAKING DIFFERENT TYPES OF TESTS

The Objective Test

True/False Test

1. **Listen and read carefully.** Read the entire question carefully before you answer it. For the question to be true, the entire question must be true. If any part of the statement is false, the entire statement is false.

2. **Pay attention to details.** Read dates, names, and places carefully. Sometimes the dates are changed around (1494 instead of 1449) or the wording is changed slightly. Any changes like these can change the meaning.

3. **Watch for qualifiers.** Watch for such words as *always, all, never,* and *every.* The question is often false because there are almost always exceptions. If you can think of one exception, then the statement is false. Ask yourself, "Does this statement overstate or understate what I know to be true?"

4. **Watch for faulty cause and effect.** Two true statements may be connected by a word that implies cause and effect, and this word may make the statement false. For example, temperature is measured on the centigrade scale *because* water freezes at zero degrees centigrade.

5. **Always answer every question.** Unless there is a penalty for wrong answers, answer every question. You have a 50 percent chance of being right.

6. **Trust your instincts.** Often your first impression is correct. Don't change an answer unless you are certain it is wrong. Don't spend time pondering until you have finished the entire test and have time to spare.

7. **Watch for the word "always."** The use of the word *always* in a statement usually makes the statement false.

Multiple-Choice Test

1. **Read the question carefully.** Are you being asked for the correct answer or the best choice? Is there more than one answer? Preview the test to see if an answer may be included in a statement or question.

2. **Rephrase the question.** Sometimes it helps to rephrase the question in your own words. You may also want to answer the question yourself before looking at the possible answers.

3. **Eliminate choices.** Narrow your choices by reading through all of them and eliminating those that you know are incorrect.

4. **Go from easy to difficult.** Go through the test and complete those questions for which you know the answers. This will give you a feeling of confidence. Don't use all your time on a few questions.

5. **Watch for combinations.** Read the question carefully and don't just choose what appears to be the one correct answer. Some questions offer a combination of choices such as, "All of the above" or "None of the above."

6. **Look at sentence structure.** Make sure the grammatical structure of the question agrees with your choice.

Matching Test

1. **Read carefully.** Read both lists quickly and watch for cues.

2. **Eliminate.** As you match the items you know, cross them out unless the directions mention that an item can be used more than once. Elimination is the key in a matching test.

3. **Look at sentence structure.** Often verbs are matched to verbs. Read the entire sentence. Does it make sense?

Fill-in-the-Blank Test

1. **Watch for clues.** If the word before the blank is *an,* the word in the blank generally begins with a vowel. If the word before the blank is *a,* the word in the blank generally begins with a consonant.

2. **Count the number of blanks.** The number of blanks often indicates the number of words in an answer.

3. **Watch for the length of the blank.** A longer blank may indicate a longer answer.

4. **Answer the questions you know first.** As with all tests, answer the questions you know first and then go back to those that are more difficult. Rephrase and look for key words.

5. **Answer all questions.** Try never to leave a question unanswered.

Open-Book Test

The key to an open-book test is to prepare. Students often think that open-book tests will be easy, so they don't study. Generally these tests go beyond basic recall and require critical thinking and analysis. Put markers in your book to indicate important areas. Write formulas, definitions, key words, sample questions, and main points on note cards. Bring along your detailed study sheet. The key is to be able to find information quickly. Use your own words to summarize. Don't copy from the book.

TRAILMARKER 7.1

Test-Taking Factors

The factors involved in taking tests and performing well on them are:

1. Preparing yourself both mentally and physically.

2. Determining what information is important.

3. Processing information.

4. Linking new material with known information.

5. Creating associations.

6. Creating a willingness to remember.

7. Staying focused.

8. Reasoning logically.

9. Overcoming fear.

10. Evaluating.

Test Taking

Do the following activities:

1. Go to each of your instructors and ask how you are doing in each class.
2. Discuss your expectations and the style of test questions you can expect on one of their tests. Ask the instructors what you can do to earn a good grade. This exercise involves a lot of risks and you may be tempted to avoid it. But do it! Students almost always find it to be helpful.

The Essay Test

Being prepared is essential when taking an essay test. Make certain that you understand concepts and relationships and not just specific facts. (See Trailmarker 7.2 on page 7-10 for a sample essay test.)

Organizing your notes and reading material will help you outline important topics. An outline will provide a framework to help you remember dates, main points, names, places, and supporting material. In addition,

1. **Read the question carefully.** Make certain you understand what is being asked in the question. Respond to key words such as *explain, classify, define,* and *compare.* Rephrase the question into a main thesis. Always answer what is being asked directly. Don't skirt around an issue. If you are being asked to compare and contrast, you do not want to describe or you will not answer the question correctly.

2. **Organize the material.** Organize your main points in an outline so that you won't leave out important information.

3. **Write concisely and correctly.** Get directly to the point and use short, clear sentences.

4. **Write neatly.** Appearance and legibility are important. Use an erasable pen. Use wide margins and don't crowd your words. Write on one side of the paper only. Leave space between answers so you can add to an answer if time permits.

5. **Focus on main points.** Your opening sentence should state your thesis, followed by supporting information. Make certain that the question is answered completely, with supporting documentation. Cover the main points thoroughly and logically.

6. **Use all the available time.** Don't hurry. Pace yourself and always use all the available time for review, revisions, reflection, additions, and corrections. Proofread carefully. Answer all questions unless otherwise directed.

CRITICAL THINKING LOG 7.2

Essay Tests

Pretend you are taking an essay test on a personal topic—your life history. Your instructor has written the following essay question on the board:

Write a brief essay on your progress through life so far, covering the highs and lows, major triumphs and challenges.

Before you begin writing, you want to remind yourself of the topics you want to cover in this essay. What key words, phrases, events, and dates would you jot down in the margin of your essay paper? List your thoughts on the lines provided.

_____

_____

_____

_____

_____

_____

_____

_____

_____

_____

_____

_____

_____

_____

_____

_____

_____

_____

_____

_____

_____

Sample Essay Test

Steve Hackett, Ph.D.
Intro. to Economics Quiz
January 12, 2000

Question:

Describe the general circumstances under which economists argue that government intervention in a market economy enhances efficiency.

Thesis statement:

Well-functioning competitive markets are efficient resource allocators, but they can fail in certain circumstances. Government intervention can generate its own inefficiencies, and so economists promote those forms of government intervention that enhance efficiency under conditions of market failure.

Outline:

I. Well-functioning competitive markets are efficient

    A. Incentive for firms to minimize costs and waste

    B. Price approximates cost of production

    C. Effort, quality, and successful innovation are rewarded

    D. Shortages and surpluses eliminated by price adjustment

II. Markets fail to allocate scarce resources efficiently under some circumstances

    A. Externalities affect other people

        1. Negative externalities like pollution

        2. Positive externalities and collectively consumed goods

    B. Lack of adequate information

    C. Firms with market power

III. Government intervention can create its own inefficiencies

    A. Rigid, bureaucratic rules can stifle innovative solutions and dilute incentives

    B. Politically powerful groups can subvert the process

IV. Efficient intervention policy balances market and government inefficiencies

LAST-MINUTE STUDY TIPS

Cramming isn't effective if you haven't studied or attended classes. You might ask yourself, however, "What is the best use of my time the night before the test?" or "What can I do right now in just a few minutes to prepare for a test?"

- *Focus on a few points.* Decide what is important. Focus on a few of the most important points or formulas instead of trying to cram everything into a short study time. Preview the chapter quickly.

- *Intend to be positive.* Don't panic or waste precious time being negative. State your intention of being receptive and open, gaining an overview of the material, and learning a few supporting points.

Sample answer:

Well-functioning competitive markets allocate resources efficiently in the context of scarcity. They do so in several different ways. First, in market systems, firms are profit maximizers and thus have an incentive to minimize their private costs of production. In contrast, those who manage government agencies lack the profit motive and thus the financial incentive to minimize costs. Second, under competitive market conditions, the market price is bid down by rival firms to reflect their unit production costs. Thus, for the last unit sold, the value (price) to the consumer is equal to the cost to produce that unit, meaning that neither too much nor too little is produced. Third, firms and individuals have an incentive to work hard to produce new products and services preferred by consumers because, if successful, these innovators will gain an advantage over their rivals in the marketplace. Fourth, competitive markets react to surpluses with lower prices and to shortages with higher prices, which work to resolve these imbalances.

Markets can fail to allocate scarce resources efficiently in several different situations. First, profit-maximizing firms have an incentive to emit negative externalities (uncompensated harms generated by market activity that fall on others), such as pollution, when doing so lowers their production costs and is not prevented by law. Individual firms also have an incentive not to provide positive externalities (unpaid-for benefits) that benefit the group, such as police patrol, fire protection, public parks, and roads. A second source of market failure is incomplete information regarding product safety, quality, and workplace safety. A third source of market failure occurs when competition is subverted by a small number of firms that can manipulate prices, such as monopolies and cartels.

Government intervention can take various forms, including regulatory constraints, information provision, and direct government provision of goods and services. Government intervention may also be subject to inefficiencies. Examples include rigid regulations that stifle the incentive for innovation, onerous compliance costs imposed on firms, political subversion of the regulatory process by powerful interest groups, and lack of cost-minimizing incentives on the part of government agencies. Thus, efficient government intervention can be said to occur when markets fail in some substantial way, and when the particular intervention policy generates inefficiencies that do not exceed those associated with the market failure.

- *Use critical thinking.* What are the key words and points? Think logically.

- *Get a tutor or study partner.* Focus on main points and summarize. Do practice problems and tests. Several hours of intense study with a tutor can be far more effective than several late nights studying by yourself.

- *Focus on key words.* Write on note cards formulas, key words, dates, definitions, and important points.

- *Review your note cards.* In just a few minutes you can review important points. Keep it simple, review quickly, and review often. Use flash cards or mind maps and review again in short segments. Carry your note cards with you.

- *Affirm your memory.* The mind is capable of learning and memorizing material in just a short time if you focus, concentrate, and apply it. Look for connections.

TRAILMARKER 7.3

Important Words in Essay Questions

The following words are used frequently in essay questions. Read them and become comfortable with their meanings so that you will be able to answer any essay questions succinctly and accurately.

Compare	Look for characteristics that are similar.
Contrast	Look for differences between objects, events, or problems.
Define	Give concise, clear meanings and definitions.
Describe	Relate in a story form or sequence.
Discuss	Give a complete discussion, including pros and cons, and give reasons as you examine the problem.
Evaluate	Carefully appraise the problem, citing authorities.
Explain	Clarify, analyze, and give examples of the problem.
Illustrate	Draw a picture or diagram to explain or clarify the problem.
Interpret	Comment on a problem or translate, giving examples and your opinion or judgment about a problem or situation.
Justify	Convince or give reasons for conclusions or decisions.
List	Enumerate or write a list of points, one by one.
Outline	Organize main points and subordinate supporting points in a logical arrangement.
Prove	Give factual evidence and logical reasons that something is true.

Studying or Cramming

Read the following and write your comments on the lines provided.

1. Recall the last time you didn't study in advance for a test and had to cram. How did you feel?

_____

_____

_____

_____

_____

_____

_____

_____

_____

_____

2. What have you learned about preparing for and taking tests that will help you commit yourself to changing to new, productive behaviors?

_____

_____

_____

_____

_____

_____

_____

_____

_____

_____

TRAILMARKER 7.4

Special Strategies for Math and Science Tests

During your years of study, you will probably take math and science courses. Here are some strategies for preparing to take a math or science test.

1. **Use note cards.** Write formulas, definitions, rules, and theories on note cards and review them often. Write out examples for each theorem.

2. **Write notes.** As soon as you are given the test, jot down formulas, theorems, and formulas in the margins.

3. **Survey the test.** Determine the number of questions and the worth and difficulty of each question.

4. **Easy to hard.** Do the easy questions first. Spend more time on questions that are worth the most points.

5. **General to specific.** First, read to understand the big picture. "Why is this subject in the book? How does it connect with other topics?"

6. **Write the problem in longhand.** For example, $A = 1/2\ bh$ "For a triangle, the area is one-half the base times the height."

7. **Think.** Use critical thinking and creative problem solving. Let your mind ponder possibilities and what-ifs.

8. **Make an estimate.** A calculated guess will give you an approximate answer. This helps you when you double-check the answer.

9. **Illustrate the problem.** Draw a picture, diagram, or chart that will help you understand the problem. For example: The length of a field is 6 ft. more than twice its width. If the perimeter of the field is 228 ft., find the dimensions of the field.

Let l = the length of the field.

Let w = the width of the field.

Then $l = 6 + 2w$

So $6w + 6 = 228$

$6w + 12 = 228$

$6w = 216$

$w = 36$

So $l = 62w = 6 + 236 = 78$

Translating: The width of the field is 36 ft. and its length is 78 ft.

Checking: The perimeter is $2w + 2l = 236 + 278 = 72 + 156 = 228$.

10. **Ask yourself questions.** "What is being asked? What do I already know? What are the givens? What do I need to find out? How does this connect and relate with other concepts? What is the point of question?"

11. **Show your work.** If you get stuck, try to retrace your steps.

12. **Do a similar problem.** If you get stuck, try something similar. Which formula worked? How does this formula relate to others?

13. **Be logical.** Break the problem down step by step. Look for proof of your answer.

14. **Check your work.** Does your answer make sense?

15. **Review.** Review your test as soon as you get it back. Where did you make your mistakes? What will you do differently next time?

TRAILMARKER 7.5

Stress

Take a minute to review your activities a few days before a major test.

1. Do you plan too many activities or agree to commitments that you could decline or delay?   Yes _____   No _____

   If yes, give some samples.

   _____

   _____

   _____

2. Maybe too many activities on a test day adds greatly to your stress, and it might help to eliminate some. Do you agree ?   Yes _____   No _____

   Explain your answer.

   _____

   _____

   _____

OVERCOMING TEST ANXIETY

Many people see tests and performance assessments as huge mountains where one slip can cause them to tumble down the slope. Test anxiety is the number 1 barrier to doing well on tests. Test anxiety is that anxious feeling you get when your instructor announces that there will be a test, or when you sit down to take a test and your mind goes blank. Even the thought of taking a test causes some people to feel anxious and sends others into a state of panic. Symptoms of test anxiety include nervousness, upset stomach, sweaty palms, and forgetfulness. Test anxiety is a learned response to stress. Since exams, tests, quizzes, tryouts, presentations, interviews, and performance reviews are all evaluations and part of life, it is worth your time to learn to overcome test anxiety.

The attitude you bring to a test has a lot to do with your performance. Approach tests with a positive attitude. Replace negative self-talk with affirmations such as, "I am well-prepared and will do well on this test." Tests provide a chance to learn to face fear and transform it into positive energy. Tests are opportunities to show what you have mastered in a course. They provide feedback on how well you do at taking tests. Tests do not measure how much you know, nor are tests indicators of your intelligence, creativity, self-esteem, personal qualities, character, or ability to contribute to society. Don't exaggerate the importance of tests. Keep them in their proper perspective. Even if the worst happens and you do poorly, you can meet with the instructor to discuss options. You can do additional work, take the test again, or take the class again if necessary. Here are a few more suggestions that might help:

TIP Rehearse. Get sample tests, make up questions, and rehearse taking tests with a study partner. Recite, summarize, and practice help to reduce test anxiety.

1. **Be prepared.** If you have attended every class; previewed chapters; reviewed your notes; and written, summarized, and studied the material in small chunks of time each day, you will be prepared.

2. **Practice taking a sample test.** Athletes, actors, musicians, and dancers practice and rehearse for hours. When performers are on stage, their anxiety is channeled into focused energy. Practice taking sample tests with your study team and you should be more confident during the actual test.

3. **Don't cram.** You should review the night before the test, not learn new information. Write the most important information, formulas, and key words on one note card. Don't try to cram several weeks or months of studying into one night. Last-minute, frantic cramming only creates a hectic climate and increases anxiety. Instead, go for a long walk. Exercise is great for reducing stress.

4. **Stay calm.** Make your test day peaceful by laying out your clothes, books, supplies, and keys the night before. Review your note cards just before you go to sleep, repeat a few affirmations, and then get a good night's rest. Set an alarm so you'll be awake in plenty of time. Before you jump out of bed, relax and visualize your day unfolding in a positive way. Eat a light breakfast that includes protein, such as toast, cheese, yogurt, or cereal. Keep a piece of fruit or nuts and bottled water in your knapsack for energy.

5. **Get to class early.** Use the few minutes before the test to take a few deep breaths. Do several head rolls. Hunch your shoulders to your ears and relax them. Review your note cards.

6. **Listen carefully to instructions.** Read all instructions on the test.

7. **Jot down notes.** On the back of your test or in the margins, write formulas, dates, or important information that you want to remember. Having this information may help you feel more confident.

8. **Preview the whole test.** Do the easiest problems first to build your confidence. Don't feel rushed. If you don't know the answer to a problem, don't panic. Move on and return to it later.

9. **Get involved.** Focus on the subject. Get involved with answering the questions and be fully in the present.

10. **Get help.** If you are experiencing severe anxiety that prevents you from taking tests or performing well on them, seek professional help from a counselor at your school.

CRITICAL THINKING LOG 7.4

Test Anxiety

Use your critical thinking skills to answer the following questions:

1. Describe your test anxiety. Write about your feelings toward test taking in general. Describe your emotions and thoughts associated with all types of tests.

_____

_____

_____

_____

2. a. Do you have different feelings about nonacademic tests, such as a driving test or a vision test, compared to academic tests, such as quizzes and exams?

_____

_____

_____

   b. What do you think is the source of these differences?

_____

_____

_____

3. What are your memories about your best and worst test-taking experiences?

_____

_____

_____

4. What factors contributed to your ease or discomfort during these tests?

_____

_____

_____

CAREER FOCUS: FOCUS ON STRENGTHS, NOT SHORTCOMINGS

It may sound strange, but people are often tested at work. The testing is not in the form of a quiz or final exam, but rather in the form of job reviews and evaluations. Knowing how to predict questions, extract important information, recall facts and details, and overcome the fear of assessment are important job skills.

Meet Saeed Bortazavi. He is an electrician who was recently promoted to a supervisory position. He knows that performance reviews are more than just a tool to determine his salary. They provide a realistic assessment of his performance, help pinpoint specific job behaviors that he wants to reinforce or discontinue, help set goals, and provide an opportunity for his boss to see how Saeed performs his job. To prepare for performance reviews, Saeed predicts certain questions that his supervisor is likely to ask. He outlines important information relevant to the job and his company and keeps this knowledge updated. Rather than wait until the night before his review to cram, Saeed keeps his boss informed regularly about what he is doing and thus prepares for reviews daily.

Saeed views performance appraisals as a motivational tool. Once he knows how others perceive him, he can lay out a specific agenda to improve his performance. He takes control of his own performance reviews and looks at feedback as valuable information to use for professional growth. Saeed's ongoing preparation for reviews includes:

- assessing his past year's accomplishments and concerns.
- demonstrating how they were met.
- recording and documenting skills and competencies.
- holding regular meetings with his boss.
- clarifying expectations.

Saeed focuses on his strengths while working to improve his overall performance. He doesn't dwell on setbacks, failures, or criticism but realizes that mistakes are only temporary stumbling blocks and can be turned into stepping-stones to lasting success. Set the stage for a formal appraisal by taking control of your own review process.

Tools and Skills

Read the following and write your comments on the lines provided.

1. Take a minute to break down some of your daily college and work tasks into the tools and skills you need to perform them.

_____

_____

_____

_____

_____

2. What personal qualities are needed to succeed?

_____

_____

_____

_____

_____

3. Describe the mental and physical skills and tools you use to get motivated for classes, tests, presentations, and reviews.

_____

_____

_____

_____

_____

4. What type of preparation would make your commute to school smooth and efficient?

_____

_____

_____

_____

_____

PREPARING FOR A PERFORMANCE APPRAISAL

In anticipation of your performance appraisal, here are some points to consider:

- Write your job description, including the duties that you perform.
- How do you view your job and the working climate?
- List goals and objectives and the results achieved.
- What areas do you see as opportunities for improvement?
- What are your strengths and how can you maximize them?
- What are your general concerns?
- What are your advancement possibilities?
- What additional training would be helpful for you?
- What new skills could assist in your advancement?
- How can you increase your problem-solving skills?
- How can you make more creative and sound decisions?
- What can you do to prepare yourself for stressful projects and deadlines?
- Give examples of how you have contributed to the company's profits.
- What relationships could you develop to help you achieve results?
- What project would be rewarding and challenging this year?
- What resources do you need to complete this project?

Technology FOCUS: Computers and Tests

Computers can help you prepare for tests. Use the computer to

- practice test problems, organize lecture and reading notes, and summarize material. You are integrating learning styles, organizing information, and practicing doing test questions.

- try the book's Web site to explore sites about test anxiety, study tips, and math anxiety:

  http://peak.glencoe.com

Performance Reviews

Read the following and write your comments on the lines provided.

1. Describe your first performance review. Explain how you felt.

   _____

   _____

   _____

   _____

   _____

2. How did you prepare?

   _____

   _____

   _____

   _____

   _____

3. Were you motivated by the feedback you heard? Did you become defensive after hearing criticism?

   _____

   _____

   _____

   _____

   _____

4. What would you do differently?

   _____

   _____

   _____

   _____

   _____

BEN COHEN AND JERRY GREENFIELD

What's a Chunky Monkey®? Who's a Cherry Garcia®? If you are an ice cream fan or looked recently in your local grocer's freezer, you know they are popular flavors of Ben & Jerry's Ice Cream. Officially known as Ben & Jerry's, Vermont's Finest Ice Cream and Frozen Yogurt, this corporation was founded by two childhood buddies transplanted from Long Island—Ben Cohen and Jerry Greenfield. From its small beginnings in a renovated gas station, this Vermont-based corporation now distributes its products in all fifty states.

Ben Cohen, who loved ice cream as a kid and liked to experiment by adding cookies and candies to his ice cream concoctions, attended Skidmore College. He studied pottery and jewelry making and taught at a small residential community high school on a working farm. He began experimenting with making ice cream for his students. In the late seventies, he decided to go into an ice cream venture with Jerry Greenfield.

Jerry was a premed major at Oberlin College in Ohio. He worked as an ice cream scooper in the school's cafeteria. After graduation, he applied twice to medical school but was rejected each time. So, he and Ben began researching the ice cream business. They took a correspondence course in ice cream making and finally opened Ben & Jerry's Ice Cream Parlor in Burlington, Vermont, in May 1978 with a $12,000 investment. They soon became well-known for their unusual flavors and socially responsible business practices.

Ben & Jerry's is a company with a strong set of unique values. Its philosophy has been called "caring capitalism." Both Ben and Jerry wanted to be a force for social change and improve the quality of life for their employees. To accomplish this, the Ben & Jerry's Joy Gang was created. It is a group of employees dedicated to bringing more joy into the workplace. Employees plan fun activities that create a strong team spirit and fun work climate.

Ben & Jerry's community spirit is shown by sponsorship for projects that entail creative problem solving and hopefulness. They were recognized with the Corporate Giving Award by the Council on Economic Priorities in 1988, for donating 7.5 percent of their pretax earnings to nonprofit organizations. Their commitment to give back to the community was also recognized by the U.S. Small Business Administration.

Ben continues to be an active founding member of Businesses for Social Responsibility and both he and Jerry speak about these issues publicly.

Ben Cohen and Jerry Greenfield are Peak Performers. They have combined innovation and management skills with compassion, integrity, and character.

Souce: See this book's Web site at http://peak.glencoe.com

7

REVIEW AND STUDY NOTES

Affirmations

- I prepare for tests starting on the first day of class.
- I feel in control and competent by reviewing every day.
- I practice making up test questions and I feel good about answering them.
- I enjoy studying for tests in groups.
- I am calm, centered, and relaxed when taking a test.
- I breathe deeply and feel energized and focused.
- I recall information easily.

Visualization

Visualize yourself calm and relaxed. You are well prepared and organized, and you look forward to showing what you have mastered. Imagine that all your muscles are relaxed, yet your mind is alert and focused. Feel your sense of accomplishment when you answer questions easily. Visualize yourself effortlessly recalling dates, facts, figures, key words, and information. You welcome feedback on the tests and can receive it in a calm, detached manner. You know you can do well on tests and you have the confidence to handle any situation.

Performance Strategies for Test Taking

1. Prepare early.
2. Clarify expectations.
3. Observe and question.
4. Review.
5. Rehearse by pretesting yourself.
6. Study with your team or a partner.
7. Organize yourself.
8. Move through the test quickly.
9. Reread, recheck, rethink, and reward.
10. Analyze, assess, and reprogram.

CASE Studies

CASE A — In the Classroom

Latrice Yoshimoto is bright and hardworking. She studies long hours, attends all her classes, and participates in class discussions. When it comes to taking tests, however, she panics. She stays up late cramming, tells herself that she will fail, gets headaches and stomach pains, and sometimes breaks out in a cold sweat. Her mind goes blank when she takes the test, and she has trouble organizing her thoughts. Latrice could get much better grades and enjoy school more if she could control her stress and apply some test-taking strategies.

1. What advice would you give Latrice?

_____

2. What techniques from this chapter would be most useful to her?

_____

3. What one habit could she adopt that would empower her to be more successful?

_____

In the Workplace

Latrice now works for a large company as a graphic designer. She likes having control over her work and is an excellent employee. She is hardworking, highly skilled, and willing to learn new skills. There is a great deal of pressure in her job to meet deadlines, learn new techniques, and compete with other firms. She handles most of these responsibilities well unless she is being evaluated. Despite her competency, Latrice panics before her performance reviews. She feels pressure to perform perfectly and does not take criticism or even advice well.

1. What strategies in this chapter would be most helpful to Latrice?

_____

2. What would you suggest she do to control performance anxiety?

_____

CASE B

Abdul Sabie is a design and technology major at a career school. He is bright and creative, and describes himself as a free spirit. He likes to push the limits of art using color and unusual designs. Abdul doesn't take negative feedback or suggestions well and becomes defensive when his instructors mention ways to make his design work more effective. He believes that others simply don't understand his creative flair and that his test results are not a reflection of his talent.

1. What suggestions would you give Abdul for making the most of feedback?

   _____

   _____

2. How can he use the strategies in this chapter to perform better on tests and evaluations?

   _____

   _____

In the Workplace

Abdul is now a jewelry designer for a small jewelry manufacturer. His peers regard him as a talented and creative designer. He has a good relationship with his supervisor and is usually left alone to do his job. His reviews are informal. However, a large manufacturer is about to buy the company Abdul works for. He is wary of formal performance reviews because he is an artist, not a production person. Just thinking about being evaluated by the new management makes him nervous.

1. How can Abdul approach reviews more positively?

   _____

   _____

2. What can he learn about evaluations as feedback, rather than as criticism?

   _____

   _____

TIP From the Workplace

Performance reviews are part of life. I keep track of all my achievements, goals, and support letters. I manage my performance and write my own reviews. I also meet with my supervisor often and discuss goals and objectives. When I have my annual review, there are no surprises.

—Video store manager

Chapter Application   WORKSHEET 7.1

Exam Schedule

Use the following chart as a reminder of your exams as they occur throughout the semester or term.

Course	Date	Time	Room	Type of Exam

Chapter Application   WORKSHEET 7.2

Preparing for Tests and Exams

Before you take a quiz, test, or exam, use this form to help you plan your study strategy.

Course: _____
Date of test: _____   **Test number:** (If any) _____
Pretest(s)   Date given _____   Results _____
                    Date given _____   Results _____
                    Date given _____   Results _____
Present grade in course: _____

Met with instructor: Yes ___ No ___ Date(s) of meeting(s):_____

Study team members: Date(s) of meeting(s): _____
Name: _____ Phone number: _____
Name: _____ Phone number: _____
Name: _____ Phone number: _____
Name: _____ Phone number: _____

Expected test format: (Circle. There can be more than one test format.)
Objective   Essay   True/False   Multiple-Choice
Other _____

Importance: (Circle one)
Quiz   Midterm   Final exam   Other _____

Chapters covered in the test: _____
Date for chapter review: _____

Chapter notes: (Use additional paper)
_____
_____
_____
_____

Date for review of chapter notes: _____
Note cards: Yes _____ No _____ Date note cards reviewed: _____
List of key words:
Word: _____ Meaning: _____
Word: _____ Meaning: _____
Word: _____ Meaning: _____
Word: _____ Meaning: _____

WORKSHEET 7.2 (CONTINUED)

Possible Essay Questions:

Question: _____

Thesis Statement: _____

    Outline:

      I. _____

         A. _____

         B. _____

         C. _____

         D. _____

      II. _____

         A. _____

         B. _____

         C. _____

         D. _____

Main Points:

_____

_____

Examples:

_____

_____

Question: _____

Thesis Statement: _____

    Outline:

      I. _____

         A. _____

         B. _____

         C. _____

         D. _____

      II. _____

         A. _____

         B. _____

         C. _____

         D. _____

Main Points:

_____

_____

Examples:

_____

_____

Chapter Application   WORKSHEET 7.3

Performance Reviews

Listed below are qualities and competencies that may be included in many performance reviews.

Acceptance of diversity*   Safety practices
Effectiveness in working with others   Personal growth and development
Quality of work   Workplace security
Quantity of work   Technology
Positive attitude   Willingness to learn

*Diversity: Getting along with people from diverse backgrounds and cultures.

1. Using this page and a separate sheet of paper, indicate how you would demonstrate each of these competences and qualities to an employer.

   _____

   _____

   _____

   _____

   _____

   _____

   _____

2. Give examples of your willingness to accept assessment and feedback from an employer. Include sample performance reviews in your portfolio.

   _____

   _____

   _____

   _____

   _____

   _____

   _____

Chapter Application   WORKSHEET 7.4

Matrix for Test Taking

Prepare early and often.

Plan your time.

Clarify expectations.

Check your work.

	Prepare				Rehearse				Organize				Assess			
	Go to every class; ask questions.	Keep up with homework.	Develop and predict questions.	Review often; join study team.	Clarify expectations.	Rehearse by summarizing.	Rehearse by predicting questions.	Take sample test.	Organize notes and materials.	Read and listen to all instructions.	Preview test and pace yourself.	Organize thoughts; jot down words, formulas.	Reread, recheck, rethink.	Analyze and assess results.	Reward yourself.	Modify and adjust.
Test 1																
Test 2																
Test 3																
Test 4																

CAREER DEVELOPMENT PORTFOLIO

Listed below are typical qualities and competencies that are included in many performance reviews.

1. Communication skills:
   • Writing
   • Speaking
   • Reading
2. Integrity
3. Willingness to learn

4. Decision making skills
5. Delegation
6. Planning
7. Organization skills
8. Positive attitude
9. Ability to accept change

In the lines below, indicate how you would demonstrate each of the listed qualities and competencies to an employer.

_____

_____

_____

_____

_____

_____

_____

_____

_____

_____

_____

_____

_____

_____

_____

_____

_____

_____

_____

_____

_____

_____

EXPRESSING YOURSELF IN WRITING AND SPEECH

"Being good at something is only half the battle. The other half is mastering the art of self-presentation, positioning, and connecting."

—Adele Scheele, career counselor and author

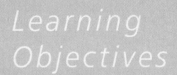

Learning Objectives

In Chapter 8 you will learn

- how to prepare research papers and speeches.
- how to use the library and take your research online.
- strategies for writing effective papers.
- strategies for giving effective presentations.
- how to overcome writer's block.

ew things in life are as difficult as writing research papers and speaking before a group. Famed sportswriter Red Smith commented, "Writing is very easy. All you do is sit in front of a typewriter keyboard until little drops of blood appear on your forehead." Public speaking can cause even more anxiety. To some students, just the thought of speaking in front of a group produces feelings of sheer terror. In fact, research indicates that public speaking is the number 1 fear of most people, outranking even fear of death. For many students, writing not only produces feelings of doubt but also demands their focused attention, intense thinking, and detailed research. You can't avoid writing or speaking in school or at work, but you can learn strategies that will make both easier and more effective. Once you master the skills and confidence required for speaking and writing effectively, you will experience a strong sense of accomplishment.

THE IMPORTANCE OF WRITING AND SPEAKING

The ability to communicate clearly, both orally and in writing, is the most important skill you will ever master. Peter Drucker, noted management expert and author, remarked, "Colleges teach the one thing that is perhaps most valuable for the future employee to know. But very few students bother to learn it. This one basic skill is the ability to organize and express ideas in writing and speaking."

You may be asked to do research on new ideas, products, procedures, and programs and compile the results in a report. You will most likely write business letters, memos, and reports. You may have to give formal speeches before a large group, preside at meetings, or present ideas to a small group. You will be expected to present both written and spoken ideas in a clear, concise, and organized manner. Writing papers and preparing speeches in school prepare you for on-the-job reports and correspondence. These assignments give you a chance to show initiative, use judgment, apply and interpret information, research resources, organize ideas, and polish your style. Public-speaking skills also help you inform and persuade others at informal meetings and presentations. Good writers and speakers are not born, nor is there a secret to their success. Like other skills, speaking and writing can be learned with practice and effort.

This chapter won't tell you how to write a great novel or deliver the keynote speech at a political convention, but it will give you strategies for handling every step of the paper-writing and speech-giving process, from choosing a topic to turning in the paper or delivering the speech. Keep four basic steps in mind as you prepare your paper or speech.

1. Prepare
2. Organize
3. Write
4. Edit

Success Principle 8: Focus on **EXCELLENCE**, not *Perfection*.

PREPARE FOR WRITING

1. **Choose a general topic.** Choose a topic that meets with your instructor's requirements, one that is narrow enough to handle in the time available and one in which you have an interest. If you have any questions concerning expectations, talk with your instructor and clarify length, format and style, purpose, and method of citation. Determine if your purpose is to entertain, inform, explain, persuade, gain or maintain goodwill, gain respect and trust, or gather information. Consider the age, education level, size of your audience, and their knowledge of the topic.

2. **Set a schedule.** Estimate how long each step will take and leave plenty of time for proofing. Work backward from the due date and allow yourself ample time for each step. See Figure 8–1 on page 8-4 for an example.

3. **Do preliminary reading.** Begin to gather general information by reviewing reference materials, such as articles or an encyclopedia. Your initial research is intended to give you an overview of the subject and key issues. Ask questions to help you begin structuring your topic and compiling a working bibliography. Make certain you check the list of related references at the end of reference books and reference book articles. You may want to develop a list of questions that can lead to new directions and additional research.

   • What do I already know about the topic? What do I want to know?

   • What questions do I want to explore? What interests me most?

   • What is the point I want to research?

   Write these questions on note cards and include them later with your research cards.

4. **Narrow your topic.** After you have finished your preliminary reading, you can narrow and focus on a specific topic. For example, instead of "Health Problems in America," narrow the subject to "Cigarette Smoking Among Teenage Girls" or "Should Cigarette Advertising Be Banned?"

5. **Write a thesis statement.** Writing a thesis statement will help you clarify what you plan to cover in your paper. The thesis is the main point or central idea of a paper. In one sentence, your thesis should describe your topic and what you want to convey about it. A good thesis statement is unified and clear; for example, Smoking among teenage girls is on the rise.

6. **Prepare a bibliography.** Go through the on-line catalog in the library. Most libraries now have electronic access and as with the card catalog, you brouse by subject or author. You can also use the Internet to discover what is available on your topic and start putting together a preliminary bibliography. Skim the references to see if they contain useful information. List all materials available on your topic. Put them in alphabetical order and number them in the corner. Write down the author's full name (last name first), exact title (underline newspapers, magazines, and book titles and put article titles in quotations marks), place of publication, name of the publisher, and date of publication, and write the call number in the upper left-hand corner.

Term Paper for Criminal Justice Class Due April 3

Final check. Make copy.	April 2.
Edit, revise, and polish.	March 29. (Put away for one or two days.)
Complete bibliography.	March 28.
Revise.	March 26.
Edit, review, revise.	March 24. (Confer with instructor.)
Final draft completed.	March 22. (Proof and review with a good writer.)
Complete second draft.	March 20.
Add, delete, and rearrange information.	March 17.
First draft completed.	March 15. (Share with writing group.)
Write conclusion.	March 12.
Continue research and flesh out main ideas.	February 16.
Introduction.	February 10.
Organize and outline.	February 3.
Gather information and compile bibliography and notes.	January 29.
Narrow topic and write thesis statement.	January 23.
Do preliminary reading.	January 20.
Choose a topic.	January 16.
Brainstorm ideas.	January 15.
Clarify expectations and determine purpose.	January 14.

Figure 8–1   Sample Schedule

7. **Take notes.** Jot down quotations and ideas that clarify your research topic. Put this information on note cards. At the top of the card, write the topic and below it, a summary in your own words, a brief statement, or a direct quotation. Unless you are quoting for support, write in your own words. If you are quoting, use quotation marks and be sure to write the words exactly as they appear and the source. If there is an error in the text insert, in brackets, the term *sic*, which means "thus in the original." If you omit words, indicate missing words with ellipses points (three dots with a space between each dot or period). Also write down each reference source on a separate card. You will need exact information for your final bibliography and footnotes and for researching material. Put a rubber band around your cards and keep them in a small folder. Sorting these cards into subject or topic divisions will help you prepare your outline. See Figure 8-2 for a sample bibliography card.

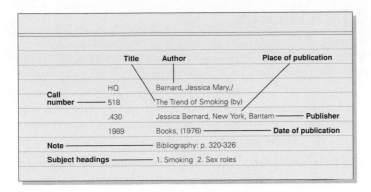

Figure 8–2   Bibliography Card

ORGANIZE A WRITING PLAN

1. **Organize and outline information.** Organize your note cards into a logical order using either a traditional or mind map outline. This outline should contain main points and subtopics. An outline is a road map that illustrates your entire project. If you use a computer, check applicable software packages that offer an outline feature.

2. **Continue your research.** Look for specific information and data that support your main points and thesis. Research the books and articles that you wrote on your bibliography cards. Organize and separate information and format consistently.

3. **Revise your outline.** Revise your outline as you continue to research. You may also want to refine your writing strategy by focusing on how best to accomplish your purpose. What is your major topic? What subtopics do you want to include? What examples, definitions, quotations, statistics, stories, or personal comments would be most interesting and supportive? Continue to look for specific information to support your thesis.

Sample Traditional Outline

I. Smoking among teenage girls is increasing.
   A. Smoking has increased by 24 percent.
      1. Supporting information.
      2. Supporting information.
   B. Girls are smoking at younger ages.
II. Advertising targets young girls directly.
   A. Example of advertising.
      1. Supporting information.
      2. Supporting information.
   B. Effects of advertising.

WRITING STRATEGIES

1. **Write your first draft.** Now is the time to organize all your note cards according to sections and headings and write in your own words according to your revised outline. Write freely and don't worry about spelling, grammar, or format. The key is to begin writing and keep the momentum going. Both papers and speeches should have three sections: an introduction, a main body, and a conclusion.

2. **Write the introduction.** The introduction should be a strong opening that clearly states your purpose, captures the attention of your audience, defines terms, and sets the stage for the main points. "Over 450,000 people will die this year from the effects of cigarette smoking" is a stronger introduction than "This paper will present the dangers of smoking."

3. **Write the main body.** The main body is the heart of your paper or speech. Each main point should be presented logically and stand out as a unit. Explain main points in your own words and use direct quotes when you want to state the original source. Refer often to your outline and your thesis statement. Your research note cards will help you find the support you need. If you find gaps, do more research.

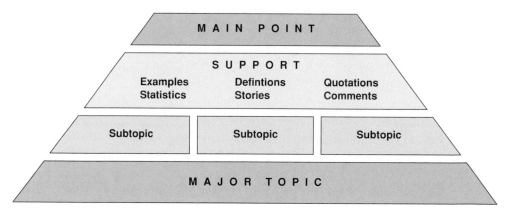

Figure 8–3   Hierarchy of Writing

4. **Write the conclusion.** Your final paragraph should tie together important points. Your reader or listener should have an understanding of the topic and an awareness that you have achieved your purpose. Use a story, a quotation, or a call to action. You may want to refer again to the introduction, reemphasize main points, or rephrase an important position. Keep your conclusion brief, interesting, and powerful.

TRAILMARKER 8.1

How to Generate Topic Ideas

- *Brainstorm.* Brainstorming is generating as many ideas as possible without evaluating their merit. The brainstorming process often works best in small groups. Your goal is to get a list of as many topics as you can in the specific time you have set aside. No one should evaluate the ideas. Within ten minutes you can often generate a sizable list of potential topics.
- *Go to the library.* Look in *The Readers Guide to Periodical Literature* for possible ideas. Look through newspapers, magazines, and new books.
- *Brainstorm on-line.* The Internet is a valuable source of ideas.
- *Keep a journal.* Keeping a journal is a great way to generate ideas for a paper or speech and is also a good way to practice your writing skills. Write down ideas, feelings, opinions, summaries of books and articles, and reactions to other speeches or papers.
- *Keep a file.* Collect articles, poems, and a list of topics that you find interesting. Listen to good speeches and collect stories or ideas from current newspapers that you could research and write about from a different perspective.
- *Develop observation skills.* Be aware of life around you. Think of possible topics as you read, watch television and movies, and talk with friends. What topics are in the news? What are people talking about?
- *Complete a sentence.* This technique can help generate potential topics. Write open-ended sentences and brainstorm completions. For example:

The world would be better if _____.

Too many people _____.

In the future _____.

A major problem today is _____.

A most wondrous event in life is _____.

The best thing about _____.

What I enjoy most is _____.

I learned that _____.

It always makes me laugh when _____.

The components of a perfect day are _____.

If I had unlimited funds, I would buy _____.

I get through a tough day by _____.

EDIT

1. **Revise.**

   - Revise your first draft the first time for attention to overall meaning and effect. Revise again for punctuation, grammar, and style.

   - Read your paper out loud to get an overall sense of meaning and the flow of your words. Vary sentence lengths and arrangements to add interest and variety. For example, don't start each sentence with the subject or overuse the same words or phrases.

   - Rework paragraphs for clarity and appropriate transitions. Does each paragraph contain one idea in a topic sentence? Is the idea well supported? Transitions should be smooth and unobtrusive. In a speech, they should be defined clearly so that listeners stay focused.

   - Recheck your outline. Have you followed your outline logically? Have you included supporting information in the correct places? Break up the narrative with lists if you are presenting series of data. As you revise, stay focused on your purpose rather than on the ideas that support your conclusion. Make sure your points are clearly and concisely presented with supporting stories, quotes, and explanations.

   - The paper should be concise and clear. Information should contribute, not just fill in space. Revision also involves deleting and/or moving information from one section to another. If you are using a computer or word processor, you can cut and paste with your word processing program. Save often and make a copy of the disk.

   - Review sentence structure, punctuation, grammar, and unity of thought. Check carefully for typographical and spelling errors, grammatical mistakes, and poor transitions.

2. **Revise again.** Often the difference between an *A* paper and a *B* paper or speech is that extra polish. If you can set it aside for a day or two before you give it a final revision, you can approach what you have written with a fresh view. Go through your entire paper or speech. Is your central theme clear and concise? Read your paper out loud. Recite your speech to a friend or tape it. Does it flow? Could it use more stories or quotes to add flair? Is it too wordy or confusing? Can you make it more concise? Does it have an interesting introduction and conclusion? Share your paper with a friend or member of your study team. Ask one of them to proofread your work. Other people can sometimes see errors that you can't and can provide a fresh viewpoint.

3. **Use a computer to compile footnotes and bibliography.** There are many ways to write citations. The Modern Language Association (MLA) of America format is often the preferred method for English and classical languages. The American Psychological Association (APA) format is commonly used for social sciences majors. Computer programs are available to format according to MLA and APA. Make sure you have written references according to your instructor's preferences. Footnotes can be placed at the bottom of a page or listed at the end of the paper, where where they are referred to as endnotes. The bibliography is a list of books or articles and is found at the end of the paper after the endnotes if they follow the conclusion.

Footnote:

1. Lee, Ann. *Office Reference Manual.* New York: Irwin, 1993.

Bibliography:

- Book: one author
  Allen, James D. *Coming of Age.* New York: Macmillan, 1992.

- Book: two authors
  Arkin, Terry C., and Nancy A. Kelly. *Smoking Too Soon.* New York: Basic Books, 1991.

- Government publication
  Congressional Quarterly Service. "A Review of Smoking." Washington, D.C., 1989, 28.

- Nonprint source
  Morgan, David E. "Reference Software for Smoking Studies." DOS Version. New York: Macmillan, 1995. Computer software.

- Journal
  "Risking the Future Adolescent." *National Research Council Journal.* Washington, D.C.: National Academy Press, 1990.

- Editorial
  "Some Better Ways to Curb Teen Smoking." Editorial, *Los Angeles Times* , August 14, 1995, sec. 1:2.

- Encyclopedia or other reference work
  Walton, Tom E. "Smoking." *World Book Encyclopedia.* New York: Macmillan, 1989.

Check this book's Web site for additional suggestions.
http:///peak.glencoe.com

4. **Confer with your instructor.** Make an appointment with your instructor to review your paper. Some students make an appointment when they have completed their outline or first draft. Other students like to wait until they have proofed their second draft. Most instructors will review your paper with you and give you suggestions. Discuss what to add and what to revise and the preferred method of citation. Follow these suggestions exactly as you prepare your final draft.

5. **Prepare your final draft.** Following your instructor's guidelines and suggestions, prepare your final draft. Leave a margin of 1 inch on all sides, except for the first page, which should have a 3-inch margin at the top of the paper. Double-space your entire paper except for the footnotes and the bibliography, which are often single-spaced. With a word processor or computer, you need only to make corrections, revise, and print out a clean, corrected copy on good quality paper. It's always a good idea to proofread this hard copy, however, because it's often easy to miss errors when you proofread on a computer screen.

6. **Number your pages.** Number all pages except the first page or the cover page. You can number the pages in the upper right-hand corner one-half inch from the top of the page. Number your end notes and bibliography as part of the text.

7. **Add a title page.** To create a title page, center the title one-third of the page from the top. Two-thirds from the top, center your name, instructor's name, course title, and date. See Figure 8-4 for a sample of a title page.

The Importance of Learning Public Speaking

Karena R. Davis
Ms. J. Williams
Verbal Communications 102
February 17, 2000

Figure 8–4   Sample Title Page

REVIEW AND ASSESS
. . . .

1. **Final review.** Do a final check of your paper by reading through all of it one more time. You want your paper to be error-free.

2. **Make a copy.** Copy your final paper or speech in case your instructor loses the original. You should also keep copies of your major research papers in your Career Development Portfolio to show documentation of writing, speaking, and research skills.

3. **Present your paper or speech on time.** Deliver your paper on time and be prepared to give your speech when it's due. Delaying the date just adds to the anxiety and may result in a lower grade.

4. **Assess and evaluate.** Review your graded paper or speech when it is returned to you. Ask your instructor for improvement tips and note them for future papers or speeches.

TRAILMARKER 8.2

Writing Do's

Be concise.
Eliminate unnecessary words. Write in plain language and avoid wordiness.

Be concrete.
Emphasize verbs for active, powerful writing. Use vivid action words rather than vague, general terms. The sentence, "Jill wrote the paper," is in the active voice and is easy to understand; "The paper was written by Jill" is in the passive voice and sounds weak. Favor familiar words over the unfamiliar. Include stories and quotes for interest and support. Avoid vague adjectives and adverbs such as *nice, good, greatly,* and *badly.*

Be clear.
Keep in mind the purpose of your writing. Make certain that your message is complete and includes all the information the audience needs to understand your intent. Never assume that the audience has any prior information. Use simple words and avoid stuffy, technical terms, clichés, slang, and jargon. If you must be technical, include simple definitions for your audience.

Be correct.
Choose precise words and grammatically correct sentences. Make sure your supporting details are factual and that you interpret them correctly.

Be coherent.
Your message should flow smoothly. Transitions between topics should be clear and logical.

Be complete.
Make certain you have included all necessary information. Will your listeners or readers understand your message? Reread your speech or paper from their point of view. What questions might the audience have? If there are any unanswered questions, answer them.

Be considerate.
Use a respectful tone. Don't talk down to your audience or use pompous language. Always write with courtesy, tact, and consideration.

Be interesting.
Use variety. Vary the length of sentences for interest and a sense of rhythm. Include stories, examples, and interesting facts.

Be neat.
Neatness counts. Papers should always be typed. If you find an error in the final draft, it's okay to use white-out fluid or pen to make a correction. A word processor or computer, of course, can help you make the correction quickly and print out a flawless page.

Edit and proofread several times.
Make certain you use correct grammar and check spelling and punctuation carefully. It is easy to miss errors with only one proofing, so proof at least twice.

Avoid biased language.
Make substitutions for biased words. Language is so powerful that it is important to avoid using words that are biased in terms of sex, disabilities, or ethnic groups. For example:

Instead of . . .	You can substitute . . .
mankind	humanity, people, humankind
manmade	manufactured, handcrafted
policeman	police officer
fireman	firefighter
housewife	homemaker
crippled	disabled, a person with disabilities
Indian (American)	Native American
Negro	African American
Oriental	Asian American
Chicano	Mexican American

USING THE LIBRARY FOR RESEARCH

The library contains a wealth of information. Besides books, libraries have newspapers, magazines, encyclopedias, dictionaries, indexes, audiovisual equipment, telephone directories, maps, catalogs, research aides, computer software, and computers. Librarians are trained to find information about every subject. They can often order special materials from other libraries or direct you to other sources. Asking for their guidance at the beginning of your search can save you hours of time and frustration. When designing your research strategy, remember the three basic types of sources found in most libraries: books, periodicals, and reference materials.

- *Books.* Books make up a large part of every library. Books are designed to treat a subject in depth and offer a broad scope. In your research project, use books for historical context; thorough, detailed discussions of a subject; or varied perspectives on a topic.

- *Periodicals.* A periodical is anything published regularly, such as daily or weekly newspapers, and weekly or monthly news magazines, professional and scholarly journals, and trade and industry magazines. Articles in periodicals provide current printed information. For your research, use periodicals when you need recent data.

- *Reference materials.* Reference materials may be in print or on the computer. Examples of reference materials include encyclopedias, dictionaries, chronologies, abstracts, indexes, and compilations of statistics. In your research strategy, use reference materials when you want to obtain or verify specific facts.

The *Reader's Guide to Periodical Literature* is a helpful source for locating articles. Other standard reference materials that may give you a general understanding of specific topics and help you develop questions include *The Encyclopedia Americana,* the *Encyclopaedia Britannica, The New York Times* index, and the *Wall Street Journal* index.

Check these sources for historical speeches.

- Speech Index.
- Index to American Women Speakers, 1828–1978.
- Representative American Speeches, 1937+.
- Facts on File, 1941+.
- Vital Speeches of the Day, 1941+.
- Historic Documents of [Year].
- Public Papers of the Presidents of the United States.

Many libraries now have World Wide Web access. Use this book's Web site to find these sources.

http://peak.glencoe.com

TAKE YOUR SEARCH ONLINE

The Internet is the world's largest information network. The Internet is often referred to as the information superhighway because it is a vast network of computers connecting people and resources worldwide. The Internet began in the 1960s when the U.S. Department of Defense was interested in creating a network through which leaders could communicate after a nuclear attack. The Rand Corporation, a military think tank, worked on a system that evolved into the Internet.

The Internet is an exciting medium to help you access the latest information. You can access data from others online and access resources such as dictionaries, encyclopedias, and library catalogs; news publications and electronic journals; and databases from universities and government agencies. You can learn about companies by visiting their Web sites. Anyone with a computer and a modem can be on the Internet.

- The World Wide Web is a collection of mechanisms used to locate, display, and access information available on the Internet. A Web site or page is multimedia and uses colored pictures, video, sound, images, and text. You can use browser software such as Netscape or Explorer and click on highlighted words, called hyperlinks, to investigate additional information. The World Wide Web is a popular way to advertise businesses, departments, and products.
- Telnet is an Internet tool that allows you to access another computer without having a special account. For example, some Telnet sites, such as libraries, allow you to log on from a home computer.
- File Transfer Protocol is a tool to transfer files between two Internet sites. You can send (upload) or retrieve (download) a file from a remote site to your own. Thousands of files are available to any Internet user.

Use this book's Web site to find online writing resources:

http://peak.glencoe.com

TRAILMARKER 8.3

Overcoming Writer's Block

- *Read.* Reading will give you ideas and improve your writing. Read novels, classic literature, biographies, and newspapers. Read other students' papers and exchange papers with your study team. Reading helps you become a better writer.

- *Write e-mail and letters.* Keep in shape by writing e-mail and letters every day. Yes, it takes time, but nothing improves your writing like daily practice.

- *Keep a journal.* Again, there is no better way to become a writer than to write.

- *Write in a conversational tone.* Don't use technical, artificial, or stilted language. Use everyday, common words as if you were talking to someone. Try using a tape recorder to dictate your paper so it sounds as if you are speaking and not writing.

- *Write in short blocks of time.* Like any other large task, you'll become discouraged if you sit down to write a large paper. Write a little every day—anywhere you happen to be. Write for five minutes before bed, when you get up in the morning, or between classes. Practice writing in short blocks of time.

- *Review your purpose.* Have a clear understanding of your purpose. Make a list of key points you want to make. In one or two words or phrases, write what you want to accomplish. What exactly is it that you want to say? This short exercise is often enough to get you started.

- *Go to a restaurant.* Go out for a cup of coffee or tea and give yourself an hour of uninterrupted time to outline or mind map your paper or speech. If you are a visual learner, you may find that a mind map breaks your writing block. Start with your central purpose and topic. Outline main points, subtopics, and so on, and fill in with additional ideas. A map allows your ideas to flow freely and lets you work on different topics and see the connections between topics. You can then use this visual map as you type your paper. Don't feel that you must start with the introduction and work in a linear fashion.

- *Find a conference room or classroom.* You may need space to be alone, spread out papers, and work without interruptions.

- *Free write.* After you have completed your map outline, write for thirty or forty minutes. Don't worry about spelling, organization, or grammar; just keep writing. Timed free writing is a powerful writing tool to break a writing block. Free writing is especially useful if you start early, allow the first draft to sit for a few days, and then return to it and revise.

- *Take a break or vary your routine.* It's often best to at least do an outline or first draft to break the fear of the blank computer screen. But if you get frustrated, take a short break or change the pace and work on your conclusion instead of starting with the introduction. Write your conclusion in one sentence to check for clarity. Is it compelling and clear? Now you can go back and write your paper by supporting your conclusion.

- *Set a deadline.* Write a schedule and stick to it. Complete each task, even if it isn't what you would like it to be. You can revise and change, but perfectionism and procrastination will keep you frozen.

- Here's a Web site for writer's block: http://peak. glencoe.com

TIP Everyone has time to write. You will become a better writer when you stop making excuses and start writing.

PUBLIC SPEAKING STRATEGIES

Many of the strategies for choosing a topic and organizing a speech are similar to those for writing papers. Here are a few additional strategies pertinent to public speaking:

- *Be prepared.* Practice giving your speech several times.

- *Look at the audience.* Establish eye contact and speak to the audience members. Smile, develop rapport, and notice when your audience agrees with you or looks puzzled or confused.

- *Develop visuals.* When it is appropriate, use overheads, slides, handouts, and demonstrations. They can focus audience attention, add drama, reduce your stress, and reinforce your speech. Make sure that the type on your visuals is large enough to read, the projector works, and you have practiced working with the visual aids.

- *Prepare your prompters.* Don't memorize the speech but be acquainted well enough with your topic that you are comfortable talking about it. Prepare simple notes to prompt yourself. Write key phrases in large letters. Write key phrases, stories, and quotes on note cards.

- *Practice.* Rehearsal is everything! Practice the speech aloud several times in front of a mirror, an empty classroom, or friends. Practice speaking slowly and calmly, but louder than usual. Vary the pitch and speed for emphasis.

- *Be in the present.* Take a deep breath before beginning your speech. Look at your audience and smile. Keep your purpose in mind and stay focused on the message and the audience. Remember to pause at important points for emphasis and to connect with your audience.

- *Avoid unnecessary words.* Use clear, concise words. Don't use pauses as fillers, irritating nonwords, or overused slang such as *uh, um, you know, stuff like that, sort of, like,* and so on. Use brief pauses for emphasis, then take a deep breath and continue.

- *Review your performance.* Ask your instructor and fellow students for feedback. Be open to learning and strive to improve. Review the sample speech evaluation form shown in Figure 8–5.

Name:_____	Topic: _____	
Introduction	**Delivery**	**Suggestions**
__ Gained attention and interest	__ Spoke without rushing and at an appropriate rate	_____
__ Introduced topic	__ Maintained eye contact	_____
__ Topic related to audience	__ Maintained volume and projection	_____
__ Established credibility	__ Avoided distracting mannerisms	_____
__ Previewed body of speech	__ Used gestures effectively	_____
Body	__ Articulated clearly	_____
__ Main points clear	__ Used vocal variety and dynamics	_____
__ Organizational pattern evident	__ Presented visual aids effectively	**General Notes**
__ Established need	__ Departed appropriately	_____
__ Presented clear plan	__ Other: _____	_____
__ Demonstrated practicality	**Conclusion**	_____
__ Language accurate and clear	__ Prepared audience for ending	_____
__ Gave evidence to support main points	__ Reinforced central idea	_____
__ Sources and citations clear	__ Called audience to agreement/action	_____
__ Reasoning sound and clear	__ Used a vivid ending	_____
__ Used emotional appeals if appropriate		_____
__ Connectives effective		_____

Key: Superior (1), Effective (2), Average (3), Weak (4)

Figure 8–5
Speech Evaluation Form

TRAILMARKER 8.4

Taking Your Search Online

Work with another student in class who has not logged onto the Internet. Write directions and illustrate how one logs on. Your assignment is to find references and information for a paper or speech. Use technology to brainstorm ideas. Try the Internet for a list of possible topics, information on federal or state programs, or tap into governmental and industrial databases in the field you are interested in writing about.

Besides browsing for topics and references, the Internet is now a powerful research database. Web pages include pictures, sound files, or video presentations. From *The Wall Street Journal* to job and music lists, the Internet offers a massive amount of information.

Use this book's Web site for more information to links about this topic.

http://peak.glencoe.com

Controlling Stage Fright and Writer's Block

A. Use your critical thinking skills to answer the following questions. Be prepared to discuss your answers in your study teams.

1. Describe your typical physical reaction to giving a speech.

   _____

2. What has helped you control stage fright?

   _____

3. Describe the processes of writing that are easiest for you and those that are the hardest.

   _____

B. Read the common reasons and excuses below that some students use for not writing effective speeches. Add to this list. Use creative problem solving to list strategies for overcoming these barriers.

Reasons/Excuses

1. I have panic attacks before I write or give speeches.

   Strategy: _____

   _____

2. I can't decide on a topic.

   Strategy: _____

   _____

3. I don't know how to research.

   Strategy: _____

   _____

4. I procrastinate until the last minute.

   Strategy: _____

   _____

5. I don't know what my instructor wants.

   Strategy: _____

   _____

6. My mind goes blank when I start to write or give a speech.

   Strategy: _____

   _____

Technology FOCUS:
Computers and Research

Computers can help you research papers and write speeches. With a computer, you can gather information, take notes, outline ideas, write a rough draft, cut and paste, spell check, and print out a flawless paper. Computers save time in the revision stage of writing. Certain computer programs can help spot incorrect sentences and grammatical errors and compile contents, indexes, footnotes, and bibliographies.

The Internet is a wonderful source for research and can access the following:

- information collections and databases.
- research papers.
- government documents.
- publications.
- news.
- online educational events.
- the most current information on a topic.

Use this book's Web sites to find more information on this topic

http://peak.glencoe.com

CAREER FOCUS: COMMUNICATION SKILLS

Many times during your career you may have to deal with stage fright, anxiety, and writer's block. The higher up the career ladder you go, the more you will use public speaking and writing skills. Employees who can give effective presentations, give clear directions, write short reports, conduct meetings, and write effectively will succeed.

Writing and giving presentations are part of most jobs. Even accountants, computer programmers, and forest rangers write memos, letters, annual reports, and proposals, and give short presentations and speeches.

Meet Hiro Yuji, a public relations and academic resources director at a local community college. She edits the catalog, news releases, and alumni reports and prepares letters and memos for the university president. She works with the college's advisory board to present new marketing ideas, growth trends, lists of alumni donating contributions, and academic resources for alumni. Hiro knows it is important to be clear, accurate, and brief. She sets deadlines and allows herself several days to review and polish important material before it is printed. She has other people edit her work to ensure that it is error-free, clear, and to the point. See Figure 8-6 on page 8-20 for an example of a memo that Yuji wrote to the accounting department.

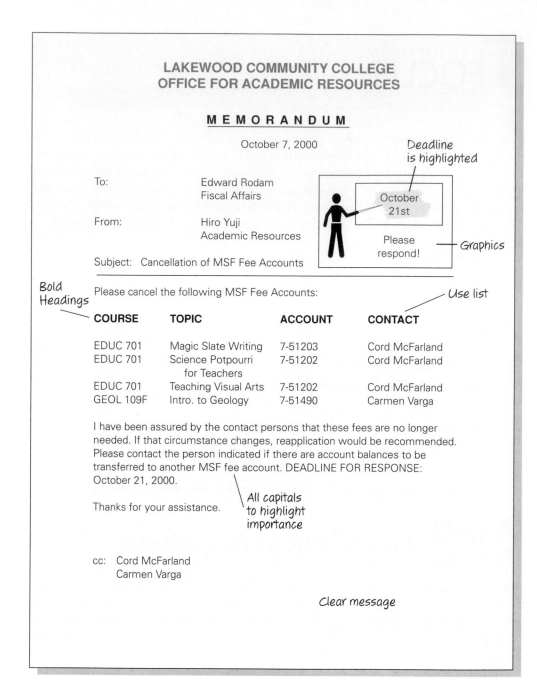

LAKEWOOD COMMUNITY COLLEGE
OFFICE FOR ACADEMIC RESOURCES

M E M O R A N D U M

October 7, 2000

Deadline is highlighted

To: Edward Rodam
             Fiscal Affairs

From: Hiro Yuji
             Academic Resources

October 21st

Please respond! — *Graphics*

Subject: Cancellation of MSF Fee Accounts

Bold Headings

Please cancel the following MSF Fee Accounts:

Use list

COURSE	TOPIC	ACCOUNT	CONTACT
EDUC 701	Magic Slate Writing	7-51203	Cord McFarland
EDUC 701	Science Potpourri for Teachers	7-51202	Cord McFarland
EDUC 701	Teaching Visual Arts	7-51202	Cord McFarland
GEOL 109F	Intro. to Geology	7-51490	Carmen Varga

I have been assured by the contact persons that these fees are no longer needed. If that circumstance changes, reapplication would be recommended. Please contact the person indicated if there are account balances to be transferred to another MSF fee account. DEADLINE FOR RESPONSE: October 21, 2000.

All capitals to highlight importance

Thanks for your assistance.

cc: Cord McFarland
     Carmen Varga

Clear message

Figure 8-6   Sample Memo

TRAILMARKER 8.5

Checklists for Writing Papers and Giving Speeches

Review these checklists before submitting a paper or giving a speech.

Papers and Speeches

___ Appropriate and focused topic

___ Attention-getting introduction

___ Thesis statement clear

___ Word choice appropriate

___ Plenty of factual support

___ Good examples

___ Good visuals

___ Sources credited

___ Smooth transitions

___ Effective summary/conclusions

Papers

___ Spelling and grammar checked

___ Proofread at least twice

___ Pages numbered

___ Neat appearance/format

___ Deadline met

___ Copies made

Speeches

___ Eye contact

___ Appropriate voice level and tone

___ No slang or distracting words

___ Relaxed body language

___ Appropriate attire

___ Access to watch or clock

MAYA ANGELOU

Maya Angelou is a poet, historian, author, actress, civil-rights activist, producer, director, and playwright. This talented woman, who stood in front of millions of people to read her poetry at Clinton's inauguration in 1992, had her beginnings in an abusive household. A mute and withdrawn child for five years after being raped by her mother's boyfriend, she finally found her voice after her grandmother introduced her to books and literature.

Angelou is among the first African-Americans to hit the best-seller's list with her book, *I Know Why the Caged Bird Sings,* which was also nominated for a National Book Award. Angelou has served in many prestigious posts, beginning with Martin Luther King, Jr.'s request for her to act as the Northern coordinator for the Southern Christian Leadership Conference. In 1975, President Jimmy Carter appointed her to the National Commission on the Observance of International Women's Year.

Angelou has also been involved in script writing and directing. She was nominated for an Emmy award for her acting in *Roots* and *Georgia. Georgia* was the first screenplay written by a black woman (Angelou) to be produced as a film. She received the Golden Eagle Award for writing several documentaries, including *Afro-Americans in the Arts.*

Her writings have earned her numerous awards, and she has been nominated for a Tony Award and a Pulitzer Prize. Through her powerful and moving writings, Angelou has inspired all people who have faced challenges.

Angelou is a Peak Performer. You may be interested in reading some of her works, which are available in libraries. Here are some titles to start:

- *The Complete Collected Poems of Maya Angelou*

- *I Shall Not Be Moved*

- *Black Pearls: The Poetry of Maya Angelou*

- *Kofi and His Magic*

- *Making Magic in the World*

- *Phenomenal Women: Four Poems Celebrating Women*

Source: http://peak.glencoe.com

Review and Study Notes

Affirmations

- I have many creative ideas for papers and speeches and enjoy looking in the library for additional ideas. I choose my topics quickly.
- I schedule my projects and feel comfortable knowing I can meet each deadline.
- I enjoy using the library and online resources for information.
- It is fun to write the first draft quickly and feel a sense of accomplishment when my ideas are taking shape.
- It is easy to edit and proof my papers and practice my speeches.

Visualization

See yourself writing interesting papers and giving excellent speeches. You are organized, calm, concise, and prepared. As you take deep breaths, you are in control of your thoughts and behavior. You use feelings of anxiety and stage fright to focus and give you energy. You maintain comfortable eye contact and look directly at your audience. See yourself building a bond with your audience. You enjoy communicating both by writing and speaking.

Peak Performance Strategies for Writing Papers and Giving Speeches

1. Determine your purpose and set a schedule.
2. Brainstorm ideas and choose the best. Limit your topic.
3. Read and research. Prepare a bibliography.
4. Develop an outline.
5. Analyze and continue to research.
6. Refine your purpose and start writing and speaking.
7. Edit and proof. Practice!
8. Revise and polish. Practice!

CASE Studies

CASE A *In the Classroom*

Kumi Russell is a good student but goes blank when she
has to write a paper. She has problems choosing a topic
and delays the paper as long as she can. Recently Kumi
was assigned a paper that is due in three weeks. This time is even
worse because the paper includes an oral presentation. If there is one thing that is
even more difficult for her than writing papers, it is giving speeches.

After changing topics four times, Kumi has finally chosen one. However, she is
experiencing writer's block. She sits in front of her computer and her mind goes
blank. She is also terrified at the thought of giving this formal speaking presentation.

1. What would you suggest to Kumi that would get her started?

    _____

2. What are three strategies mentioned in this chapter that would help her most?

    _____

3. What could she do to reduce stage fright and anxiety? Suggest one habit that
    would be helpful in writing papers and giving speeches.

    _____

In the Workplace

Kumi is now a park ranger. She chose this field because of her love of the outdoors
and the chance to work with nature. She is surprised at the amount of writing and
speaking that she has to do. She has to write daily reports, annual reports, brochures,
and fliers. She is required to give park tours and presentations and lead staff meetings. At first, the writing demands bothered her, but she is getting better at compos-
ing and meeting deadlines. However, Kumi is still experiencing anxiety every time
she gives a presentation. She knows she must overcome this terrifying stage fright.

1. What strategies would help Kumi become both a better writer and a more confi-
    dent public speaker?

    _____

2. What tips from this chapter would be most helpful?

    _____

CASE B

Steve Novak is a bookkeeping student at a career school. He likes numbers and feels comfortable with order, structure, and right or wrong answers. As part of the graduation requirements, all students must take classes in speech and writing. Steve becomes nervous about writing reports or giving speeches and doesn't see the connection between the required class and his bookkeeping studies. One of Steve's biggest stumbling blocks is thinking of topics. He experiences writer's block and generally delays any writing project until the last possible moment.

1. What strategies in this chapter would help Steve think of topics and meet his deadlines?

   _____

   _____

2. What would you suggest to help him see the value of speaking and writing well?

   _____

   _____

In the Workplace

Steve has recently been promoted to district manager for an accounting firm. He feels very secure with the accounting part of his job; however, with the new promotion comes the responsibility of presenting bimonthly speeches to top management, as well as running daily meetings and writing dozens of letters, memos, and reports. He must give motivational seminars at least twice a year to his department heads. Steve would like to make his writing and presentations more clear, concise, and motivational.

1. What suggestions would you give Steve to help make his presentations more professional and interesting?

   _____

   _____

2. What strategies could he use to improve his writing?

   _____

   _____

> **TIP** From the Classroom
>
> Set up a timetable and stick to it! Also, see your instructor when you have written the first draft and get suggestions and ideas. Follow them.
>
> —Community college student advisor

Chapter Application **WORKSHEET 8.1**

Preparing Research Papers

When you start thinking about upcoming research papers, use this guide to prepare and to take action.

Topic: _____ Date Due: _____

Thesis: _____

Introduction: _____

Interest and importance: _____

Introduce thesis in concise statement: _____

_____

Main Body:

    Background of topic.

    Thesis emphasized.

    Terminology, facts, data.

    Key words.

    Main points and arguments.

    Supporting points.

Conclusion:

    Restate thesis.

    Summarize key points.

    Present clear and strong conclusion.

Name _____   Date _____

Chapter Application   WORKSHEET 8.2

Project Board

Project _____   Due Date _____

Today's Date _____

Key Activities   Date Completed

_____   _____

_____   _____

_____   _____

_____   _____

_____   _____

_____   _____

_____   _____

_____   _____

_____   _____

_____   _____

_____   _____

_____   _____

_____   _____

_____   _____

_____   _____

_____   _____

Chapter Application   WORKSHEET 8.3

Rehearsing

Today your boss told you about an important presentation you must deliver to the management staff about a program you have been developing for budgeting. You want to start preparing for the presentation and to give yourself enough time to create a unique way to present your new ideas and information. You want to enhance your own delivery style and improve your performance so that management will understand your budget program fully.

Listed below are some ideas about presentations. Read this list and then add your own ideas:

1. Begin gathering materials and taking notes.
2. Practice visualizing yourself speaking successfully.
3. Prepare a rough draft of your presentation.
4. List the main points you want to make.
5. Prepare your handouts and overheads or visuals.
6. Recite material out loud.
7. Listen to how your presentation sounds.
8. Practice while you are jogging.
9. Give the presentation to a friend.
10. Go to the room where the presentation will be given.
11. Write a summary of the material on the board.
12. Integrate different learning styles as you explain material to your audience.
13. Time yourself.
14. Get a sense of the room, where you should stand, how you would arrange the chairs, etc. Now sit and review.
15. Eat a light meal, take a walk, or do a few jumping jacks before your presentation. Eat a nutritious and light breakfast.
16. Wear a professional outfit and follow good grooming habits.
17. Walk to the front of class with confidence.

18. _____

19. _____

20. _____

21. _____

Chapter Application   WORKSHEET 8.4

Essay Writing Tips

An essay is more than the right topic, thorough research, and a finely tuned thesis statement. It is also *good writing*. Good writing involves using

- good grammar.
- complete sentences.
- accurate punctuation.

- past tense instead of present whenever possible.
- appropriate vocabulary.

Here are areas of grammar that sometimes present problems for writers. Check yourself.

A. Subject-Verb Agreement

Sentences should always have subjects and verbs agree. This means that when the subject in a sentence is singular like *John, girl,* or *car,* the verb will also be singular like *walks, sings,* or *is.* However, if the subject in a sentence is plural like *John and Mary, girls,* or *cars,* then the verb will also be plural like *walk, sing,* or *are.*

Examples:

John walks to school.   John and Mary walk to school.
The girl sings very well.   The girls sing together.
The car is old.   The cars are old.

Write the correct verb that agrees with the subject on the line.

1. Parents often _____ their children nicknames. (give, gives)

2. A baby might _____ the nickname Red because of his hair color. (get, gets)

3. Most people _____ their nicknames. (enjoy, enjoys)

4. Nicknames _____ people. (interest, interests)

5. The seats _____ very uncomfortable in the stadium. (is, are)

B. Proper Use of Pronouns

The pronouns *I* and *we* should be used as subjects. The pronouns *me* and *us* should be used as objects.

Subject Examples:

Joe and I went to the concert.   We also went to the concert.

Object Examples:

The usher stood between   The music sounded wonderful
the stage and me.   to us.

Write the correct verb that agrees with the subject on the line.

1. The boss gave raises to _____ . (us, we)

2. All of _____ couldn't wait to begin. (we, us)

3. _____ watched the sunset. (We, Us)

4. Marge and _____ enjoyed the party. (I, me)

5. The next day, she told _____ about the party. (I, me)

C. Indefinite Pronouns and Verb Agreement

Do you know indefinite pronouns? Indefinite pronouns can be either singular or plural depending upon the meaning of the sentence. But they must always agree with the verb in the sentence. Use singular verbs with singular indefinite pronouns. Use plural verbs with plural indefinite pronouns. Here is a list to help you. Refer to it when you are writing. Use it to fill in the exercise below.

Indefinite Pronouns

Singular		Plural	Singular or Plural
one	nobody	few	most
no one	anybody	both	none
each	anyone	others	either
someone	anything	many	neither
something	everybody		
everyone			

Write the correct verb on the line.

1. Every night something _____ over our trash can. (knock, knocks)

2. Everybody _____ the game tic-tac-toe. (play, plays)

3. Most _____ their lunch to school. (bring, brings)

4. Others _____ their lunch. (buy, buys)

5. Someone _____ me a fax. (sent, sents)

D. Commas

A comma has many uses. Here are just a few of those uses.
- to set off the part of an address.
  I am going to Buffalo, New York.

- to set off parts of a date.
  I will be leaving on Monday, August 8, 2000.

- to set off introductory words or phrases.
  Wake her up, Vicki!
  No, I don't want to go.

- to set off a series of words.
  Bring a pen, pencil, and paper to class.
  Joe, Margo, Liz, and Pete are going to class.

Add commas where they are needed in the sentences below.

1. Put those boxes in the attic Sam.

2. On August 10 2000 I will deliver my report.

3. I invited Jill Mary Tom and Sue to the party.

4. I live in Williamsburg Virginia.

5. His sales call is at ZZZ Company 34 Putnam Street Olean New York.

Chapter Application WORKSHEET 8.5

Planning Grid

Use this grid as you prepare your written assignments and speeches.

Prewriting
Writing
Rewriting
Postwriting

	Preparation					Writing					Rewriting						Final Review			
	Topic: general, narrow topic.	Focus: thesis statement.	Identify audience and gather information.	Compile bibliography and notes.	Organize and outline.	Introduction.	Flesh out main idea.	Conclusion.	Write first draft.	Review.	Add, delete, rearrange information.	Write second draft.	Proof.	Confer with instructor.	Revise/share with writing group.	Revise again/compile bibliography.	Final check: grammar, spelling, documentation.	Make copy and meet deadline.	Evaluate results.	
Paper #1																				
Speech #1																				

CAREER DEVELOPMENT PORTFOLIO

Looking back: Try to recall any activities and events where you learned to write and speak. Jot down examples of classes, presentations, essays, journals, and papers.

Taking stock:

1. What are your strengths in writing and speaking?

   _____

   _____

2. What would you like to improve?

   _____

   _____

3. What are your feelings about writing and speaking?

   _____

   _____

Looking forward: Indicate how you would demonstrate writing and speaking skills to employers.

Documentation: Include letters, essays, speeches, and other examples. Who could write a letter of recommendation for you demonstrating that you have learned writing and speaking skills?

Application:

1. How can you demonstrate to employers that you have effective writing and speaking skills?

   _____

   _____

2. Include samples of speeches you have given in your portfolio. List titles below.

   _____

   _____

3. Include samples of your writing in your portfolio. List titles below.

   _____

   _____

4. Include samples of your research in your portfolio. List titles below.

   _____

   _____

CRITICAL THINKING AND CREATIVE PROBLEM SOLVING

"A problem is a picture with a piece missing; the answer is the missing piece."

—John Holt, educator and author

Learning Objectives

In Chapter 9 you will learn

- to prepare your mind for problem solving.

- the importance of critical thinking.

- common fallacies and errors in judgment.

- how to use problem solving for mathematics and science.

- how to overcome math anxiety.

- the importance of creativity in problem solving.

All problem solving—whether personal or academic—involves decision making. You have to make decisions to solve the problem, or some problems occur because of the decisions you have made. For example, in your private life you may decide to smoke cigarettes; later, you face the problem of nicotine addiction. In your school life, you may decide not to study mathematics and science because you consider them too hard. Because of this decision, many career opportunities will be closed to you. You can see that many events in your life do not just happen; they are the result of your choices and decisions. In this chapter, you will learn to use critical thinking and creativity to help solve both personal and academic problems. Mathematics and science will provide the framework in which to look at problem solving.

PREPARE YOUR MIND FOR PROBLEM SOLVING

The following strategies, based on a logical and scientific approach to problem solving, may help when you face a decision or try to solve a problem:

1. **Have a positive attitude.** Your attitude has a lot to do with how you approach and solve a problem or make a decision. Approach science and math courses with a positive and inquisitive attitude. Perceive problems as puzzles to solve rather than homework to avoid.

2. **Use critical thinking.** Critical thinking is a multidimensional process that involves decoding, analyzing, processing, reasoning, and evaluating information. It is also an attitude: a willingness and a passion to explore, probe, question, and search for answers and solutions. Critical thinking is fundamental to problem solving.

3. **Persistence pays off.** Coming to a solution requires sustained effort. A problem may not always be solved with your first effort. Sometimes a second or third try will see the results you need or want.

ATTRIBUTES OF A CRITICAL THINKER

- Willingness to ask pertinent questions and assess statements and arguments.
- Ability to suspend judgment and tolerate ambiguity.
- Ability to admit a lack of information or understanding.
- Curiosity and interest in seeking new solutions.
- Ability to define clearly a set of criteria for analyzing ideas.
- Willingness to examine beliefs, assumptions, and opinions against facts.

Success Principle 9: Focus on **DECISION MAKING**, not *Snap judgments*.

COMMON ERRORS IN JUDGMENT

Here are some common errors in judgment that interfere with critical thinking:

- Stereotypes are judgments and overgeneralizations held by a person or a group about members of another group, for example: "All instructors are absent-minded intellectuals." Learn to see individual differences between people and situations.

- Snap judgments are decisions made before all necessary information or facts are gathered. Too often people attempt to solve a problem before it is even determined what the problem is exactly.

- Unwarranted assumptions are beliefs and ideas that are taken for granted: Your business instructor allows papers to be turned in late, so you assume that your real estate instructor will allow the same.

- Projection is the tendency to attribute to others some of our own traits: "I cheat because everyone else is cheating."

- The halo effect is the tendency to label a person good at many things based on one or two qualities; for example, Serena sits in the front row, attends every class, and gets good grades on papers. Based on this observation, you decide that she is smart, organized, and nice, and a great student in all her classes. First impressions are important in the halo effect and are difficult to change.

- Sweeping generalizations are based on one experience and generalized to a whole group. For example, if research was conducted using college students as subjects, you cannot generalize the results to the overall work population.

PROBLEM-SOLVING STRATEGIES FOR MATH AND SCIENCE CLASSES

1. **Define the problem.** The first step in problem solving is to understand and define the problem before you can determine what is required to solve it. What is the situation or context of the problem? Can you separate the problem into various parts? Analyze the problem and the situation. The way you perceive a problem defines the problem. To define the problem clearly, state the problem in one or two sentences.

2. **Gather information and facts.** The next step is to make certain that you have all the necessary information to solve the problem. Scientists observe and ask questions. They ask themselves:

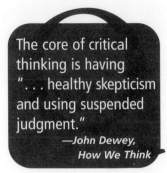

> The core of critical thinking is having "... healthy skepticism and using suspended judgment."
> —*John Dewey, How We Think*

- What is being asked?
- What do I know?
- What do I need to know?
- How do I set up this problem?
- What is my hypothesis?
- What is my theory?
- What are the main points?
- What are the relationships?
- What am I trying to find out?
- What factors will influence the outcome?
- What formulas, calculations, and constructions will be helpful?
- What theories, principles, or research will help me with this problem?

3. **Go from the general to the specific.** Look at the big picture as you gain a general understanding. Think of a more general problem. Then break the problem down step by step.

4. **Develop a plan.** Scientists formulate a hypothesis based on their observations, and this hypothesis becomes a statement or plan to be tested. What method will best help you solve this problem? Outline your step-by-step plan.

5. **Make connections.** Look for relationships and connections among different items. Use critical thinking skills to raise questions, separate facts from opinions, develop reasonable solutions, and make logical decisions. Make connections to unknown information and new information. Students who are successful with making connections often say, "This situation is similar to . . ." or "This reminds me of. . . . " Use all the data, conditions, and known factors in the problem. Connect what you learn in science and math classes to real life situations and to other classes.

6. **Be flexible and creative.** Approach the problem from a different direction and explore options. Intuition, estimation, and speculation are important. Don't erase your work. Ask questions and explore options. If you can't solve a problem in one of your academic subjects—like math, science, or accounting—write out a similar problem that you can do and examine the similarities and differences. If you still can't find a solution to the problem, take a break. Sometimes it helps to take a quick walk or relax for a few minutes and come back to the problem refreshed. When working on homework or test questions, always do the easiest problems first. Success builds success.

TRAILMARKER 9.1

Mathematics and Science Checklist

When you enroll in a math or science course, ask yourself these questions:

- Have you approached the class with a positive attitude?

- Have you built confidence by getting involved in problems?

- Have you clearly defined the problems?

- What do you want to know and what are you being asked to find out?

- Have you separated essential information from the unessential?

- Have you separated the known from the unknown?

- Have you asked a series of questions: How? When? Where? What? If?

- Have you devised a plan for solving the problem?

- Have you gone from the general to the specific?

- Have you explored formulas, theories, etc.?

- Have you made an estimate?

- Have you illustrated or organized the problem?

- Have you made a table or a diagram, drawn a picture, or summarized data?

- Have you written the problem?

- Have you discovered a pattern to the problem?

- Have you alternated intense concentration with frequent breaks?

- Have you tried working backward, completing similar problems, solving small parts?

- Have you determined if you made careless errors or do not understand the concepts?

- Do you think, apply, reflect, and practice?

- Have you asked for help early?

- Have you been willing to put in the time required to solve problems?

- Have you analyzed the problem? Was your guess close? Did your plan work? How else can you approach the problem?

- Have you rewarded yourself for facing your fears, overcoming anxiety, and learning valuable skills that will increase your success in school, your job, and in life?

The History of Your Anxiety

1. Try to recall your earliest experiences with math and science. Were those experiences positive or negative? Explain what made them negative or positive.

    _____

    _____

    _____

    _____

    _____

2. a. Did you struggle with math or science?

    _____

    _____

    b. Did you get help?

    _____

    c. Recall these memories as vividly as possible and write them down.

    _____

    _____

    _____

    _____

3. a. Summarize your feelings now about math.

    _____

    _____

    _____

    b. List all the reasons you want to succeed at math.

    _____

    _____

    _____

    _____

ASSESS AND REVIEW

1. **Summarize.** Summarize the problem in your own words and talk through the problem aloud. Explain the problem to someone else.

2. **Evaluate.** Go through each step and examine your work. Look at what you know and don't know and examine your hypotheses. Can you prove that each step is correct? Scientists analyze their findings. Examine the solution carefully. Can you obtain the solution differently? Investigate the connections of the problem. What formulas did you use? Can you use this same method for other problems? Can this study be reproduced to verify the results?

3. **Practice and be persistent.** Problem solving requires discipline and focused effort. It takes time, practice, and patience to learn any new skill. Don't look for quick, easy answers. Stay with the problem and concentrate.

Technology FOCUS: Math Anxiety

Check out this book's Web site to help you find sites that address math anxiety and how to deal with it.

http://www.peak.glencoe.com

CREATIVITY

One of the first steps in unlocking your creativity is to realize that you have control over your thinking; it doesn't control you. Creativity is thinking of something different, using new approaches to solve problems. Many inventions involved a breakthrough in traditional thinking and resulted in an "aha!" experience. For example, Einstein broke with tradition by trying many unusual approaches that revolutionized scientific thought. Your attitudes can form mental blocks that keep you from being creative. If you find yourself imprisoned by routines, afraid to look foolish, and reluctant to challenge the rules or allow failure, you may be in a rut. Before long, you may abandon your dreams; ignore your intuition; deny problems; and follow a safe, no-risk path. Try the following strategies to unlock your mind's natural creativity:

1. **Use games, puzzles, and humor.** Turn problems into puzzles to be solved. Rethinking an assignment as a puzzle, a challenge, or a game instead of a difficult problem allows an open frame of mind and encourages your creative side to operate. Creative people often get fresh ideas when they are having fun and are involved in an unrelated activity. When your defenses are down, your brain is relaxed and your subconscious is alive; creative thoughts can flow.

2. **Challenge the rules.** Habit often restricts you from trying new approaches to problem solving. Often there is more than one solution. List many alternatives, choices, and solutions and imagine the likely consequences of each. Empty your mind of the "right" way of looking at a problem and strive to see situations in a fresh, new way. How many times have you told yourself that you must follow certain rules and perform tasks a certain way? If you want to be creative, you must try new approaches, look at things in a new order, break the pattern, and challenge the rules. Try your hand at challenging the rules by completing the nine-dot exercise in Figure 9-1.

   Connect the following nine dots by drawing only four straight lines (or fewer, if you can). Do not retrace any lines and don't lift the pencil from the paper. (The answer is on page 9-11, Figure 9-2.)

Figure 9-1
Nine-Dot Exercise

3. **Brainstorm.** Brainstorming is a common creativity strategy that frees the imagination. With this strategy, a group throws out as many ideas as possible. Brainstorming encourages the mind to explore new approaches without judging the merit of these ideas. In fact, sometimes silly and irrelevant ideas can lead to truly inventive ideas. While brainstorming ideas for a speech, one study group started making jokes about the topic, and new ideas came from all directions. Again, humor generates ideas, puts you in a creative state of mind, and can make work fun. Top executives, scientists, doctors, and artists know that they can extend the boundaries of their knowledge by allowing themselves to extend their limits. They ask, What if?

CRITICAL
THINKING LOG
9.2

Mind-Sets

Look at the figure below. Do you see an attractive young woman or an old woman with a hooked nose? I see an _____.

If you saw the young woman, it is very hard to see the old woman. If you saw the old woman first, it is just as hard to see the young woman.

4. **Work to change mind-sets.** It is difficult to see another frame of reference once your mind is set. The exercise in Critical Thinking Log 9.2 was an "aha" exercise. It is exciting to watch people really *see* the other picture. There is enormous power in shifting your perception and gaining new ways of seeing things, events, and people. Perceptual exercises of this kind clearly demonstrate that we see what we focus on. You are conditioned to see certain things, depending on your beliefs and attitudes. Rather than seeing facts, you see your interpretation of reality. Perceptual distortion can influence how you solve problems and make decisions. To solve problems effectively, you need to see objects and events objectively, not through perceptual filters.

5. **Change your routine.** Try a different route to work or school. Order new dishes. Read different kinds of books. Become totally involved in a project. Stay in bed and read all day. Spend time with people who are different from you. In other words, break away occasionally from your daily routine and take time every day to relax, daydream, putter, and renew your energy. Look at unexpected events as an opportunity to retreat from constant activity and hurried thoughts. Perhaps this is a good time to brainstorm ideas for a speech assignment or outline an assigned paper. Many creative people need an incubation period in which ideas have time to develop.

TIP Try not to let your previous experiences influence your expectations on how to solve a new problem.

Creative Problem-Solving Techniques

Here are some easy techniques for identifying new ways to solve problems:

1. Act it out.

2. Move it around.

3. Picture it.

4. Take it apart.

5. Translate and summarize.

6. Simplify.

7. Estimate.

8. Work with a partner.

9. Ask questions.

10. Sleep on it.

6. **Allow failure.** Creative people know that if they don't fail occasionally, they are not risking anything. Mistakes are stepping-stones to growth and creativity. Fear of failure undermines the creative process by forcing us to play it safe. You must eliminate the fear and shame of failure experienced in earlier years and learn to admit mistakes. Looking at your mistakes as stepping-stones and opportunities for growth will allow this shift. Ask yourself, "What did I learn from this mistake? How can I handle the same type of situation the next time? How can I prepare for a situation like this the next time?"

   Creative people aren't afraid to look foolish at times, to generate unusual ideas, and to be nonconformists. They tend not to take themselves too seriously. Being creative has a lot to do with risk-taking and courage. It takes courage to explore new ways of thinking and to risk looking different, foolish, impractical, and even wrong.

7. **Expect to be creative.** To be a creative person, you must try to see yourself as a creative person. Use affirmations that reinforce your innate creativity:

   ● I am a creative and resourceful person.

   ● I have many imaginative and unusual ideas.

- Creative ideas flow to me many times a day.
- I live creatively in the present.
- I act on many of these ideas.
- When in the action stage, I act responsibly, use critical thinking, check details carefully, and take calculated risks.

TIP Practice problems and keep up with assignments. Working with a study partner is a great way to understand and practice math. Use creativity strategies to think outside the box.

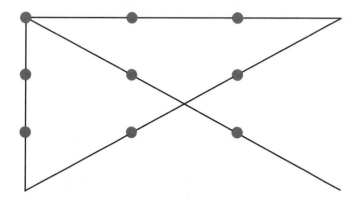

Figure 9-2
Answer to Nine-Dot Exercise

8. **Support, acknowledge, and reward creativity.** If you honor new ideas, they will grow. Get excited about new ideas and approaches, and acknowledge and reward yourself and others for creative ideas. Give yourself many opportunities to get involved with projects that encourage you to explore and be creative. Monitor your daily life as well. How often do you put your creative ideas into action? Is there anything you want to change but keep putting it off? What new hobby or skill have you wanted to try? If you find yourself getting lazy, set a firm deadline to complete a specific project. If you find yourself running frantically, then take an hour or so to review your life's goals and to set new priorities. If you are feeling shy and inhibited, clear some time to socialize and risk meeting new people. Reward your creativity and risk-taking by acknowledging it.

9. **Use both sides of the brain.** You use the logical, analytical side of your brain for certain activities and your imaginative and multidimensional side for others. When you develop and integrate both the left and the right sides of your brain, you become more imaginative, creative, and productive. Learn to be attentive to details and to trust intuition.

10. **Keep a journal.** Keep a journal of creative ideas, dreams, and thoughts and make a commitment to complete journal entries daily. Collect stories of creative people. Write in your journal about the risks you take and your imaginative and different ideas.

Solving Problems

Stating a problem clearly, exploring alternatives, reasoning logically, choosing the best alternative, creating an action plan, and evaluating your plan are all critical thinking skills involved in making decisions and solving problems. Use critical thinking to answer the following questions. Be prepared to discuss your answers in your study teams.

1. Do you consider yourself to be a creative person? Explain.

_____

_____

2. Describe a recent period when you were creative. What did you do?

_____

_____

3. Where were you when you came up with your last creative idea?

_____

_____

4. Look at the common reasons and excuses that some students use for not solving problems creatively or making sound decisions. Add to this list and use creative problem solving to list strategies for overcoming these barriers.

Reasons

I'm not a creative person.
Strategy: _____

_____

Facts can be misleading. I like to follow my emotions.
Strategy: _____

_____

I avoid conflict.
Strategy: _____

_____

I postpone making decisions.
Strategy: _____

_____

I worry that I'll make the wrong decision.
Strategy: _____

_____

CREATIVITY AT WORK

Creativity is a trait often associated with artists, writers, and performers. We can all see how important creativity is for a cartoonist or a comedian, but it is also important in most jobs. Fast-food workers are creative when they come up with new ways to be efficient in a competitive industry. Manufacturers are creative when they raise productivity and reduce costs. Salespeople are creative when they design ways to increase customer satisfaction and sales. Creativity is exploring different alternatives in making decisions and solving problems.

Of course, creativity is a valuable job skill. Too often employees fall into the routines they've always followed, which leads to burnout and negative thinking. The employee who can see situations and problems in a fresh way, explore alternatives and options, and come up with innovative ideas and thoughts is certain to be hired and promoted.

Let's look at one approach to creative problem solving on the job. Basil Clay manages a pizza parlor. He knows there is stiff competition and many small pizza businesses fail. He considers what extra touches his business could offer while maintaining a profit. Since the business is located in a college town, Basil has decided to create a college night. On this night, he will show movies and offer free popcorn at the restaurant. Saturday nights, he will feature family-type movies and give prizes for children. There will also be a special senior's night, when he will show old movies. After just a few weeks, Basil's ideas work. With just a little creativity, his business now makes a larger profit and keeps customers interested and loyal.

Basil also uses creativity and brainstorming to solve workload issues. His staff agrees that production and service cannot be kept at a high level unless additional work hours are added to the regular schedule. Should Basil hire new employees, or ask regular employees to work overtime? An example of his brainstorming notes are shown in Figure 9–3 on page 9-14.

Basil's Pizza   Sept. 29, 2000

Brainstorming Notes

Problem: Should I hire temporary employees or increase overtime of
my regular employees to meet new production schedule?

Ideas	Evaluation	Plus + or Minus –	Selection
hire temp. employees	may lack training	–	1. hire temps
	additional benefits	–	
work regular employees			
overtime	may result in fatigue	–	
	extra $ for employee	+	
	higher morale	+	
	possible advancement	+	
	cross training	+	
	save on overhead		
	& benefits	+	
turn down contract	not possible		
reduce hours store is open	not feasible		
reduce product line	not acceptable		

2. work overtime
explore further

Figure 9–3
Brainstorming Notes

Sometimes it's not just enough to create an idea—you have to sell it! (Meaning, convince others—because when you come up with a new idea, it's just you at that point.) How can Basil sell his ideas to his staff?

_____

_____

_____

_____

_____

_____

_____

_____

_____

CRITICAL THINKING LOG 9.4

Can Child Care Be a Problem?

Read the following paragraph and the accompanying questions. Then write your comments on the lines provided. Be ready to discuss your thoughts in class or with your study team.

Having and caring for a child is expensive. Experts estimate that it costs over $250,000 to raise a child. This sizable commitment is only part of the cost. It takes an enormous commitment of time and an emotional investment as well to raise a child. Add all the costs of having a baby and think critically about how every aspect of someone's life would change with the entrance of a child.

1. What changes would occur in your life if you were to be responsible for a child nine months from now?

   _____

   _____

2. How would having a child affect your education?

   _____

   _____

3. Can you afford a child?

   _____

   _____

4. Could you be the main source of support, both emotionally and financially, for a child?

   _____

   _____

5. What do you think are the main causes of unplanned pregnancies? Consider, for example, ignorance, poor judgment, pressure, and a romantic and unrealistic image of babies?

   _____

   _____

"Whether you believe you can, or whether you believe you can't, you're absolutely right."
— *auto inventor Henry Ford*

TRAILMARKER 9.3

Creative Ideas Checklist

Use this checklist to challenge usual thought patterns. When exploring alternative approaches to problem solving, you can put each category on separate cards. Here are some examples you might find helpful:

- What other idea does this situation suggest?
- How can I modify?
- What can I subtract? Can I take it apart?
- What can I streamline?
- What can I rearrange?
- Can I translate?
- Can I combine or blend?
- What are other uses if modified?
- What can I model?
- Can I use another approach?
- Can I interchange components?
- Are there any opposites?
- What are the positives and negatives?
- Have I used a mind map?
- Have I used a drawing?
- Have I acted it out?
- Can I draw a picture or visualize it?
- Should I sleep on it?
- List some of your own suggestions for creative problem solving.

_____

_____

_____

_____

_____

_____

"A hunch is creativity trying to tell you something."

— *Hollywood director Frank Capra*

Technology
FOCUS:
Computers and **C**ritical **T**hinking

Computers can help you with critical thinking and creative problem solving. Use the computer to

1. help you define problems; gather information; brainstorm ideas and solutions; create diagrams and flow charts; and make columns listing pros, cons, and likely consequences.

2. increase your creativity.

3. explore majors and careers.

4. explore this book's Web site for additional information about decision making and critical thinking.

http://peak.glencoe.com

TRAILMARKER 9.4

You Can Solve the Problem

Every day you solve problems. You make choices. Some problems are easy to solve. *What's for dinner?* Some problems are harder. *Can I afford to buy a car?* Some problems change a life forever. *Should I get married?*

You will face problems and choices. You might make good or poor choices. You don't know how a choice will turn out. However, you can follow some steps. They may help you see chances. Show you risks. Point out other choices. The steps are:

Step 1 Know what the problem really is.
Is it a daily problem?
Is it a once-in-a-lifetime problem?

Step 2 List the things you know about the problem. List the things you don't.
Ask questions. Seek help and advise.

Step 3 Know the other choices.

Step 4 Think about the "good" and "bad" for the other choices. Rank them from best to worst choice.

Step 5 Pick the choice you feel good about.

Step 6 After choosing, study what happens. Are you happy about the choice?
Would you make it again?

Read about José.

José is fifty years old. He has a wife and three kids. He has worked twenty years for the same company. The company is relocating. Only a few people will move with the company. Many workers will be losing their jobs.

José's boss says he can keep his job, but he has to move. If he doesn't, he won't have a job. The family has always lived in this town. José's daughter is a senior in high school and wants to go to the local college next year. His twin boys will be in junior high and are looking forward to playing next year for the ninth-grade football team. José's wife works part-time in a bakery. She has many friends and all her family live nearby.

The family talked about the move. His wife is afraid. His daughter doesn't want to move. The twins will miss their friends. The family has to decide about the move. What is their problem? What are the choices? Can you help them? Use the steps below.

Step 1 The problem is _____

_____

_____.

Is it a daily problem? _____

Is it a once-in-a-lifetime problem? _____

Step 2 You know _____

_____

_____

You don't know _____

_____

_____

Step 3 The other choices are _____

_____

_____.

Step 4 Rank the choices. _____

_____

_____

Step 5 Pick a choice the family might feel good about. _____

_____

_____

Step 6 What might happen _____

_____

_____.

SCOTT ADAMS

A popular comic strip is *Dilbert,* the creation of cartoonist Scott Adams. This left-brain, technologically trained and experienced artist has been described as creative. He is a good example of how creativity can be combined successfully with critical thinking.

Scott Adams earned a degree in economics in 1979 from Harwick College in Oneonta, New York, and moved to the San Francisco Bay Area. He worked at a series of low-paying jobs at a bank (he was robbed twice at gunpoint) while he completed his MBA. From 1986 until 1995, he worked at a major communications company in a technical job. While working in a cubicle, he observed office politics and relationships and saw the funny and absurd side of work. He had no drawing experience, but he practiced doodling during boring meetings and during his free time. These cartoons were eventually circulated in his office, and he used them in business presentations. Positive responses prompted him to send sample strips to major cartoon syndicates. Adams is now a syndicated cartoonist and *Dilbert* appears in 1700 newspapers in fifty-one countries. There are thirteen *Dilbert* books in print, and *Dilbert* is also the first comic strip to be made available on the Internet.

His advice to students is to combine technical and communication skills: "My single greatest piece of advice, and the one thing that separates the engineers and technicians in cubicles from other people who become speakers and leaders, is to have great communication skills." He also stresses the importance of reading widely and developing all your talents and interests. "I have a deep interest in a wide variety of technologies, and I'm also a certified hypnotist." Scott Adams is a Peak Performer.

Source: http://peak.glencoe.com

9 Review and Study Notes

Affirmations

- I see all problems as opportunities for practicing my skills and for growth.
- I know I have the wisdom, confidence, and good judgment to handle any problem or to make any decision.
- I am a creative person and act on many creative ideas.
- I use critical thinking to solve problems and make decisions.

Visualization

See yourself as a receptor of many creative ideas. They flow through you, and you can act on the best ones. You are aware, alive, and alert. You view problems as opportunities and challenges to test your problem-solving strategies and gain confidence. You make decisions easily but with care and learn from your mistakes. You look forward with enthusiasm, never backward with regret.

Peak Performance Strategies for Math and Science

1. Create a positive attitude and focus on the benefits.
2. Be realistic.
3. Go to every class.
4. Be creative and patient.
5. Make connections.
6. Go from general to specific.
7. Ask questions.
8. Use all your senses.
9. Use study teams.
10. Use precise language.
11. Review and practice often.

CASE Studies

CASE A | In the Classroom

Martha Lee Brody is a single mom who works part-time and lives and goes to school in the inner city. She is an electronics student who wants her classes to be practical and relevant. She is required to take a class in critical thinking, a class she is resisting because she sees no practical application to her job. Her attitude is affecting her attendance and participation.

1. Can you offer ideas to help Martha see the importance of critical thinking in decision making?

_____

_____

_____

_____

2. Can you help her connect decisions in school with job decisions?

_____

_____

_____

_____

Some of these decisions include the following:

School

Should I go to school full-time?   What major should I choose?
Where should I go to school?   Is there a penalty for missing classes?
Which classes should I take?

Career

Should I work full-time?   Which career should I consider?
Where should I work?   Will my career suffer if I miss deadlines?
Which projects should I work on?

CASE A

Martha is now a manager in a small electronics business. She is also taking evening classes working toward a business degree. She has received promotions quickly on her job, but she knows that she needs further management training.

Martha is keenly interested in the electronics field and loves to solve problems. She is faced daily with issues to solve and decisions to make. She has lots of practice predicting consequences and using critical thinking for problem solving.

Martha enjoys most of the business classes, but she doesn't want to take some of the classes in finance and statistics. Martha has math anxiety and is dreading the upper division math and statistics classes.

1. What strategies in this chapter can help Martha overcome math anxiety?

_____

_____

_____

_____

2. What are some affirmations Martha could use to help develop a positive attitude about math?

_____

_____

_____

_____

3. What other suggestions would you share with Martha?

_____

_____

_____

_____

CASE B

Cody Senkow is a computer student at a career school. He takes a full load of classes and also works full-time. He could handle this schedule during his first year, but now he has more demanding classes and a valuable internship. Cody faces a decision: should he stay in school full-time, concentrate on getting good grades, and give his all to the internship? This decision would mean a reduction in his work hours or on-campus employment as a work-study student. Or should he go to school part-time and continue to work full-time? Going to school full-time would get him into the workforce earlier, but he has grown accustomed to having money for a nice car, clothes, and social expenses. He lives close to his school and if he worked only part-time on campus, he could sell his car and take the bus or bike around town and campus.

1. What decision would be the most economical?

_____

_____

2. What suggestions can you give Cody to help him make a sound decision?

_____

_____

In the Workplace

Two years ago Cody founded a small computer firm of his own. He had one of the most outstanding sales records ever achieved at a small computer company. Now he has to decide if he should expand or streamline his product line. If he is to serve the needs of local businesses and colleges, he must diversify. If Cody expands his company, he will need to add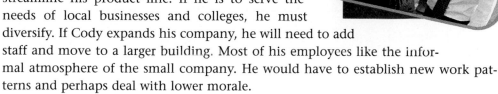
staff and move to a larger building. Most of his employees like the informal atmosphere of the small company. He would have to establish new work patterns and perhaps deal with lower morale.

1. What suggestions can you offer to help Cody make a sound decision about expanding his company?

_____

_____

2. What problem-solving strategies from this chapter can help Cody?

_____

_____

> **TIP** From the Workplace
>
> The classes I took in college on critical thinking (math, science, logic) were very helpful on the job. I use a problem-solving approach to think through management decisions. I use a combination of intuition and critical thinking to make good decisions. This is something I use daily.
> —Water resource engineer, manager

Chapter Application   WORKSHEET 9.1

Preparing for Critical Thinking

Brainstorm alternative approaches and solutions to the problems that arise in your day-to-day activities. By using critical thinking, you will be able to explore new ideas.

Issue/Problem in Day-to-Day Activities:

_____

_____

_____

_____

Alternative A

Benefits	Limit	Consequences	Cost	Timing

Alternative B

Benefits	Limit	Consequences	Cost	Timing

Chapter Application   WORKSHEET 9.1 (CONTINUED)

Alternative C

Benefits	Limit	Consequences	Cost	Timing

Alternative D

Benefits	Limit	Consequences	Cost	Timing

Alternative E

Benefits	Limit	Consequences	Cost	Timing

Chapter Application   WORKSHEET 9.2

You Can Solve the Problem

Every day you solve problems. Some problems are easy to solve. Should I do my shopping now or later? Some problems are harder. My car is in the shop. How will I get to work? Some problems change a life forever. Can I afford to go to school?

Every day life brings problems and choices. The kinds of choices you make can make your life easier or harder. Things may go right or wrong. Often, you do not know which way it will go. But there are ways to help you be more certain. There are steps you can take. You can look at your choices before you make them. You can see some of the problems you may face. You may find you have other or better choices. Here are some steps to help you make choices.

Step 1   Know what the problem really is. Is it a daily problem? Is it a once in a lifetime problem?

Step 2   List the things you know about the problem. List the things you don't know. Ask questions. Get help and advice.

Step 3   Know your other choices.

Step 4   Think about a good and a bad for the other choices. Put them in order from best to worst.

Step 5   Pick the choice you feel good about.

Step 6   Study what happens after you make your choice. Are you happy about the choice? Would you make it again?

Read the story below:

Sue has cancer. Her doctor told her that it is in only one place in her body. The doctor wants to operate on Sue's cancer. He thinks that will take all of it away, but he still wants Sue to do something else. He wants her to take medicine for four months. The medicine will make her feel very sick. It will make her tired, but the medicine can help keep the cancer from coming back.

Sue is not sure what to do. She has two small children who are not in school. Sue's husband works days and cannot help care for the children during the day. Sue's family lives far away and she cannot afford day care. She asks herself, "How will I be able to care for my children if I am sick?"

The doctor told Sue that she must make her own choice. Will she take the medicine? Sue must decide. She will talk with her husband and they will make a choice together.

What is Sue's problem? What are her choices? What would you decide? Write in the steps that follow that would help you make a choice:

Name _____   Date _____

Step 1   The problem is _____

_____

_____

Step 2

a. You know these things about the problem:

_____

_____

b. You don't know these things about the problem:

_____

_____

Step 3   The other choices are:

_____

_____

Step 4   Rank the choices, best to worst.

_____

_____

Step 5   Pick a choice the family might feel good about. _____

_____

_____

Step 6   What might happen to Sue and her family?

_____

_____

Chapter Application   WORKSHEET 9.3

Overcoming Barriers to Creativity

Keep an ongoing list of barriers to creative thinking and methods for overcoming these barriers.

Creativity Builders	Creativity Barriers
Bright colors	Fear
Music	Worry
Creative, fun people	People who say, "You act silly."

Chapter Application   WORKSHEET 9.4

You Can Solve the Problem

You make choices and solve problems every day. Some choices are automatic and don't require much thought like stopping a car at the red light or stepping on the gas pedal when the light turns green. Other problems require you to make easy choices such as which TV show to watch. Other problems are more difficult to solve, for example, what to say to your teenage son or daughter when he or she comes home past curfew smelling like beer.

In your life you will face many problems and choices. You might make good or poor choices because you don't always know how a choice will turn out.

There are some steps you can follow to help you make a good choice and solve your problem. These steps can help you think of options and improve your problem-solving skills. The steps are:

Step 1   Stop and think. Take a deep breath before you say or do something you will regret.

Step 2   Write a problem statement. Be sure to include who has the problem and state it clearly.

Step 3   Write a goal statement. Check to see that it has simple, realistic, and positive words.

Step 4   List all your choices, both the good and the bad choices.

Step 5   Remove choices that don't match your goal, will hurt others, or will cause more problems than they will solve.

Step 6   Make your best choice. Check Step 3 to be sure your choice matches your goal.

Read the story below:

Casey has been divorced for three years and her children visit their father every other weekend. When he brought the children home this weekend he told Casey that he is planning to remarry.

Now her children will have a stepmother and Casey is worried how everyone will get along. She wants her children to still visit their dad and enjoy the visits.

Can you help Casey solve this problem? Follow the six steps to help Casey make a good choice.

Name _____   Date _____

1. What is the first thing Casey should do? (See Step 1.)

   _____

   _____

2. Write a problem statement.

   _____

   _____

   _____

3. What is Casey's goal?

   _____

   _____

   _____

4. List as many choices as you can for Casey.

   _____

   _____

   _____

5. Which choices should Casey cross off her list?

   _____

   _____

6. What is the best choice for Casey to make?

   _____

   _____

   _____

7. Does the choice she made match her goal in Step 3?

   _____

   _____

Name _____   Date _____

Matrix for Critical Thinking

Question
Cause and Effect
Check
Assess

	Question				Anticipate				Analyze				Assess			
	Clearly state the problem.	Question your assumptions.	Question credentials.	Make a list of questions.	Anticipate outcomes and probabilities.	Predict consequences.	Look for cause and effect.	Anticipate trends and patterns.	Analyze facts.	Interpret data.	Make inferences and analyze.	Analyze flaws and inconsistencies.	Assess accuracy.	Assess facts and data.	Ensure that information is objective and reliable.	Adjust and modify.
Decision #1:																
Decision #2:																
Decision #3:																
Decision #4:																

ASSESSING AND DEMONSTRATING CRITICAL THINKING

Looking back: Review your worksheets to find activities in which you learned to make decisions and solve problems creatively. Jot down examples. Also look for examples of how you learned to apply critical thinking skills to math and science.

_____

_____

_____

_____

Taking stock: What are your strengths in making decisions and in using critical thinking. Are you a creative person? What areas would you like to improve?

_____

_____

_____

_____

Looking forward: How would you demonstrate critical thinking and creative problem-solving skills to an employer?

_____

_____

_____

_____

Documentation: Include documentation of your critical thinking and creative problem-solving skills. Find an instructor or employer who will write a letter of recommendation. Add this letter to your portfolio.

_____

_____

_____

_____

10

HEALTH AND STRESS

"If there is one coefficient of entrepreneurial success, it is energy. You may have all the ambition in the world, gobs of capital, a gambling man's soul, and business degrees covering an entire wall, but if you are not a human dynamo, forget it."

—Joseph R. Mancuso, author of
Have You Got What It Takes?

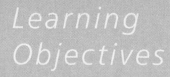

Learning Objectives

In Chapter 10 you will learn

- the importance of health.
- how to make healthy choices in your diet.
- the importance of a regular exercise program.
- how to protect yourself from disease, unplanned pregnancy, and rape.
- how to make sound decisions about alcohol and drugs.
- how to control stress and reduce anxiety.
- how to recognize depression and suicidal tendencies.

Creating balance, increasing energy, and providing time for renewal are some of the keys to becoming a Peak Performer. The purpose of this chapter is to present principles and guidelines to help you develop the most effective methods of maintaining your health while dealing with daily demands.

YOUR BODY AS A SYSTEM

Your body is good example of a working system. If you take an aspirin for a headache, the tablet doesn't just isolate the pain in your head but travels through your bloodstream and affects other parts of your body. Many factors affect your health and energy and are interrelated, factors such as exercise, food, sleep, drugs, stress, and your state of mind.

You will encounter many demands that require an enormous amount of effort at various times. Papers, reports, deadlines, tests, performance reviews, conflicts, committees, commuting, family responsibilities, and presentations are all part of school, career, and life. These demands will also bring an enormous amount of stress. Stress is not an external event but part of a larger system, and it affects every part of your body and mind.

AWARENESS

The first step in managing your health is awareness. Observe how your body feels, the thoughts going through your mind, and your level of stress. Be aware of negative habits. You may not even realize that you eat every time you watch television, drink several cans of soda while you study, nibble while you fix dinner, or eat your children's leftovers. You may discover that fast food has become a routine to save time or that you have developed the habit of skipping breakfast. Observe your daily habits and begin to replace unproductive ones with beneficial choices.

Have you gained excess weight, or experienced discomfort or a change in your body? If you can identify symptoms and early warning signs of illness, you can take appropriate action.

OBSERVE CAUTION SIGNS
The American Cancer Society provides the following guidelines for monitoring your own health. See your doctor if you notice any of the following:

C   Change in bowel or bladder habits.
A   A sore that does not heal.
U   Unusual bleeding or discharge.
T   Thickening or lump in the breast or elsewhere.
I   Indigestion or difficulty in swallowing.
O   Obvious changes in a wart or mole.
N   Nagging cough or hoarseness.

Source: See this book's Web site for further information about cancer research.
http://peak.glencoe.com

Success Principle 10:
Focus on **QUALITY,**
not *Quantity*.

CRITICAL THINKING LOG 10.1

Becoming Attuned to Your Body

Set aside a few minutes of quiet, private time. Stop what you are doing and close your eyes. Try to focus on your body. Observe its reactions to these few minutes of quiet. Notice your breathing. Write your observations on the lines provided.

1. How were you sitting? _____

2. What was your state of mind? _____

3. Were you feeling rested, energetic, or tired? _____ Yes _____ No

4. Did you observe pain anywhere in your body? If so, where?

   _____

5. Was there any feeling of tension? _____Yes _____ No

6. Were you holding your shoulders up? _____Yes _____ No

7. Were you clenching your jaw? _____ Yes _____ No

Try to stop and discern how you're feeling, several times a day.

FIVE STRATEGIES FOR GOOD HEALTH MANAGEMENT

1. **Eat healthy foods for high energy.** You must eat a nutritional diet daily to control obesity and high blood pressure and to reduce depression, anxiety, headaches, fatigue, and insomnia. Many theories try to explain which foods are best to keep you healthy and whether or not you need vitamin and mineral supplements. Some nutritionists say that a healthy diet supplies all the vitamins and minerals you need. Others disagree. The recommended daily allowances (RDAs) developed by the U.S. Senate Select Committee on Nutrition provide guidelines for determining if you consume enough vitamins and minerals.

   - *Eat a variety of foods.* Include whole grains, lots of fruits and vegetables, milk, meats, poultry, fish, and breads and cereals in your diet.

   - *Cut down on salt and caffeine.* Caffeine is found in soft drinks, coffee, tea, and chocolate. Salt is often an ingredient in prepared foods.

   - *Eat plenty of fresh fruits and vegetables.* Fruits and vegetables are excellent sources not only of cancer-preventing fiber but also of vitamins.

- *Take a multivitamin supplement every day.* Many experts advise taking vitamin and mineral supplements for optimal health. Some recommend extra C, E, B complex, and A vitamins if you are under stress.
- *Increase whole grain cereals and breads.* Whole grains contain fiber, vitamins, and minerals. They are also filling and will keep you from snacking.
- *Reduce the amount of animal fat in your diet.* Too much animal fat can clog your cardiovascular system, which causes your body to get less oxygen.
- *Broil, bake, or steam meats rather than fry them.* Use olive oil or other mono-unsaturated fat instead of butter or lard.
- *Cut down on sugar.* Sugar has no nutritional value and promotes tooth decay. You don't have to eliminate treats, but keep in mind that they do not build health and are filled with empty calories.
- *Use alcohol in moderation.* If you drink alcoholic beverages, drink only one or two a day. Too much alcohol increases the risk of certain cancers, cirrhosis of the liver, damage to the heart and brain, and hemorrhage strokes. Never drink and drive.

2. **Maintain your ideal weight.** You will have more energy and higher self-esteem, and you will be generally healthier when you maintain your ideal weight. Weight maintenance is a major problem for many people, and millions of dollars are spent every year on fad diets, exercise equipment, and promises of a quick fix. There are many support groups for weight control that can be very helpful. If you do need to lose weight, don't try to do it too quickly with fad diets or fasting. Consult a physician to discuss the best method for you. Slow weight loss is more effective and helps to keep the weight off longer. Fasting can lead to major health problems. Dieting suggests a quick fix or short-term solution. Building energy by nourishing and helping the body to do its job effectively takes a long-term commitment to changing habits. Try taking a walk when you have the urge to snack.

- *Eat only when you're hungry.* Make sure you eat to sustain your body and not because you are depressed, lonely, bored, or worried.
- *Don't fast.* When a person fasts or dramatically reduces daily caloric intake, the body's metabolic rate decreases, so the body burns calories more slowly than before. After starving, the body has an urge to binge, which is nature's way of trying to survive famine.
- *Eat regularly.* Don't skip meals. If you are really rushed, carry a banana, an apple, raw vegetables, or nuts with you. Establish a three-meals-a-day pattern. You must eat regularly and have a balanced diet to lose weight and keep it off. Don't eat big meals, especially right before a test or when you need to study.

You and Your Health

Read the following and write your comments on the lines provided.

1. Do you maintain your ideal weight? If not, what can you do to achieve your ideal weight?

   _____

   _____

2. Describe a few of your healthy eating habits.

   _____

   _____

3. Describe a few of your unhealthy eating habits.

   _____

   _____

4. Do you feel you have control over your eating? Explain.

   _____

   _____

5. What can you do to make positive and lasting changes in your eating habits?

   _____

   _____

- *Create healthy patterns.* Eat slowly and enjoy your food. Eat in one or two main places. For example, eat in the dining room or at the kitchen table. Resist the urge to eat on the run, sample food while you are cooking, munch in bed, eat while watching television, or snack throughout the day.

- *Get help.* Do you have a problem with weight control or are you overly concerned with being thin? Do you have a problem with eating too little or with fasting? Do you eat and then throw up as a way to control your weight? Bulimia and anorexia are illnesses and need a doctor's treatment. Many resources can offer help. Look in the Yellow Pages or discuss your problem frankly with your doctor.

Eating for Health and Energy

Benefical eating and exercise habits can pay off big dividends for career and life success. Researchers have studied the effects of diet for years and attempt to agree on the best diet for most people. In 1993, the Harvard School of Public Health sponsored a major conference on nutrition. Scientists and nutritionists from the United States and Europe met to look at the traditional Mediterranean diet, which has prolonged life and prevented disease for centuries in Mediterranean countries. The experts released a model similar to that of the United States Department of Agriculture food guide pyramid. The Mediterranean model suggests more beans and legumes over animal-based proteins and advocates the use of olive oil in a daily diet.

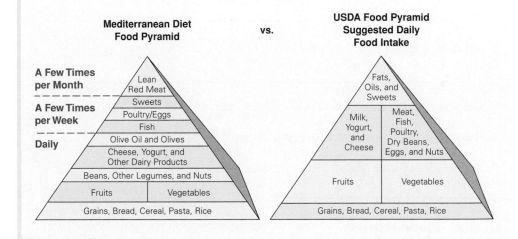

3. **Renew energy through rest.** It is important for good health and energy to get enough rest. Although amounts vary from one person to the next, most people need between six and nine hours of sound sleep a night. The answer is not to be concerned about the number of hours of sleep that you require, but whether or not you feel rested, alert, and energized. Some people wake up rested after five hours of sleep; others need at least nine hours to feel energized and refreshed. If you wake up tired, try going to bed earlier for a night or two and then establish a consistent bedtime. Notice if you are using sleep to escape conflict, depression, or boredom. It is also important to find time to relax each day. Your body requires activity and rest every day to stay healthy. Some people say they need less sleep when they exercise regularly.

4. Exercise for energy. Aerobic exercise raises the heart rate above its normal rate and keeps it there for twenty or more minutes. Regular aerobic exercise is essential for keeping your body at peak performance. Aerobics strengthens every organ in the body (especially the heart), reduces stress, strengthens the immune system, increases muscle strength, reduces excess fat, stimulates the lymph system, and increases your endurance and stamina. Exercise can also alter body chemistry by changing hormones, adjusting metabolism, and stimulating the brain to release more endorphins. Endorphins are natural chemicals in the body that affect your state of mind. How much exercise you need to stay in good physical health depends on your goals, your present fitness level, overall health, and your physician's advice. For most healthy people, a regular program of twenty to thirty minutes of aerobic exercise is needed at least three times a week for optimum health. There are many ways to exercise aerobically. Brisk walking, swimming, bicycling, dancing, jogging, jumping rope, and doing tae bo are some of the popular ways. The key is to start slowly, build up gradually, and be consistent! If you experience pain during aerobic exercise, stop.

CRITICAL THINKING LOG 10.3   Exercise Commitment

Read the following and write your comments on the lines provided.

1. Describe your commitment to exercising your body.

   _____

   _____

2. What excuses do you give for not exercising? What can you do to overcome these barriers and make exercise a daily habit?

   _____

   _____

CAFFEINE IS A DRUG TOO

A small amount of caffeine can enhance alertness and effectiveness and be a source of pleasure and comfort. A cup or two of coffee in the morning can give you a burst of energy, create a sense of well-being, and does not pose a health problem for most people. Caffeine is not found just in coffee, however; it is also found in tea, many soft drinks, chocolate, and some medications. Thus, it is easy to consume too much caffeine and become anxious, nervous, jittery, irritable, and insomnia-prone. Too much caffeine may deplete your B vitamins, minerals, and other nutrients that your body needs to cope with stress. Caffeine can be addictive; the more you take in, the more it takes to produce that desired burst of energy. If you find yourself experiencing caffeine-induced symptoms, reduce your intake but do so gradually. Headaches can result from rapid caffeine withdrawal. Try substituting decaffeinated coffee, tea, or soft drinks, or herbal tea. Check labels to confirm that your substitutions are indeed caffeine-free.

CRITICAL THINKING LOG 10.4

Proper Rest

Read the following and write your comments on the lines provided.

1. Do you wake up in the morning feeling rested and eager to start the day?

_____

_____

_____

2. What else rests and renews your body and spirit besides sleep?

_____

_____

_____

5. **Healthy relationships provide energy.** Healthy relationships can be a wonderful source of increased energy. We all know the deep satisfaction of sharing a good talk or a wonderful evening with a friend, or the sense of pride and accomplishment when we've completed a team project. Indeed, people can help us think through problems, develop self-confidence, conquer fears, develop courage, brainstorm ideas, overcome boredom and fatigue, and increase our joy and laughter. Some barriers to healthy relationships are

- getting so busy at school and work or with your goals that you ignore your friends and family.

- being shy and finding it difficult to build friendships.

- approaching friendship as a competitive sport.

It takes sensitivity and awareness to value others' needs and confidence to overcome shyness. The key is to see the enormous value of friendships. Personal friends bring a deep sense of joy and fellowship to life. Life's sorrows and setbacks are lessened when you have friends to support and help you through difficult times. You will find yourself energized by good friends.

ALCOHOL ABUSE

Alcohol is one of the biggest energy drains to your body. As a drug, it can alter moods, become habit-forming, and cause changes in the body. As a depressant, it actually depresses the central nervous system.

Alcoholism can begin as early as childhood and usually results from peer pressure. A major life lesson is to think for yourself and be responsible for your choices and behavior. For most adults, a glass of wine or a beer at dinner will not be a problem; but it is important to realize that even a small amount of alcohol can result in slowed reactions and poor judgment.

CRITICAL THINKING ABOUT ALCOHOL

It is important to use critical thinking to make sound decisions about drinking. High school and college drinking have become a major social problem. U.S. students consume over 430 million gallons of alcohol per year. There are more than 25 million alcoholics in the United States today, and most began drinking in high school and college.

Students often believe that there isn't a problem if they drink just beer, but you can become an alcoholic by drinking only beer. A six-pack of beer contains the same amount of alcohol as six drinks of hard liquor. Take a close look at some of the facts about alcohol and alcoholism in Figure 10-1.

- Alcohol costs the American society over $130 billion annually.

- Students spend $5.5 billion on alcohol each year. This exceeds the total operating costs of all college libraries, including scholarships and fellowships. In fact, the typical student spends more money on alcohol than on textbooks.

- Alcohol kills over 100,000 people every year. Every day, almost 80 people are killed in alcohol-related automobile accidents, the leading cause of death of people between the ages of 16 and 24. You don't have to be drunk, only under the influence, to be arrested and prosecuted.

- Alcohol has been linked with a high incidence of aggression, physical abuse, and violence and is almost always a factor in domestic violence and date rape.

- College administrators believe that alcohol is a factor in over half of academic problems.

Figure 10-1
Facts About the Costs and Dangers of Alcohol

THE DANGERS OF CIGARETTE SMOKING

It is hard to believe that anyone would still be smoking after the public awareness campaigns that present the risks of cigarette smoking and the energy drain it causes. Perhaps the billions of dollars advertisers spend each year convince enough people that smoking makes you more attractive, sexier, cooler, and calmer, and will solve all your problems. That advertising is in stark contrast to the facts shown in Figure 10–2.

- Cigarette smoke is composed of over 4000 chemicals, forty-three of which are known to cause cancer. These chemicals include cyanide, formaldehyde, acetone, ammonia, carbon monoxide, and, of course, addictive nicotine.

- Nicotine is a stimulant that saps your energy. Close to 500,000 people die every year from smoking-related illnesses.

- Nonsmokers who are married to smokers have a 30 percent greater risk of developing lung cancer than those who are married to nonsmokers. The effects of secondhand smoke (especially on children) are now documented. They include respiratory problems, colds, and illnesses.

Figure 10-2
Facts About the Dangers of Cigarette Smoking

THE DANGERS OF ILLEGAL DRUGS

Drug addiction is another major social problem. Almost 80 percent of people in their mid-twenties have tried illegal drugs. Here are some pertinent facts concerning drug abuse in this country:

- The cost of drug abuse to our society is almost $50 billion a year.

- According to the National Council on Alcoholism and Drug Dependence, marijuana releases five times as much carbon dioxide and three times as much tar into the lungs as tobacco does. Smoking three to five joints per week has the same carcinogenic effect as smoking sixteen tobacco cigarettes per day, seven days a week.

- There are certain patterns of behavior among marijuana users, especially adolescents, that show a loss of memory and intellectual reasoning.

- Crack addiction can occur in less than two months of occasional use; it is extremely addictive.

- Intravenous drug use is responsible for 24 percent of the AIDS cases in the United States.

Go to this book's Web site for helpful resources on substance abuse and addiction: http://peak.glencoe. com

CRITICAL THINKING ABOUT DRUGS

Drugs (both legal and illegal), alcohol, and tobacco are everywhere. People like to get high, feel good, and forget their pain and troubles. Every drug-induced high, however, has a crashing low. Peak Performers rely on their own inner strength, not on external means, to feel good enough about life. They are aware of the facts about alcohol and drug abuse and the high cost of addiction.

You need peak energy and concentration if you are to be successful at school and in your job. Only you can take responsibility for your life and determine if harmful substances are costing you more than the pleasure you get from them. Ask yourself if you really need to complicate your life, if this drug will actually make your life better. The answers are most likely *no.*

DEALING WITH ADDICTIONS

Here is a list of steps for dealing with an addiction:

- *Admit you have a problem.* The only way to solve a problem is to face it. Denial is a major reaction for someone with a substance abuse problem or addiction. An alcoholic may do well in school or hold down a job and therefore doesn't see a problem. If you think you have lost control or are involved with someone who has, admit it and take charge of your life.

- *Take full responsibility for your addiction and your recovery.* You are responsible for your life. Alcoholism may be inherited, but that doesn't mean you are not responsible for your behavior. Alcoholism isn't a disease like cancer; it's preventable, and you have a choice. If drinking to excess runs in your family, then don't drink. You cannot become an alcoholic or a drug addict if you don't start. Look at the consequences and the cost of addiction. Several support groups and treatment programs can help if you have an addiction. Try an Alcoholics Anonymous (AA) meeting. AA has over one million members and is one of the most successful programs in the world for many kinds of addiction. To obtain the location of your local chapter of Alcoholics Anonymous, look in the phone book or contact:

World Services
PO Box 459
Grand Central Station
New York, NY 10163
212-686-1100

National Council on Alcoholism
and Drug Dependence
12 West 21st Street
New York, NY 10010
212-206-1100

DEALING WITH CODEPENDENCY

Even if you are not directly involved with alcohol or drugs, your life may be affected by someone who is. Families and friends can find themselves affected by the addicted person. A common term often used when discussing people whose lives are affected by an addict is *codependency.* There are many definitions of codependency, and they include numerous self-defeating behaviors such as low self-esteem; lack of strong, solid, and emotionally fulfilling relationships; and lack of self-control. A codependent person may:

- avoid facing the problem of addiction. Denying, making excuses, justifying, rationalizing, blaming, controlling, and covering up are all games that a codependent person plays in an effort to cope with living with an addict.
- take responsibility for the addict's life. This may include lying; taking over a job, assignment, or deadline; or somehow rescuing the addict.
- be obsessed with controlling the addict's behavior. For example, the codependent may hide bottles, put on a happy face, hide feelings of anger, confuse love and pity, and sometimes feel that if only he or she could help more, the addict would quit.

If you feel that you have problems in your life as a result of growing up in an alcoholic family or that you may be codependent, get help. There are many agencies and support groups that can make a real difference.

PROTECT YOUR BODY

Reliable information about sex can help you handle the many physical and emotional changes you will experience in life. It can also help you make better decisions about difficult choices. Although sex is a basic human drive and a natural part of life, there are also dangers that include unplanned pregnancies, sexually transmitted diseases, and rape. Your level of sexual activity is a personal choice and can change with knowledge, understanding, and awareness. Just because you were sexually active at one time does not mean you cannot choose to be celibate now. No one should pressure you into sexual intercourse. If you decide to be sexually active, you need to make responsible choices and decisions and to be aware of the risks. Know the facts and protect your body.

You are totally responsible for your behavior.

Avoid Sexually Transmitted Diseases (STDs)

Sexually transmitted diseases are spread through sexual contact (including genital, vaginal, anal, and oral contact) with an infected partner. A person may be infected yet appear healthy and symptom-free. See Figure 10-3 on page 10-14 for a list of STDs and their symptoms, treatments, and risks. Despite public health efforts and classes in health and sexuality, STDs continue to infect significant numbers of young adults. Even if treated early, STDs are a major health risk and can have a devastating effect on your life. In some cases they can result in damage to the reproductive organs, infertility, or cancer. AIDS (acquired immune deficiency syndrome) is a fatal STD. It weakens the immune system and leads to an inability to fight infection. AIDS is transmitted through sexual or other contact with the semen, blood, or vaginal secretions of someone with the human immunodeficiency virus (HIV), or by sharing unsterile intravenous needles with someone who is HIV-positive. Occasionally, but rarely, it is contracted via a blood transfusion. AIDS is not a "gay" disease; in fact, worldwide, it is most commonly spread by heterosexual intercourse. AIDS cannot be transmitted by saliva or casual contact, such as by sharing utensils or shaking hands. There is currently no cure for AIDS.

To avoid contracting an STD, ask prospective partners about their health; *no matter what their health status is*, explain that you always use safety precautions. For any type of sex, prevention is the best rule. Latex condoms and dental dams can help protect against most sexually transmitted diseases. *However, abstinence is the only method totally effective in preventing the spread of sexually transmitted diseases.* It is important to know the facts, latest treatments, and the ways you can protect your body.

Sexually Transmitted Diseases	Common Symptoms	Treatment	Risks
Genital herpes Cold sores can spread genitally via oral sex.	Sores or blisters around genitals.	Medicated ointment may help; there is no cure.	Higher risk of cervical cancer (highly contagious).
Genital warts	Warts around genitals.	Laser, cryotherapy, or chemical treatment.	May contribute to precancerous cell changes; may recur.
Chlamydia	Discharge from genitals or stinging when urinating.	Antibiotics.	Painful infections that may result in infertility.
Crab lice	Itching.	Chemical treatment.	None known.
AIDS/HIV	No symptoms for years. Some carriers can be HIV–.	Medications slow the disease. No known cure.	Life-threatening infections.

Figure 10-3

Symptoms, Treatment, and Risks of Some Sexually Transmitted Diseases

Birth Control

If your relationship is intimate enough for sex, it should be open enough to discuss birth control, venereal diseases, pregnancy, and options if birth control fails. Both men and women need to stop and ask, "How would an unwanted pregnancy change my life?"

More contraceptives are available currently, but you must understand that none are 100 percent foolproof (except abstinence). Current contraceptives include the birth control pill, condoms, diaphragms, sponges, spermicidal foams, cervical caps, IUDs, and long-term implants. Douching and withdrawal are not effective and should never be used for birth control. Discuss birth control methods with your partner and with a qualified health professional. Make an informed decision and thus choose what is best for you.

Preventing Rape

Rape is a serious problem. To help prevent rape, you need to be proactive. Make certain you know your campus well. Ask the campus police or security what you can do to prevent a sexual assault or rape. If you are taking a night class, find the safest place to park your car. Find out if the school has a security escort policy for students taking a night class or using the library in the evening. (If such a service does not exist, perhaps you can organize one.) If there is no campus escort policy, arrange to walk to your car with a friend or group from your class. Another preventive measure is taking a course on self-defense. Consult a rape crisis counseling center or the campus police to learn if a course is available.

Date Rape

Date rape often goes unreported because the victim knows the attacker. Sometimes the victim blames herself because she had too much to drink or wonders if she said or did something to give the attacker the wrong idea. Date rape is *not* your fault! Check with the counseling center, health center, or campus police for ways to prevent date rape. Here are a few preventive measures:

1. **Use assertive language.** In a direct, forceful, and serious tone, let others know when their advances are not welcome.

2. **Trust your intuition.** Be attuned to body cues and trust your intuition. If it doesn't feel right, leave the situation and get help as soon as you can.

3. **Take your time.** Take the time to know a person before you spend time alone with him or her. Meet someone you don't know very well in a public place, or double date with a couple you know well. If you are going to a party or to a movie, or for a walk at night, ask a friend to accompany you. Don't take chances because someone looks nice or knows someone that you know.

4. **Recognize that drugs and alcohol can be dangerous.** Everyone is aware of how dangerous it is to drive while under the influence of drugs or alcohol. Drugs and alcohol are also dangerous while dating and are often factors in date rape. If you are intoxicated, you may not be able to protect yourself or be aware of the signals that would otherwise warn you of danger.

5. **Be aware of the danger signals of an unhealthy relationship.** Be concerned if you are dating someone who

   - pressures you sexually.
   - refers to people as sex objects.
   - doesn't respect your wants.
   - is possessive.
   - is bossy or aggressive.
   - has a temper and acts rashly.
   - is emotionally or physically abusive.

6. **Don't send mixed messages.** Make certain that your body language, tone of voice, and choice of words match your feelings, or your date may become confused. If you do not want to get physically intimate, don't allow anyone to talk you into it. Be aware of your own limits and feelings and communicate them assertively to your date. Respect yourself. Don't do anything that you do not feel comfortable doing. Say no loudly and clearly. Scream for help if you need it. An effective tactic is to yell "Fire!" to ensure other people's assistance.

7. **Get professional help.** Date rape is a traumatic experience and a violent crime. Report it immediately to a rape crisis center or call the local police. Make certain you get counseling to deal with the trauma. *It is not your fault!*

What Men Should Know About Rape

1. **Rape is not just a woman's problem.** Be aware and speak up against such stereotypical attitudes that women who are raped ask for it or that women are sex objects. No one asks to be raped because of their clothing or behavior. Forced sexual intercourse is degrading and humiliating and it is rape. You can challenge demeaning and cruel jokes, attitudes, and violence against women by taking a mature, caring stand against violence.

2. **Rape is a serious and crime.** Rape is a violent crime and can result in the offender spending years in prison. It is an act of violence, aggression, force, and power.

3. **Your date has the right to say no.** Respect another person's right to say no under any conditions or at any time. Don't expect sex in exchange for dinner or just because you have had sex with this person before. People have a right to change their minds, and this right should be respected.

4. **Alcohol and drugs can be dangerous.** Alcohol and drugs reduce sexual inhibition and the ability to read body language and cues. Some people blame alcohol consumption for their actions that take advantage of someone else or for their aggressive behavior. This is a very weak excuse.

5. **Understand and state your intentions.** Be clear about your feelings and intentions and respect your date's feelings and intentions. If you believe you are getting mixed messages, talk about it and clear any miscommunication. Listen to your intuition. If the situation doesn't feel right, leave.

6. **Take your time getting to know someone.** Rushing a relationship is a danger sign. Take your time and get to know someone as a person and not an object. Look for and model healthy relationships.

Go to this book's Web site for helpful resources on current medical research: http://peak.glencoe.com

CRITICAL THINKING LOG 10.5

Better Health

Read the following and write your comments on the lines provided.

List at least four ways you can improve your health.

_____

_____

_____

_____

MANAGING STRESS

Stress is a natural reaction of the body to any demand, pleasant or unpleasant. Stress is simply your body's reaction to external events (taking an exam or giving a speech) or internal events (fear, worry, or unresolved anger). Everything you experience stimulates your body to react and respond. Stress is normal and in fact necessary for a vital life. With too little stress, many people are bored and unproductive. The key is knowing how to channel stress.

Life is a series of changes, and these changes require adaptive responses. The death of a close family member or friend, a serious illness, exams, divorce, financial problems, losing a job, or moving are all examples of changes that require adjustment and cause some types of stress. It is important to emphasize, however, that your perception of these inescapable life events determines how they affect you. Even positive events can be stressful. Events such as marriage, a promotion, the birth of a baby, going away to school, a new romantic relationship, a new roommate, graduation, even vacations and holidays may be disruptive and demanding for some people and therefore stressful. Public speaking may be exciting and fun for one person and may cause an anxiety attack in another. Stress isn't "out there"; it is something you create and can manage. You can choose to respond in a calm, centered way.

Go to this book's Web site for helpful resources on mental health information: http://peak.glencoe.com

Stress-Reduction Strategies

Prolonged stress can wear you down and produce burnout. It can lead to physical problems, such as migraine headaches, ulcers, high blood pressure, or serious illnesses. Research has indicated that constant change over a long period of time can cause excessive levels of stress. Too many negative or positive changes stimulate the production of certain hormones and chemicals that affect the body. The solution is not to avoid stress but to acknowledge it directly and learn to manage and channel it. Try the following strategies:

1. **Become attuned to your body and emotions.** Many of us have been taught to deny emotions or physical symptoms and ignore stress. Become aware of your body and its reactions. Stress produces physical symptoms. Are you having physical symptoms of stress such as frequent headaches? Are you finding it difficult to relax? Are you emotionally upset, depressed, or irritable?

   The transition to college forces you to become more self-reliant and self-sufficient. Give yourself permission to feel several different emotions, but also learn strategies to pull yourself out of a slump. You might set a time limit: "I accept that I'm feeling overwhelmed or down today. I will allow a few hours to feel these emotions; then I will do what I know works to make me feel better."

   You have the power to change negative, hurtful thoughts and to create positive habits.

Figure 10-4
Common Student Stress Factors

2. **Exercise regularly.** Experts say that exercise is one of the best ways to reduce stress, relax muscles, and promote a sense of well-being. Most people find that they have more energy when they exercise regularly. Students often find it difficult to take the time to exercise. Sometimes the best way is to make exercise a daily habit and a top priority in your life.

3. **Rest and renew your body and mind.** Everyone needs to rest, not only through sleep but also through deep relaxation. Too little of either causes irritability, depression, inability to concentrate, and memory loss. Yoga is a great way to unwind, stretch and tone the muscles, and focus energy. Many people find that meditation is essential for relaxation and renewal. You don't have to practice a certain type of meditation; just create a time for yourself when your mind is free to rest and quiet itself. Other people find that a massage relieves physical and mental tension. Visualization is another powerful technique for relaxing your body.

   Build serenity and peace into your life in any number of ways: dance, listen to music, garden, swim, hike, or fly a kite, for example.

4. **Develop hobbies and interests.** Hobbies can release stress. Sports, painting, quilting, reading, and collecting can add a sense of fun and meaning to your life. Many find satisfaction and focus by developing an interest in the environment, the elderly, politics, children, animals, or the homeless. Investigate volunteering opportunities in your area.

5. **Use breathing methods**. Deep breathing reduces stress and energizes the body. If you are like many people, you breathe in short, shallow breaths, especially when under stress. Begin by sitting or standing up straight, breathe through your nose, fill your lungs completely, and push out your abdomen and exhale slowly and fully. Focus on a word, a sound, or your breathing and give it your full attention for about ten minutes. You can do a variation of this any time during the day, even if you can't escape to a quiet spot.

6. **Develop a support system.** The support and comfort of family and friends can help you clear your mind, sort out confusion, and make better decisions. Express your feelings, fears, and problems to people you trust. Make friends with nonworriers. Negative, chronic complainers who worry but don't act to solve their problems are stressful. Dozens of support groups can help you cope with stress. A group of people with similar experiences and goals can give you a sense of security, personal fulfillment, and motivation.

7. **Take minivacations.** Next time you are put on hold or kept waiting in line, pull out a novel and enjoy a few moments of reading. Practice deep breathing or head rolls, or visualize the tension flowing out of your body. Get up and stretch periodically while you're studying. These minivacations can keep you relaxed and expand your creativity.

TIP From the Classroom

I gained 15 pounds my first year in college. I wasn't exercising and I didn't know how to cook well-balanced meals. I soon learned to save money and eat healthy by buying rice, beans, flour, oatmeal, and grains in bulk. I also built exercise into my life. I now have energy and am determined to stay in shape.

—Sophomore in fashion design

"Breathing exercises can calm your emotions, clarify your mind, and benefit your involuntary nervous system and metabolism."

—*Dr. Andrew Weil*

8. **Rehearse the feared event.** When you mentally rehearse beforehand, you are inoculating yourself against a stressful event. Your fears become known and manageable. Visualization is an excellent technique for rehearsing an event.

9. **Exercise and stretch the mind.** Mental exercise can refresh and stimulate your entire life. Reading, doing crossword puzzles, and playing challenging board games renew the spirit and stretch the mind. Attend lectures, take workshops and seminars, and brainstorm creative ideas or current subjects with well-read friends. Think of all the ways that you can renew and expand your thinking. Make friends with creative people who inspire you and renew your perspective.

10. **Create balance in your life.** Peak Performers recognize the importance of balance between work and play in their lives. They want quality and a balanced life, not one filled of unfulfilling activities. Assess your activities and determine if they are distractions or opportunities. Learn to say no to requests that do not enrich your life or the lives of others. Set a time limit on work, demands from other people, and study, and reward yourself for tasks accomplished.

11. **Develop a sense of humor.** Nothing reduces stress like a hearty laugh or spontaneous fun. Discovering the child within helps us release our natural creativity. Laughing produces endorphins, natural chemicals that strengthen the immune system and produce a sense of well-being. Laughter also increases oxygen flow to the brain and causes positive physiological changes.

12. **Plan, don't worry.** Leading a disorganized life is stressful. Write down what has to be done each day; don't rely on your memory. Take a few minutes the night before to lay out your clothes, pack your lunch, and jot down a list of the next day's priorities. Get up twenty minutes early so you don't have to dash about. Worrying is stressful and depletes your energy. You can have only one thought in your mind at a time, so don't allow self-defeating thoughts to enter. Set aside twenty minutes a day to plan, solve problems, and explore solutions. Get involved in the solutions, not the problem. When your time is up, leave the problems until your next scheduled session.

13. **Be assertive.** Stand up for your rights, express your preferences, and acknowledge your feelings. Assertive communication helps you solve problems rather than build resentment and anger and increases confidence and control over your life.

    Part of being assertive is clarifying expectations. Take a few moments to make certain that you understand. Repeat the directions, expectations, meeting time and place, or assignment, and have a contingency plan for unexpected changes or problems.

"The old man laughed loud and joyously, shook up the details of his anatomy from head to foot, and ended by saying such a laugh was money in a man's pocket, because it cut down the doctor's bills."

—*Mark Twain*

TRAILMARKER 10.2

Stress Leads to Burnout

Here are early warning signs that your body is pushing too hard and too long and may be on its way to burnout. If you have more than four of the following symptoms, you may want to consider getting help for dealing with stress overload.

1. Frequent headaches, backaches, neck pain, or stomach aches, or tensed muscles.
2. Insomnia or disturbed sleep patterns.
3. No sense of humor; nothing sounds like fun.
4. Feeling fatigued, listless, and hopeless, and having low energy.
5. Increase in alcohol intake, smoking, or taking drugs.
6. Depression, moodiness, or hopelessness.
7. Heart racing.
8. Appetite changes (eating too much or too little).
9. Frequent colds, flu, or other illnesses.
10. Feeling anxious, nervous; difficulty concentrating.
11. Irritability, losing your temper, and overreacting.
12. Lack of motivation, energy, or zest for living.
13. Feeling that you have too much responsibility.
14. Lack of interest in relationships.

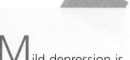
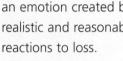

Mild depression is an emotion created by realistic and reasonable reactions to loss.

14. **Keep a log.** A log can be helpful in gaining insight into the types of situations that are stressful for you and how you respond to them. Write journal entries in this book. Be honest with yourself and record daily events and your reactions. Writing in a journal also helps clarify concerns and decisions and can give you a fresh perspective.

15. **Get professional help.** It is normal to experience grief after a loss or a major transition, and you should allow yourself to grieve and experience your emotional pain fully. However, if your sadness, depression, or anger continues despite your best efforts, or if you are suicidal, get professional help. Call a crisis hotline, health center, counseling center on campus or in the community, or mental health department for a list of agencies that can provide help. With a counselor's guidance, you can gain insight into your pattern of reacting to stress and modify your perception and behavior.

EMOTIONAL HEALTH

Everyone has the blues occasionally. Sometimes stress and emotional problems interfere with your goals or ability to cope. Here are a few descriptions of emotional problems that affect college students and professionals from all walks of life.

Go to this book's Web site for helpful resources:

http://peak.glencoe.com

Depression

It has been estimated that over 60 million people suffer from mild forms of depression each year. Mild depression is relatively short-term. Severe depression is deeper and may last months or years. Over 6 million Americans suffer serious depression that impairs their ability to function. Depression accounts for 75 percent of all psychiatric hospitalizations. It is an emotional state of sadness ranging from mild discouragement to feelings of utter hopelessness. Depression can occur as a response to

- *Loss.* The death of a loved one, the loss of a job, or any major change or disappointment in your life can trigger depression.
- *Health changes.* Physical changes such as a serious disease or illness, childbirth, or menopause can result in chemical changes that may cause depression.
- *Conflicts in relationships.* Unresolved conflicts in relationships can cause depression.

Depression can be triggered by many events. Some of these events are tied to certain stages in life. For example, adolescents are just beginning to realize who they are and are trying to cope with the responsibilities of freedom and adulthood. Moving out of your parents' house and going away to college can make you feel insecure and lonely. Setting unrealistic goals like buying your own car, making the Dean's list, or keeping a full-time job and going to school can also cause depression. If you are facing middle age, you may feel the loss of youth or unrealized career success, or worry that your children are leaving home and won't need you. For an elderly person, the loss of physical strength, illness, the death of friends, and growing dependency may prompt depression.

SIGNS AND SYMPTOMS OF DEPRESSION

The following are a few of the common symptoms associated with depression.

- sleep disturbance (sleeping too much or too little, or waking up in the night).
- increase or loss of appetite.
- overuse of prescription drugs.
- use of nonprescription drugs.
- drinking too much.
- withdrawal from family and friends, leading to feelings of isolation.
- recurring feelings of anxiety.
- becoming angry for no apparent reason.
- loss of interest in formerly pleasurable activities.
- feeling that simple activities are too much trouble.
- feeling that other people have much more than you have.

A lengthy period of the above symptoms may indicate a more serious form of depression and treatment should be considered.

A Picture of Stress

Read the directions that follow. Then complete the assignments.

1. Use the drawing below. Surround this picture with arrows, words, or other drawings that illustrate the source and intensity of external sources of stress (school, exams, job) and internal sources of stress (fears, anger). List your stresses:

_____

_____

_____

_____

_____

2. For each stressful factor, list ways you can manage your stress.

_____

_____

_____

_____

Warning Signs for Severe Depression

When depression causes persistent sadness and continues for longer than a month, serious depression may be present. Suicidal thoughts occur when a feeling of hopelessness sets in and problems seem too much to bear. Suicidal people think that the pain will never go away.

The Suicidal Person

Typically, suicidal people respond to help. Be concerned if you or others exhibit the following warning signs:

- excessive alcohol or drug use.
- significant changes in person's emotions (hyperactivity, withdrawal, mood swings).
- significant changes in sleeping, eating, studying, weight gain or loss.
- feeling hopeless or helpless.
- spending little time with or lacking close, supportive friends.
- nonsupportive family ties.
- rarely participates in group activities.
- recent loss or traumatic or stressful events.
- suicidal statements.
- close friend or family member has committed suicide.
- has attempted suicide.
- engages in dangerous activities.
- starts giving away things or has suicide plan.

You should be concerned if you know someone who exhibits several of the above warning signs. If you do know someone who is suffering from depression,

- remain calm.
- take the person seriously; don't ignore the situation.
- encourage the person to talk.
- listen without moralizing or judging. Acknowledge their feelings.
- remind the person that counseling can help and is confidential.
- remind the person that reaching out for help is a sign of strength, not weakness.
- call a suicide hotline or a counselor at school and get the name of a counselor for the person to call, or make the call with him or her.
- stay with the person to provide support when he or she makes the contact. If possible, walk or drive the person to the counselor.
- seek support yourself. Helping someone who is suicidal is stressful and draining.

Technology FOCUS: Use Your Computer to Reduce Stress

Your computer can save you time with writing papers and speeches, print out flawless copies, and generally help make your life more efficient at school and at work. There are lots of sites for giving tips on health and reducing stress. Try this book's Web sites to find links to information about stress management.

http://peak.glencoe.com

Also, use the computer to keep a computer journal of your energy level, your exercise and eating patterns, and your general level of wellness.

CAREER FOCUS: PREVENT STRESS AND FATIGUE AT WORK

Working full-time can be demanding. Long working hours, deadlines, meetings, and lack of time can play havoc with your health. The ability to manage stress, maintain health, and increase energy is critical for job success. Hannah, an emergency rescue technician, has a stressful and demanding job. Being alert, physically fit, energized, calm, and clear-headed are critical for making sound decisions. To combat fatigue and stress, Hannah plans to

- limit herself to one or two cups of coffee.
- eat a healthy diet.
- get a good night's rest.
- meditate and exercise every day.
- take minivacations by closing her eyes, breathing deeply, and mentally imagining the calm of a favorite lake.
- read good books and learn something new every day.
- develop a daily program of walking.

Hannah realizes that, to be at her highest energy level, she has to respect her body, mind, and emotions. Hannah keeps a list of more energy gains over her desk that help her to feel energized:

- Take walks.
- Eat healthy meals and snacks.
- Get sufficient rest.
- Spend quality time with family and friends.
- Keep a journal.
- Watch good movies.

- Take time to enjoy a favorite sport, activity, or hobby.
- Assess goals and results.
- Sing.
- Plant a garden.
- Laugh several times a day.
- Take time off when necessary.

TIP While computers can give you lots of information, help in writing papers, and increase retention of information, you need to take frequent breaks to avoid eye strain and a sore back. Make certain you have a good chair and keep your posture straight.

In addition to physical problems, some people isolate themselves from face-to-face contact and spend too much time in front of their computer screens. It's almost an addiction and can be stressful. Net Anonymous is now available for people who use the Internet too much.

Warning Signs of Stress Overload

Stress Performance Test

Read the statements below. Now think back over the last few months. Have you experienced stress as described in the statements? If so, put a checkmark under the number column that best indicates the amount of stress you have experienced.

	Severe (3)	Moderate (2)	Little (1)	None (0)
1. No time for goals	_____	_____	_____	_____
2. Lack of money	_____	_____	_____	_____
3. Uncomfortable living and study areas	_____	_____	_____	_____
4. Long working hours	_____	_____	_____	_____
5. Boring, uninteresting job	_____	_____	_____	_____
6. Conflict with roommate, family, etc.	_____	_____	_____	_____
7. Conflict with instructors	_____	_____	_____	_____
8. Too many responsibilities	_____	_____	_____	_____
9. Deadline pressures	_____	_____	_____	_____
10. Boring classes	_____	_____	_____	_____
11. Too many changes in life	_____	_____	_____	_____
12. Lack of motivation	_____	_____	_____	_____
13. Difficulty finding housing	_____	_____	_____	_____
14. Little emotional support from family	_____	_____	_____	_____

(Continued)

	Severe (3)	Moderate (2)	Little (1)	None (0)
15. Poor grades	_____	_____	_____	_____
16. Parents/partners have set standards and expectations that are too high	_____	_____	_____	_____
17. Unclear on goals	_____	_____	_____	_____
18. Too many interruptions	_____	_____	_____	_____
19. Health problems	_____	_____	_____	_____
20. Dependency on alcohol, drugs	_____	_____	_____	_____
21. Too much socializing	_____	_____	_____	_____
22. Lack of career/life goals	_____	_____	_____	_____
23. Speaking/test-taking anxiety	_____	_____	_____	_____
24. Lack of relationships, friends	_____	_____	_____	_____
25. Lack of self-esteem	_____	_____	_____	_____

Add your 1s, 2s, and 3s to give yourself a total score.

Totals   (3s) _____   (2s) _____   (1s) _____

Scores:
24–36:   Peak Performer (you have learned how to function effectively under stress).
37–48:   Persistent coper (you cope and handle stress in most situations, but you have some difficulty coping and feel overwhelmed sometimes).
49–60:   Stress walker (you have frequent feelings of being overwhelmed and exhausted, and they affect your performance).
Over 60: Burnout disaster (you need help coping; stress is taking its toll on your health and emotions and you are facing real burnout).

GARY SOTO

Do you like to read poetry? Do you write your own poems? Then, perhaps you are familiar with the poetry and stories written by Gary Soto. His writings deal with the lives of Mexican-Americans. As the son of Mexican-American parents and a former resident of the Mexican-American community in Fresno, California, he is familiar with this topic.

Becoming a writer and poet may have been far from Gary's aspirations as he worked as a migrant laborer, but today he is one of the youngest poets to appear in *The Norton Anthology of Modern Poetry*. Unsure of his direction and potential, Gary began pursuing a degree at Fresno City College in the seventies. He ultimately attained an M.F.A. degree from the University of California.

Today Soto lives with his wife and daughter near San Francisco. He recently gave up teaching at the University of California at Berkeley to write full-time. Gary Soto is a poet, playwright, essayist, and the author of several children's books. His *Living Up the Street* won the American Book Award. In addition, he has received the Andrew Carnegie Medal, Discovery—The Nation Prize, and was a finalist for the 1995 National Book Award for Poetry. He has had many fellowships from The National Endowment for the Arts and the Guggenheim Foundation.

Gary Soto drives around California visiting schools in small towns and reading his poetry, playing his guitar, and singing to children in Spanish. His goal is to make readers out of every young Latino in the state. He is well on his way to fulfilling his mission of creating a dynamic and living body of literature for Mexican-American children. Soto has found an audience. His books have become staples in school libraries across the country.

Gary Soto is a successful Hispanic poet who writes beautifully about fatherhood; Fresno, California; Catholicism; and love, but he is at his best when he writes about childhood. In 1990, he published his first book for young adults, *Baseball in April*. It was one of the few books written for Mexican-American children and was an instant success. In the last five years, he has published eighteen books for children and has sold more than 500,000 copies. Soto creates vivid images of life as a young Mexican boy in *Selected Poems,* the collection that made him a finalist for the 1995 National Book Award. Gary Soto has created a literary world for Mexican-American children.

Source: http://peak.glencoe.com

Review and Study Notes

CHAPTER 10

Affirmations

- I am aware of my body, emotions, and level of stress.
- I am relaxed and calm.
- I have confidence that I can handle any situation.
- I enjoy eating healthy foods, exercising, resting, and supporting my body.
- I avoid addicting substances and prefer to feel high from my inner strength.

Visualization

Imagine yourself at a favorite place that is relaxing and peaceful for you. You could be strolling on the beach, climbing a mountain, or hiking in the woods. Feel all your muscles relaxing; feel the sunshine on your shoulders and a cool breeze on your face. Breathe in the fresh air and feel your body unwind. All the tension and stress is released with each deep breath. Start at the top of your head and go through each part of your body until it is relaxed. Now imagine yourself in this perfect place, and give thanks mentally to all the resources, friends, strengths, prosperity, and blessings you have in your life. Next, see yourself accomplishing your most important priorities. Perhaps you are preparing for a speech. You see yourself working consistently to finish the speech, polish it, and practice it. You see yourself the day of the speech looking poised, confident, and prepared. You feel your success and the pleasure of accomplishment.

Peak Performance Strategies for Increasing Energy

1. Be aware of your body and emotions.
2. Eat healthy foods for high energy.
3. Maintain your ideal weight; exercise for energy.
4. Renew energy through rest.
5. Avoid harmful substances.
6. Protect your body from accidents or illnesses.
7. Plan, don't worry. Reduce and manage stress.
8. Develop healthy relationships.
9. Develop hobbies and interests; take minivacations.
10. Develop a support system.
11. Create balance in your life.
12. Get help for physical and mental distress.

CASE Studies

CASE A — *In the Classroom*

Melia Martins has a weight problem. She fasts to lose weight and then binges. She has lost and gained hundreds of pounds over the years and is becoming discouraged. She is under a lot of stress because she is taking a full course load at business college and working twenty-five hours a week as well.

Melia also comes from an alcoholic family, and her boyfriend, Scott, drinks to excess, even driving when he's drunk. He says that he doesn't have a problem and is just doing what others do when they party in college. Scott almost always has a hangover on the weekends, and his drinking is starting to affect his grades and his relationships. Melia is a Supporter personality type who dislikes conflict and doesn't want to upset Scott.

1. What strategies from this chapter would you suggest to help Melia control her weight, her health, and her anxiety?

   _____

2. What strategies would you suggest to help her cope with Scott's drinking problem?

   _____

3. What would you do if you were Scott's best friend?

   _____

In the Workplace

Melia is now a journalist at a medium-sized newspaper. She has always lived a fast-paced life and has had difficulty coping with stress. Her job requires traveling, meeting deadlines, skipping lunches, late nights, and the temptation to socialize too much with coworkers. As a result, Melia finds it difficult to maintain a high level of energy and good health because she can't find time to exercise, meditate, or eat healthy meals.

1. What strategies in this chapter would help Melia increase her energy and decrease her stress?

   _____

2. Write a list that Melia could place above her desk or on her mirror to refer to.

   _____

CASE B

In the Classroom

Rauel Dominguez is a business major in finance, works part-time at a sporting goods store, is president of his fraternity, and is on the crew team. This demanding schedule is manageable because Rauel's energy is high, but around midterm he finds that the stress becomes overwhelming. He needs to find ways to increase his energy, stay in good health, and manage stress.

What strategies would you suggest to Rauel that would increase his energy level and reduce his stress?

_____

_____

_____

_____

_____

_____

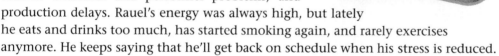

In the Workplace

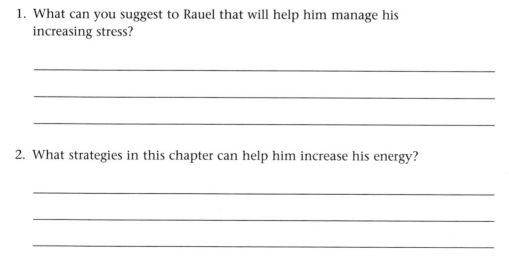

Rauel is now a manager for a large automobile manufacturer. He is often on the road three or four days a week visiting various dealerships. When Rauel returns, he finds work piled on his desk, endless customer and personnel problems, and production delays. Rauel's energy was always high, but lately he eats and drinks too much, has started smoking again, and rarely exercises anymore. He keeps saying that he'll get back on schedule when his stress is reduced.

1. What can you suggest to Rauel that will help him manage his increasing stress?

_____

_____

_____

2. What strategies in this chapter can help him increase his energy?

_____

_____

_____

TIP From the Workplace

I thought I was stressed in college. But my job and demands on my time are very stressful. I am working over forty-five hours a week, traveling, trying to keep up a house, and spend time with my wife and a baby. I need to find time to exercise, relax, have time for my hobbies, and give back to the community. I'm working on ways to get back in balance.

—Environmental lobbyist

ASSESSING INTERESTS

Developing outside interests can be a helpful way to reduce stress in your life. Remember, interests are activities that you enjoy and pique your curiosity. Besides helping to reduce your stress level, they may help you determine your life's work and career path. For example, an interest in the outdoors may lead to a major in natural resources, which could lead to a career as a park ranger. A passion for working with cars may lead to a certificate in auto mechanics and thus to your own auto repair shop. Include in your Career Portfolio a list of at least five current interests.

1. My interests are:

   _____

   _____

   _____

   _____

   _____

TIP Make exercise part of your life. Take care of your physical and mental health every day. *Get help immediately* if you experience physical or emotional distress.

2. Answer the following:

   a. What magazines do I like to read?

   _____

   _____

   b. What kinds of books do I like to read?

   _____

   _____

3. When you have a day off, what do you like to do? Check the areas that interest you.

Reading	_____	Wilderness activities	_____
Writing	_____	Working with people	_____
Fishing	_____	Working with computers	_____
Sports	_____	Building or remodeling	_____
Hiking	_____	Creating (such as painting or	
Rafting	_____	modeling)	_____
Traveling	_____	Public speaking	_____

   Others: _____

   _____

   _____

11

BUILDING DIVERSE AND HEALTHY RELATIONSHIPS

Management is getting work done through people.

—Mary Parker Follett, management theorist

Learning Objectives

In Chapter 11 you will learn

- strategies for communicating and building rapport.

- to understand and appreciate college and workplace diversity.

- assertive communication.

- how to build rapport with instructors and advisors.

- how to accept criticism.

- how to overcome shyness.

- how to create healthy relationships.

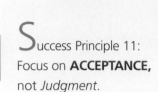
No one exists in a vacuum. You can learn to read more efficiently, write more fluid prose, take tests well, or memorize anything you want, but success will elude you if you don't have the ability to communicate and build rapport with different people. People spend nearly 70 percent of their waking hours communicating—listening, speaking, writing, and reading. Communication skills and the ability to build rapport and foster diverse relationships are key strengths for school and job success. SCANS lists interpersonal relationships, communication, understanding diversity, and team skills as important for job success.

This chapter will discuss ways to improve your ability to understand and relate to people. Developing these skills is one of the most important challenges you will face in your personal, school, and work life.

THE IMPORTANCE OF COMMUNICATION

Communication is the giving and receiving of ideas, feelings, and information. Note the word *receiving*. Some people are good at speaking but are not effective listeners. Poor listening is one of the biggest barriers to effective communication. Miscommunication is common and wastes billions of dollars in the business world and damages relationships.

Think of what you really want when you communicate with someone else. Do you want people to really listen to you, understand your feelings, and relate to your message? Building rapport is more than just giving and receiving information. It is the ability to find common ground with another person based on respect, empathy, and trust. Common ground is the intent to focus on similarities and core values that are diverse or cross-cultural.

Some people seem to have a knack for building rapport and making others feel comfortable and accepted. Spend a few minutes with a person like this and you feel as if you've known him or her for years. They are highly sensitive to nonverbal cues and the responses that they elicit from other people. They have developed empathy and make you feel valued. They are comfortable with themselves and comfortable communicating with people from different cultures and backgrounds. They can put themselves aside and focus on the other person with genuine interest and appreciation. You can learn this skill, too. People will want to be near you because you will make them feel good about themselves, give them a sense of importance, and create a climate in which they feel comfortable. People who are good at building rapport not only look for similarities in others, they also appreciate and value differences.

STRATEGIES FOR BUILDING RAPPORT

Let's look at a few strategies for building rapport:

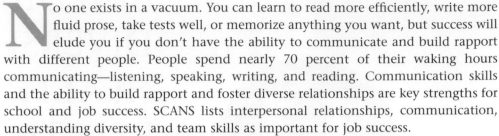

I will pay more for the ability to deal with people than any other commodity under the sun.

—*John D. Rockefeller,*
business tycoon

1. **Assess and clarify intention.** The first step in building rapport is to assess your intention. Your intention sets the tone and direction and often determines the results. If your goal is to build understanding, acceptance, and rapport, it will usually be reflected in your tone, body language, and style. If you are judgmental, however, this message will come through regardless of your choice of words. For example, let's say that your arms are crossed and you frown, lean back in your chair, have indirect eye contact, sigh, and shake your head. You indicate that you are

willing to listen, but your nonverbal body language is shouting, "I don't like you and I don't want to listen." Choose to listen for understanding and to find common ground.

2. **Be an active listener.** Here are a few tips:

   - *Listen, don't talk.* Don't change the subject unless the speaker is finished. Be patient and don't interrupt others. Listen for feelings and the undertones and meanings of what people are really saying. You can accomplish this by being attuned to nonverbal cues—posture, tone of voice, eye contact, body movements, and facial expressions.

   - *Put the speaker at ease.* Listeners who want to build rapport put the talker at ease by creating a supportive and open climate. Being warm and friendly, showing interest, and smiling all help put others at ease.

   - *Withhold criticism.* Criticizing puts people on the defensive and blocks communication. Arguing almost never changes someone's mind.

   - *Paraphrase.* Restating what the speaker has said shows that you are really interested in understanding, not just in getting your point across. Encourage others to talk and explain. Ask questions and seek to understand another person's point of view.

   - *Know when you cannot listen.* If you know you do not have time to pay close attention to the speaker, say so. For example, if you have a lot of studying to do and your roommate wants to talk about a date, you may want to say in a kind and respectful tone, "I'd like to know more about your date, but I have to read this chapter. Can we have a cup of tea in an hour and talk about it?" You also may want to delay talking and listening if you are angry, tired, or stressed. Just make certain you respond in a respectful tone of voice.

3. **Look attentive, alert, and interested.** Look at the speaker and appear interested. When your eyes wander, it makes it seem as if you are uninterested or bored. You can create an attentive and supportive climate by communicating openness with facial expression, relaxed and uncrossed arms, and leaning slightly toward the person. Try not to sit behind a desk but closer to the other person. Some experts say that 70 percent of what is communicated is done through nonverbal communication or body language. If you intend to build rapport, your body language must be warm and open and convey interest and acceptance.

4. **Be respectful.** Many organizations are implementing employee training programs that emphasize the importance of business etiquette—respect and consideration of the feelings and needs of others. Good manners and respect are the foundation of all healthy relationships. People need to feel they are getting the consideration and appreciation that they deserve—whether it is in the classroom, on the job, or at home. Therefore, if you want to build rapport with others, be respectful.

5. **Use warmth and humor.** People who have a knack for building rapport know how to use humor. They are never sarcastic. They never make jokes at the expense of another person's feelings, nor do they take themselves too seriously. They are able to laugh at life and themselves. Humor

is warming and puts people at ease. A joke or easy laughter can dissipate tension. Use humor, wit, and a sincere smile to add warmth and understanding.

6. **Review your team style inventory.** There are many different types of people in this world who learn, think, and relate differently. Knowing this can help you interact and work more effectively with diverse people and teams. For example, if your boss has an Analyzer type of personality, you will want to make certain that your report is based on facts and that your presentation is clear, concise, and correct.

7. **Relate to a person's preferred learning style.** You can build rapport with your instructors, coworkers, and supervisors by relating to their personality, learning, and teaching styles. For example, perhaps your instructor prefers the visual mode. She writes on the board, shows overheads and films, and uses phrases such as, "Do you see what I'm saying?" For an instructor who prefers a visual mode, you will want to enhance your visual presentation. Turn in an especially attractive visual paper by taking note of neatness and spelling, and using pictures, diagrams, and drawings whenever appropriate. You should maintain eye contact while this instructor is lecturing and return visual clues, such as nodding, smiling, and other reassurances.

PROFICIENT PEAK PERFORMER

Acts on commitment to eliminate oppressions in all forms

Truly values and appreciates people from diverse cultural and social backgrounds

Actively seeks to include full participation of diverse cultural groups in decision making

CULTURALLY SENSITIVE AND RESPECTFUL

Respects people from diverse cultural and social backgrounds
Seeks out contacts with people from diverse backgrounds
Encourages people to value and respect their cultural identity

CULTURALLY AWARE

Attempts to understand and increase awareness
Is aware that experiences differ for people based on their culture

CULTURALLY IN DENIAL

There is no problem. Everyone is the same.

Figure 11–1
Diversity Pyramid

UNDERSTANDING DIVERSITY

Colleges and workplaces are becoming more and more diverse. Diversity includes factors such as gender, race, age, ethnicity, physical ability, social and economic background, and religion. College is an excellent place to get to know, understand, and value other cultures.

More and more people travel to different countries for business or personal reasons, and they en-counter varied cultures and customs. Coupled with television, news-papers, computers, the Internet, telephones, and fax machines, the opportunities to link nations and interact with many cultures are on the rise. Statistics provided by the Bureau of Labor projects that the workforce of the

twenty-first century will include more women, minorities, and part-time workers. These diverse people will bring a different and broader worldview to schools, society, and organizations. As a result of this cultural explosion, many organizations offer diversity awareness training to help employees relate comfortably and appreciate diversity. These programs provide opportunities for employees to develop and strengthen critical thinking skills and reduce stereotypical thinking and prejudice.

As a contributing member of society and the workforce, it is essential that you use critical thinking to assess your assumptions, judgments, and views about people who are different from you. Building cultural sensitivity will be the foundation for building common ground with diverse groups.

Stereotype is a mental or emotional picture held in common by members of a group that repre-sents an oversimplified belief, opinion, or judg-ment about members of another group.

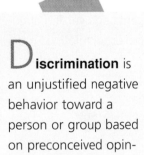

Prejudice is an unjustified negative feeling directed at a person or group based upon preconceived opinions, judgments, and stereotypes.

Discrimination is an unjustified negative behavior toward a person or group based on preconceived opinions, judgments, and stereotypes.

COMMUNICATION STRATEGIES

Here are a few strategies you may wish to use when developing acceptable communication with diverse groups:

1. **Be aware of your feelings.** If you have a negative reaction to a group or person, examine it and see where it is coming from. Be aware of how you talk to yourself about other people. Be aware of the words you use. Be willing to admit your own prejudices. This is the first step toward change.

2. **See the value in diversity.** We are a rich nation because of different races and cultures. Knowledge and understanding can break through barriers. The value of education is the appreciation of different views and the tools for building understanding and tolerance. Learn to think instead of react. Look for the value that different views can bring to your study team, group discussions, and work situations. By sharing different viewpoints, you can learn new and interesting ways of seeing situations and approaching problems.

3. **Treat people as individuals.** It is important to look beyond preconceived notions and see people as individuals and not members of a particular group. Try to see people as unique and valued.

4. **Treat people with respect.** Treat people with respect, consideration, and civility. You can be respectful even if you find someone's behavior unacceptable.

5. **Be aware of differences.** It is important to focus on similarities. We are 99.99 percent alike in our humanness. Don't let differences dominate your interactions. However, don't act as if people are all alike and that their experiences are the same. Be aware that values and experiences differ for people based on their culture, religion, and background.

6. **Listen.** Avoid telling other people what it means to be a member of their particular ethnic, cultural, religious, or gender group. Ask questions and be willing to learn.

7. **Get involved.** Take a cultural diversity course at college or in the community. Visit with people from other religions. Be willing to seek out international students and people from different cultures. Attend open events for various ethnic groups. Go to lectures, read, and look for opportunities to become acquainted with other cultures.

8. **Take risks.** Don't avoid contact with other cultures because you may be afraid of making a mistake, saying the wrong thing, or inadvertently offending someone. Cultivate friendships with people from different cultures and races. Share your own culture's traditional foods and customs with others. Knowledge of other cultures can help you appreciate your own roots. When you take a risk, you become more aware of how other people relate to you and you will become more comfortable dealing with diversity.

9. **Apologize when you make a mistake.** The only way you can bridge the gaps between cultures is to risk getting involved. Mistakes happen even with the best intentions. Ask for clarification and apologize. However, be prepared at times for strong feelings or misunderstandings that may result from past experiences with racism or sexism. Don't take it personally if someone does not respond as positively as you had hoped. Sometimes bridging the gap requires that you make an extra effort to understand.

10. **Speak out.** It is not enough to be aware that values and experiences differ for people from different cultures; you must act on this knowledge. Stand up and speak out whenever you hear or see discrimination in school or at work. Encourage your school to welcome and celebrate diversity.

11. **Encourage representation.** Encourage active participation by members of diverse cultural and social groups in various clubs, student government, local government, college meetings and boards, community groups and boards, and any decision-making groups.

Stereotypical Thinking

Do you know someone who views people in a stereotypical way? Can you describe some stereotypical reactions you may have observed or heard concerning people like those listed below? Write your comments on the lines provided.

1. Welfare recipient _____

2. Asian female _____

3. Truck driver _____

4. Housewife _____

5. Lawyer _____

6. Biker _____

7. Farmer _____

TRAILMARKER 11.1

Thinking About Diversity

If you could shrink earth's population to a village of precisely 100 females and males—but maintain the existing demographic ratios—the group would look like this:

- 57 Asians.
- 21 Europeans.
- 14 Western Hemisphere dwellers (North and South Americans).
- 8 Africans.
- 70 nonwhite.
- 30 white.
- 70 non-Christian.
- 30 Christian.
- 70 unable to read.
- 50 malnourished.
- 80 living in substandard housing.
- 1 university graduate.
- 50 percent of the wealth worldwide would be in the hands of six people—all citizens of the United States.

Cultural and Gender Diversity at Work

Attention to cultural and gender diversity is increasingly important because the workplace is becoming more diverse. Attitudes and behavior from top management set the tone for the whole company. Many top managers approach the issue by asking themselves, "How can I instruct others to tolerate differences in race, gender, religion, and sexual preference?" Perhaps a better question would be, "How can I set an example, create a climate of respect, and encourage people to value differences?" Managers can create an atmosphere of respect and understanding.

There are many seminars and workshops that offer ideas on working successfully with people of different cultures and genders. Firm guidelines need to be established and clearly communicated about the consequences of discrimination.

Discrimination is illegal and can be grounds for court action. Organizations have a responsibility and an obligation to make certain that all employees know what behaviors are illegal and inappropriate and the consequences for such behavior. Top managers are responsible for establishing procedures and need to offer a safe atmosphere for complaints. In short, companies must provide education, create guidelines and procedures, and set a tone of serious concern and respect toward all differences in the workplace.

Sexual Harassment at School and at Work

Sexual harassment is destructive to the school and work climate. It is also costly. Employee turnover, loss of productivity, expensive lawsuits, and a negative work environment are just some of the consequences of sexual harassment.

Organizations are responsible for establishing accepted guidelines. Most campuses and companies employ someone you can talk to if you have a complaint or concern. Organizations that have over twenty-five employees are legally required to have written procedures concerning sexual harassment. Organizations should also

Sexual harassment is behavior that is unwelcome, unwanted, and degrading.

- define sexual harassment and the disciplinary actions that may result because of inappropriate behavior.
- make certain that all employees are informed of the policy and are aware of the procedures for filing a complaint.
- designate a person to handle confidential complaints and concerns.
- ensure that common work practices are in compliance with the policy.

Assertive Communication

You may not always feel that you have the right to speak up for what you need, particularly in new situations where you see yourself as powerless and dependent. Assertive communication should help in these situations. Assertive communication is expressing yourself in a direct, above-board, and civil manner. Only you can take responsibility for clarifying expectations, expressing your needs, and making your own decisions. You might find yourself acting passively in some situations, aggressively in others, and assertively in still others. In most situations, however, strive to communicate in an assertive, direct, clear, and respectful manner.

- Passive people rarely express feelings, opinions, or desires. They have little self-confidence and low self-esteem, have difficulty accepting compliments, and often compare themselves unfavorably with others. Sometimes they feel that others take advantage of them, which creates resentment.
- Aggressive people are often sarcastic, critical, and controlling. They want to win at any cost and sometimes blame others for making them angry. They sometimes resort to insults and criticisms, which breaks down communication and harms relationships.
- Passive-aggressive people appear passive but act aggressively. For example, a passive-aggressive student will not respond in class when asked if there are any questions about an assignment but will then go to the dean to complain. A passive-aggressive roommate will leave nasty notes or complain to others rather than confront a roommate directly.
- Assertive people state their views and needs directly; use confident body language; and speak in a clear, strong voice. They take responsibility for their actions. Assertive people respect themselves and others.

Assertive Communication Role Playing

Read the following situations. Then develop an assertive response for each one.

1. **Situation:** You receive a *B* on your test, and you think you deserve an *A*. What would you say to your instructor?

   Assertive response: _____

2. **Situation:** A friend asks you to read her term paper. She tells you it is the best paper that she has ever written. However, you find several glaring errors.

   Assertive response: _____

3. **Situation:** Your roommate asks to borrow your new car. You don't want to lend it.

   Assertive response: _____

4. **Situation:** An acquaintance makes sexual advances. You are not interested.

   Assertive response: _____

5. **Situation:** You go to a party and your date pressures you to drink.

   Assertive response: _____

6. **Situation:** Your roommate's friend has moved in and doesn't pay rent.

   Assertive response: _____

7. **Situation:** Your sister borrowed your favorite sweater and stained it.

   Assertive response: _____

8. **Situation:** A friend lights up a cigarette, and you are allergic to smoke.

   Assertive response: _____

9. **Situation:** You want your roommate or spouse to help you to keep the apartment clean.

   Assertive response: _____

10. **Situation:** Your mother wants you to come home for the weekend, but you have a major test to study for.

    Assertive response: _____

11. **Situation:** Your team member has not done his share of work on a major project.

    Assertive response: _____

COMMUNICATING WITH INSTRUCTORS AND ADVISORS

Develop professional relationships with your instructors and advisors just as you would with your supervisor at work. Try a few of these tips to increase rapport:

1. **Clarify expectations.** Make certain you understand the objectives and expectations of your instructors and advisors. Most instructors will give you extra help and feedback if you take the initiative. For instance, before a paper is due, hand in a draft and say, "I want to make sure I am covering the important points in this paper. Am I on the right track? What reference sources would you like me to use? What can I add to make this an *A* paper?"

2. **Clarify concerns.** If you don't understand or you disagree with a grade you have received on a test or paper, ask for an appointment with the instructor. Approach the situation with a supportive attitude. "I like this course and want to do well in it. I don't know why I got a *C* on this paper because I thought I had met the objectives. Could you show me exactly what points you think should be changed? Could I make these corrections for a higher grade?" Make certain you are respectful and appreciative of your instructor's time and help.

3. **Adapt to your instructor's teaching style.** Approach each class with a positive attitude and don't expect that all instructors will teach to your learning style.

4. **Be open to learn.** Attend every class with an inquisitive and open mind. Some instructors may be less interesting, but you owe it to yourself to be as supportive as possible. If you are a returning student, you may find that the instructor is younger than you are and may lack life experiences. Be open to learn and value the training, education, and knowledge that the instructor brings to class. The same rule applies in the workplace too. Be supportive and open to learning, and consider yourself on the same team.

5. **Take responsibility for your own learning.** Don't expect your instructor to feed you information. Take an active role in each class. You are ultimately responsible for your own learning and your own career. You may be tempted to cut classes when you don't like your instructor, but you will miss valuable class discussions, question-and-answer sessions, explanations, reviews of concepts, expectations about tests, contact with students, and structure to help you stay focused. Furthermore, you miss the opportunity to see your instructor improve because your initial impression may be false. Students have reported that once they gave the instructor a chance and worked hard, their attitude changed. In fact, in some instances, this instructor became their favorite and they excelled in the class.

6. **Take an interest in your instructors.** Visit them during office hours to discuss your work, goals, grades, and future coursework. When it is appropriate, ask about your instructor's academic background as a guide for yours. Ask about degrees, colleges attended, work experience, and what projects they are working on for professional growth. A large part of building rapport is showing genuine interest, appreciation, and respect.

7. **Ask for a letter of reference.** If you have built rapport with your instructor or advisor, ask for a letter of recommendation soon after the class is over. Your instructor and advisor can help you in school and in your career.

TRAILMARKER 11.2

Pre-Registration Questions for Your Advisor

- What general education courses should I take this term?

- Where can I find out what "general education" is and what courses are approved for it?

- What course do I need to take first?

- Do I need placement tests? Which ones?

- When should I declare a major?

- Can I repeat a course to replace a bad grade?

- Is there a course I can take this summer at a community college to meet my general education or major?

- How do I change my major?

- Is there an option to develop a special or interdisciplinary major?

- How do I take an educational leave, withdraw from the university, or transfer to another college?

- How do I make certain that courses I take "on exchange" will apply to my major or to my general education?

- If I change majors, will I lose credit for some of my general education courses?

- How many credits can I sign up for each quarter or semester?

- Do my general education courses count toward my major?

ACCEPTING CRITICISM

Being reminded that you aren't perfect is never easy or pleasant. However, try to listen with an open mind when your instructor, boss, coworker, roommate, spouse, or other students point out mistakes, mention concerns, or make suggestions. Learning to accept and grow from feedback is key to job success. Start with the attitude that the critic has good intentions and goodwill. Also admit that you have shortcomings. Here are a few more tips on how to receive criticism:

1. **Stay calm.** Don't lose your temper. Take time to compose a response. If your critic is angry, try to diffuse his or her emotions. Ask questions. Ask him or her to calm down: "I can see that you are upset and I really want to know what your concerns are. Please talk more slowly." It is important to listen to the message without overreacting or becoming defensive.

2. **Establish an open environment.** It helps if you can create an open dialogue that invites feedback. People need to feel safe when giving feedback or criticism. Let people know that you like them and you will not get angry if they give you negative feedback or suggestions. For example, get to know your instructors and bosses. Don't wait for formalized feedback in the form of grades; ask the instructors how you are doing in class, on quizzes, on papers, and so on. Keep copies or records of your quizzes and papers and review them with your instructors. Just as a hiker needs a compass to check direction, check your own direction at times. Open communication keeps issues from reaching a boiling point.

3. **Be open to nonverbal cues.** Sometimes people have difficulty expressing criticism, so look for nonverbal criticism. If the person is aloof, angry, or sad, ask if you did something to offend him or her. If he or she is sarcastic, perhaps there is underlying hostility. You can say something like, "You have been very quiet today. Is there something that I did to offend you?"

4. **Listen.** Listening is key. Don't interrupt or start your defense. Really concentrate on the other person's perceptions, feelings, and expectations. Listen for understanding and stay calm and detached.

5. **Don't justify.** Practice saying, "Thank you. I appreciate your viewpoint and your courage in telling me what is bothering you." It's fine if you need to explain a situation, but don't make excuses for your behavior. If the criticism is true, change your behavior. If not, then continue without arguing or becoming sarcastic. Criticism is feedback about how another person views your behavior. It is not necessarily reality but an interpretation. Relax and put it in perspective. Someone is reacting to a certain behavior at a specific time, not to your whole personality or the way you really are at all times. You might try being more detached and observing your behavior with more awareness, or ask others if it is offensive.

6. **Ask for clarification.** If you are unclear, ask for specific details, the time of the incident, and clarification. "Can you give a specific incident

or time when you think that I was rude?" Keep comments in perspective, and ask for clarification. The key is to understand the issue at hand.

7. **Focus on the problem.** Don't use detours and attack the person. For example, "You think I'm messy? Look at your room. You're a real pig." Instead, focus on the problem. "If I do the dishes the same evening I cook, will that make you feel more comfortable?" Trust that you can both speak your minds in a calm and nondefensive manner without destroying your relationship.

8. **Ask for specific instructive feedback.** Remember, you have a right to ask for clarification. Make certain you understand. For example, "Professor Walker, you gave me a *B* on this paper. Could you explain what points you consider to be inadequate? How can I improve it?" Summarize the discussion.

9. **Focus on solutions.** Focus on the problem and possible solutions instead of the person. You might say, "I can see that this is a problem for you. What can I do to solve it? What procedures or options can we explore?"

10. **Apologize.** If you think the situation warrants it, apologize. If you feel the criticism is unfair, discuss it openly. You don't want to let resentments smolder and build.

CRITICAL THINKING LOG 11.3   Observe

Read the following questions and write your comments on the lines provided.

1. Observe how others handle conflict, compliments, and criticism. Note any ineffective behaviors. List them.

_____

_____

2. If you were a consultant in conflict resolution, what are some conflict resolution tips you would provide?

_____

_____

3. What behaviors do you use under stress that you would like to change?

_____

_____

4. What do you intend to do the next time you are in a conflict with someone else?

_____

_____

OVERCOMING THE BARRIERS TO EFFECTIVE COMMUNICATION

The number one barrier to effective communication is the assumption that the other person knows what you meant. It is easy to think that what you say is what the other person hears. Communication is a complex system with so many barriers to overcome that it is a wonder anyone ever really communicates. Other barriers include

- faulty perception.
- misunderstandings.
- cultural, religious, social, and gender differences.
- poor listening skills.
- the need to be right.

Communication is the lifeblood of personal relationships and the foundation of effective team and work groups. Learning how to work effectively with your study team, advisors, instructors, roommates, coworkers, and supervisors will help you be successful at school, at work, and in personal relationships. There are few professional or personal problems that don't involve a failure in communication.

The first step to effective communication is the desire and willingness to understand and build rapport with others. Seek to clarify intentions and be an active listener. Show that you are interested in others and establish common bonds. Paraphrase conversations to assess mutual understanding. Develop healthy relationships based on integrity, respect, trust, and honesty.

CRITICAL THINKING LOG 11.4

Conflict Resolution

Describe a conflict that you have not yet resolved. What techniques do you intend to use that would be helpful? Write a script that you can follow.

1. Describe the problem:

   _____

   _____

2. Express your feelings:

   _____

   _____

3. State what you want:

   _____

   _____

4. Predict the consequences:

   _____

   _____

OVERCOMING SHYNESS

Shyness is common. Some behavioral experts say it affects thousands of people. Shyness is not a problem unless it interferes with your life. It is perfectly acceptable to enjoy your privacy, be quiet, be modest, prefer a few close friends to many, and even embarrass easily. However, if shyness prevents you from speaking up in class, getting to know your instructors and other students, giving presentations, or making new friends, it is keeping you from fulfilling your potential for success. In school and in the workplace, it is important to ask questions, clarify assignments, and ask for help. The inability to ask for help is one of the biggest barriers in being shy. In addition, shy people often don't contribute to classroom discussions, ask stimulating questions, build rapport with instructors, or offer positive feedback. In short, they can appear emotionally detached and withdrawn. Shyness is not a condition you were born with or that others forced upon you. You can change any behavior you choose, and you can overcome your shyness, build rapport, and be an effective conversationalist by following these tips:

1. **Use positive self-talk.** Reinforce your self-confidence and self-image by using positive talk. Instead of saying, "I'm shy. I can't change," tell yourself, "I am confident, people like me, and I like people. I find it easy and enjoyable to get to know new people. I am accepted, appreciated, and admired."

2. **Use direct and relaxed eye contact.** Many shy people look down or avoid making eye contact. Direct eye contact reinforces your confidence and shows interest and empathy. Look at your instructors and show interest in what they are presenting.

3. **Ask questions.** You don't have to talk a lot to be an effective conversationalist. In fact, you don't want to deliver monologues. Ask questions and give others a chance to talk and to change the subject. Asking open-ended questions shows interest and concern. For example, instead of asking Jennifer if she is in your English class, ask her how she is progressing with the assigned term paper. If you are asking questions of an instructor, be clear and to the point and focus on understanding the concept.

4. **Listen to other points of view.** You don't have to agree with other people's points of view, but you can listen and respond tactfully and thoughtfully. You have something to contribute, and exchanging different views is a great way to learn and grow.

5. **Use humor.** Most people like to laugh. Poking good-natured fun at yourself lightens the conversation, as does a funny joke or story. Just make certain to be sensitive; don't tell off-color or racial jokes or stories. Smiling at others will lighten your own outlook.

> We conceal and camouflage our true being before others, to foster a sense of safety, to protect ourselves against unwanted but expected criticism, hurt, or rejection. But without disclosure, others do not know us and we lose touch with our real selves.
>
> —*Sidney Jourard*
> *author*

CRITICAL THINKING LOG 11.5

Patterns

Look at the pattern of some of your relationships. Recall situations that occur again and again. Once you see the pattern and consequences of your interactions, you can begin to think and act differently. When you take responsibility for changing your inner world of beliefs and thoughts, your outer world will also change. What seems to be a recurring theme or pattern in your relationships?

_____

_____

_____

_____

_____

_____

GREAT RELATIONSHIPS
• •

Problems in relationships can consume a great deal of your time and energy. Because feeling good about yourself is one key to all-around success, it is important to look at friendships and romantic relationships, too. Here are a few tips to help you build healthy relationships:

1. **Progress slowly.** A healthy relationship progresses slowly. Take the time to get to know the person and how he or she feels and reacts to situations. Relationships that move too fast or have intense and instant sexuality as a basis generally end quickly. Some people go from casual to intimate in one date. Solid relationships need time to grow and develop through the stages of companionship and friendship. Take the time to know people in many different situations. Peak Performers have many good acquaintances and solid friendships. And perhaps, from one of these friendships, a romantic relationship may develop.

2. **Expectations are realistic.** Some people think that having a good love relationship will magically improve their lives, even if they make no effort to change their thinking or behavior. If you are a poor student, are unmotivated, are depressed, or lack confidence, you will still have these problems even if you have a great love relationship. It is unrealistic to expect a love relationship to solve life's problems or transform them; only you can solve your problems. Knowing this, you can put more energy into improving your life than you do in looking for someone else to change it.

3. **Honesty.** A healthy relationship is based on commitment to the truth. You certainly don't want to reveal to a casual acquaintance or a first date everything in your past. At the appropriate time, however, honesty about your feelings, basic values, and major life experiences is the foundation of a healthy relationship. For example, if you are an alcoholic or have been married before, the other person should know that as your relationship progresses.

4. **Support.** A healthy relationship is supportive of the growth and well-being of each partner; an unhealthy relationship is not. No one owns another person, nor does anyone have a right to physically or emotionally harm another. An unhealthy relationship is possessive and controlling. A healthy relationship is mutually supportive.

5. **Respect.** A healthy relationship is based on respect for the feelings and rights of the other person. An unhealthy relationship is self-centered and disrespectful.

6. **Trust.** A healthy relationship works in a relaxed, loving, and comfortable way. When an occasional problem comes up, there is an inherent trust that it will be faced and resolved. If a relationship is obsessive, controlling, and distrustful, it is unhealthy. When problems arise, the focus should be on solving them, not on assigning blame. You don't need to worry about, control, or work on a healthy relationship all the time.

7. **Change can occur.** It is easy for healthy relationships to change. Emotionally healthy people know that not all relationships will develop into romantic and intimate commitments. Letting go and knowing how to end a relationship is just as important as knowing how to form healthy relationships. It is acceptable and normal to say no to an acquaintance who asks you out or to decide that you don't want a romantic relationship or a friendship to continue after a few dates. No one should date, have sex, or stay in a relationship out of guilt, fear, or obligation. It is more difficult to terminate a relationship that has progressed too fast or one where the expectations for the relationship are perceived differently. Talk about your expectations and realize that your sense of personal worth does not depend on someone's wanting or not wanting to date you.

8. **Open lines of communication.** Healthy relationships are based on open communication. Trouble occurs in relationships when you think you know how the other person feels or would react to a situation. For example, you may assume that a relationship is intimate, but the other person may regard it as a casual affair. Expectations for the relationship can be vastly different. Make certain that you make your expectations clear and that your body language matches your words. Communication in a healthy relationship is open enough to discuss even sensitive topics such as birth control, sexually transmitted diseases, and unplanned pregnancy.

GETTING ALONG WITH ROOMMATES OR FAMILY

The following suggestions will help you create rapport and improve communication with your roommates or family members:

1. **Clarify expectations.** List the factors that you feel are important for a roommate on the housing application or in an ad. If you don't want a smoker or pets, be honest about it.

2. **Discuss expectations during the first meeting.** Define what neatness means to both of you. Discuss how both of you feel about overnight guests.

3. **Clarify concerns and agree to communicate with each other.** Don't mope or whine about a grievance or leave nasty notes. Communicate honestly and kindly.

4. **Treat your roommate with respect.** Don't give orders or make demands. Communicate openly and calmly. Listen to each other's needs. Treat each other with courtesy and civility. Be especially respectful of your roommate's need to study or sleep. Don't interrupt or make noise.

5. **Don't borrow unless necessary.** A lot of problems result over borrowing money, clothes, jewelry, bikes, cars, and CDs. The best advice is not to borrow. If you do, however, ask permission first and make certain you return the item in good shape or replace it if you lose or damage it. Fill the tank of a borrowed car with gas, for instance. Immediately pay back all money borrowed.

6. **Take responsibility for your life.** It isn't your roommate's responsibility to loan you money or food, clean up after you, entertain or feed your friends, or pay the bills.

7. **Keep your agreements.** Agree on chores and do your share. Make a list of chores. You should both feel as if you are keeping up a fair share of the load.

8. **Accept your roommate's beliefs.** Don't try to reform or change a roommate's beliefs. Listen openly, and when necessary, agree that your viewpoints are different.

9. **Accept your roommate's privacy.** Don't enter each other's bedroom or private space without asking. Don't pry, read personal mail, or eavesdrop on conversations. Don't expect to share activities unless you are invited. Give each other space.

10. **Get to know each other.** Set aside time for shared activities. Cook a meal, go for walks, or go to a movie.

11. **Keep your agreements.** Your life will improve greatly if you adopt this quality. When you say you will do something, do it. When you agree on a time, be punctual. Try to be flexible, however, so that annoyances don't build. Appreciate your roommate and don't focus on little faults.

 **CRITICAL THINKING LOG 11.6**

Healthy Relationships

Read the statements and questions below and write your comments on the lines provided.

1. List the factors that you believe are essential for a healthy relationship.

   _____

   _____

   _____

2. What do you believe contributes to unhealthy relationships?

   _____

   _____

   _____

3. Who are your friends?

   _____

   _____

   _____

4. Describe some of your other relationships, such as support groups and study teams.

_____

_____

5. List the ways that your relationships support you and your goals.

_____

_____

6. List the ways that unhealthy relationships may undermine you and your goals.

_____

_____

7. Describe your relationships with your instructors.

_____

_____

echnology
FOCUS:
Computers and Relationships

Computers can help you build better relationships when you use them to

- keep in touch with friends and family through e-mail.
- e-mail your academic advisor and instructors several times during the semester. Your e-mail could be just a few lines recapping a conversation, confirming a meeting, or clarifying expectations, but it improves communication and builds rapport.
- explore this book's Web site for multicultural issues.

http://peak.glencoe.com

Once you have an Internet account, username, password, and instructions on how to log on and log off, you can access the following:

- Electronic mail is a great way to send messages to friends and professional colleagues almost anywhere in the world who also have e-mail addresses.
- Chatrooms are popular Internet features that allow you to talk with others who share your interests. You can enter chat rooms about any subject and collaborate with others who share your research interests.

CAREER FOCUS: TEAM BUILDING AT WORK

Success at work, like success at school, begins with confidence, a sense of identity, and rapport. Being committed to warmth, sensitivity, and respect toward others is a winning combination for building teamwork in any organizational setting. Using assertiveness skills to work effectively as a team member will increase your productivity and satisfaction.

Meet Brad Timmons. He is an environmental planner and department head. Brad finds that he works more effectively when he works in small teams. The team members come up with more solutions, brainstorm ideas, edit and review each other's projects, and divide the work based on expertise and interest. Brad's team-building strategies include open communication, respect for differences, focusing on the task instead of the personalities, and solving conflicts. Most organizations are run by teams, and even the most educated and skillful people will falter if they fail to work effectively and cooperatively with others. The key is to review the effectiveness of your team periodically. Brad uses this team-building exercise.

Team Effectiveness Scale

	Low Effectiveness	High Effectiveness
	1 2 3 4 5 6	7 8 9 10

Team Function

Commitment to task _____

Oral communication skills _____

Listening skills _____

Writing skills _____

Conflict resolution _____

Decision-making skills _____

Creative problem solving _____

Openness to brainstorming and new ideas _____

Team spirit and cohesiveness _____

Encouragement of critical thinking _____

Interest in quality decisions _____

	Low Effectiveness	High Effectiveness
	1 2 3 4 5 6 7 8 9 10	

Professionalism   _____

Team integrity and concern for ethics   _____

Starting and ending meetings on time   _____

Scoring: The higher the number, the greater is the
team's effectiveness.   _____

How can this team be more effective?

_____

_____

_____

_____

_____

_____

What can individual members do to strengthen the team?

_____

_____

_____

_____

_____

_____

Acceptance

TIP Accepting and valuing individuals instead of stereotyping groups requires critical thinking skills.

A. Read the following and write your comments on the lines provided.

1. What is your attitude toward people who are different from you in gender, race, sexual orientation, or culture?

_____

2. Is your attitude one of acceptance or exclusion?

_____

3. Would you speak up if someone's gender, cultural, racial, sexual, or ethnic background were discussed in a stereotypical manner?

_____

4. Do you consider yourself to be a sensitive and respectful person?

_____

5. How do you show a sensitive and respectful attitude?

_____

B. Look at the reasons and excuses some students use for *not* meeting different types of people. Add to the list and write strategies for overcoming these excuses.

1. **Reason:** It's not polite to notice differences.

   Strategy:_____

2. **Reason:** I'm afraid of rejection.

   Strategy:_____

3. **Reason:** People who are different want to stick with their own kind.

   Strategy:_____

4. **Reason:** I feel uncomfortable around people who are different from me.

   Strategy:_____

5. **Reason:** I might say something embarrassing.

   Strategy:_____

6. **Reason:** People who are different from me wouldn't want me in their group.

   Strategy:_____

GLORIA STEINEM

Gloria Steinem is the founder and champion of the women's movement. She is a successful writer and activist. For the last twenty years, she has traveled, written books and articles, and has lectured widely. Steinem is extremely intelligent and determined to succeed. She won a scholarship to Smith College based on the strength of her outstanding entrance examinations. After college, she launched her career as a writer with assignments from *Esquire* and as a scriptwriter for NBC-TV.

Steinem went on to co-found *Ms.* magazine, becoming a frequent columnist and consulting editor. Author of numerous books, including *The Thousand Indias* and *Outrageous Acts and Everyday Rebellions,* she seems to have no limit to her energy, talent, or dedication. She was also active in the civil rights movement, and she was a founding member of the Coalition of Labor Unions for Women and a member of the International Women's Year committee. She is the recipient of many honors and awards, including the Penny-Missouri Journalism award and the Bill of Rights award. She was named Woman of the Year by *McCalls* magazine. Recently, with other investors, she became co-owner of *Ms.*

Steinem is a born leader with self-esteem and self-confidence. In her latest book, however, we see a vulnerable side. After almost twenty-five years of devoting herself to leading social revolutions, she is now exploring avenues of inner growth. She focuses on the impact of self-esteem as a source of authority and empowerment.

Source: http://peak.glencoe.com

11

Review and Study Notes

Affirmations

- I value relationships and make time for them.
- I listen actively to others.
- My intention is to build understanding and rapport.
- I communicate in a clear, calm, direct, yet kind manner.
- My relationships are supportive, satisfying, and nurturing.

Visualization

See yourself communicating with others openly and directly. You build rapport easily with others. People instinctively like you. You attract supportive and loving relationships that are allowed to change and grow. You are comfortable with yourself and are accepting of others. Feel the warm glow of satisfaction that comes from your healthy and satisfying relationships.

Peak Performance Strategies for Building Rapport

1. Assess and clarify intention.
2. Listen to understand.
3. Maintain a comfortable level of eye contact, tone of voice, and posture.
4. Remember names.
5. Show interest and empathy and ask questions.
6. Use warmth and humor.
7. Establish common bonds.

CASE A   *In the Classroom*

Anna Vitale is a business student in a two-year business college. She also works part-time on campus. She is friendly and outgoing and loves to visit with other people. Friends of hers often stop by to chat during her work hours, but she avoids telling them that she should be working. She likes people, but she has trouble being assertive and direct. Anna can be easily convinced to attend parties, even when she has homework to do. She often interrupts others, even when she knows they should be studying.

1. What advice would you give to Anna to help her be more assertive?

   _____

2. Is it unethical to use work time for socializing?

   _____

In the Workplace

Anna is now an office manager of a small company. She has little supervision. Because she is so sociable, coworkers stop by to chat throughout the day.

    Anna went recently to a workshop on ethics. The presenter made the point that time is money and should be viewed as an investment and not as an endless resource to be squandered. Anna would never steal money or supplies from her employer, but she realizes that she is stealing valuable time when she socializes too much on work time. Read and discuss the following guidelines Anna brought back from her workshop.

1. Give your employer your full attention while at work. You want to build good working relationships with your coworkers, but focus on work priorities while on the job.

2. Give your employer a full day's work. Ask yourself how you are adding to the value of the office rather than just putting in time.

3. Don't do unrelated business work on company time or take office supplies for personal use.

4. Don't interrupt coworkers to socialize when you know they have work to do.

   What other strategies would you suggest to Anna that would help her build rapport with others at work, yet would help her to use her time to add value to the company?

   _____

   _____

CASE B

Brent Scott is an electronics student and works part-time in an electronics firm. He likes to work with his hands and enjoys his technical classes. He has one marketing class that is difficult for him. The instructor has formed permanent class teams with weekly case studies to present and a final team project to complete. Brent dislikes relying on others for a final grade and gets frustrated trying to keep the team members focused on their task. Some people are late for meetings, others don't do their share of the work, and two people have personality conflicts.

1. What suggestions do you have for Brent to help him work more effectively with others?

   _____

   _____

2. What strategies in the chapter would increase Brent's listening and team-building skills?

   _____

   _____

In the Workplace

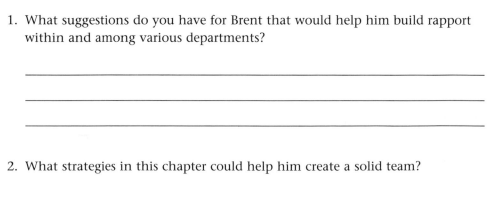

Brent is now a department manager of service technicians for a large security business that provides security equipment and alarm systems for banks, hotels, and industrial firms. His department must work closely with salespeople, systems design specialists, clerical staff, and maintenance personnel. Brent is having trouble convincing his technicians that they are part of the team. Sometimes they don't listen to the advice of the salespeople, clerical staff, or each other, which results in miscommunication and frustration.

1. What suggestions do you have for Brent that would help him build rapport within and among various departments?

   _____

   _____

   _____

2. What strategies in this chapter could help him create a solid team?

   _____

   _____

   _____

Chapter Application   WORKSHEET 11.1

Study Team Relationships

List some strategies for helping your study team be organized and effective.

Before the meeting:

_____

_____

_____

During the meeting:

_____

_____

_____

After the meeting:

_____

_____

_____

Challenges	Solutions
Latecomers or no-shows	_____
Passive members	_____
Negative attitudes	_____
Low energy	_____
Arguments	_____
Lack of preparation	_____
Socializing	_____
Members who dominate	_____

Name _____   Date _____

Chapter Application   WORKSHEET 11.2

Appreciating Diversity

Check Yes or No for each of the following comments.

	Yes	No
1. I am committed to increasing my awareness and sensitivity to diversity.	____	____
2. I ask questions and don't assume that I know about different groups.	____	____
3. I use critical thinking to question my assumptions and examine my views.	____	____
4. I strive to be sensitive and respectful of differences in people.	____	____
5. I listen carefully and seek to understand people with different views and perspectives.	____	____
6. I realize that I have certain biases, but I work to overcome prejudices and stereotypes.	____	____
7. I do not use offensive language.	____	____
8. I readily apologize if I unintentionally offend someone. I do not argue or make excuses.	____	____
9. I celebrate differences and see diversity as positive.	____	____
10. I speak up if I hear others speaking with prejudice.	____	____
11. I try to read about other cultures and customs.	____	____
12. I do not tell offensive jokes.	____	____
13. I encourage active participation of members of diverse cultural and social groups in clubs, groups, and any decision-making group.	____	____

Chapter Application   WORKSHEET 11.3

Are You Assertive, Aggressive, or Passive?

Next to each statement, write the number that best describes how you usually feel:
3 = mostly true; 2 = sometimes true; 1 = rarely true.

1. I often feel resentful because people use me. _____

2. If someone is rude, I have a right to be rude, too. _____

3. I am a confident and interesting person. _____

4. I am shy and don't like speaking in public. _____

5. I use sarcasm if I need to make my point with another person. _____

6. I can ask for a higher grade if I feel I deserve it. _____

7. People interrupt me often, but I prefer not to bring their attention to it. _____

8. I can talk louder than other people and can get them to back down. _____

9. I feel competent with my skills and accomplishments without bragging. _____

10. People take advantage of my good nature and willingness to help. _____

11. I go along with people so they will like me or to get what I want. _____

12. I ask for help when I need it and give honest compliments easily. _____

13. I can't say no when someone wants to borrow something. _____

14. I like to win arguments and control the conversation. _____

15. It is easy for me to express my true feelings directly. _____

16. I don't like to express anger, so I often keep it inside or make a joke. _____

17. People often get angry with me when I give them feedback. _____

18. I respect other people's rights and can stand up for myself. _____

19. I speak in a soft, quiet voice and don't look people in the eyes. _____

20. I speak in a loud voice, make my point forcefully, and can stare someone in the eye. _____

21. I speak clearly and concisely and use direct eye contact. _____

Scoring:

Total your answers to questions 1, 4, 10, 13, 16, 19: (Passive) _____

Total your answers to questions 3, 6, 9, 12, 15, 18, 21: (Assertive) _____

Total your answers to questions 2, 5, 8, 11, 14, 17, 20: (Aggressive) _____

Your highest score indicates your prevalent pattern.

CAREER DEVELOPMENT PORTFOLIO

Looking back: Review your worksheets to find situations where you learned to build rapport, listen, overcome shyness, resolve conflict, work with diversity, and be assertive.

_____

_____

_____

_____

_____

_____

_____

_____

Taking stock: Describe your people skills. What are your strengths in building relationships? What areas do you want to improve?

_____

_____

_____

_____

_____

_____

_____

_____

Looking forward: Indicate how you would demonstrate to an employer that you can work well with a variety of people.

_____

_____

_____

_____

_____

_____

_____

_____

Documentation: Include documentation and examples of team and relationship skills. Ask an advisor, friend, supervisor, or instructor to write a letter of support for you in this area. Keep this letter in your portfolio.

EXPLORING YOUR COMMUNITY'S RESOURCES

Coming together is the beginning.
Keeping together is progress.
Working together is success.

—Henry Ford, founder, Ford Motor Corp.

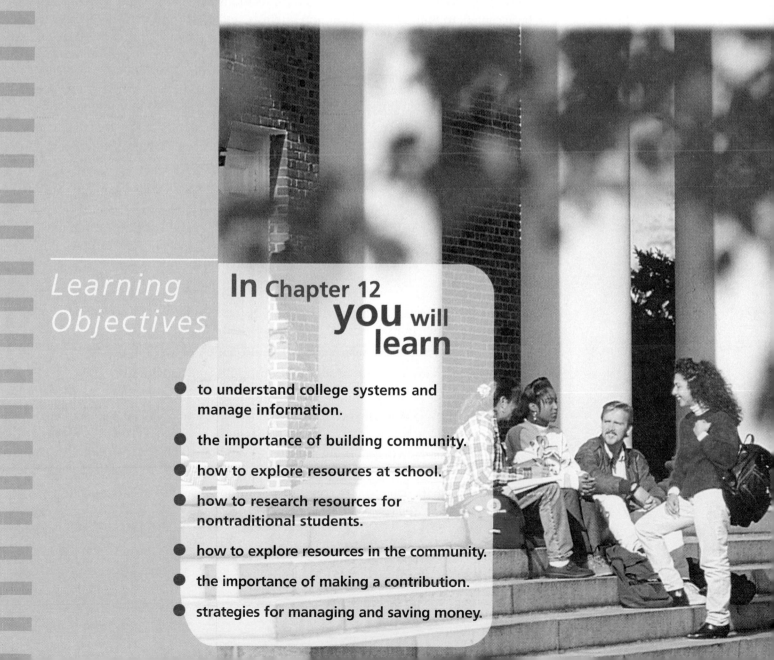

Learning Objectives

In Chapter 12 **you** will **learn**

- to understand college systems and manage information.

- the importance of building community.

- how to explore resources at school.

- how to research resources for nontraditional students.

- how to explore resources in the community.

- the importance of making a contribution.

- strategies for managing and saving money.

UNDERSTANDING THE COLLEGE SYSTEM

In this chapter, we will look at ways for using the resources of your school and the greater community, as well as your own inner resources, to build your own community. A system is a unified structure of interrelated subsystems. A school—a large school district or a private school or college—is a system composed of interrelated parts that work together to graduate students. When you enter a college or job, you are entering a system. You become responsible for understanding how the system works. This understanding includes knowing the system's rules, regulations, deadlines, procedures, and requirements.

THE IMPORTANCE OF BUILDING COMMUNITY

A sense of belonging is a basic and powerful human need. If you are a student living away from home, if you commute to school, if you live in a large urban area, or if you've moved often, you may not have experienced a sense of community or belonging. College is an ideal place to form relationships that will last a lifetime; to be accepted; to find activities, common interests, and issues; and to work together to achieve common goals.

The tools you have been learning for building rapport, listening, finding and managing resources, and forming relationships are all important for building a sense of community. Community is not just a physical place but a spirit where people are accepted despite their differences. You can create this sense of community and intimacy wherever you are.

EXPLORING CAMPUS RESOURCES

Resources are people, programs, paper and materials, facilities, time, and financial services that offer help and support for meeting goals and building community. Identify the resources most important to you, locate them on your campus, and include materials and phone numbers in a three-ring binder or your academic planner.

- *People resources.* Faculty, advisors, administrators, friends, coworkers, classmates, and counselors.
- *Paper and materials resources.* Catalogs, directories, books, and brochures.
- *Program resources.* Areas of study, groups, clubs, and activities.
- *Facility resources.* Buildings and equipment.
- *Financial resources.* Financial aid, credit agencies, and financial planning services.
- *Time resources.* Goals, priorities, activities, and scheduling.
- *Inner resources.* Personal skills, abilities, attitudes, qualities, motivation, and talents that enable you to cope, grow, contribute, and share. Your greatest resource is yourself.

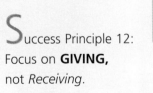

Success Principle 12: Focus on **GIVING,** not *Receiving*.

Planning

Write a list of people's names, facilities, and activities that you think you will need or use during most of your school term:

People

1. Person's Name: _____

   Phone Number: _____ Office Hours: _____

2. Person's Name: _____

   Phone Number: _____ Office Hours: _____

3. Person's Name: _____

   Phone Number: _____ Office Hours: _____

4. Person's Name: _____

   Phone Number: _____ Office Hours: _____

Facilities

1. Facility: _____ Phone Number: _____

   Purpose: _____

2. Facility: _____ Phone Number: _____

   Purpose: _____

3. Facility: _____ Phone Number: _____

   Purpose: _____

4. Facility: _____ Phone Number: _____

   Purpose: _____

Activities

1. Activity: _____

   Place: _____ Date/Time: _____

2. Activity: _____

   Place: _____ Date/Time: _____

3. Activity: _____

   Place: _____ Date/Time: _____

4. Activity: _____

   Place: _____ Date/Time: _____

Review the list of campus resources and find out where most of the offices are located on your campus.

Choose two or three offices from the above list and visit them. Discuss in your group.

People Resources

The most important resources on campus are the people with whom you work, study, and relate. Faculty, administrators, advisors, study team members, club members, sports team members, guest speakers, and all the students with whom you connect and form relationships make up your campus community. These people will help you network for jobs and will provide information and support.

Paper and Materials Resources

Most schools have a vast amount of paper resources. Here are a few that will be most helpful:

- *School catalog.* The school catalog is a great place to start. The catalog will include procedures and guidelines, academic areas, basic graduation requirements, and information on most services offered at your school. Look under academic areas. What fields of study interest you the most or the least? Which areas are so unusual you didn't even know that they existed?

- *School telephone directory.* The school telephone directory is an excellent source of information regarding staff, phone numbers, locations, activities, and services offered.

- *School newspaper.* This publication provides information about campus events and activities, jobs, roommates, rides, and so on. Working for newspapers and other campus publications is also a great way to develop writing and job skills and to meet new people.

- *Library.* When we think of libraries, most of us think of books. Indeed, the library is a rich source of books, magazines, newspapers, encyclopedias, dictionaries, pamphlets, directories, and more. Libraries also offer many services besides the written word. They may vary in size and services, but they all have information, ideas, facts, and a mountain of treasures just waiting to be explored. Besides books and periodicals, librarians and their staff are trained to find information about almost every subject. They can often order special materials from other libraries or direct you to other sources. Computer networks are now available in many libraries to retrieve information quickly. Many libraries have electronic access to books and periodicals.

- *Orientation guide.* Many colleges provide a student handbook or orientation guide.

- *Other.* (Add to this list.)

_____

_____

Program Resources

Most schools have various programs, departments, and offices that provide services and help. Use them to build your sense of community. Here are a few:

- *Orientation programs.* Many schools offer an orientation program or preview weekend. If you had the opportunity to attend an orientation program, review your information packets and keep them in your binder or academic planner.

Often there is so much information presented that it can feel overwhelming. You may want to refer to planning guides and requirements before you register for classes for next term.

- *Advising center.* A central advising center is available at most colleges to provide general education advising and to answer questions concerning policies, procedures, graduation requirements, and deadlines. In addition, you will usually be assigned an academic advisor for your major. Make certain that you keep your major contract, program changes, and graduation requirements in your binder or academic planner.

- *Admissions, records, and registration.* This office will have your transcripts, including information about grades, transfer credits, and dropping or adding classes. The registrar and staff can also assist you with graduation deadlines and requirements. Keep a copy of your transcripts, grades, grade changes, and other requirements in your binder or Career Development Portfolio.

- *Career development center.* This office provides career counseling and advising and often includes interview and résumé workshops and materials. Keep a copy of inventories, materials, and possible majors and careers in either your binder or Career Development Portfolio.

- *Job placement office.* Some schools offer a free placement service to help students find part- and full-time employment.

- *Exchange programs.* Your school may offer an exchange program, which is a great way to attend a different school without transferring. You stay enrolled at your own school but study for a term or a year at a designated school, either in this country or abroad.

- *Tutoring and special services.* Tutoring is offered through tutoring centers, academic departments, and special classes offered through student services.

- *Counseling.* Many schools offer a free counseling service for students who are trying to cope with the enormous demands of school or who want to talk about personal problems. Most professionals are trained to deal with addiction, eating disorders, depression, excessive shyness, and relationship conflicts, or they can refer students to agencies for specific problems. Many counseling centers also offer classes in study skills, time and stress management, and other topics to help students succeed.

- *Clubs, campus events, and activities.* Whether you have moved to a new college or are attending a local school, join campus events. Approach these events with a positive attitude and a sense of adventure. Create a new sense of community by joining clubs and making new friends. Developing a support system of people who are facing the same problems and changes as you are can be very helpful. For example, returning students often find the reentry center to be a wonderful resource of information, support, and friends.

- *Other.* (Add to the list.)

_____

_____

_____

CRITICAL
THINKING LOG
12.2

Discussion

Read the following statements and questions and write your comments in the lines provided. Be prepared to discuss your thoughts in class or with your study team.

1. When you hear the word *community,* what comes to mind?

   _____

   _____

2. Describe your experiences with community.

   _____

   _____

3. Did you grow up in a close-knit small town or rural community where you knew everyone?

   _____

   _____

4. Did you enjoy pancake suppers or ice cream socials at churches or community centers? What community events did you attend?

   _____

   _____

5. Did you grow up in a city and didn't know your neighbor two doors away?

   _____

   _____

6. Can that same sense of community that many people experienced years ago in small communities be created in the new millennium, or have people become too isolated, busy, independent, or uncaring? Explain your answer.

   _____

   _____

7. What factors kept you out of certain groups in the past?

   _____

   _____

8. Would you like to have a stronger sense of community? If so, what are the barriers involved? Add to this list of common reasons for not exploring or building a sense of community:

   _____

   _____

Reasons	Strategies
I'm not good at making new friends.	a. _____ b. _____ c. _____
This new campus or community overwhelms me.	a. _____ b. _____ c. _____
I work and I have a family. I don't have time.	a. _____ b. _____ c. _____
I like to figure things out for myself.	a. _____ b. _____ c. _____
People aren't friendly, so I stick to myself.	a. _____ b. _____ c. _____
I go to class and come home.	a. _____ b. _____ c. _____
I'm a returning student, so I don't need any of the school's resources.	a. _____ b. _____ c. _____
Jobs are impossible to find in this town.	a. _____ b. _____ c. _____

Financial Resources

Most schools provide many sources of jobs and financial aid. Be sure to explore them on your campus. Thousands of dollars of financial aid are available and go unclaimed each year. If you are having trouble paying for your education, check the financial aid office for loans, grants, scholarships, and information on programs available to students. Generally, scholarships and grants do not have to be paid back. However, student loans must be repaid! Make certain that you know the payback policy and treat your school loan with the same respect you would treat any loan. Unpaid loans hurt the lending agency or school and, of course, other students who want loans. They also hurt you because this information appears on credit reports. Here are some of the programs that are available:

- *School scholarships and grants.* Scholarships and grants are awarded at most schools on the basis of academic achievement, athletics, music, art, or writing and usually do not have to be paid back.

- *Pell Grants.* This is the largest student aid program financed by the federal government and does not have to be repaid. Check with your school.

- *Loans.* Stafford and Perkins loans are low-interest loans to be repaid after you complete your education. Plus loans and supplemental loans for students (SLS) have variable interest rates; repayment of the principal and interest begins after the last loan payment. Check with the financial aid office for a complete list of loans.

- *Work-study.* Student employment, or work-study, is an excellent way to earn money and gain valuable experience.

- *Other sources.* Loans, assistance programs, and aid programs may be available if you have special needs such as visual impairments, hearing problems, speech difficulties, or a deceased parent.

- *Veterans Programs.* Veterans can take advantage of money available through the Veterans Administration.

- *Programs for Native American students.* Native American students can find financial aid from the U.S. Bureau of Indian Affairs.

- *Unemployed.* Training programs such as WIN (Work INcentive) are available for the unemployed. There are also scholarships, grants, fellowships, and loans available.

Check with your school's financial aid office for a complete listing, or send for a copy of the Federal Student Aid Fact Sheet by writing to the U.S. Department of Education, Office of Student Financial Assistance, Washington, D.C. 20202-5464.

TRAILMARKER 12.1

Campus Facilities

Many campus facilities provide equipment and services. Here are a few:

- *Student union or center.* This office often houses student organizations, clubs, the bookstore, student government, and student activities. It will also have information on various student vacations, special classes, religious organizations, retreats, sports, and political groups. Get involved with your school, meet new people, and contribute your talents.

- *The health center.* There is usually an office or center that offers free or low-cost medical treatment and information for students.

- *Alumni association.* This organization provides special discounts, travel arrangements, benefits, and information for graduates. These services are often available to all students.

- *Gymnasium and sports complex.* Some schools have athletic centers or field houses, weight rooms, swimming pools, and basketball and racquetball courts that are open to all students.

- *Security.* Many schools have security or police departments that provide information about safety, parking, and traffic rules. Some even provide safe escort for night-class students.

- *Child care center.* Child care is often provided on campus, and sometimes there is a children's center sponsored by the early childhood education department.

- *Ride and carpooling boards.* There is often a bulletin board that lists information on rides, carpooling, and public transportation.

- *Off-campus housing.* Check for posted lists of available apartments, houses, people requesting roommates, and so on.

- *Other.* (Add to the list.)

_____

_____

_____

_____

_____

_____

_____

_____

_____

STUDENTS WITH DISABILITIES

Most schools realize the importance of providing services and resources for students with learning disabilities, chronic illnesses, and physical limitations.

- *Check out resources.* The first step is to learn what is available at your school, perhaps a center for disabled students or a learning skills center. Maybe special services are provided by student services or counseling. If you are visually impaired, the library may have audiotapes or books in braille. There are often classes in sign language for the hearing impaired. There should be ramps in most buildings, and some schools offer a van to transport students to classes. Most schools have tutors, student assistants, and special materials to help students with learning disabilities.
- *Meet with instructors.* The next step is to talk to all of your instructors. You are not asking for special favors or treatment but for alternatives for meeting your goals. You may want to sit in the front row, tape the lectures, be tested orally, or use a computer instead of writing assignments longhand.
- *Be realistic.* Outline what adjustments you will need to be successful. Design your educational plans with your disabilities in mind.
- *Be assertive.* Ask for what you need and want in polite, direct language. Treat yourself and others with respect.
- *Focus on your goals.* Realize that, even though your mountain is steeper, you have what it takes to succeed.

THE RETURNING STUDENT

If you are a returning student, you have lots of company. Over one-third of all students are over age twenty-five, and many are well over forty. These students are often referred to as nontraditional students. Their numbers are growing every year as more and more people return to school. Some returning students are veterans or single parents, some work full-time, and almost all have other commitments and responsibilities. Returning students often do better than younger students because they have a sense of purpose, discipline, and years of experience to draw on.

Two of their biggest concerns are finding time and dealing with interruptions. How can they manage school as well as the demands of families and jobs? Many find that they must organize their time and use the available campus resources. More and more services are offered for the older, returning student, such as support groups, child care, tutoring, credit for work experiences, and special classes. Some of the resources that are most important for reentry students include:

- Adult reentry center
- Legal aid
- Continuing education
- Adult services

- Veterans Affairs
- Office for credit for prior experiences
- Women's center
- Counseling center
- Job placement center
- Information/referral services
- Financial aid
- On-campus child care
- Orientation programs for transfer students

TRANSFER STUDENTS

Most colleges have a special orientation or workshop for transfer students. The important point is to remember that every college is different. Don't assume you know policies and procedures because you have attended a different college.

You will also want to make certain that you have an advisor; you should know what upper division, general education courses are required, what credits were transferred, and whether they were accepted as general education or as electives. Complete a major contract or plan of study so that you have direction. If you transferred as a junior, you may have only two years of college to complete.

STUDENTS ON PROBATION

Probation is a warning that you are doing substandard work. On many campuses, this means less than a 2.0 grade point average. If you continue to maintain a grade point average below 2.0 or if it falls to a certain level, you may be disqualified. Disqualification means that you are denied further school attendance until you are reinstated. Disqualified students may petition for reinstatement generally through the Office of Admissions and Records.

Many resources are available to help you stay in school and avoid probation. Follow all the study strategies in this book. Check with the learning skills lab, advising center, counseling center, and academic support services. Most schools offer workshops on study skills.

COMMUNITY RESOURCES

As a college student you have an opportunity to get to know a city and a chance to make a contribution to the campus and community. Even if you've always lived in the same city, you may not be aware of its rich resources and opportunities. When you get involved, you gain a sense of belonging and know that one person can make a difference. Many students have found enormous satisfaction in working with children, volunteering in nursing homes and hospitals, serving in a house of worship, or working with the homeless.

People Resources

- *Business professionals.* It is important to connect with business professionals in your field of study. They offer valuable information and advice, and maybe internships, scholarships, contacts, jobs, and career opportunities. You can make contacts by volunteering your services or joining professional organizations. Many professional groups have student memberships.

- *Government officials.* You will feel more involved in the community when you learn the names of your local political leaders. Go to a city council meeting, attend a county board of supervisors meeting, or meet the mayor. Sometimes city, county, and state governments have special programs, internships, and fellowships for students. Learn the names of your state senator and representative by calling the local political office or chamber of commerce.

- *Political parties.* Political activity is a great way to meet people, become informed about local issues, and contribute your organizational talents. Political parties are always looking for volunteers.

- *Child care.* Child care is provided by both private and public agencies. Look in the yellow pages and call city hall, houses of worship, or the local school district.

- *Health care.* Know the phone number of local hospitals and health clinics. They provide inexpensive vaccinations, birth control, gynecological exams, and health care.

- *Houses of worship.* Find a spiritual balance in your life and meet new friends. Houses of worship also hold social events, workshops, support groups, and conferences.

- *Crisis centers.* Hotlines are usually available twenty-four hours a day for such crises as suicidal feelings, physical and/or emotional abuse, rape, AIDS, and severe depression.

- *Helping organizations.* The American Cancer Society, American Heart Association, Red Cross, and Salvation Army provide information, services, and help. These organizations are always looking for volunteers.

Financial Resources

Look in the yellow pages or call the chamber of commerce to obtain a list of resources that offer help with financial planning or saving money. The following lists a few examples:

- *Job placement services.* Job placement services provide career counseling, job listings, and workshops for interviewing skills and résumé writing.

> We must delight in each other, make others' conditions our own, rejoice together, mourn together, labor and suffer together, always having before our eyes our community as members of the same body.
>
> —*John Winthrop, governor of Massachusetts Bay Colony, 1630*

- *Legal aid.* You may need free or low-cost legal aid services.

- *Community scholarships and grants.* Many community organizations (such as Rotary, Kiwanis, Lions, Elks, Soroptimist, and the American Association of University Women) offer scholarships and grants that do not have to be repaid.

- *Support groups.* Whatever your needs, there may be a support group to share concerns and to offer help. Among these are support groups for alcoholism, drug addiction, friends and family of addicts or alcoholics, physical and/or emotional abuse, veterans, people making career changes, and cancer and other terminal illnesses.

- *Counseling.* Counselors, psychiatrists, clergy, and therapists can help with personal problems such as depression, excessive shyness, or destructive behavior, or just to talk about any problem you may be having.

Paper and Material Resources

- *Community telephone directory.* Scanning the yellow pages is one of the best ways to discover the services available in the area.

- *Local newspapers.* Read the local newspaper to learn about community events, services, seminars, clubs, auctions, art showings, sporting events, concerts, businesses, and entertainment. You'll also read about the local political and community leaders and the current community issues.

- *Journals and newsletters.* Almost every community has a few journals and newsletters describing the area, featuring special local-interest stories, and advertising community resources.

- *Local libraries.* Check out the city and county libraries. As we have already discussed, libraries are a tremendous resource. Besides printed material, they offer a wealth of information, films, and classes.

- *Service learning.* Many schools are now encouraging students to incorporate internships, co-op programs, volunteer, or service learning into their education. The emphasis is on students contributing their time and talents to improve the quality of the community and to learn valuable job skills. Students often earn college credits and obtain valuable experience while integrating what they learn in classes with practical, on-the-job problem solving. Students also have an opportunity to create their own learning experiences through directed study and field experience. Some students tutor or work with the homeless, elderly, or disabled. Many other students find that internships and co-op programs are great ways to earn college credit and contribute their talents to a corporation. Many internships offer wages and some lead to part-time or full-time employment after graduation.

Making Time for Commitments

Read the following questions and write your comments on the lines provided.

1. How involved are you in campus events and activities?

   _____
   _____
   _____
   _____

2. Do your studies suffer?

   _____
   _____
   _____
   _____

3. Is time a factor?

   _____
   _____
   _____
   _____

4. Do you have enough time for school when you have a relationship?

   _____
   _____
   _____
   _____

5. How do you "juggle" school and a full-time job? List some tips or ideas.

   _____
   _____
   _____
   _____

6. What activities do you make sure you do with your children while maintaining job or school commitments?

   _____
   _____
   _____
   _____

All these programs stress service to the community. Organizations are looking for people who are not focused solely on promoting their careers but who also take time to contribute to the community. Service learning is beneficial for students, the school, and the community. Ask your academic department, advisor, and the career center about the service-learning options in your community.

Program Resources

- *Chamber of commerce.* The local chamber of commerce has information about local attractions, special events, museums, bed and breakfast inns, hotels, motels, restaurants, libraries, clubs, and businesses. They also have information about economic development, the environment, political issues, and clubs and organizations.

- *Clubs and organizations.* Many clubs such as Rotary, Lions, Elks, Soroptimist, American Association of University Women, and Kiwanis also offer scholarships for students. Clubs such as Toastmasters and Sierra Club offer programs for people with a specific interest. Big Brothers, Big Sisters, YWCA, YMCA, Girls Clubs, and Boys Clubs are always looking for volunteers and lecturers, and, they offer many services free or at low cost.

- *Recreation centers.* Recreation centers, gyms, swimming pools, and local community education programs offer classes, programs, and recreation.

> Annual income twenty pounds, annual expenditure nineteen pounds six, result happiness. Annual income twenty pounds, annual expenditure twenty pounds ought and six, result misery.
>
> —*Quote from* David Copperfield *by* **Charles Dickens**

YOU ARE A GREAT RESOURCE

The most important resource you have is yourself. Call on your inner resources to make a difference in the world. School and community resources are available not just to help you; you can also become involved and contribute your talents. Making a contribution is one of the best ways to connect to a school and community and to gain a real sense of satisfaction. What resources are you particularly interested in using? In what areas do you think you can make a contribution? Make time to get involved in at least one area of interest in school, the community, or the world.

HANDLING MONEY WISELY

Like time, money is a resource to manage. Financial planning is setting goals and choosing the steps necessary to reach these goals. Once you form the habits of saving, living within your means, planning, and taking charge of your financial responsibilities, you will have a solid foundation for lifelong financial success. Follow these tips:

- *Keep a budget.* The first step in planning is to write a budget. Calculate how much money you earn and how much money you spend. Write a long-range budget for a year or more, one for the school term, and a short-term monthly budget. You will then have a big picture of large expenses such as tuition, and you will also be able to modify and monitor your expenses each month. Keep receipts, bills, canceled checks, and credit card statements in a file or box in case you want to exchange your purchases and to help you revise for accuracy in your budget. Keep one file for taxes and file applicable receipts. Be realistic and monitor your budget each month. Refine it when necessary and then stick to it.

- *Beware of credit card debt.* You will want to establish a good credit rating. Credit cards are convenient and a way to establish a credit rating. However, be careful not exceed your loan limit and make certain you have the money before you charge. Thousands of students find themselves in debt every year by using a credit card without backup funds. Many students don't even know the rate of interest that they are paying. Most cards charge at least 18 percent interest. Some people blame the financial industry for making it too easy to obtain credit cards. As an adult, however, you should take full responsibility for being informed and for your decisions and actions.

Get Financial Help if You're in Trouble

If you find that you are having financial problems and your credit rating might be damaged, get help. Don't borrow more money!

1. **First, admit to yourself that you have a problem.** Take full responsibility. Denial only makes the problem worse. Don't blame others for yoursituation.

2. **Get professional help.** Check the yellow pages or call the local chamber of commerce and ask if your community has a consumer credit agency that helps with credit counseling. Bring all your budget information, assets, bills, resources, loans, and any other requested items.

3. **Spend less than you earn.** Write a budget and be absolutely firm about sticking to it. Once the habit of living within your means is part of your life, you will reap the rewards of confidence and control.

   - *Shop wisely.* Refer to a list when you shop and don't buy on impulse. Don't shop as a means of entertainment. Avoid buying convenience items and snack foods. They all cost more and provide less nutrition. Pack your lunch rather than buying snacks at school. You can save a considerable amount of money each week.

   - *Pay cash.* Don't use a credit card. If you have one, use it only for emergencies or special items like airline tickets. Pay off the balance on a credit card immediately. Interest charges can be expensive. You will be tempted to buy more with credit, and it is difficult to monitor how much you spend. Follow this simple rule: if you don't have the money, don't buy it. Keep your money in the bank and don't carry too much with you or have too much in your home. You will be less tempted to spend if money isn't readily available.

- *Think critically.* Expensive purchases, such as a car, stereo, or computer, should be planned carefully.

- *Use public transportation.* Don't buy a car if you can avoid it. Most cities have public transportation. Biking or walking whenever possible is far cheaper and less inconvenient than searching for parking. A car is an expensive purchase, and the purchase price is only the initial cost. Make certain you have researched the cost of insurance, tires, maintenance, gasoline, and parking. The stress of trying to find a parking space on campus can add to all the other pressures of school.

- *Simplify your life.* If you don't need it, don't buy it. Savor the freedom of living a simple, uncomplicated life. Look for free or inexpensive entertainment.

- *Exchange room and board for work.* Some students exchange room or board for lawn care, child care, or housecleaning. Since rent is an expensive item in your budget, an exchange situation can save you thousands of dollars over a few years. Ask around or put an ad in the newspaper, church or synagogue newsletter, community organization publications, and so forth. Also look for opportunities to house-sit.

- *Stay healthy.* Illness is costly in terms of time, energy, missed classes, and medical bills. You can avoid many illnesses by respecting your body and using common sense. Avoid unhealthy snacks and poor eating habits. Fresh fruit, vegetables, beans, brown rice, and whole grains are nutritious and cost less than processed and convenience foods. Get plenty of exercise and rest, and avoid harmful substances. Cigarette smoking is expensive, and smokers are sick more often, pay higher health premiums, and have more difficulty getting roommates.

- *Conserve energy.* Save money on utilities by turning down the heat, turning off lights, taking quick showers, and turning the water off while you brush your teeth.

- *Get a job.* Working while you go to school can help earn extra money, but make sure you are not working long hours and neglecting your education. Check with the career center or placement office for a list of on- and off-campus jobs.

Money In/Money Out

A. Monitor your spending for a month. To keep your budget simple, list money in and money out. Suggested categories are earnings, food, travel, school items, etc. At the end of the month, total your monthly income and your monthly expenses. Put them in the appropriate categories. Subtract your total expenses from your total income. The money left is your monthly surplus. If you have a deficit, you will need to explore ways of increasing revenue or decreasing expenses. An example budget follows.

Date	Money In	Money Out
Monday, Jan. 2	$28.00 (typed paper)	
Tuesday, Jan. 3		$14.00 (dinner/movie) $12.00 (gas for car)
Wednesday, Jan. 4	$58.00 (snow removal)	

How can you increase your earnings?

_____

_____

_____

_____

How can you decrease your spending?

_____

_____

_____

_____

B. List all the free or inexpensive entertainment available in your community. Discuss this list with your study team.

_____

_____

_____

_____

Technology FOCUS:
Computers and Organizational Information

Computers can help you find and organize information. Use the computer to

- check your college library's online database. Most college libraries offer Web access and online searches.
- explore resources at your career school or college.
- explore business sites.
- research information about student disabilities.

Use this book's Web site to link with other business sites and information about financial aid:

http://peak.glencoe.com

CAREER FOCUS:
KNOWING THE WORK SYSTEM

The more you give to your job, the more you get out of it. People, paper, programs, equipment, and financial and health plans are all an essential part of most businesses. You will be more successful in your job and daily activities will proceed more smoothly when you tap into the structure and procedures of your organization.

Meet Susan Weaton. She is a stress-reduction counselor and recreation director of a large airline manufacturing plant. She taps into all the resources of the company to serve both employees and clients. She uses memos, fliers, brochures, the telephone, guest speakers, departmental meetings, retreats, the informal grapevine, and films to reach all company employees. Her department is best known for its fully equipped, state-of-the-art gym and health facilities and its extensive stress-reduction programs. Susan's current challenge is to inform employees of the department's alcohol and drug prevention program. Employees can take advantage of excellent, confidential help for substance abuse, free of charge.

Susan has also discovered the satisfaction of contributing to the company. Besides being an active speaker and promoter of health and fitness, she is also a mentor to several young employees. She gives them advice, follows their careers, encourages them to obtain additional training, and looks for appropriate job opportunities. Susan insists that focusing on the resources available, rather than what is unavailable, is empowering.

PROFILE of A Peak Performer

BEVERLY J. HARVARD

We regard our community as a system made of many subsystems—people, services, machines, transportation, etc.—working together. We expect this interaction to create a safe, happy, and flourishing environment. When one subsystem of the community is not working properly, then the entire system cannot reach or maintain its goals. The result is chaos or crime.

To help a community reach its goals, rules and regulations are put in place. Community members like Beverly J. Harvard are called on to assist in achieving its goals. Harvard makes an important contribution of her time and talents as a Chief of Police to improve the quality of the community called Atlanta, Georgia. Juggling this high profile position and family responsibilities, this former sociology major has more than twenty years on the force. From patrolling the streets of Atlanta to various administrative positions in the department, she was in 1994 appointed the city's twenty-first police chief.

Her position is a multifaceted challenge and grand contribution to her community for many reasons. One is that she is the *first* African-American woman to lead a major metropolitan police department. Another is that she is making an impact in a once male-dominated work environment. And as the top police person, her daily challenge has been to maintain law and order in a city that was once ranked in FBI statistics as one of the most crime-ridden cities in the United States.

Recipient of many awards and citations—Metro Atlanta YMCA Woman of Achievement Award, Georgia's 100 Most Influential People, to name two—she has also appeared on televised broadcasts such as CNN and the *Today Show*.

Harvard is making a mark on her community. Her entire philosophy is about service and helping people. Responsible for over 2000 officers, she believes that the Atlanta police force can build positive relationships with its community's members. Community policing and community involvement will help reduce the crime rate.

A community is not just a physical place, but a spirit where people are accepted and can flourish. How do you think a police force builds positive relationships with its community?

Source: http://peak.glencoe.com

Review and Study Notes

CHAPTER 12

Affirmations

- I enjoy learning about campus resources.
- I enjoy learning about community resources.
- I own a manual that lists important resources.
- I contribute both on campus and in the community.
- I enjoy saving, and I save every month.
- I choose to live on less than I make.
- I feel prosperous, and I focus on my blessings.

Visualization

Visualize all the rich resources that surround you at school. Think of the community resources that support and enliven your life. Think of all the positives in your life—food, friends, family, and many opportunities. Feel prosperous, not deprived.

Peak Performance Strategies

1. Explore campus resources.
2. Explore community resources.
3. Find ways to get involved.
4. Find ways to contribute.
5. Budget your finances.

CASE Studies

CASE A

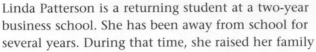

In the Classroom

Linda Patterson is a returning student at a two-year business school. She has been away from school for several years. During that time, she raised her family and is now eager to become involved in school and school activities. On returning to school, she happily discovered other returning students. Several of them get together for coffee regularly.

Linda wants to become more involved with the school community and is especially interested in foreign students and international business. She also wants to learn more about available computer services, guest speakers, marketing associations, and scholarships.

1. What suggestions do you have for Linda about involvement in campus and community events?

   _____

2. How would you define the term *school community*?

   _____

3. How can she find out about scholarships and explore all the resources that would increase her success as a returning student?

   _____

In the Workplace

Linda has been a salesperson for several years with a large cosmetics firm. She recently was promoted to district manager for sales. Part of her job is to offer motivational seminars on the benefits of working for her firm. She wants to point out opportunities and special resources available to employees, for example, training programs, support groups, demonstrations, sales meetings, and conferences. The company also donates money for scholarships and sponsors community events. An elaborate incentive system offers awards and prizes for increased sales.

1. How can Linda publicize these resources to her sales staff?

   _____

2. What strategies in this chapter would help her communicate the importance of contributing time and talents to the community and the company?

   _____

CASE B

Joseph Montero is a full-time computer programming student. His parents are helping him with most of his expenses. He lives at home and works summers with his father to help pay for his tuition. He can get along without a car but recently decided that he wanted one. He must work more than part-time to save enough money for a down payment. Because of his job, he eats out a lot and finds he isn't able to save as much as he'd like. Working has cut into his study time, and he has had to drop most activities. He'd like to take a math class at night and join the computer club, but these would interfere with his job. Help Joseph decide the pros and cons of buying a car.

1. If Joseph doesn't have to work to go to school, is it hurting or helping his future chances for career success?

   _____

   _____

2. What strategies in this chapter would you use to help Joseph save money and take control of his finances?

   _____

   _____

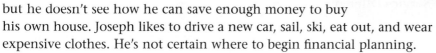

In the Workplace

Joseph is now a computer programmer for a large computer firm. He makes a good salary and can earn extra money by consulting or teaching part-time at the local business college. However, he never seems to save any money and lives from paycheck to paycheck. He lives in an expensive suburb of San Francisco. He loves living on the West Coast, but he doesn't see how he can save enough money to buy his own house. Joseph likes to drive a new car, sail, ski, eat out, and wear expensive clothes. He's not certain where to begin financial planning.

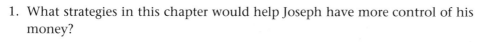

1. What strategies in this chapter would help Joseph have more control of his money?

   _____

   _____

2. What resources may be available in the community or at the local college that could help Joseph?

   _____

   _____

Chapter Application   WORKSHEET 12.1

Resources

List resources in your community. Check those you have visited.

Check

_____   Resource: _____

            Service Offered: _____

            _____

            Contact Person: _____

            Phone Number: _____

_____   Resource: _____

            Service Offered: _____

            _____

            Contact Person: _____

            Phone Number: _____

_____   Resource: _____

            Service Offered: _____

            _____

            Contact Person: _____

            Phone Number: _____

_____   Resource: _____

            Service Offered: _____

            _____

            Contact Person: _____

            Phone Number: _____

Name

Date

_____   Resource: _____

Service Offered: _____

_____

Contact Person: _____

Phone Number: _____

_____   Resource: _____

Service Offered: _____

_____

Contact Person: _____

Phone Number: _____

_____   Resource: _____

Service Offered: _____

_____

Contact Person: _____

Phone Number: _____

_____   Resource: _____

Service Offered: _____

_____

Contact Person: _____

Phone Number: _____

Name _____   Date _____

Keep a Budget Each Term

Budget for Each School Term		Estimated Expenses for the Year	
Tuition	$ _____	Tuition	$ _____
Books and supplies	$ _____	Books and supplies	$ _____
Housing	$ _____	Housing	$ _____
Transportation	$ _____	Transportation	$ _____
Insurance	$ _____	Insurance	$ _____
Clothing	$ _____	Clothing	$ _____
Laundry	$ _____	Laundry	$ _____
Food	$ _____	Food	$ _____
Entertainment	$ _____	Entertainment	$ _____
Utilities	$ _____	Utilities	$ _____
Phone	$ _____	Phone	$ _____
Health care	$ _____	Health care	$ _____
Household items	$ _____	Household items	$ _____
Savings	$ _____	Other	$ _____
Miscellaneous	$ _____	Loans	$ _____

Estimated Resources

	Month/Term
Parental contribution	$ _____
Summer savings	$ _____
Student savings	$ _____
Job	$ _____
Loans	$ _____
Other	$ _____
Total	$ _____

Chapter Application WORKSHEET 12.3

Money Management

A. List ways to increase income.

_____

_____

_____

_____

_____

_____

_____

_____

_____

B. List ways to decrease spending.

_____

_____

_____

_____

_____

_____

_____

_____

_____

Chapter Application   WORKSHEET 12.4

Building Community

Fill in the grid.

Read:
1. Catalog
2. School newspaper
3. Schedule of classes
4. Library publications

	People				Program				Facilities				Financial			
	Do you know your advisor?	Do you know your instructors?	Do you know key administrators?	Do you know your study team?	Have you attended orientation?	Do you know how to use computers?	Have you chosen a major?	Do you know about key programs?	Have you been to the student union?	Have you explored the library?	Have you used the computer facilities?	Have you explored key administrative offices?	Have you researched financial aid?	Work study	Student employment	Loans, grants, internships
First Month																
Second Month																
Third Month																
Fourth Month																
Fifth Month																
Sixth Month																
Seventh Month																
Eighth Month																

Chapter Application   WORKSHEET 12.5

Assessing Community Involvement

The purpose of this worksheet is to look back and assess how involved you have been in community service.

1. In what ways have you integrated academic course work with real life hands-on experiences?

   _____

   _____

   _____

2. List clubs and activities in which you were involved in high school.

   _____

   _____

   _____

3. List clubs and activities in which you are involved in college.

   _____

   _____

   _____

4. List internships.

   _____

   _____

   _____

5. List volunteer organizations in the community.

   _____

   _____

   _____

Chapter Application   WORKSHEET 12.5 (CONTINUED)

6. List professional clubs or organizations to which you belong.

   _____

   _____

7. List your role in those clubs.

   _____

8. What activities does your school club or organization involve itself in?

   _____

9. Choose two organizations from the following list. Use the Internet and other sources of information to find out about these organizations.

   United Way

   Volunteers of America

   Lions Club

   Salvation Army

   AmVets

   Other _____

10. Using the information you found for Question 9, answer the following questions for one of the organizations you researched.

    a. Who founded the organization?

       _____

    b. When was it founded? Where?

       _____

    c. Is it a

       _____ local organization

       _____ national organization

       _____ international organization

    d. Where is its main headquarters?

       _____

    e. What is its purpose or mission statement?

       _____

Chapter Application   WORKSHEET 12.6

Networking

Keep information about your network of people on the form below.

Name: _____

Company: _____

Phone: _____

Type of work: _____

Name: _____

Company: _____

Phone: _____

Type of work: _____

Name: _____

Company: _____

Phone: _____

Type of work: _____

Name: _____

Company: _____

Phone: _____

Type of work: _____

ASSESSING YOUR COMMUNITY INVOLVEMENT

1. Describe your ability to manage resources. What are your strengths in managing time, money, information, and determining what resources are available to solve problems?

    _____
    _____
    _____
    _____
    _____

2. Indicate how you would demonstrate to an employer that you have made a contribution to the community.

    _____
    _____
    _____
    _____
    _____

3. Indicate how you would demonstrate to an employer that you know how to explore and manage resources.

    _____
    _____
    _____
    _____
    _____

4. Indicate how you would demonstrate to an employer that you have learned leadership skills.

    _____
    _____
    _____
    _____
    _____

13

DEVELOPING GOOD HABITS

*All great bosses do one thing:
They engage. They capture
imagination and energy,
and by doing so get people to
move mountains.*

—Nancy Austin, management consultant

Learning Objectives

In Chapter 13 you will learn

- the importance of positive habits.

- the importance of commitment.

- how to change a negative habit.

- the seven positive attitudes of Peak Performers.

- the top tips for school success.

You can use many strategies for doing well in your school, career, and personal life. Many techniques are also available on how to manage your time, how to succeed at taking tests, and how to develop healthy relationships. Reading about and discussing them is one thing, but actually making these techniques and strategies part of your everyday life is another. You will find that embracing them will prove rewarding and helpful as you begin developing and working on your goals. Knowing that you have the motivational skills to succeed in school and in your career can give you the confidence to risk, grow, contribute, and overcome life's setbacks. You have what it takes to keep going even when you feel frustrated and unproductive. This chapter will show you how to take strategies and turn them into lasting habits. It will also look at the importance of effort and commitment, without which there is no great achievement. Look at great athletes. The difference in their levels of physical skill is often not dramatic, but their sense of commitment is what separates the good from the truly great. Peak Performers also achieve results by being committed.

MAKE A COMMITMENT TO CHANGE YOUR HABITS

Most people resist change. Even when you are aware of a bad habit, it is difficult to change it. Consequently, you may find it hard to integrate into your life some of the skills and strategies that you have encountered in this book.

Old habits become comfortable, familiar parts of your life. Giving them up leaves you feeling insecure. For example, you want to get better grades, and you know it's a good idea to study only in a quiet study area rather than while watching television or listening to the radio. However, you have always read your assignments while watching television. You might even try studying at your desk for a few days, but then you lapse into your old habit. Many people give up at this point rather than acknowledge their resistance. Some find it useful to take stock of what common resistors, or barriers, keep them from meeting their goals. But you, as a potential Peak Performer, will begin to adopt positive techniques to help change your old habits.

STRATEGIES FOR CREATING POSITIVE CHANGE

If you have trouble making changes, realize that habits are learned and can be unlearned. Adopting new habits requires a desire to change, consistent effort, time, and a commitment. Try the following strategies for eliminating old habits and acquiring new ones.

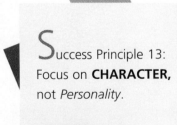

Success Principle 13: Focus on **CHARACTER,** not *Personality*.

1. **You must want to change.** To change, you must have a real desire and see the value of the change. It helps to identify important goals: "I really want to get better grades. I have a real desire to graduate from business college and own my own small retail business. I see the benefit and value in continuing my education." Your motivation has to be channeled into constructive action.

PART THREE   Application

2. **Develop specific goals.** Setting specific goals is a beginning for change. Statements such as, "I wish I could get better grades" or "I hope I can study more" are too general and only help to continue your bad habits. Stating goals such as "I will study for forty minutes, two times a day, in my study area" are specific and can be assessed and measured for achievement.

3. **Change only one habit at a time.** You will become discouraged if you try to change too many things about yourself at the same time. If you have decided to study for forty minutes, two times a day, in your study area, then do this for a month, then two months, then three, and so on, it will become a habit. After you have made one change move onto the next. Perhaps you want to exercise more, or give better speeches, or get up earlier.

4. **Be patient.** It takes at least thirty days to change a habit. Lasting change requires a pattern of consistent behavior. With time and patience, the change will eventually begin to feel comfortable and normal. Don't become discouraged and give up if you haven't seen a complete change in your behavior in a few weeks. Give yourself at least a month of progressing toward your goal. If you fall short one day, get back on track the next. Don't expect to get all *A*'s the first few weeks of studying longer hours. Don't become discouraged if you don't feel comfortable instantly studying at your desk instead of lying on the couch.

5. **Imagine success.** Imagine yourself progressing through all the steps toward your desired goal. For example, see yourself sitting at your desk in your quiet study area. You are calm and find it easy to concentrate. You enjoy studying and feel good about completing projects. Think back to a time in your life when you had these same positive feelings. Think of a time when you felt warm, confident, safe, and relaxed. Imagine enjoying these feelings and create that same state of mind. Remember, the mind and body produce your state of mind, and this state determines your behaviors.

6. **Observe and model others.** How do successful people think, act, and relate to others? Do students who get good grades have certain habits that contribute to their success? Basic success principles produce successful results. Research indicates that successful students study regularly in a quiet study area. They attend every class, are punctual, and sit in the front row. Observe successful students. Are they interested, involved, and well prepared in class? Do they seem confident and focused? Now model this behavior until it feels comfortable and natural. Form study groups with people who are good students, are motivated, and have effective study habits.

7. **Self-awareness.** Sometimes paying attention to your own behavior can help you to change habits. For example, you may notice that the school work you complete late at night is not as thorough as the work you complete earlier in the day. Becoming aware of this characteristic may prompt you to change your time frame for studying and completing school work.

> So few of my prisons are built by others. My sorrows, my loneliness, my despair are all of my own design. If there is confinement in my soul, it is of my own making.
>
> —*Bob Samples,*
> *author*

8. **Reward yourself.** One of the best ways to change a habit is to reward the completion of the desired behavior. Increase your motivation with specific payoffs. Suppose you want to reward yourself for studying for a certain length of time in your study area or for completing a project. You might say to yourself, "After I outline this chapter and look up the key words, I'll watch television for twenty minutes," or "When I finish reading these two chapters, I'll call Brent and talk for ten minutes." Watching television or talking with friends may make you feel relaxed, warm, or safe. Of course, the reward should come after the results are achieved and be limited in duration.

9. **Use affirmations.** Talking to yourself means that you are reprogramming your thoughts, a successful technique for making change. When you have negative thoughts, tell yourself, "Stop!" Counter negative thoughts with positive statements. Replace the negative thought with something like "I am centered and focused. I have control over my thoughts. When they wander, I gently bring them back. I can concentrate for the next forty minutes, and then I'll take a short break and have a snack."

10. **Write a contract for change.** Write a contract with yourself for overcoming your barriers. State the payoffs for meeting your goals: "I agree to take an honest look at where I am now and at my resistors, my shortcomings, my negative thoughts, the ways I sabotage myself, and the barriers I experience. I agree to learn new skills, choose positive thoughts and attitudes, and try new behaviors. I will reward myself for meeting my goals." You may want to discuss this with a study partner. Complete Critical Thinking Log 13.1, Self-Help Contract.

Make a Commitment to Contribute

Peak Performers are concerned about making a contribution to the world. They are committed to making the world a better place by improving themselves, giving to their families, and volunteering their time in the community. They want to leave a legacy that is positive and inspiring. They focus on this purpose and not just accumulating money, possessions, prestige, and career advancement. They want their family and friends to remember them for being a giving and service-minded person. Think about the contribution you make, the kind of person you want to be when you are eighty-five, and the legacy you want to leave behind.

Self-Help Contract

Complete the following statements in your own words.

1. I most want to change _____

   _____

   _____

   _____

2. My biggest barrier is _____

   _____

   _____

   _____

3. The resources I will use to be successful are _____

   _____

   _____

   _____

4. I will reward myself by _____

   _____

   _____

   _____

5. The consequences for not achieving the results I want will be _____

   _____

   _____

   _____

Date: _____

Signature: _____

Witness: _____

TRAILMARKER 13.1

Make a Commitment to Learn and Apply Positive Habits

Committing yourself to good habits is really the foundation for reinforcing the cycle of success. Read the following statements concerning habits for success. Check either Yes or No as each statement applies to you.

Success Habit	Yes	No
1. Have you created a study area that helps you concentrate?	_____	_____
2. Do you make learning physical?	_____	_____
3. Do you preview each chapter before you read it?	_____	_____
4. Do you preview chapters?	_____	_____
5. Do you rewrite your notes before class?	_____	_____
6. Do you outline your papers?	_____	_____
7. Do you proofread your papers several times?	_____	_____
8. Do you rehearse your speeches until you are confident and well prepared?	_____	_____
9. Do you attend every class?	_____	_____
10. Do you sit in the front of the class?	_____	_____
11. Do you actively listen and take good notes?	_____	_____
12. Do you rewrite your notes and review them within twenty-four hours?	_____	_____
13. Do you monitor your work?	_____	_____
14. Do you get help early, if necessary?	_____	_____
15. Do you participate in class and ask questions?	_____	_____

		Yes	No
16.	Have you developed rapport with each of your instructors?	___	___
17.	Have you joined a study team?	___	___
18.	Do you study and review regularly each day?	___	___
19.	Do you complete tasks and assignments first and then socialize?	___	___
20.	Do you recite and restate to enhance your memory skills?	___	___
21.	Do you take advantage of campus and community activities?	___	___
22.	Can you create a motivated and resourceful state of mind?	___	___
23.	Do you know how to solve problems creatively?	___	___
24.	Do you use critical thinking in making decisions?	___	___
25.	Do you exercise daily?	___	___
26.	Do you maintain your ideal weight?	___	___
27.	Do you keep your body free of harmful substances and addictions?	___	___
28.	Do you support your body by eating healthy foods?	___	___
29.	Do you practice techniques for managing your stress?	___	___
30.	Have you developed an effective budget?	___	___
31.	Do you take the time for career planning?	___	___

If you find you've answered No to many of these questions, don't be alarmed. When old habits are ingrained, it's difficult to change them. By observing your thoughts, rethinking your beliefs, and reframing your experiences, you can alter your behavior and make lasting changes.

Seven Positive Attitudes of Peak Performers

1. *A flexible attitude* means that you are open to new ideas and situations. You are willing to learn new skills and are interested in continual growth.

2. *A mindful attitude* means that you are focused on lasting values. You are mindful of living in the moment, being a person of integrity and character, and acting with kindness and civility. Being is more important than acquiring or doing.

3. *A responsible attitude* means that you take an active role in school and work. You take responsibility for your life and don't rely on others to motivate you. You are a self-starter who takes the initiative to produce positive results.

4. *A supportive attitude* means that you encourage, listen, show empathy, and work well with others. You look for the best and are more concerned about understanding than persuading others. You look for win/win solutions and communicate clearly, concisely, and directly.

5. *A confident attitude* means that you have a balanced perspective about your strengths and limitations. You commit time and effort to grow and to renew yourself physically, mentally, emotionally, and spiritually. You are confident because you use the whole of your intelligence and you are self-disciplined.

6. *A follow-through attitude* means that you are aware of the big picture but are also attentive to details and follow through on essential steps. You see whole systems while attending to essential parts. This perspective can make the difference between success and disaster. For example, there were not enough lifeboats on the Titanic nor were there binoculars in the crow's nest. A limiting and arrogant mind-set convinced many that the Titanic was unsinkable; therefore, details were not addressed. As a result, the iceberg was not spotted soon enough to avoid it, and many people could not be saved because of the lack of lifeboats.

7. *An innovative attitude* means that you are upbeat, optimistic, and enthusiastic. You use creative problem solving and critical thinking to solve problems.

Make a Commitment to Develop a Positive Attitude

Achieving excellence is a combination of a positive attitude and specific skills. When you commit yourself to being successful, you learn to go with your own natural energy and strengths. You learn to be your own best friend by working for yourself. You begin by telling the truth about who you are: your current skills; abilities; goals; barriers; and habits, both good and bad. You learn to be aware of the common barriers and setbacks that cause others to fail. Then you set goals to focus your energy on a certain path. Next, you create the specific thoughts and behaviors that will produce the results you want.

Everyone loses course at times; thus, it is important to build in observation and feedback so that you can correct and modify. You will learn to alter your actions to get back on track. Even when you are equipped with the best skills, self-understanding, and a motivated attitude, you will still face occasional setbacks and periods of frustration. At times you may question your decisions, become discouraged, and feel your confidence and self-esteem dip. Focus on the positive and learn to be resilient.

Make a Commitment to Be Resilient

The key to being a Peak Performer is to make adversity work for you. Successful people see their failures as temporary setbacks and learning experiences; unsuccessful people see their failures as barriers and dead ends. Use the power of reframing to see your setbacks as stepping-stones to your final goal. Children have a natural resiliency and can bounce back after a disappointment. You can reclaim resiliency by using your creativity to see what options are still available.

Make a Commitment to Be a Person of Character and Integrity

The word *integrity* comes from the Latin word *integer*, meaning "a sense of wholeness." This book has stressed using the *whole* of your intelligence for school and job success. When you have a sense of wholeness, you are confident about thinking, speaking, living, and walking on the right path. You know that you can trust yourself to do the right thing, keep your commitments, and play by the rules. You are a complete human when you use your skills, competencies, and essential personal qualities, such as integrity. You have effective communication skills, strive to be sociable and personable, but you put character first. It is not difficult to work out a code of ethics or a moral code that most of us can agree on. Most people believe in core values of honesty, truthfulness, fairness, kindness, compassion, and respect for others. Doing the right thing is a decision and a habit. The key is to assess your integrity as you would any skill and use critical thinking to reflect on your actions.

As an adult, you teach values by example. To choose to teach deliberately and consistently is the challenge. Becoming a responsible, motivated, emotionally mature person makes you smarter than you think. You may have a high IQ, talent, skills, and experience, but if you lack responsibility, effort, commitment, a positive attitude, interpersonal skills, and especially character and integrity, you will have difficulty in college, in the workplace, and in your relationships.

TRAILMARKER 13.2

Success Principles

Focus on **REALITY,** not *Illusion.*

Focus on **RESPONSIBILITY,** not *Blame.*

Focus on **PRIORITIES,** not *Activities.*

Focus on **INTENTION,** not your own *Message.*

Focus on the **PRESENT,** not the *Past.*

Focus on **WHOLENESS,** not *Fragmented parts.*

Focus on **STRENGTHS,** not *Weaknesses.*

Focus on **EXCELLENCE,** not *Perfection.*

Focus on **DECISION MAKING,** not *Snap judgments.*

Focus on **QUALITY,** not *Quantity.*

Focus on **ACCEPTANCE,** not *Judgment.*

Focus on **GIVING,** not *Receiving.*

Focus on **CHARACTER,** not *Personality.*

Focus on **ESSENTIALS,** not *Nonessentials.*

More Success Principles

Focus on **EFFORT,** not *Ability.*

Focus on **RESULTS,** not *Time.*

Focus on **NOW,** not the *Past.*

Focus on **SUCCESS,** not *Failure.*

Focus on **PROBLEMS,** not *Inconveniences.*

Focus on **AGREEMENT,** not *Excuses.*

Focus on **FORGIVENESS,** not *Grievances.*

ON THE ROAD TO SUCCESS

You are beginning to feel that you have a positive attitude. You practice imagery and affirmations daily. You have read the Trailmarkers in each chapter and completed all the Critical Thinking Logs and Career Development Portfolio exercises. What else can you do to promote your success in school, on the job, and in your life?

1. **Face your fears.** Psychologists suggest that many self-limiting and self-defeating behaviors are motivated by fear—of failure, success, the unknown, looking foolish, letting go, giving up, not being perfect, losing, and being lonely. Fear blocks creativity, causes the imagination to run wild, and makes everyday problems look catastrophic. Fear can devastate your sense of self-confidence, make recall difficult, and harm your performance in school and in life. When you are faced with a new

situation, a public speaking class, a math exam, a new roommate, dating someone new, or talking to your instructor about a poor grade, don't fall into the black hole of fear. It is easy to focus on the worst that could happen, but you can learn to face and overcome fear. Many students have been on academic probation and have still been able to graduate with honors and do well in careers. Many successful managers became Peak Performers only after being fired, picking themselves up, and starting anew. Indeed, many successful people experience failure and use it as a stepping-stone to success. They dare to risk and fail.

2. **Be a good listener.** The ability to listen is one of the most important skills. Active listening is listening with the intention of really understanding the other person. Assuming you know what the other person feels or thinks is a major problem in communicating and listening. Ask yourself, "How can I see this differently?" and "What can I do to increase understanding?"

3. **Assume responsibility.** Assuming responsibility and having the strength to follow through with commitments and agreements are key qualities of people who are successful in all areas of their lives. You may not always feel like keeping your commitments to yourself, to your instructors, or to your supervisors, but in the long run, meeting obligations will serve you well. You will get ahead in school and in life when you are reliable, conscientious, and honorable. Often, a major obligation for students is repayment of student loans after completing a course of study. Deciding to pursue higher education is an extremely important commitment to yourself as you enter a partnership with your school. You'll want to honor all aspects of this and other commitments.

4. **Be a team player.** Some people resist authority. No one likes to be controlled, supervised, or given orders. To be successful, it is important to change your perception and begin to look at instructors, advisors, and supervisors as part of your team. They deserve your support, tolerance, and willingness to be a team player. Unless an instructor, advisor, or supervisor does something that is immoral, illegal, or unethical, they deserve your loyalty and support.

Students sometimes criticize instructors and advisors and do their best to make them look bad. Employees go to their supervisor's supervisor with complaints and demands. Most schools give students an opportunity to evaluate instructors. A candid evaluation of the instructor is an appropriate method to voice any complaints. However, even if you think your instructor or supervisor is incompetent, only upper management will decide when, and if, he or she should be fired. Why not begin to see a person in authority as an ally who can help you and whom you can help? Adopt an attitude of "How can I support this person? What can I do to make him or her look good?"

The working relationship you establish should be based on respect. You will find that most instructors and advisors will go the extra mile to help you if they know who you are and if you show interest and a willingness to apply yourself. The team player attitude also extends to time spent with your study teams. They are important, and you will learn so much more by being a team player and studying in teams.

Peak Performers Whose Lives Showed Resiliency and Courage

Elizabeth Garrett Anderson—Although rejected by medical schools because she was female, she still became the first female member of the British Medical Association.

Abraham Lincoln—Although raised in poverty and teased because of his appearance, he still was elected President of the United States.

Glen Cunningham—Although he was told he would never walk after he was severely burned when he was three, in 1934 he set the world's record for running a mile in just over four minutes.

5. **Be willing to learn.** Some students feel that learning new information is not important for success. They cling to their own traditions or argue with everything the instructor says. Talented professionals can also find themselves in the dead-end lane of their careers if they refuse to learn. Everyone must keep up with new ideas, techniques, and information. The willingness to learn is key to success in school and life. Keep an open mind and be willing to learn new information, and unlearn and revise your map of the world.

6. **Be tolerant.** Often we enter school or the business world with a set of prejudices and an intolerant attitude about others that is faulty and negative. Be tolerant of different cultures, backgrounds, views, and lifestyles. Never assume that people see the world as you do. School is an excellent opportunity to begin to understand and cooperate with people from different cultures, nationalities, and backgrounds. Tolerance is essential in the business world and for every aspect of life.

7. **Keep on top of it.** Everyone starts the school year or a new job with a measure of enthusiasm, but often complacency sets in before the semester or year is over. Don't indulge in pity, self-satisfaction, or complacency. Keep up with assignments, set goals and priorities, study, and review every day. We all need a breather to set new goals, but your supervisor or instructor will know when you are coasting and, most important, so will you. Keep up with your assignments and don't fall behind.

8. **Be enthusiastic.** One way to sabotage your classes or career is to expect that your supervisor or instructor will make your life interesting. Don't fall into the boredom trap. All careers are boring at times, and some classes are less than spellbinding. You can use your imagination and creativity to make any tedious situation challenging and fun. You are responsible for creating a motivated and resourceful state of mind. No one is responsible for entertaining you. Boredom can be stressful. Some students have received their worst grades when they haven't had enough to keep them busy because they took only a few classes. Ask yourself, "What can I do to get more out of this class?" Assume more responsibility, ask if you can take on additional projects, help with tutoring or grading other classes, or learn a new job area.

9. **Be independent.** Being independent is more than being responsible. It means you can spend time alone, and you can make decisions based on your values and not allow others to talk you into anything. Enjoy the company of others, but also learn to enjoy yourself and solitude.

10. **Be supportive.** A supportive attitude is important in your interactions with others. Pettiness is a major barrier to school or career success. It is often how something is said, not what is said, that makes a difference. Listen to what you say and your tone of voice. Ask yourself, "How can I be direct and kind? Does this tone of voice sound hostile? How can I give a more supportive and respectful response?" Whether you are a student or a business professional, you can be perceived as petty by your actions. Try not to complain constantly, criticize coworkers or fellow students, or belittle others' accomplishments.

11. **Be sincerely happy for others.** Life often seems like a comparison game, with competition for grades, jobs, relationships, and money. Sometimes others seem to have more and your own life is lacking. Realize that there is enough of everything in life to go around. Make a decision to be happy when others get good grades. Don't let jealous feelings sour your life. Focus on your blessings, strengths, and talents, not on comparing your life to others.

12. **Keep things in perspective.** Is it a problem or an inconvenience? Some people spend a great deal of time and energy focusing and getting angry at events that they cannot change. They complain about the weather, become angry when their plane is late, become annoyed because other people are difficult, or are upset because they had to wait in line. For example, a plane crash is a problem, the plane being late is an inconvenience. A serious car accident is a problem; a fender bender is an inconvenience. Cancer or another life-threatening disease is a problem; a cold is an inconvenience. Put events in perspective and focus on what is important. Even good students can lose papers, forget assignments, and do poorly on a test. Don't turn one mistake into a recipe for continued failure. Focus on all the tasks you do well and on your accomplishments. Take responsibility, but don't blow the situation out of proportion.

CRITICAL THINKING LOG 13.3   Advise Others

Answer the questions below before you write a letter to your daughter, your son, or a close friend about success.

1. What can you write that would help them face and overcome setbacks and disappointments?

   _____

   _____

   _____

   _____

2. What would make their climb toward becoming a Peak Performer easier?

   _____

   _____

   _____

   _____

   _____

PEAK PERFORMANCE SUCCESS FORMULA

There isn't any secret to producing an outstanding athlete, a skilled musician, an accomplished performer, or an experienced mountain climber—or academic excellence and success. The training required to get into Olympic form is the same as that which produces results in school and in work.

W hat is *intrinsic vision?* It is encouraging self-talk and imagery. It is your positive voice and vision telling you that you can accomplish your goals.

Formula for Success

The Formula for Success can be broken down into four components:

1. *Confidence* is believing in yourself, knowing your worth, and recognizing that you have what it takes to do well. Self-confidence is one of the most important mental qualities you can have for producing results. When you build on the accomplishments of small victories and successes, you realize that you can achieve almost any goal you set. Confidence is your resolve to win.

2. *Vision* is mental rehearsal of your victory. You must know clearly what you want to achieve. Be realistic about seeing this vision become a reality. Vision requires you to focus internally and to imagine yourself in detail achieving your goal.

3. *Method* is the process for achieving your goal and knowing the strategies, techniques, tools, and tactics that produce tangible results. Method involves monitoring your actions and techniques so that you can change, modify, and adapt them to excel consistently.

4. *Training* is the actual practice and the consistent effort required to improve your skills. Training requires the capacity to stay with a vigorous program and endless hours of rehearsal. Athletes know that they must practice relentlessly to see what may often be only small improvements. Practice is what separates the Peak Performer from the average person.

Positive **H**abits

You can use the computer to create an electronic file of the positive habits and personal qualities you are developing. Keep a journal in which you list the changes you want to make each semester. Log in your goals and keep track of your progress. Include in your journal samples of quotes and inspiring stories. Save supportive e-mails from friends and family.

You can also use the Internet to explore resources, tips on creating positive habits, and ways to manage change. Keep in mind that sites often change.

Use this book's Web site http://peak.glencoe.com. to find links to sites that will explore resistance to adapting positive habits, managing change, and coping with instructors. These sites may lead you to other sites.

MAKE A COMMITMENT TO LIFELONG LEARNING

Self-awareness provides some understanding of why and how you make choices. You can learn strategies for the short-term, but true learning is lifelong and depends on the ability to manage change. Regardless of occupation, age, education level, or job status, all of us must be involved in the exciting, frightening, and frustrating business of change.

The workplace is experiencing major changes. Shifts in the economy can result in layoffs for competent, highly educated, and skilled workers. Corporate buyouts, downsizing, and mergers may also cause job turnovers, layoffs, and forced retirement. The competition for good jobs is fierce. Pick up any newspaper or magazine and you'll find articles about slow job growth and predictions of slow recovery in the job market. Given this information, it is imperative that all employees learn new skills, obtain job training, and learn to adapt to change.

As we've seen throughout this book, the ability to transfer learning habits and skills is crucial to successful learning. The same holds true on the job. Be prepared to transfer basic job and career skills such as problem solving, active learning, effective communication, and maintaining healthy relationships between jobs and throughout a career. Flexibility is the key to managing change.

However, some employees resist change. Just as poor habits and a secure comfort zone can limit a student's sense of worth and result in discouragement and poor study habits, workers may also feel powerless and unwilling to make the effort unless they can be guaranteed job security. The fact is, surviving in today's business world means that everyone must adapt to change. Many business opportunities are lost because a manager clung to outdated business practices. A willingness to change doesn't mean adopting every new trend or change for the sake of change. It means being aware and open to new trends, taking responsibility for creating a positive climate, and taking a lead in developing policies and procedures to prevent problems before they occur. Clearly, the ability to adapt to change, learn new skills, and solve problems concerning workplace trends are crucial job skills.

> To be conscious that you are ignorant of the facts is a great step to knowledge.
>
> —*Benjamin Disraeli,*
> *former prime minister of*
> *Great Britain*

TRAILMARKER 13.3

Assessment Is Lifelong

Read the skills listed below. Then rate yourself on a scale of 1 to 5 (1 being poor and 5 being peak or excellent).

Area	Peak Performance		Satisfactory		Poor
	5	4	3	2	1
1. Reading			_____		
2. Writing			_____		
3. Speaking			_____		
4. Mathematics			_____		
5. Listening			_____		
6. Critical thinking and reasoning			_____		
7. Decision making			_____		
8. Creative problem solving			_____		
9. Mental visualization			_____		
10. Knowing how to learn			_____		
11. Personal qualities (honesty, character, responsibility)			_____		
12. Sociability			_____		

CREATING GOOD HABITS

Make a commitment to take responsibility for your thoughts, feelings, words, behaviors, and habits. The way you feel and interpret events around you has a direct bearing on all of them. Consequently, the first step is to take control of how you interpret events and your reactions and behaviors toward them. Negative interpretations can entail placing the blame on others, always seeing dissenting ulterior motives, or turning minor events into major problems. On the positive side, you can interpret events and people's intentions so that you see the best in others and situations.

	Peak Performance		Satisfactory		Poor
	5	4	3	2	1

13. Self-management and control   _____

14. Self-esteem and confidence   _____

15. Management of time, money, space, and people   _____

16. Interpersonal, team, and leadership skills   _____

17. Working well with cultural diversity   _____

18. Organization and evaluation of information   _____

19. Understanding systems   _____

20. Understanding technology   _____

21. Commitment and effort   _____

Assess your results. Do you have a better understanding of how you learned these skills and competencies? Do you know how to document and demonstrate these skills and competencies? Your major or career choice may include other skills. Assess additional skills that can be transferred to many situations or jobs. For example, here are six broad skill areas:

- Communication skills
- Human relations skills
- Organization, management, and leadership skills
- Technical and mechanical skills
- Innovation and creativity skills
- Research and planning skills

Create a system for thinking and behaving in positive ways. Practice a behavior or habit you want to adopt until it becomes a way of life. This kind of change will take commitment, time, and practice. The results, however, will be uplifting. You will find yourself exhibiting self-discipline, emotional control, and habits that will keep you centered, calm, rational, productive, and peaceful even in the midst of confusion and turmoil.

RESISTORS AND FEARS

Listed below are a few resistors that may make lasting change difficult.

- *Fear of the unknown.* What will happen if I really can't get good grades? Can I compete? I was not that good a student in high school. What makes me think I can do college work? Everyone else seems so much smarter.

- *It's familiar and comfortable.* I have a familiar routine of going to work, coming home, preparing dinner, and taking care of the house. How will I find time to study, work, and take care of my family?

- *Independence.* I don't work well in groups. I'd rather study by myself. Besides, some of the students are so young that I may not have anything in common with them.

- *Security.* I felt secure with my beliefs and views. Some of the new ideas that I'm learning are so different. I had thought through my opinions, but now I see that there are lots of ways of looking at issues. This is exciting, but it also makes me feel insecure.

- *Tradition.* I come from a conservative family. I was always expected to stay home and raise my family and take a job only to help supplement the family income. My desire for a college education and career of my own contradicts family tradition. My sister-in-law says that I'm selfish and foolish to go back to school at this time in my life.

- *Embarrassment.* Will I feel embarrassed being in classes with younger students? Can I hold up my end of the team projects and class discussions? I haven't had a math course in twenty years and my study skills are rusty.

- *Responsibility.* I am overwhelmed by the responsibility of working, going to school, and caring for my family. I know I am responsible for my life, but sometimes it would be easier if someone would just tell me what to do.

- *Expectations.* I have certain expectations of myself. If I go to college, I want to do well. I will not feel successful unless I get mostly *A*s.

- *Environment.* My physical environment is not supportive for studying. Our home is noisy and there is no place where I can create my own study area. My husband and children say they are proud of me, but they complain about hurried meals and a messy house. They resent the time I spend studying.

- *Cost.* I am concerned about the cost of going to school. Tuition, textbooks, a computer, day care, and supplies all add up. Is it worth it? Maybe I should be saving for my children's education instead.

- *Giving up.* I love my classes, the new ideas I'm learning, and the people I've met. My study group is accepting, and they value my opinions and contributions. It is my dream to earn a college degree. But, it's too overwhelming. I might as well quit now because I don't want to invest more time and money and then fail.

BE RESPONSIBLE

Career enhancement suggestions are useless unless you actually change your behavior and develop positive, consistent, and long-lasting work habits. Habits free you from making constant decisions about daily events. Good habits can transform you into a true professional. Commit yourself to taking responsibility for your career by developing habits that produce results.

Meet Laura Makay. She is a sales assistant in a refrigeration plant. As a student, she was undisciplined and never developed effective techniques for making her workload easier. In her new job, Laura was offered the opportunity to take a sales training course. She was told that a great deal would be expected of her, but it was also a tremendous opportunity for advancement. Fortunately, Laura has a supervisor that is aware of the importance of good habits. She encourages Laura to assess her strengths and weaknesses and to develop goals for better health and energy; better relationships; better work habits; and more effective memory, reading, note-taking, listening, problem-solving, and decision-making skills. Laura also plans to focus on clear communication. Instead of trying just a few strategies, Laura works with her supervisor and the training department to develop good habits. She assesses herself often and adjusts her behavior when necessary to get herself on track.

Trailmarker 13.4 lists ten habits you can develop that will go a long way toward a successful career. Commit yourself to them!

TRAILMARKER 13.4

Ten Habits for Peak Career Performance

1. Be dependable. Keep your agreements and always be on time!

2. Be an active team player. Get involved and contribute your time and talents.

3. Be enthusiastic, motivated, and interested in your work.

4. Be an active learner and continually acquire new skills.

5. Be a self-starter.

6. Be a creative problem solver and use critical thinking to make decisions.

7. Follow up on details.

8. Always project a professional, well-groomed image.

9. Use communication skills (active listening, writing, and speaking) consistently.

10. Always act from a point of integrity. Consistently follow high business ethics. Your reputation is your most important asset.

Building on Success

1. Read the following statement: Success builds on success.

2. In your own words, explain what the above statement means.

   _____

   _____

   _____

   _____

3. Cite some examples of successful events or projects that have led to other successful endeavors (sports, promotions, personal).

   _____

   _____

   _____

   _____

COMPUTERS AND YOUR CAREER

Exciting new career options and changes in the workplace will appear as two divergent technologies, telecom and cablecom, merge. This merger will result in a sophisticated data communication system that will include the Internet, protocols, e-mail, cable, and digital video. People who have a background and experience in these emerging cable and telephony technologies will be in demand. These professionals will include cable pros versed in radio frequency transmission, analog cable engineers, networking experts, and electricians capable of running advanced protocols on the same wiring. Marketing professionals will also be needed.

Take this opportunity to explore new exciting career options.

Computers can also help you organize. Keep a file of changes in your chosen field and in the business world in general. This research will help ease your transition from college to career and help you keep up with rapid changes. Try: http://peak.glencoe.com

PART THREE   Application

TRAILMARKER 13.5

The Best Strategies for Success in School

1. Attend every class.

2. Go early and stay until the end.

3. Sit in the front, participate, and ask questions.

4. Choose the best instructors and get to know them.

5. Give the first three weeks of classes your best effort.

6. Use the power of synergy; form study teams.

7. Preview all reading assignments before classes.

8. Write key words, phrases, and formulas on note cards.

9. Write a summary of the chapter in your own words.

10. Study in short blocks of time and take frequent breaks.

11. See your advisors and instructors regularly. E-mail them.

12. Review class notes after every class and again within twenty-four hours.

13. Carry note cards for formulas and key words with you.

14. Make up sample tests and pretest yourself.

15. Set goals and daily priorities. Do first things first.

16. Turn in all assignments on time. Do extra credit work.

17. Create an organized, well-lit, and quiet study space.

18. Eat healthy foods, exercise, get enough rest, and avoid drugs.

19. Study when you are most alert.

20. Adapt to your instructor's teaching style.

21. Integrate learning styles. Make learning physical and personal.

22. Use a mind map for outlining and brainstorming.

23. Practice speeches until you are comfortable and confident.

24. Read and exchange term papers. Proofread several times.

25. Program your mind with positive affirmations and visualizations.

26. Neatness counts. Focus on details of papers.

27. Negotiate for a better grade *before* grades are sent in.

28. Review expectations for every class.

29. Value and develop positive personal qualities.

30. Don't procrastinate. Set up a schedule and project board.

31. Keep a journal and write letters to improve your writing skills.

32. Be positive and upbeat.

33. Be tolerant of others.

34. Focus on your priorities. Don't become distracted.

35. Use an erasable pen for neat, organized essay questions.

36. Reframe your circumstances and see the positive side of life.

37. Make questions out of chapter headings. Read chapter summaries.

38. When taking notes in class, watch for clues from your instructor.

39. Use waiting time for reviewing notes and using note cards.

40. Read standing up. Read out loud. Summarize your reading.

41. Welcome feedback and use it to monitor your results.

42. Ask for help early.

43. Connect patterns, link concepts, and look for relationships.

44. Summarize chapters in your own words. Recite out loud.

45. Use listening and good communication skills to build rapport.

46. Take time to explore campus and community resources.

47. Know the course objectives and the instructor's expectations.

48. Anticipate questions and ask why. Good questions deserve good answers.

49. Make information personal, applicable, and alive.

50. Focus on the present and absorb yourself in the moment.

51. Surround yourself with students who are motivated.

COLIN POWELL

Colin Powell was the first African-American to hold the office of the Chairman of the Joint Chiefs of Staff. He was regarded by many political leaders of both parties as successful and intelligent, and as the most powerful military person in the nation. No one would have been able to predict his success based on his earliest academic record.

Powell was the son of Jamaican immigrants and grew up in a poor neighborhood of New York City. In elementary school he was placed in the slow-learners group, and in high school he was a *C* student. He went to the City College of New York, where he continued to struggle with his grades. His first success came when he enrolled in a Reserve Officer Training Corps (ROTC) class. Finally, Powell was on the right path. He not only found something in which he could excel, but he discovered his life's work. He received *A*s in all his ROTC classes and was graduated first in his ROTC class. He began to show unusual leadership skills and to clarify his life's mission. He became president of the Cadets Officers Club and a cadet colonel. After serving in Vietnam, Powell applied to graduate school. He was turned down initially because of poor grades, but eventually he was graduated second out of a class of 1244.

He attributes his success to his philosophy. "Hard work generates good luck and opportunities. . . Yes, I climbed and I climbed well, and I climbed hard and I climbed over the cliff, but always on the backs and contributions of those who went before. Now, on the top of that cliff and looking ahead, there are still more rivers to be crossed."

Powell is now retired but still active. He was knighted by the Queen of England and received the Presidential Medal of Freedom (the highest United States nonmilitary award) and the Presidential Medal of Freedom With Distinction. He is a popular and sought-after speaker and has been asked to run for political office. He has said that neither of the two major parties fits his phi-losophy and he is not willing to com-promise. However, he does not rule out a political future. It is clear that with his talent, vision, and character, Powell will once again assume a strong leadership role in some aspect of American life. Powell is a Peak Performer.

Source: http://peak.glencoe.com

13

Review and Study Notes

Affirmations

- I have the creative resources to overcome boredom and frustration.
- Nothing can destroy my deep, inner peace.
- I choose positive thoughts and words.
- I am inspired to live life to the fullest.
- Today I will do everything to support my health, happiness, and goals.

Visualization

As soon as you wake in the morning, take five minutes to set the tone for the day. Close your eyes and take several deep breaths. Imagine within you a bright light that illuminates all your thoughts and feelings. This light spreads throughout your body, giving warmth and strengthening your inner resources. Imagine your success instincts becoming strong and focused. Feel the certainty and commitment. You have everything it takes to be successful. Feel the confidence and sense of being alive spread through your body as you take a deep breath.

Peak Performance Strategies for Creating Positive Habits

1. You must want to change.
2. Set specific goals.
3. Work on only one habit at a time.
4. Give yourself thirty days to change a habit.
5. Imagine success.
6. Observe and model successful people.
7. Observe and monitor yourself.
8. Reward yourself.
9. Use positive self-talk.
10. Write a contract for change.

CASE A In the Classroom

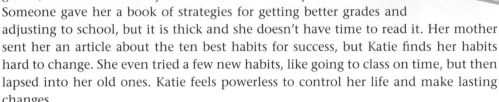

Katie Lyons is smart, attractive, fun, and energetic, and she works well with other people. She wants to get better grades, but she is too busy to take a class on study skills. Someone gave her a book of strategies for getting better grades and adjusting to school, but it is thick and she doesn't have time to read it. Her mother sent her an article about the ten best habits for success, but Katie finds her habits hard to change. She even tried a few new habits, like going to class on time, but then lapsed into her old ones. Katie feels powerless to control her life and make lasting changes.

What strategies would you suggest to Katie to help her adopt positive habits?

_____

_____

_____

_____

In the Workplace

Katie is now an assistant buyer at a sportswear company. She talks endlessly about the excitement of this field, opportunities for travel, contacts with interesting people, and the fun of seeing new fashions. Her dream is to become a buyer with a large sportswear company. She knows that she will have to make some major changes. First, she should get additional training in computer skills, management, and accounting, but when can she find the time? She also knows that she has to follow through on details more carefully, but that part of her job bores her. In addition, Katie has fallen into the habits of coming to work and meetings late, and turning in reports that are overdue and incomplete. She also must learn to work with diverse groups of people, but she finds different people hard to relate to. Clearly, Katie has the desire for advancement, but she finds it difficult to make real, lasting changes or committing herself to changing poor work habits.

What strategies would you suggest to Katie for changing her habits and making the commitment to the results she wants for her career?

_____

_____

_____

_____

CASE B

Cody Brady is a welding student. He never liked high school, but his natural mechanical ability helped him get into a trade school. He wants to be successful and knows that this is an opportunity for him to get a good job. Cody's parents both worked, so he and his sister had to get themselves off to school, supervise their own homework, and prepare many of their own meals. Money was tight and he didn't often receive encouragement for positive behavior. He never learned positive study or work habits.

1. What kind of a study plan can you suggest to Cody to build his confidence and help him be successful?

   _____

   _____

   _____

2. What strategies in this chapter can help him develop positive, lasting habits?

   _____

   _____

   _____

In the Workplace

Cody is now working in a large farm equipment manufacturing plant. He has just been promoted to general supervisor in charge of welding and plumbing. He is a valued employee at the firm and has worked hard for several years for this promotion. Cody wants to ensure his success in his new job by getting training in motivation, teambuilding, quality customer service, and communication skills.

1. What suggestions do you have for Cody to help him establish and train his staff in good habits?

   _____

   _____

   _____

2. What strategies in this chapter can help him be more successful?

   _____

   _____

   _____

Chapter Application   WORKSHEET 13.1

Overcoming Resistance to Change

Fill in the following:

1. I resist _____

2. I resist _____

3. I resist _____

4. I resist _____

5. I resist _____

6. I resist _____

7. I resist _____

8. I resist _____

9. I resist _____

10. I resist _____

Strategies to Overcome Resistance:

1. _____

2. _____

3. _____

4. _____

5. _____

6. _____

7. _____

8. _____

9. _____

10. _____

Chapter Application   WORKSHEET 13.2

Changing a Habit

1. Write a study habit you want to change and the steps for creating lasting change.

   _____

   _____

   Results wanted: _____

   _____

   Practice new behavior: _____

   Reward: _____

   Write an affirmation _____

2. Write a personal habit you want to change and the steps for creating lasting change.

   _____

   _____

   Results wanted: _____

   _____

   Practice new behavior: _____

   Reward: _____

   Write an affirmation _____

3. Write a habit at work you want to change and the steps for creating lasting change.

   _____

   _____

   Results wanted: _____

   _____

   Practice new behavior: _____

   Reward: _____

   Write an affirmation _____

Chapter Application WORKSHEET 13.3

Planning Your Career

Use the following plan to develop a career action plan.

Career Objective: _____

What type of job? _____

When do you plan to apply? _____

Where is this job? _____

- City _____

- State _____

- Company _____

Whom should you contact? _____

How should you contact? _____

- phone _____

- letter _____

- walk-in _____

Why do you want this job? _____

Resources available: _____

Skills applicable for this job: _____

Education: _____

- Internship _____

- Courses taken _____

- Grade Point Average _____

- References _____

_____

_____

Chapter Application   WORKSHEET 13.4

Changing Habits

Fill in the grid. You can list more than one habit under each category.

	Habit				Change Perception				Reinforce				Practice			
Take responsibility Be willing to learn Be a team player Be honest Identify	Make a commitment to change.	Set a specific goal.	Work on only one habit at a time.	Give yourself time.	Choose to do things differently.	Change negative self-talk to positive.	Imagine success.	Observe and model others.	Reward yourself.	Set negative consequences for setbacks.	Keep a journal of successes.	Write a contract for change.	Act as if you have succeeded.	Practice, practice, practice.	Be persistent and resilient.	Never give up.
Work Habit																
Study Habit																
Personal Habit																

Name _____   Date _____

Final Exam Schedule

Course	Date	Time	Room	Type of Exam

CAREER DEVELOPMENT PORTFOLIO

PREPARING YOUR RÉSUMÉ

In anticipation of preparing your résumé, start thinking about the information that will appear on it. No matter what résumé format you use, you will need to summarize your skills and qualifications and match them to the requirements of the job you are seeking.

As you continue with your courses of study in preparation for entering the job market, gather materials and phrases that capture your developing skills and accomplishments. Add them to your career development portfolio so you will have a selection to choose from when it is time to write a résumé. Use proactive words and action verbs when writing information for your résumé. Here are some examples:

- *organized* a group of after-school tutors for math and accounting courses.
- *wrote* and *published* articles for the school newspaper.
- *participated* in a student academic advisory board.
- *developed* a new accounting system.
- *managed* the petty cash accounts for the PTA.
- *can keyboard* 60 wpm.

Now try your hand at writing some action phrases that demonstrate your accomplishments as a student, employee, or participant in a club or organization. Begin your phrases with verbs like *organized, participated, developed, accomplished,* or *managed.*

1. _____

2. _____

3. _____

4. _____

5. _____

6. _____

7. _____

8. _____

Do not be discouraged if you have few action phrases to write at this time. Keep this activity in your portfolio and add to your list as you continue your studies and become an active participant on your campus and with your courses of study.

TIP You can write a résumé in either of two basic forms: the chronological form or the functional form.

CAREER DEVELOPMENT PORTFOLIO

Your vision will become clear only when you can look into your own heart. Who looks outside, dreams; who looks inside, awakes.

—Carl Jung, psychologist

Learning Objectives

In Chapter 14 you will learn

- how to plan your Career Development Portfolio.

- the contents of your portfolio.

- how to assemble your portfolio.

- how to use your portfolio for writing an effective résumé.

- how to use your portfolio to prepare for interviewing.

- how to explore majors and careers.

Y ou need assessment and feedback as you progress through the various aspects of your life: school, work, community, family, and personal. One method of assessment is to keep an up-to-date Career Development Portfolio. This chapter will show you how to take control and plan your career by using this assessment tool. Maintaining your Career Development Portfolio will become a lifelong process. Just as you change and grow, you will want to change and update your portfolio. You will discover that the strategies that helped you plan your education successfully are the same techniques that can help you plan your career.

CREATING A CAREER DEVELOPMENT PORTFOLIO

Artists have traditionally compiled samples of their work in portfolios. Showing samples of their best work, style, and talent was fundamental to getting a job. You can also gain a competitive edge by showing the best of your work and accomplishments in your Career Development Portfolio. It is a tool designed to highlight your strengths, skills, and competencies to other people.

The Importance of a Career Development Portfolio

A Career Development Portfolio helps you to

- plan and design your educational program and postgraduate learning.
- record significant life experiences.
- reflect on these experiences and assess what you have learned.
- describe how your experiences have helped you grow professionally.
- document clearly skills and accomplishments in and out of the classroom.
- see the connections among educational, extracurricular, community service, internship, job, and leadership learning experiences.
- apply patterns of interests, skills, and competencies to career planning.
- identify areas you want to enhance, augment, or improve.
- record and organize experiences for your résumé and job interviews.

Using Your Career Development Portfolio

A portfolio can be used for many different goals. Use it to

- satisfy entry requirements for a job even if you do not have the degree qualifications.
- enter an educational program even if you do not have the required course requirements.
- obtain a certain level job and demonstrate that you have transferable skills and experience that are not evident from your present position.
- receive college credit for prior learning for work you have completed through other colleges; internships; and learning, work, or life experiences.

Success Principle 14: Focus on **ESSENTIALS**, not *Nonessentials*.

- prepare for a job change.
- prepare a résumé.
- document accomplishments during an interview.
- organize a file for tenure and/or promotion.
- express talents creatively and artistically.

The Career Development Portfolio can also help you connect what you have learned in school to your work, and it serves as an organized and documented system to demonstrate that you have the necessary skills, competencies, and personal qualities to perform a job. For example, Janet convinced an employer to hire her based on her portfolio: she showed the manager samples of her work and the certificates she had earned. Jake used his portfolio to receive a promotion: he was able to stress his strengths based on documentation of his skills and experiences in his portfolio.

The Career Development Portfolio is an organized place to file documentation of courses, certificates, degrees, and samples of your work. It helps colleges place you in the right courses; it helps employers make the best use of your skills; and it helps you determine what you need to do to obtain a job, internship, leadership position, or promotion, or to reach a career goal.

When Should You Start Your Portfolio?

You can start your portfolio at any time. Ideally your first year or first term in school is the time to begin your Career Development Portfolio. By the time you graduate, you will have a tool that is distinctly personal and persuasive. A sample planning guide follows. This guide can be used for students in both two- and four-year schools. (Students in a two-year school include freshman and sophomore years in their first year and junior and senior years in their second year.) Modify the planning guide to fit your needs.

HOW TO ORGANIZE AND ASSEMBLE YOUR PORTFOLIO

The exercises, log entries, and worksheets that you have completed throughout this book form the basis of your Career Development Portfolio. You will want to keyboard an edited copy of this information on the computer and save it so you can easily make changes and update it often. You will also need

- a three-ring notebook.
- sheet protectors to hold documents and work samples.
- labels and tabs.
- a box to store work samples and information.

Sample Career Development Portfolio Planning Guide

Freshman Year

- Begin your Career Development Portfolio.
- Assess your interests, skills, values, goals, and personality.

- Go to the career center in your school and explore majors and careers.
- Set goals for your first year.
- Write a résumé.
- Network with professors and students. Concentrate on getting good grades.
- Keep a journal. Label the first section Self-Assessment. Begin to write your autobiography. Label another section Exploring Careers.

Sophomore Year

- Add to your Career Development Portfolio.
- Start a file about careers and majors.
- Join clubs and take a leadership role.
- Read articles and books about your major area.
- Find a part-time job or volunteer your time.
- Update your résumé.
- Explore internships and co-op programs.
- Add a section to your journal called Job Skills and Qualities.

Junior Year

- Update and expand your Career Development Portfolio.
- Choose a major and career and gain more job experience.
- Network. Join student organizations and professional organizations.
- Develop relationships with faculty, administrators, and other students.
- Obtain an internship or gain additional job experience.
- Update your journal with job tips and articles about your field.
- Update your résumé.
- Visit the career center on campus for help with your résumé, internships, and job opportunities.

Senior Year

- Refine your Career Development Portfolio.
- Put your job search into high gear. Go to the career center for advice.
- Read recruitment materials. Schedule interviews with companies.
- Update and polish your résumé and print copies. Write drafts of standard cover letters.
- Network.
- Keep a list of contacts and their telephone numbers.
- Join professional organizations and attend conferences.
- Start sending out résumés and attending job fairs.
- Find a mentor to help you with your job search and career planning.
- Log interviews in your journal or notebook.
- Continue your journal with strategies for promotion.

The steps for organizing and assembling your portfolio will vary depending on your purpose and the school you are attending. However, they generally include procedures such as these:

- *Step 1: Determine your purpose.* You may want to keep a portfolio as a general documented system of achievements and professional growth, or you may have a specific reason such as attempting to receive credit for prior learning experiences.

- *Step 2: Determine criteria.* The U.S. Department of Labor's Secretary's Commission on Achieving Necessary Skills (SCANS) identified skills and competencies needed for success in the workplace. They apply to all kinds of jobs in every occupation. You may add specific criteria to this list as they apply to your situation.

- *Step 3: Do your homework.* Make certain that you have completed the Career Development Portfolio at the end of each chapter. Assess and review your worksheets.

- *Step 4: Assemble your portfolio.* Print computer copies using quality paper. It often works best to work with a study partner. The following is a general guideline for the contents of your portfolio.

Cover Letter

Your cover letter should indicate the purpose of the letter, indicate documents enclosed, give a brief review, and ask for an interview. See Figure 14-1 on page 14-6 for an example of a cover letter.

Cover Page

Your cover should include a title, your name, college, and the date. You may want to use heavy card stock and put your own logo on the cover to make it unique. Do not number this page. See Figure 14-2 on page 14-6 for an example of a portfolio cover.

Title Page

Your title page should include the title of your document, where you are submitting the portfolio, name, and date. See Figure 14-3 on page 14-6 for an example of a title page.

Contents Page(s)

The contents lists the contents of the portfolio. You can make a draft when you start your portfolio, but it will be the last item you finish so that the page numbers and titles are correct. See Figure 14-4 on page 14-6 for an example of a contents page.

Introduction

The introduction should discuss why you are submitting the document, your plan of development, and the contents. See Figure 14-5 on page 14-7 for an example of an introduction page.

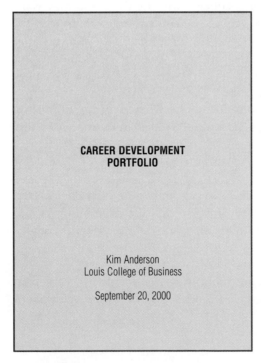

737 Grandview Avenue
Euclid, Ohio 43322
October 2, 2000

Dr. Kathryn Keys
Director of Assessment of Prior Learning
Louis College of Business
333 West Street
Columbus, OH 43082

Dear Dr. Keys:

I am submitting my portfolio for credit for prior learning. I am applying for credit for the following courses:

Marketing 201   Retail Marketing
Management 180   Introduction to Management
Business Writing 100   Introduction to Business Writing

I completed my portfolio while taking the course Special Topics 350. My experiences are detailed in the portfolio and I believe they qualify me for six units of college credit.

I look forward to meeting with you to discuss this further. I will call your office next week to arrange an interview at your convenience. If you have questions, please call me at 202-555-5556.
Sincerely,

Kim Anderson
Kim Anderson

Figure 14-1
Sample Cover Letter

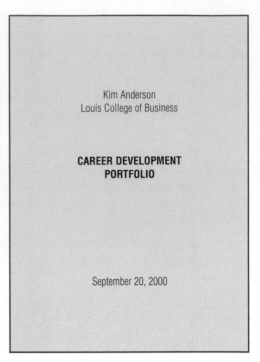

Kim Anderson
Louis College of Business

**CAREER DEVELOPMENT
PORTFOLIO**

September 20, 2000

Figure 14-2
Sample Cover Page

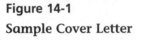

**CAREER DEVELOPMENT
PORTFOLIO**

Kim Anderson
Louis College of Business

September 20, 2000

Figure 14-3
Sample Title Page

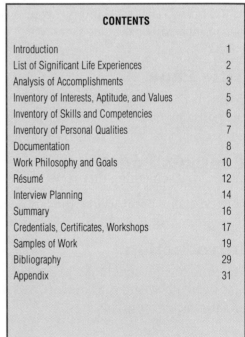

CONTENTS

Figure 14-4
Sample Contents Page

INTRODUCTION

The Career Development Portfolio I am submitting reflects many hours of introspection and documentation. The purpose of this portfolio is to gain college credit for similar courses that I completed at Wake View Community College.

I am submitting this portfolio to Dr. Kathryn Keys in the Office of Prior Learning at Louis College of Business.

I recently made a career change and want to enter the marketing field. The reason for the change is personal growth and development. I had an internship in marketing, and I know I will excel in this area. I plan to complete my degree in Business Administration at Louis College of Business. Eventually I want to work my way up to store manager or director of marketing at a large store.

This portfolio contains:

- A list of significant life experiences
- Analysis of accomplishments
- Inventory of interests, aptitudes, and values
- Inventory of skills and competencies
- Inventory of personal competencies
- Work philosophy and goals
- Résumé
- Documentation
- Interview planning
- Samples of work
- Summary of transcripts
- Credentials, certificates, workshops
- Bibliography
- Appendix

Figure 14-5
Sample Introduction

List of Significant Life Experiences

This section should include a year-by-year account of all your significant life experiences (turning points) in your life. You are preparing a chronological record or time line. Resources that can help you besides your memory are family members and friends, photo albums, and journals. Don't be concerned at this point about what you learned but concentrate on experiences that are important because you

- found the experience enjoyable.
- found the experience painful.
- learned something new about yourself.
- achieved something that you value.
- received recognition.
- expended considerable time, energy, or money.
- experienced a major change in your life.

This section can also be written as an autobiography. It can include:

- graduation and formal education.
- jobs/promotions.
- marriage/divorce.
- special projects.
- volunteer work.
- training, workshops.
- self-study, re-entry into college.
- extensive travel.
- hobbies and crafts.
- relocation.
- military service.
- events in family.

Analysis of Accomplishments

Once you have completed your list of significant life experiences, you are now ready to identify and describe what you have learned and how you learned it. Specifically identify what you learned in terms of knowledge, skills, competencies, and values and how you can demonstrate the learning. Whenever possible, include evidence or a measurement of the learning. What valuable attitudes have you developed as a result of your experiences? Review your list of significant experiences and look for patterns, themes, or trends. Assess your accomplishments and analyze your experiences. Did these experiences

- help you make decisions?
- help you clarify and set goals?
- help you learn something new?
- broaden your view of life?
- accept diversity in people?
- help you take responsibility?

- increase your confidence and self-esteem?
- result in self-understanding?
- change your attitude?
- change your values?

Inventory of Skills and Competencies

Use your completed Career Development Portfolio worksheets to record skills and competencies. Your college may also provide you with a list of specific courses, competencies, or categories. Consider as a guide the report we have discussed throughout this book from the Department of Labor Secretary's Commission on Achieving Necessary Skills (**SCANS**). Indicate how you have learned each of these skills and competencies:

1. **Foundation skills.** These basic skills include reading, writing, mathematics, speaking, and listening.
2. **Thinking skills.** Thinking skills include critical thinking, creative thinking, decision making, problem solving, knowing how to learn, reasoning, and ability to visualize mentally.
3. **Personal qualities.** Personal qualities include responsibility, dependability, self-esteem, sociability, integrity, and self-management.
4. **Resource management.** Resource management skills include management of time, management of money, management of space and facilities, management of human resources, and working well with cultural diversity.
5. **Information management.** Information management skills include acquiring, organizing, maintaining, and evaluating information, and using computers to process information.
6. **Systems.** Systems skills include maintaining systems, improving systems, and understanding systems.
7. **Technology.** Technology skills include selecting and applying technology and maintaining technology.

Documentation

For your Career Development Portfolio, document each of the SCANS skills and competencies and personal qualities. Indicate how and when you learned each. Write the names of people who can vouch that you have these skills, competencies, and personal qualities. Include letters of support and recommendation. These letters could be from your employer verifying your skills, letters of support from coworkers and community members, and letters of thanks and appreciation from clients or customers. These skills and competencies may have been learned at college, in vocational training programs, in community work, through on-the-job training, or through travel.

Work Philosophy and Goals

Your work philosophy is a statement about how you approach work. It can also include changes you believe are important in your career field.

For example, define your educational goals. An example statement defining educational goals would be:

My immediate educational goal is to graduate with a certificate in fashion design. In five years, I plan to earn a college degree in business with an emphasis in marketing.

Define your career goals. Two examples are shown below:

- to hold a leadership role in fashion design.
- to belong to at least one professional organization.

Expand on your short-term, medium-range, and long-term goals. Include a mission statement and career objectives. You may also write your goals according to the roles you perform. What is it you hope to accomplish in each area of your life? Figure 14-6 on page 14-11 is an example of a mission statement. Ask yourself, Do I want to

- improve my skills?
- change careers or jobs?
- become more competent in my present job or earn a promotion?
- obtain a college degree?
- spend more time in one or more areas of my life?
- learn a new hobby or explore areas of interest?
- improve personal qualities?
- spend more time with my family?

Valued employee qualities:
- Honesty, character, integrity
- Responsibility
- Positive, motivated attitude
- Dependability
- Sociability
- Self-management and self-control
- Confidence and high self-esteem
- Empathy
- Good communication skills
- Listening skills
- Creative problem solving
- Sound decision making
- Team player
- Essential job skills
- Willingness to learn new skills
- Openness to suggestions and feedback
- Willingness to work hard
- Ability to follow through
- Confidence
- Loyalty
- Neatness and attractive appearance
- Respect and consideration
- Civility and good manners
- High energy
- Ability to cope with stress

Inventory of Personal Qualities

SCANS lists several important personal qualities necessary for success in the workplace: responsibility, dependability, self-esteem, sociability, integrity, and self-management. Indicate below how you have learned and demonstrated each of these qualities. Next, indicate how you would demonstrate each to an employer. Add personal qualities that you think are important. Use additional pages if needed. The first item has been filled in as an example.

1. Responsibility: *Learned responsibility by having a paper route, later working as a lifeguard at a community pool. I was also responsible for chores at home and helping to care for my younger sister and grandparent.*

   I am a responsible person because I turn in work on time, keep commitments with study team, take responsibility for mistakes, attend all classes, on time, am on time at work, pay attention to details.

2. Dependability: _____

   _____

   _____

3. Self-esteem: _____

   _____

   _____

4. Sociability: _____

   _____

   _____

5. Integrity: _____

   _____

   _____

6. Self-management: _____

   _____

   _____

Name _____

My mission is to use my talent in fashion design to create beauty and art. I want to influence the future development of fashion. I seek to be a lifelong learner because learning keeps me creative and alive. In my family, I want to build strong, healthy, and loving relationships. At work, I want to build creative and open teams. In life, I want to be kind, helpful, and supportive to others. I will live each day with integrity and be an example of outstanding character.

Long-Term Goals

Career goals: I want to own my own fashion design company.

Educational goals: I want to teach and lead workshops.

Family goals: I want to be a supportive parent.

Community goals: I want to belong to different community organizations.

Financial goals: I want to earn enough money to live comfortably and provide my family with the basic needs and more.

Medium-Range Goals

Career goals: I want to be a manager of a fashion company.

Educational goals: I want to earn a college degree in business and marketing.

Short-Term Goals

Career goals: I want to obtain an entry-level job in fashion design.

Educational goals: I want to earn a certificate in fashion design.

Figure 14-6
Sample Mission Statement

Résumé

The purpose of the résumé is to show the connections between your strengths, accomplishments, and skills and the needs of a company or employer. The résumé is a critical tool because it is a first impression, and first impressions do count! Your résumé is almost always the first contact an employer will have with you. You want it to look professional, to stand out, and to highlight your skills and competencies. Computer programs can help you format your résumé, and classes may be offered in the career center. See Figure 14-7 on page 14-12 for a sample résumé.

Your résumé should
- be honest.
- be error free.
- be clear and concise.
- use action words.
- be printed on high-quality paper.
- focus on skills, achievements, and accomplishments.

KATIE J. JENSEN

Present address: Permanent address:
1423 10th Street   812 La Jolla Avenue
Arlin, Minnesota 52561   Burlingate, Wisconsin 53791
(320) 555-2896   (414) 555-1928

JOB OBJECTIVE: To obtain an entry-level job as a travel agent.

EDUCATION:
Arlin Community College, Arlin, Minnesota
Associate of Arts in Business, June 1994
    Magna Cum Laude graduate
    Cross Pointe Career School, Arlin, Minnesota
    Certificate in Tourism, June 1992

HONORS AND AWARDS:
Academic Dean's list
Recipient of Burlingate Rotary Scholarship, 1992

WORK EXPERIENCE:
University Travel Agency, Arlin, Minnesota

Tour Guide, August 1993–present
- Arrange tours to historic sites in a four-state area. Responsibilities include contacting rail and bus carriers, arranging for local guides at each site, making hotel and restaurant reservations, and providing historical information about points of interest.
- Develop tours for holidays and special events. Responsibilities include pre-event planning, ticketing, and coordination of travel and event schedules.
- Specialized tour planning resulted in 24 percent increase in tour revenues over the preceding year.

Burlingate Area Convention Center, Burlingate, Minnesota
- Intern Tourist Coordinator, December 1992–June 1993
- Established initial contact with prospective speakers, coordinated schedules, and finalized all arrangements. Set up computerized database of tours using dBase IV.
- Organized receptions for groups up to 250, including reserving meeting rooms, contacting caterers, finalizing menus, preparing seating charts.

CAMPUS AND COMMUNITY ACTIVITIES:
Vice President Tourist Club, 1993–1994.
Co-chaired 1992 home-tour fundraising event for Big Sisters.

PROFESSIONAL MEMBERSHIP:
Burlingate Area Convention and Visitors Bureau

Figure 14-7
Sample Résumé

You may want to include the following components in your résumé:
- personal information (name, address, phone number, e-mail address)
- job objective.
- educational background.
- awards and honors.
- campus and community activities.
- work experience.
- professional memberships and activities.
- references.

1. **Personal information.** Write your name, address, and telephone number. If you have a temporary or school address, you will also want to include a permanent address and phone number. Don't include marital status, height, weight, health, interests, picture, or hobbies unless you think they are relevant to the job. Keep your résumé simple. Adding unessential information only clutters it and detracts from the essential information.

2. **Job objective.** It is not essential that you include a job objective on your résumé. The rule is to include a job objective if you will accept only a specific job. You may be willing to accept various jobs in a company, especially if you're a new graduate with little experience. If you decide not to list a job objective, you can use your cover letter to relate your résumé to the specific job for which you are applying.

3. **Educational background.** List your highest degree first, school attended, dates, and major field of study. Include educational experience that may be relevant to the job, such as certification, licensing, advanced training, intensive seminars, and summer study programs. Don't list individual classes on your résumé. If you have special classes that relate directly to the job you are applying for, list them in your cover letter.

4. **Awards and honors.** List awards and honors that are related to the job or indicate excellence. In addition, you may want to list special qualifications that relate to the job, such as fluency in a foreign language. Highlight this information prominently rather than write it as an afterthought. Pack a persuasive punch by displaying your best qualifications at the beginning.

5. **Campus and community activities.** List activities that show leadership abilities and a willingness to contribute.

6. **Work experience.** List the title of your last job first, dates worked, and a brief description of your duties. Don't clutter your résumé with needless detail or irrelevant jobs. You can elaborate on specific duties in your cover letter and in the interview.

7. **Professional memberships and activities.** List professional memberships, speeches, or research projects connected with your profession.

8. **References.** You will want three to five references, including employment, academic, and character references. Ask instructors for a general letter *before* you leave their last class or soon after. Ask someone from your church, synagogue, or mosque; fellow member of professional associations, club advisors, a coach, or students who have worked with you on projects and can provide good character references. See Figure 14-8 on page 14-15 for a sample request for a recommendation letter. Ask your supervisor for a letter before you leave the job. Make certain you ask your references for permission to use their names and phone numbers. Update a list of possible references and their addresses and phone numbers. Don't print your references on the bottom of your résumé. List them on a separate sheet of paper so you can update the list when it is appropriate. Also, you may not want your references to be called until you have an interview. Include recommendations in your Career Development Portfolio. See Figure 14-9 on page 14-15 for an example of a letter of recommendation.

TIP Follow up with a phone call in a week or two to make certain that your résumé was received. This is also the time to ask if additional information is needed and when a decision will be made. Call or write in a month if you haven't heard.

PUTTING YOUR RÉSUMÉ ONLINE

Many people put their résumé online and create their own home page on the World Wide Web. In addition, you can highlight essential aspects of your Career Development Portfolio. Many services are available to scan your résumé and help you place it in an electronic database. Some services will help you design your résumé and also identify trends in your field. Check with your campus career center or a job search agency.

Check this book's Web site for posting your résumé online:

http://peak.glencoe.com

COVER LETTER

A cover letter is a written introduction and should state the job you are applying for and what you can contribute to the company. If possible, find out to whom you should address your cover letter. Often a call to the personnel office will yield the correct name and title. Express enthusiasm and highlight how your education, skills, and experience relate to the job and will benefit the company.

Include sample cover letters and other letters that you may find useful in your Career Development Portfolio. See Figure 14-10 for a sample of a block-style cover letter.

CRITICAL THINKING LOG 14.2

Inventory of Interests, Aptitudes, and Values

Aptitudes are abilities or natural inclinations that you have in certain areas. Some people learn certain skills easily and are described by these aptitudes; for example, Joe is a natural salesman or Mary is a born speaker.

Check the areas below in which you have an aptitude. Add to the list.

Mechanical _____   Gardening _____

Clerical _____   Investigative _____

Musical _____   Artistic _____

Drama/acting _____   Working with numbers _____

Writing _____   Working with people _____

Persuasive speaking _____   Working with animals _____

Sales _____   Working with things _____

_____

May 2, 2000

Professor Eva Atkins
Chair of the Fashion Department
Green Briar Business Institute
100 North Bank Street
Glenwood, New Hampshire 03827

Dear Professor Atkins:

I was a student of yours last term in Fashion Design
and earned an *A* in your class. I am currently assembling my career development portfolio so I can apply
for summer positions in the fashion business. Would
you please write a letter of recommendation addressing
the following skills and competencies?
• my positive attitude and enthusiasm.
• my ability to work with diverse people in teams.
• my computer and technical skills.
• my skills in design and art.

I have also included my résumé, which highlights my
experience, GPA, and selected classes. If it is convenient, I would like to stop by your office next week and
pick up this letter of recommendation.

Your advice and counsel have meant so much to me
over the last three years. You have served as a instructor, advisor, and mentor. Thank you again for all your
help and support. Please call or e-mail me if you have
questions.

Sincerely,

Susan Sanchos

Susan Sanchos
242 Cherry Lane
Glenwood, New Hampshire 03827
Home phone: 304-555-8293
e-mail: susans@edu.glow.com

Figure 14-8

**Sample Letter of Request
(Block-Style Format)**

August 12, 2000

Mr. Jason Bently
University Travel Agency
902 Sunnybrae Lane
Pinehill, New Mexico 88503

Dear Mr. Bently:

It is a pleasure to write a letter of support for Ms. Mary
Anne Myers. I have worked with Mary Anne for five
years at Computer Divisions Corporation. We were part
of the same project team for two years and worked well
together. For the last year, I have been her supervisor at
Computer Divisions. Mary Anne is a team player and
works well with a variety of people. She is also well-prepared, knowledgeable, and hard-working. Recently, a
major report was due and Mary Anne worked weekends
and nights to meet the deadline.

Mary Anne has a positive attitude and is willing to
tackle any assignment. She is self-motivated and creative. In 1995, she won our Creative Employee Award
for her new marketing design. Mary Anne is also an
excellent listener. She takes the time to build rapport
and listen to customers and, as a result, many repeat
customers ask for her by name.

Mary Anne is a lifelong learner. She is attending classes
for her college degree in the evenings and she regularly
takes additional training in computers.

I highly recommend Mary Anne Myers. She is an excellent employee. Call or e-mail me if you have questions.

Sincerely,

Joyce Morocco, MBA

Joyce Morocco, MBA
Computer Divisions Manager
388 Maple Street
Midland, New Mexico 85802
Office Phone: 606-555-3948
e-mail: joycem@CDCorp.com

Figure 14-9

**Sample Letter of Recommendation
(Block-Style Format)**

July 2, 2000

Dr. Sonia Murphy
North Clinic Health Care
2331 Terrace Street
Chicago, Illinois 69691

Dear Dr. Murphy:

Mr. David Leeland, Director of Internship at Bakers College, gave me a copy of your
advertisement for a medical assistant. I am interested in being considered for the
position.

Your medical office has an excellent reputation, especially regarding health care for
women. I have taken several courses in women's health and volunteer at the hospital
in a women's health support group. I believe I can make a significant contribution to
your office.

My work experiences and internships have provided valuable hands-on experience. I
set up a new computer-designed program for payroll in my internship position. In
addition to excellent office skills, I also have clinical experience and people skills. I
speak Spanish and have used it often in my volunteer work in hospitals.

I have paid for most of my college education. My grades are excellent and I have been
on the Dean's list in my medical and health classes. I have also completed advanced
computer and advanced office procedures classes.

I will call you on Tuesday, July 22, to make sure you received this letter and to find out
when you might be able to arrange an interview.

Sincerely,

Julia Andrews

Julia Andrews
Green Briar Business Institute
242 Cherry Lane
Chicago, Illinois 69692
Home phone: 304-555-5593
e-mail: juliaa@edu.BakersC.com

Figure 14-10

Sample Cover Letter (Block-Style Format)

TRAILMARKER 14.1

Tips for Exploring Majors and Careers

1. *Self-assessment* is important when determining your interests, values, strengths, likes, dislikes, abilities, skills, and personality. Take various personality inventories. For example, the Strong Interest Inventory matches your interests with careers. Review your worksheets, and reflect on the following comments and questions:
   - Describe your perfect day in detail. If money were no object, what would you do and where would you live?
   - If you were independently wealthy but you still wanted to make a contribution to the world, how would you use your talents?
   - What community organization would you like to help?

2. *Take introductory classes* and general education classes to review specific majors, gain skills, and explore possible careers. Ask instructors what majors and careers relate to the classes you are taking.

3. *Talk with professionals* and try to obtain a realistic view of their various occupations. Visit with four or five people in the top three or four different careers that you would like to explore further. Find out what they like and dislike about their work.

4. *Explore campus resources* such as the library, advising center, and career center. They are tremendous resources for information on various majors and careers. Many campuses have a majors' fair and career day where various majors and careers are discussed. Explore other resources, such as
   - clubs and college organizations
   - student government

5. *Work experience* is a great way to learn about work conditions in the fields you want to pursue. A part-time job, volunteer work, or an internship can provide valuable experience and help you determine if a specific major or career path is for you.

6. *Checking the newspaper's classified ads;* scanning professional journals; checking the job board in various academic departments; obtaining job listings from the career center; and telling your advisors, other students, friends, and instructors that you are interested in finding a job may lead to part- or full-time work.

7. *Apply for jobs with a company you are interested in.* Take your résumé and inquire about vacancies. Some companies say that they are not hiring, but if you can present your résumé and show how valuable you would be, they might find a place for you.

8. *Volunteer* in organizations or clubs, a library, a museum, or a newspaper. A political campaign will help you get to know people of different ages and cultural and political backgrounds. Ask questions and find out what people do for a living.

9. *Internships and work-study programs* are excellent ways to gain experience, make connections, and practice positive job skills and habits. You will also see how many skills learned in school apply to the business world.

10. *Explore careers in depth.* Narrow your list to four or five possible careers. Many careers do not have traditional titles; for example, you could describe your career goals as follows: "I love to cook, and cheesecake is my specialty. I'm majoring in retailing. I'd like to use my marketing and cooking skills to produce and market the best cheesecake," or "I was a welder by trade and am now enrolled in business school. I like to make jewelry as a hobby. I would like to produce my own line of jewelry, travel the world to find other interesting jewelry, and create a wholesale business."

11. *Explore all options.* Students can often create their own majors in school. For example, many colleges have a special or interdisciplinary major that allows students to create their own major from various disciplines. Most campuses also have a general liberal arts major. These majors are often ideal for students who have various interests and find it difficult to choose one major.

12. *Networking and personal contacts* are excellent ways to explore majors and careers and to find a job. Networking provides access to several people who can serve as mentors and help connect you to jobs and opportunities. This referral system is critical for your career. Personal and professional contacts must be created, cultivated, and expanded. Use campus and community resources to begin to structure and build your network. Here are a few tips that can help you:
    - brainstorm a list of contacts.
    - talk with instructors, advisors, and counselors.
    - talk with other students.
    - collect business cards.
    - join professional organizations.

Interview Planning

Just as the résumé is important for opening the door, the job interview is critical for putting your best foot forward and clearly articulating why you are the best person for the job. Many of the tips discussed in this text about getting hired and being successful in a career center around both verbal and nonverbal communication skills. These communication skills will be assets during your job interview. Here are some interview strategies that will help you make full use of these skills and others:

1. **Be punctual.** A good first impression is important and can be lasting. If you arrive late, you have already said a great deal about yourself. Make certain you know the location and the time of the interview. Allow time for parking and other preliminaries.

2. **Be professional.** Being too familiar can be a barrier to a professional interview. Never call anyone by their first name unless you are asked to. Know the name, title, and the pronunciation of the interviewer's name, and don't sit down until the interviewer does.

3. **Dress appropriately.** Since nonverbal communication is 90 percent of communication, dressing appropriately for the interview is important. In most situations, you will be safe if you wear clean, pressed, conservative business clothes in a neutral color. Pay special attention to grooming. Keep makeup light and wear little jewelry. Make certain your nails and hair are clean, trimmed, and neat. Don't carry a large purse, backpack, books, coat, or hat. Leave extra clothing in an outside office, and simply carry a pen, pad of paper, and a small folder with extra copies of your résumé and references.

4. **Learn about the company.** Be prepared; show that you have researched the company. What product(s) does it make? How is it doing? What is the competition? Always refer to the company when you give examples.

5. **Learn about the position.** Before you interview, request a job description from the personnel office. What kind of employee and skills is the company looking for to fill the position? You will likely be asked the common question, "Why are you interested in this job?" Be prepared to answer with a reference to the company.

6. **Relate your experience to the job.** Use every question as an opportunity to show how your skills relate to the job. Use examples taken from school, previous jobs, internships, volunteer work, leadership in clubs, and experiences growing up to indicate that you have the personal qualities, aptitude, and skills needed at this new job.

7. **Be honest.** While it is important to be confident and stress your strengths, it is equally important to your sense of integrity to be honest. Dishonesty always catches up with you sooner or later. Someone will verify your background, so do not exaggerate your accomplishments, grade point average, or your experience.

The key to a good interview is to stand out from all the other applicants.

8. **Focus on how you can benefit the company.** Don't ask about benefits, salary, or vacations until you are offered the job. During a first interview, try to show how you can contribute to the organization. Don't appear to be too eager to move up through the company or suggest that you are more interested in gaining experience than in contributing to the company.

9. **Be poised and relaxed.** Avoid nervous habits such as tapping your pencil, playing with your hair, or covering your mouth with your hand. Watch language such as *you know, ah, stuff like that.* Don't smoke, chew gum, fidget, or bite your nails.

10. **Maintain comfortable eye contact.** Look people in the eye and speak with confidence. Your eyes reveal much about you; use them to show interest, confidence, poise, and sincerity. Use other nonverbal techniques such as a firm handshake to reinforce your confidence.

11. **Practice interviewing.** Consider videotaping a mock interview. Most college campuses have this service available through the career center or media department. Rehearse questions and be prepared to answer directly.

12. **Anticipate question types.** Expect open-ended questions such as, "What are your strengths?" "What are your weaknesses?" "Tell me about your best work experience," and "What are your career goals?" Decide in advance what information and skills are pertinent to the position and reveal your strengths. For example, you could say, "I learned to get along with a diverse group of people when I worked for the park service."

13. **Ending the interview.** Close the interview on a positive note. Thank the interviewer for his or her time, shake hands, and say that you are looking forward to hearing from him or her.

14. **Follow up with a letter.** A follow-up letter is especially important. It serves as a reminder for the interviewer. For you, it is an opportunity to thank the interviewer and a chance to make a positive comment about the position and the company. See Figure 14-11 on page 14-20 for a sample follow-up letter.

Samples of Work

When appropriate, include samples of your work. Think of how you can demonstrate visually your expertise in your particular area or field. These samples can include articles, portions of a book, artwork, fashion sketches, drawings, photos of work, poetry, pictures, food demonstrations, brochures, a typical day at your job, job descriptions, and performance reviews. If you are in the music field, you can include visual samples of flyers and an audiotape.

Summary of Transcripts

Include a copy of all transcripts of college work.

May 29, 2000

Mr. Henry Sanders
The Mountain View Store
10 Rock Lane
Alpine, Montana 79442

Dear Mr. Sanders:

Thank you for taking the time yesterday to meet with me concerning the position of sales representative. I enjoyed meeting you and your employees, learning more about your growing company, and touring your facilities. I was especially impressed with your new line of outdoor wear. It is easy to see why you lead the industry in sales.

I am even more excited about joining your sales team now that I have visited with you. I have the education, training, enthusiasm, and personal qualities necessary to succeed in business. I am confident that I would fit in with your staff and make a real contribution to the sales team.

It has been difficult not to think of exciting possibilities and new ideas for customer service. I am attaching another résumé and would be glad to come for another interview.

Thank you again for the interview and an enjoyable morning.

Sincerely,

John A. Bennett

John A. Bennett
124 East Buttermilk Lane
LaCrosse, Wisconsin 54601
Home Phone: (608)555-4958
e-mail: johnb@shast.edu

Figure 14-11
Sample Follow-Up Letter (Block Style)

Credentials, Certificates, Workshops

Include a copy of credentials, certificates, workshops, seminars, training sessions, conferences, continuing education courses, and other examples of lifelong learning.

Bibliography

Include a bibliography of books you have read that pertain to your major, career goals, or occupation.

Appendix

Include internships, leadership experiences in clubs and sports, volunteer work, service to the community, and travel experiences that relate to your goals. You can also include awards, honors, and certificates of recognition.

OVERCOMING THE BARRIERS TO PORTFOLIO DEVELOPMENT

The biggest barrier to career success is procrastination. Maybe you're telling yourself that the idea of a portfolio sounds good, but

- I don't have the time.
- it's a lot of work.
- it won't work for me.
- I don't have enough work samples.
- I wouldn't know where to start.
- I'll do it when I'm ready for a full-time job.

A Career Development Portfolio is an ongoing process that requires time and effort. You cannot expect to pull together in a few days your work philosophy, goals, documentation of your skills and competencies, and work samples. The responsibility for career planning cannot be relegated to someone else. If you are resisting or procrastinating, work with a partner. Together you can organize supplies, brainstorm ideas, review each other's philosophies and goals, and help assemble the contents.

Another major barrier to career planning is the notion that once you choose a major and a career, you are on a straight and settled path. Change is part of life, however. The average student changes majors three times, and the average worker will have four or five career changes. Career planning is a lifelong process, and your Career Development Portfolio should be started during your freshman year and updated throughout your life. The Internet, computer technology, and telecommunications have fueled major changes.

As middle management jobs are eliminated, workers are expected to take more responsibility for managing themselves and their work progress. The job security of lifelong employment will be replaced by a reliance on employees' own portfolios of skills and competencies. Salary increases and advancement will be based on performance and production rather than seniority or entitlement. You will be responsible for managing your own career and marketing yourself. Career planning gives you the information for making sound decisions, helps you learn how to assess your skills and competencies, and creates a dynamic system that encourages you to adapt to changing jobs and careers. Being prepared, resilient, flexible, and a lifelong learner will help you overcome many barriers to effective career planning.

Technology FOCUS:
Computers and Your Career

Computers are a great help for exploring careers. The Internet has excellent sites for exploring job trends and occupations. Many professional and business associations have Web sites that link you to additional resources. Use this book's Web site to begin discovering these links.

http://peak.glencoe.com

Browse Web sites of interests to find specific information about careers. Look at Web sites of college and university departments that have majors you want to explore. Many colleges and career schools have a Web site that gives a general answer to the question, "What can I do with a major in . . . .?"

TIP Keep your résumé and sample cover letters on your computer so that you can update and print them at a moment's notice.

Interviewing the Employed

Make a list of the types of jobs you think you would like. Then make a list of contacts in those types of jobs. Ask those contacts if you can interview them about their jobs. The purpose of each interview is to find out about the person's career and what the job is really like. Below is a list of questions to ask your contacts. Keep notes for your Career Development Portfolio. (Remember to send a thank-you note after each interview.)

Person interviewed _____

Job title _____   Date _____

1. Why did you choose your career?

   _____

2. What do you do on a typical day?

   _____

3. What do you like best about your job?

   _____

4. What do you like least?

   _____

5. Would you mind telling me the salary range for your job?

   _____

6. If you had to do it again, would you choose the same job?

   _____

7. If not, what would you do differently in planning your career?

   _____

8. What advice can you give me for planning my career?

   _____

CRITICAL THINKING LOG 14.4

Values

Values are qualities that are important to you and that enhance your life. Your values are ideals that make you unique, and they often act as motivators. When your life's goals, behavior, major, career, and choices match your values, you are more centered and productive. Below is a partial list of values. You may wish to add to this list and make it more personal. Describe in a few words the values you believe are important to you and how you demonstrate them.

Values	How Values Are Demonstrated
Kindness	
Generosity	
Citizenship	
Integrity	
Friendship	
Honesty	
Work ethic	
Spirituality	

CAREER FOCUS: CAREER PLANNING IS LIFELONG

Few people can change or advance their careers simply by announcing that they are ready for a change. For most, great career opportunities don't drop into their laps. Many times it takes a great deal of planning and work experience.

Consider the case of Ryan Neuner, an airline pilot for an overnight mail company. His passion in life is flying and he never thought that he would change his career. He worked hard, had excellent skills, got along well with people, and was soon promoted into management. After two years as head of his department, he decided that the paperwork kept him away from his real interest.

After several months of self-assessment, talking with others about their past job experiences, and exploring job growth within the company, Ryan decided to become a flight instructor. The company offered a job training program, and he completed additional certificates through a local college. By taking advantage of many career planning strategies, updating his résumé, and practicing interview techniques, Ryan made a career change. He learned one important lesson from his experience: career planning is a lifelong process. Complete Critical Thinking Log 14.5 on page 14-25.

Assess Your Skills

Here is a way to assess your skills at various times during your school and work careers. Answer the following questions. Use this list at the end of a term or year or at the beginning of a new job or when considering a job change. Your answers may surprise you. They may remain the same or change dramatically. What is important is that you are assessing, changing, and growing.

- Are you a lifelong learner?

- Are you a creative problem solver?

- Do you know several jobs and have an understanding of many tasks?

- Are you an expert in one area?

- Do you constantly strive to make your job more interesting and improve your productivity?

- Do you add value to the company?

- Do you cooperate and work well with others?

- Do you manage your career professionally?

- Are you efficient, effective, professional, and accurate in your work?

- Are you both people- and task-oriented?

- Are you motivated and a self-starter?

- Do you have excellent communication skills?

- Do you have important personal qualities such as responsibility, character, and integrity?

WORKPLACE TRENDS

Keep a section in the appendix of your Career Development Portfolio for workplace trends that relate directly to your occupation. One of the important trends will be education on the job. Some of this education will be informal and consist of on-the-job-training, acquiring new job skills, learning to complete challenging projects, and shifting your work style so that you can work more effectively with others. Other education will be formal, such as seminars, courses, and workshops designed to improve or add to your job skills. These formal courses may include training in topics such as:

| Computers | Grant writing | Technical skills |
| World Wide Web | Financial planning | Report writing |

Other formal seminars, courses, or workshops may develop better human relations skills. Topics may include:

Alcohol and drug abuse	Time and stress management	Negotiation
Sexual harassment	Communication	Conflict resolution
Cultural and gender diversity	Motivation	Basic supervision
Team building		

You may decide that you need to earn an advanced degree or certificate by going to lengthy training sessions or attending college in the evenings. However you go about it, lifelong education is a new and significant job trend. The employee who learns new skills, cross-trains in various positions, and has excellent human relations skills will be sought after and promoted.

CRITICAL THINKING LOG 14.5

Action Plan/Career Planner

Fill in your goals.

Career Goals
1.
2.
3.

Personal Goals
1.
2.
3.

Lifetime Goals
1.
2.
3.

BUSINESS ETHICS

Business ethics have become an important issue in today's business world. The go-for-it-at-any-cost attitude of corporate raiders and unethical businesspeople has tarnished the image of big business and made us all more aware of ethical business practices. Each employee must make decisions based on moral values and conscience, and follow the code of ethics provided by his or her industry. Sometimes this is an unwritten code and sometimes it is an industrywide set of rules. Whether they are written or unwritten, ethical business standards must be upheld. Sometimes a seemingly small indiscretion or decision can cost a job or result in a tarnished reputation.

Top managers also have a responsibility for setting an ethical code and acting as role models for all employees. They should act with integrity and model ethical behavior. Corporations must set clear guidelines for ethical behavior and insist on accountability. Many corporations have improved their image by being socially responsible and encouraging their employees to become involved in the community and contribute their time and talents to worthwhile community agencies and causes. Make certain you review your campus and workplace codes of ethics.

CRITICAL THINKING LOG 14.6
Transferable Skills

Read the following and comment on the lines provided.

1. What transferable skills do you have?

   _____

   _____

2. What specific content skills do you have that indicate a specialized knowledge or ability, such as plumbing, computer programming, or cooking?

   _____

3. List your daily activities and determine the skills involved in each. Then consider what you like about this activity. These factors may include the environment, being alone or with people, or a certain emotional reaction; for example, "I like bike riding because I am outdoors with friends, and the exercise feels great."

Activity	Skills Involved	Factors
Bike riding	Balance, stamina, discipline	Being outdoors

TIP When you fill out a job application, write a résumé, or interview for a job, make certain that you include all the skills you have demonstrated.

JIRKA RYSAVY

The dramatic success of Jirka Rysavy is an amazing story of determination and creativity. Rysavy was born and raised in Czechoslovakia. He earned a master's degree in engineering and was also a hurdler in international track and field.

When he first arrived in the United States, he didn't speak English and took a job for $3.35 an hour in Boulder, Colorado. In three months he had saved the $600 he needed to start a company selling recycled paper. His company, Transformational Economy, made $100,000 in pretax profits in its first year.

Although he had no formal training in business, Rysavy then invested in a health-food store. He read books and articles about business and was ready to expand his health-food business when he noticed that an office supply company was for sale. The store was losing $300,000 annually in sales. He purchased the store and changed its focus from retail sales to corporate sales, expanding sales nearly eightfold within a year. He discovered that the office supply industry was riddled with inefficiencies and developed technical strategies to maintain low cost and deliver service.

In just eleven years, Rysavy came to a new country, learned a new language, learned about business, and with limited savings started a multibillion dollar, worldwide business. Jirka Rysavy is a Peak Performer who used determination, self-reliance, and creativity to produce incredible results.

Source: http://peak.glencoe.com

CHAPTER

14

Review and
Study Notes

Affirmations

- I see the value of a Career Development Portfolio.
- I see the relationship between school and careers. I know what I'm doing now builds skills and relationships.
- I make the best of every situation, and I see all experiences as opportunities to learn about myself and prepare for the world of work.
- I like to plan my education and career, and I gain a sense of confidence and direction by doing so.

Visualization

See yourself focused by a vision and purpose. You awake with zest each day and turn even the most mundane task into a learning experience. You love to dream, explore, and see the interrelationships among all your classes, jobs, and relationships. You feel good about your contributions. You can decide on any number of careers and be successful and happy.

Peak Performance Strategies for Your Career Development Portfolio

1. Invest time in planning and preparing a Career Development Portfolio.
2. Realize that your portfolio is a lifelong process.
3. Connect SCANS skills and competencies to school and work.
4. Choose to manage your career.

CASE A In the Classroom

Juanita Harris likes to make presentations, enjoys working with children, and is a crusader for equality and the environment. She also values family, home, and community. Making a lot of money is not important to her. Her motivation is a feeling that she is making a difference and enjoying what she is doing. Now that her own family is grown, she wants to complete a college degree. However, she is hesitant because she has been out of school for many years.

1. How would you help Juanita with her decision?

_____

2. What careers would you have Juanita explore?

_____

3. What strategies in this chapter would be most helpful?

_____

4. What one habit would you recommend to Juanita to help her with career planning?

_____

In the Workplace

Juanita completed a degree in Childhood Development. She has been a caregiver in a child's daycare for two years. She has enjoyed her job, but she feels that it is time for a change. If she wants to stay in her field and advance, she has to travel and go into management. She wants more time off to be with her family, write, and become more involved in community action groups. Juanita would like to stay in a related field. She still likes working with children, but she also likes giving presentations and workshops, and writing. She has thought about consulting, writing, or starting her own small business.

What strategies in this chapter would help Juanita with her career change?

_____

_____

CASE B

Mark Gryber will graduate in June with a business degree. In addition to excellent grades, Mark has solid and varied job experience, community service experience, and a track record of leadership in clubs and activities. He has also demonstrated good work habits and is personable, hard-working, positive, and organized. With all of these attributes, it is no wonder that Mark was offered a full-time job at a prestigious marketing company where he has worked part-time for two years.

His dilemma is that, after he accepted the job offer, he was asked to interview in New York City for a sales position. Mark really isn't interested in the job, but he would love to go to New York City for a few days and have the trip paid for. After a great deal of thought, Mark decided against going for the interview. Although there is nothing illegal about going, Mark's own sense of ethics dictates that it would be wrong because he is not serious about the job.

1. What would you have decided if you were faced with a similar situation?

   _____

   _____

2. How would your values and beliefs affect this decision?

   _____

   _____

In the Workplace

Mark is now a marketing representative and enjoys his job. He works a lot of overtime and is always thinking of ways to add value and profit to the company. Recently, the company downsized and several older, competent managers lost their jobs. Mark's father stayed with the same company for thirty-five years, and Mark has that same sense of loyalty to his company. But he has begun to see that the old traditional compact between worker and employer has changed. There is little job security and, as a result, many employees feel little loyalty to the company. Mark wants to continue to encourage his coworkers to make themselves more valuable to the company and to be part of the large corporate team. This task is becoming harder, however, as employees become disillusioned.

What advice do you have for Mark?

_____

_____

_____

Chapter Application   WORKSHEET 14.1

Career Planning Grid

Use the grid to help you with your career planning.

Major
Assess
Explore
Brainstorm
Choose

	Assess				Plan				Action Network				Follow-Up			
	Assess your skills.	Assess your abilities.	Assess your interests.	Assess your values and dreams.	Set goals and priorities.	Translate skills into career.	Plan network system.	Plan résumé and cover letter.	Volunteer, intern, get job experience.	Network.	Send out résumé.	Interview.	Write thank-you notes.	Follow up with phone calls.	Follow up on job leads.	Follow up on network building.
Freshman Year																
Summer																
Sophomore Year																
Summer																
Junior Year																
Summer																
Senior Year																
Summer																

EXPLORING CAREERS

Complete the following.

1. Go to the library or career center and find ten careers you've never heard of or are interested in exploring. Use the Internet to explore at least one.

_____

_____

_____

2. Can these careers be grouped into one field?

_____

_____

_____

TIP Career reference sources:

- Internet
- Your school's career counseling center
- *Encyclopedia of Careers and Vocational Guidance*
- *Occupational Outlook Handbook*
- *The American Almanac of Jobs and Salaries*
- *The Jobs Rated Almanac*

3. List your skills and interests. Then list the careers that match these skills and interests. Create names for careers if they are unusual.

Skills/Interests   Possible Careers

_____   _____

_____   _____

_____   _____

4. Review your list of skills and interests. What stands out? Do you like working with people or accomplishing tasks? Think of as many jobs as you can that relate to your skills and interests. Your skills and interests are valuable clues about your future career.

_____

_____

_____

5. Describe an ideal career that involves the skills you enjoy using the most. Include the location of this ideal career and the kinds of people you would be working with (e.g., coworkers, customers, employees).

_____

_____

_____

INDEX

INDEX

INDEX

benefits of, 2–8, 2–9
differences between high school and, 2–8

High school, differences between college and, 2–8

Hippocrates, 1–11

HIV, 10–14

Hobbies, for stress management, 10–19

Honesty, relationships and, 11–18

Houses of worship, as resource, 12–12

Housing, off-campus, 12–9

Humor
to enhance creativity, 9–8
for overcoming shyness, 11–16
rapport building and, 11–3—11–4
for stress management, 10–20

I

Illegal drugs, dangers of, 10–11

Imagery, remembering, 6–16

Independence, success and, 13–12

Information overload, reducing, 6–3

Innovative attitude, 13–8

Instructions, for tests, 7–3—7–4

Instructors
communicating with, 11–11—11–12
conferring with, 8–9

Integrity, 2–13—2–14
commitment to, 13–9

Intention
memory and, 6–2
rapport building and, 11–2—11–3

Interests
inventory of, 14–14
for stress management, 10–19

Internet, 2–22. *See also* Technology focus
research on, 8–14, 8–17

Internships, for exploring majors and careers, 14–8

Interruptions, 3–16
controlling, 3–14—3–17

Interviewing
of employed people, 14–22

for jobs, 14–18—14–19

Intrinsic vision, 13–14

Introduction
for Career Development Portfolio, 14–5, 14–7
to paper, 8–6

Introductory classes, for exploring majors and careers, 14–16

Introverts, 1–11, 1–12

Intuitives, 1–11, 1–12

Inventory of skills and competencies, for Career Development Portfolio, 14–8

"I" statements, for managing anger, 2–18

J

James, Henry, 1–19

Job applications
cover letters for, 14–14, 14–15
for exploring majors and careers, 14–16
interviewing and, 14–18—14–19

Job placement office, 12–5

Job placement services, 12–12

Job searching, 5–7

Job success
self-assessment for, 1–22—1–23
skills and competencies for, 1–3—1–4

Journals
to enhance creativity, 9–11
as resources, 12–13

Judges, 1–11, 1–12

Judgment
errors in, interfering with critical thinking, 9–3
postponing, listening and, 4–3

Jung, Carl, 1–11

K

Keeping up, 7–2
success and, 13–12

Keirsy, David, 1–11

rapport building and, 11–3
for stress management, 10–18
at work, 4–20
Mind maps, 4–9—4–11
template for, 4–10
Mind-sets, changing, 9–9
Mind shifts, for positive attitude and
motivation, 2–20
Minorities. *See* Diversity
Mission statement, 14–9, 14–11
Mnemonic devices, 6–7
Modeling, of successful behavior, 3–18
Money, handling, 12–15—12–18
Motivated attitude, importance of,
2–2—2–3
Motivation, 2–4–2–10
affirmations and visualizations
and, 2–7
overcoming barriers to, 2–20—2–22
strategies for, 2–4 –2–6
to study, 2–8, 2–9
for time management, 3–12
Motivation cycle, 2–7
Multiple-choice tests, 7–5—7–6
Myers-Briggs Type Inventory (MBTI),
1–11

N

Names, remembering, 6–15
Native American students, financial
programs for, 12–8
Needs hierarchy, 2–3—2–4
Networking, for exploring majors and
careers, 14–8
Newsletters, as resources, 12–13
Newspapers
classified ads in, for exploring
majors and careers, 14–16
as resources, 12–13
Nicotine, dangers of, 10–11
Note taking, 4–2
computers and, 4–18
effective, overcoming barriers to,
4–18

strategies for, 4–14—4–16, 4–17
systems for, 4–7—4–13
for writing, 8–4, 8–5
Numbering pages, 8–9
Nutrition, health and energy and,
10–3—10–4, 10–6

O

Objective tests, 7–5—7–7
Observing, 11–14
for active listening, 4–3
for changing habits, 13–3
to enhance memory, 6–3, 6–8
Off-campus housing, 12–9
Older students, 3–19
Online research, 8–14, 8–17
Online résumés, 14–14
Open book tests, 7–6
Organizational information,
computers and, 12–19
Organizations, in community, 12–15
Organizing
with computers, 13–20
to enhance memory, 6–6, 6–14
for juggling family, school, and
job, 3–19
for test taking, 7–3
for time management, 3–9—3–10,
3–11
of writing plans, 8–5
Orientation programs, 12–4—12–5
Outlines
for active reading, 5–5
as note-taking system, 4–7, 4–8
for writing, 8–5

P

Pacing yourself, in test taking, 7–4
Pages
numbering, 8–9
title, 8–10
Paper resources

INDEX

for job success, 1–22—1–23
of learning style, 1–6—1–14
overcoming barriers to, 1–22
of personality style, 1–13—1–14
of skills, 14–24

Self-awareness, for changing habits, 13–3

Self-control, 2–17—2–18

Self-esteem, 2–18—2–19

Self-knowledge, 5–7

Self-management, 2–17—2–18

Self-talk
for overcoming shyness, 11–16
positive, 13–14

Senses
for memory, 6–4
for note taking, 4–14—4–15

Sensors, 1–11, 1–12

Service learning, 12–13, 12–15

Sexual activity
birth control and, 10–14
preventing rape and,
10–15—10–16

Sexual harassment, 11–9

Sexually transmitted diseases (STDs),
avoiding, 10–13—10–14

Shorthand, for note taking, 4–15, 4–16

Shyness, overcoming, 11–16

Siegel, Morris (Mo), 1–25

Signal words and phrases, 4–3,
4–4—4–5

Significant life experiences list, for
Career Development Portfolio,
14–7

Silence, for active listening, 4–6

Skills
assessment of, 14–24
inventory of, for Career
Development Portfolio, 14–8
transferable, 14–26—14–27

Smith, Red, 8–2

Smoking, dangers of, 10–11

Soto, Gary, 10–28

Speaking
checklists for, 8–21
importance of, 8–2

stage fright and, 8–18
strategies for, 8–16

Special services, on campus, 12–5

Sports complex, 12–9

SQ3R reading system, 5–4

Staffing, for time management, 3–11

Stage fright, controlling, 8–18

Steinem, Gloria, 11–24

Stereotypes, 11–5

Stress, 10–23
test taking and, 7–16

Stress management, 10–17—10–21
computers for, 10–25
preventing stress at work and, 10–25
warning signs of stress overload
and, 10–26—10–27

Students, types of, 2–11—2–12

Student union/center, 12–9

Studying
at high-energy time, 3–9
in library, 3–17
place for, 3–9, 3–15
in short segments, 3–9, 6–5
in teams. See Team study
for tests, 7–3, 7–10—7–11, 7–13
time for, 3–17

Substance use and abuse
addictions and, 10–12
alcohol use and, 10–9—10–10
caffeine and, 10–8—10–9
cigarette smoking and, 10–11
codependency and,
10–12—10–13
critical thinking about, 10–12
illegal drugs and, 10–11—10–12

Success, 13–10—13–14
formula for, 13–14
imagining, 13–3
principles of, 13–10
promoting, 13–10—13–13
in school, 13–21—13–22

Suicidal persons, 10–25

Summarizing
in notes, 4–16
for problem solving, 9–7
after reading, 5–9
for tests, 7–3

INDEX

T note-taking system, 4–12

Tobacco, dangers of, 10–11

To-do lists, 3–6

Tolerance, success and, 13–12

Topics, for writing, 8–3, 8–7

Trailmarkers

    assessment is lifelong, 13–16—13–17

    benchmark plan, 1–24

    best strategies for success in school, 13–21—13–22

    campus facilities, 12–9

    checklists for writing papers and giving speeches, 8–21

    creative ideas checklist, 9–16

    creative problem-solving techniques, 9–10

    differences between high school and college, 2–8

    eating for health and energy, 10–6

    four grid personality and team profile, 1–13—1–14

    how to generate topic ideas, 8–7

    important words in essay questions, 7–12

    investing your time in high-priority items: the 80/20 rule, 3–15

    learning style inventory, 1–8—1–9

    look it up! using the dictionary, 5–12

    make a commitment to learn and apply positive habits, 13–6—13–7

    mathematics and science checklist, 9–5

    memory map—a walk down memory lane, 6–10—6–11

    mindfulness, 6–9

    overcoming barriers to effective note taking, 4–18

    overcoming writer's block, 8–15

    pre-registration questions for your advisor, 11–12

    remembering names, 6–15

    sample essay test, 7–10

    skills, school, and career, 2–11

    stress, 7–16

    stress leads to burnout, 10–21

    success principles, 13–10

    symbols, 5–9

    ten habits for peak career performance, 13–19

    test-taking factors, 7–7

    thinking about diversity, 11–8

    tips for exploring majors and careers, 14–16—14–17

    tips to build self-esteem and confidence, 2–19

    warning signs of stress overload, 10–26—10–27

    writing do's, 8–11—8–12

    you can solve the problem, 9–17—9–18

Training, success and, 13–14

Transcripts, in Career Development Profile, 14–19

Transferable skills, 14–26—14–27

Transfer students, resources for, 12–11

True/false tests, 7–5

Trust, relationships and, 11–18

Tutoring, 12–5

U

Unemployed students, programs for, 12–8

V

Values, 14–23

    inventory of, 14–14

Veterans programs, 12–8

Vision, success and, 13–14

Visualization, motivation and, 2–5, 2–7

Visual learning style, 1–6—1–7

    attitudes and motivation and, 2–10

    memory and, 6–4

Vocabulary building, 5–16—5–17

Volunteering, for exploring majors and careers, 14–8

W

INDEX